# ORIGINAL NARRATIVES OF EARLY AMERICAN HISTORY

REPRODUCED UNDER THE AUSPICES OF THE AMERICAN HISTORICAL ASSOCIATION

GENERAL EDITOR, J. FRANKLIN JAMESON, PH.D., LL.D., LITT.D.

DIRECTOR OF THE DEPARTMENT OF HISTORICAL RESEARCH IN THE CARNEGIE INSTITUTION OF WASHINGTON

---

NARRATIVES OF EARLY VIRGINIA

BRADFORD'S HISTORY OF PLYMOUTH PLANTATION

WINTHROP'S JOURNAL "HISTORY OF NEW ENGLAND" (2 vols.)

NARRATIVES OF EARLY CAROLINA

NARRATIVES OF EARLY MARYLAND

NARRATIVES OF EARLY PENNSYLVANIA, WEST NEW JERSEY, AND DELAWARE

NARRATIVES OF NEW NETHERLAND

EARLY ENGLISH AND FRENCH VOYAGES

VOYAGES OF SAMUEL DE CHAMPLAIN

SPANISH EXPLORERS IN THE SOUTHERN UNITED STATES

SPANISH EXPLORATION IN THE SOUTHWEST

NARRATIVES OF THE INSURRECTIONS

NARRATIVES OF THE INDIAN WARS

JOHNSON'S WONDER-WORKING PROVIDENCE

THE JOURNAL OF JASPAR DANCKAERTS

NARRATIVES OF THE NORTHWEST

NARRATIVES OF THE WITCHCRAFT CASES

THE NORTHMEN, COLUMBUS, AND CABOT

ORIGINAL NARRATIVES
OF EARLY AMERICAN HISTORY

# NARRATIVES
# OF EARLY VIRGINIA

## 1606—1625

EDITED BY

LYON GARDINER TYLER, LL.D.

LATE PRESIDENT OF THE COLLEGE OF WILLIAM AND MARY

*New York*

BARNES & NOBLE, INC.

CONSTABLE & CO LTD

10-12 ORANGE STREET, LONDON, W.C.2

REPRINTED, 1959



PRINTED IN THE UNITED STATES OF AMERICA

# NOTE

This volume is intended to include the most important and interesting narratives of that part of Virginian history which extends from the formation to the dissolution of the Virginia Company. In the selection, Captain John Smith's *True Relation* and the *Description of Virginia* and account of the *Proceedings of the English Colonie* which he and his friends drew up have, on well-known historical principles, been preferred to the somewhat ampler but less strictly contemporary version of the transactions of the same period which he gave in the *Generall Historie*; but the ensuing period was deemed to be in the main best covered by reproducing the fourth book of the latter treatise.

Dr. Reuben G. Thwaites, Secretary of the State Historical Society of Wisconsin, and the Burrows Brothers Company of Cleveland, the publishers, have kindly permitted use to be made in this volume of the translation of Father Biard's *Relation* which appeared in the third volume of *The Jesuit Relations*, edited by Dr. Thwaites. The Massachusetts Historical Society has permitted the use of the text of the letter of John Pory, printed in their *Collections*. The Virginia Historical Society has allowed the editor to reprint from the *Virginia Magazine of History* "The Discourse of the Old Company." Grateful acknowledgments are made for these favors.

Those texts which have been taken from books printed in the seventeenth century have been carefully collated with copies of the original editions in the Library of Congress. But the use of *u* and *v* and *i* and *j* has been modernized; many words printed in italics in the original have been put into roman type when the present practice required it; and while the spelling of the original has of course been closely followed, the punctuation of Purchas or of Captain John Smith has not been regarded as equally sacred. The punctuation has been left as in the original whenever no strong reason existed to the contrary; but where the original punctuation does not make sense, nor indicate what was without doubt the author's meaning, as for instance in the case of the *True Relation*, of which the author had no chance to examine the proof-sheets, appropriate alterations have been introduced.

J. F. J.

# CONTENTS

## NARRATIVES OF EARLY VIRGINIA

EDITED BY LYON GARDINER TYLER, LL.D.

PAGE

OBSERVATIONS BY MASTER GEORGE PERCY, 1607 . . . . . . 1
- INTRODUCTION . . . . . . . . . . . . . . 3
- The Fleet bearing the Emigrants to Virginia leaves London . . 5
- Its Adventures in the West Indies . . . . . . . . . 6
- Enters Chesapeake Bay . . . . . . . . . . . . 9
- Some of the Settlers visit Kecoughtan . . . . . . . . 11
- The Ships ascend the River . . . . . . . . . . . 13
- They reach the Place of Settlement on Jamestown Island . . . . 15
- Habits and Customs of the Indians . . . . . . . . . 18
- Captain Newport returns to England . . . . . . . . 19
- Sufferings during the Summer . . . . . . . . . . 20
- President Wingfield deposed . . . . . . . . . . . 22

A TRUE RELATION, BY CAPTAIN JOHN SMITH, 1608 . . . . . 25
- INTRODUCTION . . . . . . . . . . . . . . . 27
- Description of the Voyage . . . . . . . . . . . 32
- Settlement on Jamestown Island; Exploration of the River . . 33
- Indian Attack; Newport sails for England . . . . . . . 35
- Sufferings during the Summer . . . . . . . . . . 36
- President Wingfield deposed . . . . . . . . . . . 37
- Efforts to obtain Corn . . . . . . . . . . . . 37
- Smith explores Chickahominy River . . . . . . . . 39
- Captured by the Indians . . . . . . . . . . . 44
- Is taken to Werowocomoco . . . . . . . . . . . 47
- Description of the Pamunkey River . . . . . . . . 50
- Customs of the Indians . . . . . . . . . . . . 51
- Smith is sent back to Jamestown . . . . . . . . . 52
- Arrival of Captain Newport with the First Supply . . . . 52
- The Fort burned . . . . . . . . . . . . . . 52
- Newport and Smith visit Werowocomoco . . . . . . . 53
- Trading with the Indians . . . . . . . . . . . 55
- Visits to Pamunkey and Nansemond . . . . . . . . 60
- Captain Newport returns to England . . . . . . . . 61
- Arrival of Captain Nelson . . . . . . . . . . . 64
- Trees felled and Corn planted . . . . . . . . . . 65

PAGE

Punishment of thieving Indians . . . . . . . . . . 66
Pocahontas visits the Fort . . . . . . . . . . 69
Captain Nelson returns to England . . . . . . . . 71

DESCRIPTION OF VIRGINIA AND PROCEEDINGS OF THE COLONIE . . 73

INTRODUCTION . . . . . . . . . . . . . 75
Title and Prefaces of the *Description* . . . . . . . . 76
Indian Vocabulary . . . . . . . . . . . . 78
Climate of Virginia . . . . . . . . . . . . 80
Chesapeake Bay and Mountains . . . . . . . . . 82
Rivers . . . . . . . . . . . . . . 83
Tribes of Indians . . . . . . . . . . . . 84
Varieties of Trees . . . . . . . . . . . . 90
Berries and Roots . . . . . . . . . . . . 92
Animals . . . . . . . . . . . . . . 93
Birds . . . . . . . . . . . . . . 94
Minerals and Vegetable Products . . . . . . . . . 95
Commodities . . . . . . . . . . . . . 97
Appearance and Manners of the Natives . . . . . . . 99
Their Dwellings . . . . . . . . . . . . 100
Their Habits and Customs . . . . . . . . . . 101
Their Religion . . . . . . . . . . . . 108
Their Government . . . . . . . . . . . . 113
Smith's Explanation of the Troubles at Jamestown . . . . 117
Title and Preface of the *Proceedings* . . . . . . . 119
Beginnings of the Virginia Company . . . . . . . 121
Sailing of the Fleet . . . . . . . . . . . 122
Arrival at Jamestown . . . . . . . . . . . 123
Names of the First Planters . . . . . . . . . . 125
Experiences of the First Summer . . . . . . . . . 127
Smith's Trading Voyages . . . . . . . . . . 129
Captured by the Savages . . . . . . . . . . 130
Arrival of the First Supply . . . . . . . . . . 132
Trading with the Savages . . . . . . . . . . 133
Newport visits Powhatan at Werowocomoco . . . . . . 134
Burning of Jamestown . . . . . . . . . . . 135
The Gold Craze at Jamestown . . . . . . . . . 136
Newport returns to England . . . . . . . . . . 137
Arrival of the *Phœnix* under Captain Nelson . . . . . . 137
How Smith frightened the Savages . . . . . . . . 138
The *Phœnix* returns to England . . . . . . . . . 139
Names of those who came in the First Supply . . . . . 140
Smith's First Voyage up Chesapeake Bay . . . . . . . 141
Discovers the Potomac River . . . . . . . . . . 144
Wounded by a Stingray; returns to Jamestown . . . . . . 146
His Second Voyage up Chesapeake Bay . . . . . . . 147

PAGE
He becomes President . . . . . . . . . . . . . 151
Arrival and Return of the Second Supply . . . . . . . 152
Smith visits Werowocomoco . . . . . . . . . . 153
The Coronation of Powhatan . . . . . . . . . 155
Arrival of the First Woman in the Colony . . . . . . . 155
Newport's Explorations; Smith's Management . . . . . 156
Evils wrought by Private Trading . . . . . . . . . 158
Names of those who came in the Second Supply . . . . . 159
Smith's Voyage to York River . . . . . . . . . 161
Experiences at Werowocomoco; Discourse with Powhatan . . . 163
Visits to Opechancanough at Pamunkey . . . . . . . 170
Death of Matthew Scrivener, Peter Waldo, and Anthony Gosnoll . 174
Difficulties in settling Virginia . . . . . . . . 177
Smith's Measures as President in the Spring of 1609 . . . . 180
His Hand-to-hand Fight with the Paspahegh Chief . . . . 181
Makes Peace with the Indians . . . . . . . . . 183
The Rats eat up the Corn . . . . . . . . . . 185
Smith's Efforts to supply Provisions . . . . . . . 186
Volda's Treachery . . . . . . . . . . . . 188
Arrival of the Third Supply . . . . . . . . . 191
Dissensions with the Newcomers . . . . . . . . 192
Smith is injured by Gunpowder . . . . . . . . . 195
Sails for England . . . . . . . . . . . . 196
Review of his Administration . . . . . . . . . 197
The Starving Time . . . . . . . . . . . . 200
Arrival of Sir Thomas Gates . . . . . . . . . 201
Death of Sir George Somers . . . . . . . . . 203

THE RELATION OF THE LORD DE-LA-WARE, 1611 . . . . . . . 205
INTRODUCTION . . . . . . . . . . . . . 207
Severe Experiences . . . . . . . . . . . . 210
Condition of the Colony . . . . . . . . . . 211
Establishment of Three New Forts . . . . . . . . 212

LETTER OF DON DIEGO DE MOLINA, 1613 . . . . . . . . 215
INTRODUCTION . . . . . . . . . . . . . 217
Urges the Spanish King to destroy the Colony promptly . . . 218
Dangers which may be expected . . . . . . . . . 219
Condition of the English Settlements . . . . . . . 220
Chesapeake Bay described . . . . . . . . . . 222
Forts in Virginia . . . . . . . . . . . . 223

LETTER OF FATHER PIERRE BIARD, 1614 . . . . . . . 225
INTRODUCTION . . . . . . . . . . . . . 227
Describes the English Attack on Mount Desert Island . . . . 228

PAGE

Is carried to Virginia . . . . . 230
Is present at the Destruction of Port Royal next year . . . . . 231
Dangers of the Voyage to England . . . . . 231

LETTER OF JOHN ROLFE, 1614 . . . . . 235
INTRODUCTION . . . . . 237
His reasons for marrying Pocahontas . . . . . 239

PROCEEDINGS OF THE VIRGINIA ASSEMBLY, 1619 . . . . . 245
INTRODUCTION . . . . . 247
List of Burgesses . . . . . 249
Captain Martin's Plantation denied Representation . . . . . 251
Committees appointed . . . . . 256
Petitions to the Authorities in England . . . . . 257
The Great Charter; the Price of Tobacco . . . . . 259
Captain Martin's Patent . . . . . 261
Laws based on Instructions from England . . . . . 262
Laws proposed by Individual Burgesses . . . . . 268
Captain Spelman punished . . . . . 274
Argall's Town . . . . . 275
Final Proceedings . . . . . 276

LETTER OF JOHN PORY, 1619 . . . . . 279
INTRODUCTION . . . . . 281
Condition of the Colony . . . . . 282

GENERALL HISTORIE OF VIRGINIA BY CAPTAIN JOHN SMITH, 1624; THE FOURTH BOOKE . . . . . 289
INTRODUCTION . . . . . 291
The Starving Time . . . . . 295
Arrival of Sir Thomas Gates; Jamestown abandoned . . . . . 296
Saved by the Coming of Lord Delaware . . . . . 297
His Administration of the Colony . . . . . 299
Returns to England . . . . . 301
Arrival of Sir Thomas Dale . . . . . 302
Institutes a Severe Government; Gates returns; Henrico founded . 304
Jamestown described . . . . . 306
Capture of Pocahontas . . . . . 307
Her Marriage with John Rolfe . . . . . 310
Peace with the Indians . . . . . 311
Private Property First Instituted . . . . . 312
Ralph Hamor's Visit to Powhatan . . . . . 313
William Parker recovered . . . . . 315
Remarks of Dale and Whitaker . . . . . 316
The Lottery . . . . . 318

PAGE
Spanish Spies at Point Comfort . . . 320
The Government of Sir George Yeardley . . . 321
He reduces the Indians to Peace . . . 323
Pocahontas visits England . . . 325
Captain Smith's Letter to Queen Anne . . . 325
Death of Pocahontas . . . 330
The Government of Captain Samuel Argall . . . 330
Lord Delaware dies on the Voyage over . . . 331
Murder of Killingbeck and of William Fairfax's Family . . . 333
The State of the Colony told by Rolfe . . . 334
Death of Powhatan . . . 334
Second Government of Sir George Yeardley . . . 335
Fertility of the Land in Virginia . . . 336
The First General Assembly; the First Negroes . . . 337
Division of Lands . . . 338
Young Maidens sent over; Gifts to the College . . . 339
A Desperate Sea-fight . . . 340
Great Fortunes from Tobacco . . . 346
Mr. Stockden's Warning . . . 347
Government of Sir Francis Wyatt . . . 348
Captain Gookin settles at Newport News . . . 349
Large Emigration to Virginia . . . 350
Voyage of John Pory to Accomack . . . 351
Tenants for the College and School sent over . . . 356
The Indian Massacre . . . 357
Reflections upon it . . . 364
The Number slain at the different Settlements . . . 368
Captain Thomas Newce's Industry . . . 371
Captain Raleigh Croshaw's Voyage to Potomac . . . 372
Smith's Proposals . . . 373
Answer of the Company; its Dissensions . . . 375
Escape of Edward Waters . . . 376
Adventures of Captain Madison . . . 378
Captain Thomas Newce at Elizabeth City . . . 378
Madison attacks the King of the Potomacs . . . 381
Sir George Yeardley attacks the Nansemonds . . . 384
Smith's Suggestions . . . 386
Arrival of Captain Butler . . . 389
Adventure of John Argent . . . 389
Death of Captain Spelman . . . 392
Outfit for a Virginia Planter . . . 393
Smith's Review of his Administration . . . 395
Questions of the Commissioners and Answers by Smith . . . 399
Dissolution of the Virginia Company . . . 405

PAGE

The Virginia Planters' Answer to Captain Butler, 1623 . . . 409
Introduction . . . . . . . . . . . . . . 411
Defence as to Climate and Natural Qualities . . . . . . 412
Defence as to Prosperity and Improvements . . . . . . 414

The Tragical Relation of the Virginia Assembly, 1624 . . 419
Introduction . . . . . . . . . . . . . . 421
Martial Law complained of . . . . . . . . . . . 422
Insufficient Supplies . . . . . . . . . . . . 423
Terrible Mortality . . . . . . . . . . . . 424
Sir Thomas Smith's Government a Failure . . . . . . . 425

The Discourse of the Old Company, 1625 . . . . . . . 427
Introduction . . . . . . . . . . . . . . 429
Results of the First Twelve Years . . . . . . . . . 432
Results of the Government of Sandys and Southampton . . . . 434
Difficulties encountered in the Latter Time . . . . . . . 436
Captain Butler's Attack . . . . . . . . . . . . 438
Unhappy Results of the Revocation of the Charter . . . . 440
Troubles experienced from Factious Enemies . . . . . . 445
The Tobacco Contracts . . . . . . . . . . . . 446
History of the Revocation of the Charter . . . . . . . 450
Insufficiency of the Succeeding Management . . . . . . 455

# NARRATIVES OF EARLY VIRGINIA

# OBSERVATIONS BY MASTER GEORGE PERCY, 1607

# INTRODUCTION

George Percy was the eighth son of Henry, eighth earl of Northumberland, by his wife Catherine, eldest daughter of John Neville, Lord Latimer. He was born September 4, 1580; served for a time as a soldier in the Netherlands; sailed for Virginia in the first expedition, December 20, 1606, and was president during the terrible time from September, 1609, to the arrival of Gates in May, 1610. When Lord Delaware left Jamestown in March, 1611, Percy was again placed at the head of the colony until the arrival of Dale in May following. He left Virginia April 22, 1612, and reached England in the following summer. He never returned to Virginia, but about 1625, when war was declared with Spain, he went again to the Netherlands, where as captain of a company he distinguished himself, and lost a finger in battle. He died unmarried in 1632. The fact that he was three times trusted with the supreme command in Virginia attests the good opinion entertained of his character, courage, and abilities.

The *Observations*, etc., gives in minute detail the incidents of the first voyage to Virginia, and is the straightforward account of an eye-witness and prominent actor. The original manuscript is not preserved, and what has come down to us is only an abridgment published for the first time in 1625 by Samuel Purchas, who assigns as a reason for the omissions he made in it that "the rest is more fully set downe in Cap. Smiths Relations." The narrative is to be found in *Purchas his Pilgrimes*, IV. 1685–1690, of the original edition. It presents the fullest account we have of the voyage and of the first events of the settlement, to Newport's departure, June 22, 1607. Of the other accounts of the earliest months of the colony, Wingfield's *Discourse of Virginia*, printed in the fourth volume of the *Archaeologia Americana* and separately (Worcester, 1860), begins at that point; but it is too largely a partisan account of the author's quarrels with his fellow-members of the council to have the same sort of value as Percy's story. There is also the *Relatyon* called Newport's, though perhaps written by Archer, likewise printed in the *Archaeologia*, Vol. IV.; but this is almost confined to the exploration of James River, May 21–27. Captain John Smith's *True Relation*, the most important narrative of the early days, which begins to be explicit about where what we have of Percy leaves off, is printed next after it in this volume. Purchas's text was reprinted by Edward Arber in his edition of Smith's *Works* (Birmingham, 1884), to which Wingfield and Archer are also prefixed. It has also, of course, been reprinted in the edition of Purchas which has now (July, 1907) just finished passing through the press.

L. G. T.

# OBSERVATIONS BY MASTER GEORGE PERCY, 1607

*Observations gathered out of a Discourse of the Plantation of the Southerne Colonie in Virginia by the English, 1606. Written by that Honorable Gentleman, Master George Percy.*

On Saturday the twentieth of December in the yeere 1606. the fleet fell from London,[1] and the fift of January we anchored in the Downes: but the winds continued contrarie so long, that we were forced to stay there some time, where wee suffered great stormes, but by the skilfulnesse of the Captaine wee suffered no great losse or danger.

The twelfth day of February at night we saw a blazing Starre, and presently a storme.

The three and twentieth day [2] we fell with the Iland of Mattanenio,[3] in the West Indies. The foure and twentieth day we anchored at Dominico,[4] within fourteene degrees of the Line, a very faire Iland, the Trees full of sweet and good smels; inhabited by many Savage Indians. They were at first very scrupulous to come aboord us. Wee learned of them afterwards that the Spaniards had given them a great over-

[1] The fleet sailed down the Thames from London. The Downs is a celebrated roadstead for ships, extending six miles along the seacoast of Kent in England, protected on the sea side by the Goodwin Sands.

[2] Of March.

[3] Martinique.

[4] Dominica. Purchas says at this point in the margin, "Captaine Smith was suspected for a supposed Mutinie, though never no such matter." Smith says in his *Generall Historie*, folio 43, that "all this time from their departure from the Canaries" to June 10, he "was restrained as a prisoner upon the scandalous suggestions of some of the chiefe, who fained he intended to usurp the government, murther the Councell, and make himselfe King."

throw on this Ile, but when they knew what we were, there came many to our ships with their Canoas, bringing us many kindes of sundry fruites, as Pines, Potatoes, Plantons, Tobacco, and other fruits, and Roane Cloth abundance, which they had gotten out of certaine Spanish ships that were cast away upon that Iland. We gave them Knives, Hatchets for exchange, which they esteeme much. Wee also gave them Beades, Copper Jewels which they hang through their nosthrils, eares, and lips, very strange to behold. Their bodies are all painted red to keepe away the biting of Muscetos. They goe all naked without covering. The haire of their head is a yard long, all of a length, pleated in three plats hanging downe to their wastes. They suffer no haire to grow on their faces. They cut [1] their skinnes in divers workes. They are continually in warres, and will eate their enemies when they kill them, or any stranger if they take them. They will lap up mans spittle, whilst one spits in their mouthes, in a barbarous fashion like Dogges. These people and the rest of the Ilands in the West Indies, and Brasill, are called by the names of Canibals,[2] that will eate mans flesh. These people doe poyson their Arrow heads, which are made of a fishes bone. They worship the Devill for their God, and have no other beliefe.

Whilest we remayned at this Iland we saw a Whale chased by a Thresher and a Sword-fish. They fought for the space of two houres. We might see the Thresher with his flayle lay on the monstrous blowes which was strange to behold. In the end these two fishes brought the Whale to her end.

The sixe and twentieth day we had sight of Marigalanta,[3] and the next day, wee sailed with a slacke saile alongst the Ile of Guadalupa, where we went ashore, and found a Bath which was so hot, that no man was able to stand long by it. Our Admirall, Captaine Newport, caused a piece of Porke to be put in it; which boyled it so in the space of halfe an houre,

[1] Tattoo.

[2] See *The Northmen, Columbus and Cabot*, in this series, p. 289, note 2.

[3] Marie Galante, a French possession.

as no fire could mend it. Then we went aboord and sailed by many Ilands, as Mounserot[1] and an Iland called Saint Christopher, both uninhabited. About two o'clocke in the afternoone wee anchored at the Ile of Mevis.[2] There the Captaine landed all his men being well fitted with Muskets and other convenient Armes; marched a mile into the Woods; being commanded to stand upon their guard, fearing the treacherie of the Indians, which is an ordinary use amongst them and all other Savages on this Ile. We came to a Bath standing in a Valley betwixt two Hils, where wee bathed our selves; and found it to be of the nature of the Bathes in England, some places hot and some colder: and men may refresh themselves as they please. Finding this place to be so convenient for our men to avoid diseases which will breed in so long a Voyage, wee incamped our selves on this Ile sixe dayes, and spent none of our ships victuall, by reason our men some went a hunting, some a fouling, and some a fishing, where we got great store of Conies, sundry kinds of fowles, and great plentie of fish. We kept Centinels and Courts de gard[3] at every Captaines quarter, fearing wee should be assaulted by the Indians, that were on the other side of the Iland. Wee saw none, nor were molested by any; but some few we saw as we were a hunting on the Iland. They would not come to us by any meanes, but ranne swiftly through the Woods to the Mountaine tops; so we lost the sight of them; whereupon we made all the haste wee could to our quarter, thinking there had beene a great ambush of Indians there abouts. We past into the thickest of the Woods, where we had almost lost our selves. We had not gone above halfe a mile amongst the thicke, but we came into a most pleasant Garden, being a hundred paces square on every side, having many Cotton-trees growing in it with abundance of Cotton-wooll, and many *Guiacum* trees. Wee saw the goodliest tall trees growing so thicke about the Garden, as though they had beene set by Art, which made us marvell very much to see it.

[1] Montserrat. [2] Nevis. [3] Watches.

The third day[1] wee set saile from Mevis. The fourth day we sailed along by Castutia[2] and by Saba. This day we anchored at the Ile of Virgines[3] in an excellent Bay able to harbour a hundred Ships. If this Bay stood in England, it would be a great profit and commoditie to the Land. On this Iland wee caught great store of Fresh-fish, and abundance of Sea Tortoises, which served all our Fleet three daies, which were in number eight score persons. We also killed great store of wild Fowle. Wee cut the Barkes of certaine Trees which tasted much like Cinnamon, and very hot in the mouth. This Iland in some places hath very good ground, straight and tall Timber. But the greatest discommoditie that wee have seene on this Iland is that it hath no Fresh-water, which makes the place void of any Inhabitants.

Upon the sixt day, we set saile and passed by Becam[4] and by Saint John de porto rico.[5] The seventh day we arrived at Mona: where wee watered, which we stood in great need of, seeing that our water did smell so vildly that none of our men was able to indure it. Whilst some of the Saylers were a filling the Caskes with water, the Captaine and the rest of the Gentlemen, and other Soldiers, marched up in the Ile sixe myles, thinking to find some other provision to maintaine our victualling. As we marched we killed two wild Bores, and saw a huge wild Bull, his hornes was an ell betweene the two tops. We also killed Guanas[6] in fashion of a Serpent, and speckled like a Toade under the belly. These wayes that wee went, being so troublesome and vilde, going upon the sharpe Rockes, that many of our men fainted in the march, but by good fortune wee lost none but one Edward Brookes Gentleman, whose fat melted within him by the great heate and drought of the Countrey. We were not able to relieve him nor our selves, so he died in that great extreamitie.

[1] Of April.
[2] St. Eustatius, a Dutch island, of which Saba is a dependency.
[3] Virgin Islands.
[4] Vieques, now belonging to the United States.
[5] Porto Rico.
[6] Iguanas, a kind of lizard.

The ninth day, in the afternoone, we went off with our Boat to the Ile of Moneta,[1] some three leagues from Mona, where we had a terrible landing, and a troublesome getting up to the top of the Mountaine or Ile, being a high firme Rocke, ste[e]p, with many terrible sharpe stones. After wee got to the top of the Ile, we found it to bee a fertill and a plaine ground, full of goodly grasse, and abundance of Fowles of all kindes. They flew over our heads as thicke as drops of Hale; besides they made such a noise, that wee were not able to heare one another speake. Furthermore, wee were not able to set our feet on the ground, but either on Fowles or Egges which lay so thicke in the grasse. Wee laded two Boats full in the space of three houres, to our great refreshing.

The tenth day we set saile, and disimboged [2] out of the West Indies, and bare oure course Northerly. The fourteenth day we passed the Tropicke of Cancer. The one and twentieth day, about five a clocke at night there began a vehement tempest, which lasted all the night, with winds, raine, and thunders, in a terrible manner. Wee were forced to lie at Hull [3] that night, because we thought wee had beene neerer land then wee were. The next morning, being the two and twentieth day, wee sounded; and the three and twentieth, and foure and twenteth day; but we could find no ground. The five and twentieth day, we sounded, and had no ground at an hundred fathom.[4] The six and twentieth day of Aprill, about foure a clocke in the morning, wee descried the Land of Virginia. The same day wee entred into the Bay of Chesupioc [5] directly, without any let or hinderance. There wee landed and discovered [6] a little way, but wee could find nothing worth the speaking of, but faire meddowes and

[1] Monica.

[2] By this expression the fleet is likened to a stream of water which "pours out" into the ocean.

[3] To lie to, with sails furled.

[4] The margin says, "We were driven to try" [*i.e.*, to lie to] "that night: and by the storme were forced neere the shoare, not knowing where we were."

[5] Chesapeake Bay.

[6] Throughout this volume, it is important to bear in mind that in the texts here printed "discovered" almost always means "explored."

goodly tall Trees, with such Fresh-waters running through the woods, as I was almost ravished at the first sight thereof.

At night, when wee were going aboard, there came the Savages creeping upon all foure, from the Hills, like Beares, with their Bowes in their mouthes, charged us very desperately in the faces, hurt Captaine Gabrill Archer in both his hands, and a sayler in two places of the body very dangerous. After they had spent their Arrowes, and felt the sharpnesse of our shot, they retired into the Woods with a great noise, and so left us.

The seven and twentieth day we began to build up our Shallop. The Gentlemen and Souldiers marched eight miles up into the land. We could not see a Savage in all that march. We came to a place where they had made a great fire, and had beene newly a rosting Oysters. When they perceived our comming, they fled away to the mountaines, and left many of the Oysters in the fire. We eat some of the Oysters, which were very large and delicate in taste.

The eighteenth [1] day we lanched our Shallop. The Captaine and some Gentlemen went in her, and discovered up the Bay. We found a River [2] on the Southside running into the Maine; we entered it and found it very shoald water, not for any Boats to swim. Wee went further into the Bay, and saw a plaine plot of ground where we went on Land, and found the place five mile in compasse, without either Bush or Tree. We saw nothing there but a Cannow, which was made out of the whole tree, which was five and fortie foot long by the Rule. Upon this plot of ground we got good store of Mussels and Oysters, which lay on the ground as thicke as stones. Wee opened some, and found in many of them Pearles. Wee marched some three or foure miles further into the woods, where we saw great smoakes of fire. Wee marched to those smoakes and found that the Savages had beene there burning downe the grasse, as wee thought either to make their

[1] Rather the twenty-eighth, of April.

[2] Lynnhaven River in Princess Anne County.

plantation there, or else to give signes to bring their forces together, and so to give us battell. We past through excellent ground full of Flowers of divers kinds and colours, and as goodly trees as I have seene, as Cedar, Cipresse, and other kindes. Going a little further we came into a little plat of ground full of fine and beautifull Strawberries, foure times bigger and better then ours in England. All this march we could neither see Savage nor Towne. When it grew to be towards night, we stood backe to our Ships, we sounded and found it shallow water for a great way, which put us out of all hopes for getting any higher with our Ships, which road at the mouth of the River. Wee rowed over to a point of Land, where wee found a channell, and sounded six, eight, ten, or twelve fathom: which put us in good comfort. Therefore wee named that point of Land, Cape Comfort.[1]

The nine and twentieth day we set up a Crosse at Chesupioc Bay, and named that place Cape Henry. Thirtieth day, we came with our ships to Cape Comfort; where we saw five Savages running on the shoare. Presently the Captaine caused the shallop to be manned; so rowing to the shoare, the Captaine called to them in signe of friendship, but they were at first very timersome, until they saw the Captain lay his hand on his heart; upon that they laid downe their Bowes and Arrowes, and came very boldly to us, making signes to come a shoare to their Towne, which is called by the Savages Kecoughtan.[2] Wee coasted to their Towne, rowing over a River running into the Maine, where these Savages swam over with their Bowes and Arrowes in their mouthes.

When we came over to the other side, there was a many of other Savages which directed us to their Towne, where we

[1] In 1608 a fort called "Algernourne" was established here by Captain George Percy, and it is now the site of Fort Monroe, built in 1819 by the federal government.

[2] The town was located at the mouth of Hampton River on the east side, and was three miles from Point Comfort. The Soldiers' Home occupies very nearly the ancient site. In the Indian language the word meant "great town." At the time of the arrival of the settlers it was commanded by Pochins, a son of Powhatan

were entertained by them very kindly. When we came first a Land they made a dolefull noise, laying their faces to the ground, scratching the earth with their nailes. We did thinke they had beene at their Idolatry. When they had ended their Ceremonies, they went into their houses and brought out mats and laid upon the ground: the chiefest of them sate all in a rank; the meanest sort brought us such dainties as they had, and of their bread which they make of their Maiz or Gennea wheat.[1] They would not suffer us to eat unlesse we sate down, which we did on a Mat right against them. After we were well satisfied they gave us of their Tabacco, which they tooke in a pipe made artifically of earth as ours are, but far bigger, with the bowle fashioned together with a piece of fine copper. After they had feasted us, they shewed us, in welcome, their manner of dancing, which was in this fashion. One of the Savages standing in the midst singing, beating one hand against another, all the rest dancing about him, shouting, howling, and stamping against the ground, with many Anticke tricks and faces, making noise like so many Wolves or Devils. One thing of them I observed; when they were in their dance they kept stroke with their feet just one with another, but with their hands, heads, faces and bodies, every one of them had a severall gesture: so they continued for the space of halfe an houre. When they had ended their dance, the Captaine gave them Beades and other trifling Jewells. They hang through their eares, Fowles legs; they shave the right side of their heads with a shell, the left side they weare of an ell long tied up with an artificiall knot, with a many of Foules feathers sticking in it. They goe altogether naked, but their privities are covered with Beasts skinnes beset commonly with little bones, or beasts teeth. Some paint their bodies blacke, some red, with artificiall knots of sundry lively colours, very beautiful and pleasing to the eye, in a braver fashion then they in the West Indies.

[1] Maize was the West Indian name for Indian corn. Gennea (Guinea) wheat was a tall grass grown in Africa and familiar to us as broom corn.

The fourth day of May we came to the King or Werowance of Paspihe:[1] where they entertained us with much welcome. An old Savage made a long Oration, making a foule noise, uttering his speech with a vehement action, but we knew little what they meant. Whilst we were in company with the Paspihes, the Werowance of Rapahanna[2] came from the other side of the River in his Cannoa. He seemed to take displeasure of our being with the Paspihes. He would faine have had us come to his Towne. The Captaine was unwilling. Seeing that the day was so far spent, he returned backe to his ships for that night.

The next day, being the fift of May, the Werowance of Rapahanna sent a Messenger to have us come to him. We entertained the said Messenger, and gave him trifles which pleased him. Wee manned our shallop with Muskets and Targatiers sufficiently: this said Messenger guided us where our determination was to goe. When wee landed, the Werowance of Rapahanna came downe to the water side with all his traine, as goodly men as any I have seene of Savages or Christians: the Werowance comming before them playing on a Flute made of a Reed, with a Crown of Deares haire colloured red, in fashion of a Rose fastened about his knot of haire, and a great Plate of Copper on the other side of his head, with two long Feathers in fashion of a paire of Hornes placed in the midst of his Crowne. His body was painted all with Crimson, with a Chaine of Beads about his necke, his face painted blew, be-

[1] The territory of the Paspihes (Paspaheghs, or Pasbyhaes) stretched along the north side of James River from about Warwick River, where the territory of the Kecoughtans ended, to Sturgeon Point. Their chief town, "Old Paspaheghs," had been located until a short time before the arrival of the English on the north shore, almost a mile from Jamestown Island; but, at the time of the narrative, their chief town was at Sandy Point, a much more fertile region, about ten miles above Jamestown, on the north side of the river.

[2] The country on the south side of the James opposite to Paspahegh belonged to the Quiyoughcohanock Indians, whose chief town was at Claremont. The Rapahanna chief was a stranger, who came to the James from the Rappahannock River in order to assist in resisting the landing of the explorers.

sprinkled with silver Ore as wee thought, his eares all behung with Braslets of Pearle, and in either eare a Birds Claw through it beset with fine Copper or Gold. He entertained us in so modest a proud fashion, as though he had beene a Prince of civill government, holding his countenance without laughter or any such ill behaviour. He caused his Mat to be spred on the ground, where hee sate downe with a great Majestie, taking a pipe of Tabacco: the rest of his company standing about him. After he had rested a while he rose, and made signes to us to come to his Towne. Hee went foremost, and all the rest of his people and our selves followed him up a steepe Hill where his Palace was settled. Wee passed through the Woods in fine paths, having most pleasant Springs which issued from the Mountaines. Wee also went through the goodliest Corne fieldes that ever was seene in any Countrey. When wee came to Rapahannos Towne, hee entertained us in good humanitie.

The eight day of May we discovered up the River. We landed in the Countrey of Apamatica.[1] At our landing, there came many stout and able Savages to resist us with their Bowes and Arrowes, in a most warlike manner, with the swords at their backes beset with sharpe stones, and pieces of yron able to cleave a man in sunder. Amongst the rest one of the chiefest, standing before them cross-legged, with his Arrow readie in his Bow in one hand, and taking a Pipe of Tobacco in the other, with a bold uttering of his speech, demanded of us our being there, willing us to bee gone. Wee made signes of peace, which they perceived in the end, and let us land in quietnesse.

The twelfth day we went backe to our ships, and discovered a point of Land, called Archers Hope,[2] which was sufficient

[1] The "country of Apamatica" was the region of the Appomattox River. Thirty miles up the river is Petersburg; at its mouth is City Point, first called Charles City.

[2] This point is made by a creek, at the head of which five miles inland is situated the city of Williamsburg, made the capital of Virginia in 1699 after the burning of the State House at Jamestown.

with a little labour to defend our selves against any Enemy. The soile was good and fruitfull, with excellent good Timber. There are also great store of Vines in bignesse of a mans thigh, running up to the tops of the Trees in great abundance. We also did see many Squirels, Conies, Black Birds with crimson wings, and divers other Fowles and Birds of divers and sundrie collours of crimson, Watchet, Yellow, Greene, Murry,[1] and of divers other hewes naturally without any art using.

We found store of Turkie nests and many Egges. If it had not beene disliked, because the ship could not ride neere the shoare, we had setled there to all the Collonies contentment.

The thirteenth day, we came to our seating place in Paspihas Countrey, some eight miles[2] from the point of Land, which I made mention before: where our shippes doe lie so neere the shoare that they are moored to the Trees in six fathom water.

The fourteenth day, we landed all our men, which were set to worke about the fortification, and others some to watch and ward as it was convenient. The first night of our landing, about midnight, there came some Savages sayling close to our quarter. Presently there was an alarum given; upon that the Savages ran away, and we [were] not troubled any more by them that night. Not long after there came two Savages that seemed to be Commanders, bravely drest, with Crownes of coloured haire upon their heads, which came as Messengers from the Werowance[3] of Paspihæ, telling us that their Werowance was comming and would be merry with us with a fat Deare.

The eighteenth day, the Werowance of Paspihæ came himselfe to our quarter, with one hundred Savages armed, which garded him in a very warlike manner with Bowes and Arrowes, thinking at that time to execute their villany. Pas-

[1] Watchet is pale blue; murry is dark red.

[2] The settlement was placed about five miles above the mouth of Archer's Hope Creek at the west end of the island, where the channel of the river comes close to the shore. The margin gives the name, "Their plantation at James Towne." The early narrators also call the settlement James Fort.

[3] The word "werowance" among the Virginia Indians was equivalent to the word "sachem" in New England.

pihæ made great signes to us to lay our Armes away. But we would not trust him so far. He seeing he could not have convenient time to worke his will, at length made signes that he would give us as much land as we would desire to take. As the Savages were in a throng in the Fort, one of them stole a Hatchet from one of our company,[1] which spied him doing the deed: whereupon he tooke it from him by force, and also strooke him over the arme. Presently another Savage seeing that, came fiercely at our man with a wooden sword, thinking to beat out his braines. The Werowance of Paspiha saw us take to our Armes, went suddenly away with all his company in great anger.

The nineteenth day, my selfe and three or foure more walking into the Woods by chance wee espied a pathway like to an Irish pace:[2] wee were desirous to knowe whither it would bring us. Wee traced along some foure miles, all the way as wee went, having the pleasantest Suckles, the ground all flowing over with faire flowers of sundry colours and kindes, as though it had been in any Garden or Orchard in England. There be many Strawberries, and other fruits unknowne. Wee saw the Woods full of Cedar and Cypresse trees, with other trees, which issues out sweet Gummes like to Balsam. Wee kept on our way in this Paradise. At length, wee came to a Savage Towne, where wee found but few people. They told us the rest were gone a hunting with the Werowance of Paspiha. We stayed there a while, and had of them Strawberries and other things. In the meane time one of the Savages came running out of his house with a Bowe and Arrowes and ranne mainly through the Woods. Then I beganne to mistrust some villanie, that he went to call some companie, and so betray us. Wee made all haste away wee could. One of the Savages brought us on the way to the Wood side, where there was a Garden of Tobacco and other fruits and herbes. He gathered Tobacco, and distributed to every one of us; so wee departed.

[1] "These Savages," says the margin, "are naturally great theeves."
[2] Pass, or passage.

The twentieth day the Werowance of Paspiha sent fortie of his men with a Deere, to our quarter: but they came more in villanie than any love they bare us. They faine would have layne in our Fort all night, but wee would not suffer them for feare of their treachery. One of our Gentlemen having a Target which hee trusted in, thinking it would beare out a slight shot, hee set it up against a tree, willing one of the Savages to shoot; who tooke from his backe an Arrow of an elle long, drew it strongly in his Bowe, shoots the Target a foote thorow, or better: which was strange, being that a Pistoll could not pierce it. Wee seeing the force of his Bowe, afterwards set him up a steele Target; he shot again, and burst his arrow all to pieces. He presently pulled out another Arrow, and bit it in his teeth, and seemed to bee in a great rage; so hee went away in great anger. Their Bowes are made of tough Hasell, their strings of Leather, their Arrowes of Canes or Hasell, headed with very sharpe stones, and are made artificially like a broad Arrow: other some of their Arrowes are headed with the ends of Deeres hornes, and are feathered very artificially. Pasphia was as good as his word; for hee sent Venison, but the Sawse came within a few dayes after.

At Port Cotage [1] in our Voyage up the River, we saw a Savage Boy about the age of ten yeeres, which had a head of haire of a perfect yellow and a reasonable white skinne,[2] which is a Miracle amongst all Savages.

This River which wee have discovered is one of the famousest Rivers that ever was found by any Christian. It ebbs and flowes a hundred and threescore miles, where ships of great burthen may harbour in safetie. Wheresoever we landed upon this River, wee saw the goodliest Woods as Beech, Oke, Cedar,

[1] The writer of *A Relatyon of the Discovery of our River* says (Arber, xlii) that he gave the name of "Poor Cottage" to a place on the James River about twenty miles below the falls.

[2] Possibly a descendant of one of the lost colony of Roanoke. On the theory, not generally agreed to, that that colony was not wholly destroyed, and that descendants of some of its members are still to be found in North Carolina, see Weeks, "The Lost Colony of Roanoke: Its Fate and Survival," in *Papers of the American Historical Association*, V. 441–480.

Cypresse, Wal-nuts, Sassafras, and Vines in great abundance, which hang in great clusters on many Trees, and other Trees unknowne; and all the grounds bespred with many sweet and delicate flowres of divers colours and kindes. There are also many fruites as Strawberries, Mulberries, Rasberries, and Fruites unknowne. There are many branches of this River, which runne flowing through the Woods with great plentie of fish of all kindes; as for Sturgeon, all the World cannot be compared to it. In this Countrey I have seene many great and large Medowes having excellent good pasture for any Cattle. There is also great store of Deere both Red and Fallow. There are Beares, Foxes, Otters, Bevers, Muskats, and wild beasts unknowne.

The foure and twentieth day wee set up a Crosse at the head of this River, naming it Kings River, where we proclaimed James King of England to have the most right unto it. When wee had finished and set up our Crosse, we shipt our men and made for James Fort. By the way, wee came to Pohatans Towre, where the Captaine went on shore suffering none to goe with him. Hee presented the Commander of this place, with a Hatchet which hee tooke joyfully, and was well pleased.

But yet the Savages murmured at our planting in the Countrie, whereupon this Werowance made answere againe very wisely of a Savage, Why should you bee offended with them as long as they hurt you not, nor take any thing away by force. They take but a litle waste ground, which doth you nor any of us any good.

I saw Bread made by their women, which doe all their drugerie. The men takes their pleasure in hunting and their warres, which they are in continually, one Kingdome against another. The manner of baking of bread is thus. After they pound their wheat into flowre, with hote water they make it into paste, and worke it into round balls and Cakes, then they put it into a pot of seething water: when it is sod throughly, they lay it on a smooth stone, there they harden it as well as in an Oven.

There is notice to be taken to know married women from Maids. The Maids you shall alwayes see the fore part of their head and sides shaven close, the hinder part very long, which they tie in a pleate hanging downe to their hips. The married women weares their haire all of a length, and is tied of that fashion that the Maids are. The women kinde in this Countrey doth pounce and race their bodies, legges, thighes, armes and faces with a sharpe Iron, which makes a stampe in curious knots, and drawes the proportion of Fowles, Fish, or Beasts; then with paintings of sundry lively colours, they rub it into the stampe which will never be taken away, because it is dried into the flesh where it is sered.

The Savages beare their yeeres well, for when wee were at Pamonkies, wee saw a Savage by their report was above eight score yeeres of age. His eyes were sunke into his head, having never a tooth in his mouth, his haire all gray with a reasonable bigge beard, which was as white as any snow. It is a Miracle to see a Savage have any haire on their faces. I never saw, read, nor heard, any have the like before. This Savage was as lusty and went as fast as any of us, which was strange to behold.

The fifteenth of June we had built and finished our Fort, which was triangle wise, having three Bulwarkes, at every corner, like a halfe Moone, and foure or five pieces of Artillerie mounted in them. We had made our selves sufficiently strong for these Savages. We had also sowne most of our Corne on two Mountaines.[1] It sprang a mans height from the ground. This Countrey is a fruitfull soile, bearing many goodly and fruitfull Trees, as Mulberries, Cherries, Walnuts, Cedars, Cypresse, Sassafras, and Vines in great abundance.

Munday the two and twentieth of June, in the morning, Captaine Newport in the Admirall departed from James Port for England.

[1] The highest part of Jamestown peninsula is not over ten feet above the level of the sea; so that "the two mountaines" were only slight elevations of the soil.

Captaine Newport being gone for England, leaving us (one hundred and foure persons) verie bare and scantie of victualls, furthermore in warres and in danger of the Savages, we hoped after a supply which Captaine Newport promised within twentie weekes. But if the beginners of this action doe carefully further us, the Country being so fruitfull, it would be as great a profit to the Realme of England, as the Indies to the King of Spaine. If this River which wee have found had been discovered in the time of warre with Spaine, it would have beene a commoditie to our Realme, and a great annoyance to our enemies.

The seven and twentieth of July the King of Rapahanna demanded a Canoa, which was restored, lifted up his hand to the Sunne (which they worship as their God), besides he laid his hand on his heart, that he would be our speciall friend. It is a generall rule of these people, when they swere by their God which is the Sunne, no Christian will keep their Oath better upon this promise. These people have a great reverence to the Sunne above all other things: at the rising and setting of the same, they sit downe lifting up their hands and eyes to the Sunne, making a round Circle on the ground with dried Tobacco; then they began to pray, making many Devillish gestures with a Hellish noise, foming at the mouth, staring with their eyes, wagging their heads and hands in such a fashion and deformitie as it was monstrous to behold.

The sixt of August there died John Asbie of the bloudie Flixe.[1] The ninth day died George Flowre of the swelling. The tenth day died William Bruster Gentleman, of a wound given by the Savages, and was buried the eleventh day.

The fourteenth day, Jerome Alikock, Ancient, died of a wound, the same day, Francis Midwinter, Edward Moris Corporall died suddenly.

[1] Bloody flux or dysentery. Most of these names appear in the list of the first planters, printed in the first chapter of *The Proceedings of the English Colonie*, *post*, or in the fuller list which Smith gives on folios 43, 44, of his *Generall Historie*. These, however, read Jeremy Alicock, Edward Morish, Thomas Gore, Dru Pickhouse, Kellam Throgmorton, William Rodes and Thomas Studley.

The fifteenth day, their died Edward Browne and Stephen Galthorpe. The sixteenth day, their died Thomas Gower Gentleman. The seventeenth day, their died Thomas Mounslic. The eighteenth day, there died Robert Pennington, and John Martine Gentleman. The nineteenth day, died Drue Piggase Gentleman. The two and twentieth day of August, there died Captaine Bartholomew Gosnold,[1] one of our Councell: he was honourably buried, having all the Ordnance in the Fort shot off, with many vollies of small shot.

After Captaine Gosnols death, the Councell could hardly agree by the dissention of Captaine Kendall, which afterwards was committed about hainous matters which was proved against him.

The foure and twentieth day, died Edward Harington and George Walker, and were buried the same day. The six and twentieth day, died Kenelme Throgmortine. The seven and twentieth day died William Roods. The eight and twentieth day died Thomas Stoodie, Cape Merchant.[2]

The fourth day of September died Thomas Jacob Sergeant. The fift day, there died Benjamin Beast. Our men were destroyed with cruell diseases, as Swellings, Flixes, Burning Fevers, and by warres, and some departed suddenly, but for the most part they died of meere famine. There were never Englishmen left in a forreigne Countrey in such miserie as wee were in this new discovered Virginia. Wee watched every three nights, lying on the bare cold ground, what weather soever came, [and] warded all the next day, which brought our men to bee most feeble wretches. Our food was but a small Can of Barlie sod in water, to five men a day, our drinke cold water taken out of the River, which was at a floud verie

[1] Captain Gosnold had exerted great influence in establishing the London Company. In 1602 he had made a voyage to New England, for an account of which see Brereton's *Briefe and True Relation* in the volume of this series entitled *Early English and French Voyages*.

[2] Thomas Studley. The cape merchant was the company's general keeper of the stores.

salt, at a low tide full of slime and filth, which was the destruction of many of our men. Thus we lived for the space of five moneths in this miserable distresse, not having five able men to man our Bulwarkes upon any occasion. If it had not pleased God to have put a terrour in the Savages hearts, we had all perished by those vild and cruell Pagans, being in that weake estate as we were; our men night and day groaning in every corner of the Fort most pittifull to heare. If there were any conscience in men, it would make their harts to bleed to heare the pitifull murmurings and out-cries of our sick men without reliefe, every night and day, for the space of sixe weekes, some departing out of the World, many times three or foure in a night; in the morning, their bodies trailed out of their Cabines like Dogges to be buried. In this sort did I see the mortalitie of divers of our people.

It pleased God, after a while, to send those people which were our mortall enemies to releeve us with victuals, as Bread, Corne, Fish, and Flesh in great plentie, which was the setting up of our feeble men, otherwise wee had all perished. Also we were frequented by divers Kings in the Countrie, bringing us store of provision to our great comfort.

The eleventh day,[1] there was certaine Articles laid against Master Wingfield [2] which was then President; thereupon he was not only displaced out of his President ship, but also from being of the Councell. Afterwards Captaine John Ratcliffe was chosen President.

The eighteenth day, died one Ellis Kinistone,[3] which was starved to death with cold. The same day at night, died one Richard Simmons. The nineteenth day, there died one Thomas Mouton.

[1] Of September, 1607.

[2] Edward Maria Wingfield was born about 1560 and was a brave soldier, who served in Ireland and then in the Netherlands. He was elected May 14, 1607, first president of the first council in the first English colony in America. Suspected of being a Catholic, he lost his influence among the settlers and was deposed. See his *Discourse of Virginia*, mentioned in the introduction to this section.

[3] Smith gives this name as Kingston.

William White (having lived with the Natives) reported to us of their customes. In the morning by breake of day, before they eate or drinke, both men, women, and children, that be above tenne yeares of age, runnes into the water, there washes themselves a good while till the Sunne riseth, then offer Sacrifice to it, strewing Tobacco on the water or Land, honouring the Sunne as their God. Likewise they doe at the setting of the Sunne.

# A TRUE RELATION, BY CAPTAIN JOHN SMITH, 1608

# INTRODUCTION

THIS tract contains a brief account of the Virginia colonists from the time of their leaving London, December 20, 1606, to the departure of the *Phoenix* for England, June 2, 1608. It was entered for publication at Stationers' Hall, August 13, 1608, and some of the copies purported to be written by "a Gentleman of the said Collony." Other copies ascribed the work to "Th. Watson Gent. one of the said Collony," but a final issue identified the author as "Captain Smith Coronell of the said Collony." The editor of the tract as last presented explained the use of Thomas Watson's name as "owing to the overrashnesse or mistaking of the workemen." The pamphlet itself bears internal evidence that it was from Captain John Smith's pen. He was the son of George and Alice Smith, tenants of Peregrine Bertie, Lord Willoughby, and was baptized at Willoughby, January 9, 1580. At fifteen years of age he was apprenticed to a merchant, but the love of excitement was strong in him, and the next nine years were passed on the continent of Europe in constant travel and adventure. He served in the French, Dutch, and Transylvanian armies, and encountered many dangers. He was robbed and beaten by outlaws, was thrown into the sea for a heretic, and was a slave to a Turkish pasha. He had many hairbreadth escapes, but the most notable incident of his early career was his three combats before the city of Regall with the three Turkish champions, whose heads he cut off one after another. As a reward he received from Sigismund Bathori, a prince of Transylvania, a coat of arms with three Turks' heads in a shield.

Smith returned to England in 1604, and immediately became interested in the movement then on foot to establish a colony in Virginia. His reputation had preceded him, and he was picked out as one of the council to direct affairs in Virginia. He remained in this service till October, 1609, having been from September 20, 1608, to September 20, 1609, president of the colony. His wonderful talent for hairbreadth escapes did not desert him. He was charged on the way over with conspiracy and kept under arrest till three weeks after the settlers landed at Jamestown. In December, 1607, he was captured by the Indians and was saved from death by Pocahontas. He returned to Jamestown only to run into a new danger. He was arrested by the council and condemned to death and escaped hanging by the timely return of Captain Christopher Newport, who interfered and saved his life. Captain Smith left the colony at the end of his presidency, and for several years he was in the employment of the Plymouth Company, giving the name to New England and making a valuable chart of the country. From 1615 to his death in 1631 he lived quietly in England, where he was known as a prolific writer. In 1612 he published his *Map of Virginia*, in 1624 *The Generall Historie of Virginia, New England and the Summer Isles*, and in 1630 *The True Travels*. The absence of any reference in the *True Relation* to his rescue by Pocahontas has led some to doubt the truth of his assertions; but it appears that Smith omitted any particular mention of several other prominent incidents since his departure from London, affecting him personally. He has nothing to say of his arrest in the West Indies for mutiny, or the sentence of death imposed at Jamestown after his return from captivity. The timely arrival of Newport was in fact even more surprising than the kindly intervention of Pocahontas. Nor does he say in the *True Relation* anything of the fine of £200 imposed at Jamestown upon Wingfield for Smith's arrest in the West Indies. It is not to be forgotten that the editor of the *True Relation* expressly states that the published account does not include the entire manuscript as it came from Smith. Smith was often inaccurate in his estimates as to time and place and often very prejudiced in his judgments of others, but that is far from saying that he could mistake plain objects of sense or deliberately concoct a story having no foundation. The narrative below, in its essential features, is strongly supported by other contemporaneous documents, though for the reasons stated not much weight is to be attached to his opinions of the motives of Wingfield and the rest.

The *True Relation* was reprinted in 1866 at Boston, in a small edition, with an introduction and notes by Dr. Charles Deane.

L. G. T.

# A TRUE RELATION, BY CAPTAIN JOHN SMITH, 1608

*A True Relation of such occurrences and accidents of noate as hath hapned in Virginia since the first planting of that Collony, which is now resident in the South part thereof, till the last returne from thence.*

*Written by Captain Smith, Coronell of the said Collony, to a worshipfull friend of his in England.*

*London: Printed for John Tappe, and are to bee solde at the Greyhound in Paules-Church-yard, by W. W.* 1608.[1]

## TO THE COURTEOUS READER

Courteous, Kind, and indifferent Readers, whose willingnesse to reade and heare this following discourse, doth explaine to the world your hearty affection, to the prosecuting and furtherance of so worthy an action: so it is, that like to an unskilfull actor, who having by misconstruction of his right Cue, over-slipt himselfe, in beginning of a contrary part, and fearing the hatefull hisse of the captious multitude, with a modest blush retires himself in private; as doubting the reprehension of his whole audience in publicke, and yet againe upon further deliberation, thinking it better to know their censures at the first, and upon submission to reape pardon, then by seeking to smother it, to incurre the danger of a secret scandall: Imboldening himselfe upon the curteous kindnesse of the best, and not greatly respecting the worst, comes fourth againe, makes an Apollogie for himselfe, shewes the cause of his error, craves pardon for his rashness, and in fine, receives a generall

[1] This italic heading is from the title page of one of the original copies.

applauditie of the whole assemblie: so I gentle Readers, happening upon this relation by chance (as I take it, at the second or third hand) induced thereunto by divers well willers of the action, and none wishing better towards it then my selfe, so farre foorth as my poore abilitie can or may stretch to, I thought good to publish it: but the Author being absent from the presse, it cannot be doubted but that some faults have escaped in the printing, especially in the names of Countries, Townes, and People, which are somewhat strange unto us; but most of all, and which is the chiefe error (for want of knowledge of the Writer), some of the bookes were printed under the name of Thomas Watson, by whose occasion I know not, unlesse it were the over rashnesse, or mistaking of the workemen, but since having learned that the saide discourse was written by Captaine Smith, who is one of the Counsell there in Virginia: I thought good to make the like Apollogie, by shewing the true Author so farre as my selfe could learne, not doubting, but that the wise, noting it as an error of ignorance, will passe it over with patience; and if worthy an applauditie, to reserve it to the Author, whose paines in my judgement deserveth commendations; somewhat more was by him written, which being as I thought (fit to be private) I would not adventure to make it publicke. What more may be expected concerning the scituation of the Country, the nature of the clime, number of our people there resident, the manner of their government, and living, the commodities to be produced, and the end and effect it may come too, I can say nothing more then is here written: only what I have learned and gathered from the generall consent of all (that I have conversed withall) aswell marriners as others, which have had imployment that way, is that the Country is excellent and pleasant, the clime temperate and health full, the ground fertill and good, the commodities to be expected (if well followed) many, for our people, the worst being already past, these former having indured the heate of the day, whereby those that shall succeede, may at ease labour for their profit, in the most sweete, coole, and temperate shade: the action most honorable, and the end to the high glory of God, to the erecting of true religion among Infidells, to the overthrow of superstition and idolatrie, to the winning of many thousands of wandring sheepe, unto Christs fold, who now, and till now, have strayed in the unknowne paths of Paganisme, Idolatrie, and superstition: yea, I say the Action being well followed, as by the grave Senators, and worthy adventurors, it hath beene worthily begunne: will tend to the everlasting renowne of our Nation, and to the exceeding good and benefit of our Weale publicke in generall: whose Counsells, labours, godly and industrious endeavours, I beseech the mighty Jehovah to blesse, prosper, and further, with his heavenly ayde, and holy assistance.

*Farewell.*

*I. H.*

*A True relation of such occurrences and accidents of note, as hath hapned at Virginia, since the first planting of that Collony, which is now resident in the South part thereof, till the last returne.*

KINDE SIR, commendations remembred, &c. You shall understand that after many crosses in the downes[1] by tempests, wee arrived safely uppon the Southwest part of the great Canaries: within foure or five daies after we set saile for Dominica, the 26. of Aprill: the first land we made, wee fell with Cape Henry, the verie mouth of the Bay of Chissiapiacke, which at that present we little expected, having by a cruell storme bene put to the Northward. Anchoring in this Bay twentie or thirtie went a shore with the Captain, and in comming aboard, they were assalted with certaine Indians which charged them within Pistoll shot: in which conflict, Captaine Archer and Mathew Morton were shot: wherupon Captaine Newport seconding them, made a shot at them, which the Indians little respected, but having spent their arrowes retyred without harme. And in that place was the Box opened, wherin the Counsell for Virginia was nominated:

[1] The Downs is the part of the North Sea immediately east of Kent, between its coast and the Goodwin Sands.

and arriving at the place where wee are now seated. the Counsel was sworn, and the President elected, which for that yeare was Maister Edm. Maria Wingfield, where was made choice for our scituation, a verie fit place for the erecting of a great cittie, about which some contention passed betwixt Captaine Wingfield and Captaine Gosnold: notwithstanding, all our provision was brought a shore, and with as much speede as might bee wee went about our fortification.

The two and twenty day of Aprill,[1] Captain Newport and my selfe with divers others, to the number of twenty two persons, set forward to discover the River, some fiftie or sixtie miles, finding it in some places broader, and in some narrower, the Countrie (for the moste part) on each side plaine high ground, with many fresh Springes, the people in all places kindely intreating us, daunsing and feasting us with strawberries Mulberies, Bread, Fish, and other their Countrie provisions wherof we had plenty: for which Captaine Newport kindely requited their least favours with Bels, Pinnes, Needles, beades, or Glasses, which so contented them that his liberallitie made them follow us from place to place, and ever kindely to respect us. In the midway staying to refresh our selves in a little Ile foure or five savages came unto us which described unto us the course of the River, and after in our journey, they often met us, trading with us for such provision as wee had, and ariving at Arsatecke,[2] hee whom we supposed to bee the chiefe King of all the rest, moste kindely entertained us, giving us in a guide to go with us up the River to Powhatan, of which place their great Emperor taketh his name, where he that they honored for King[3] used us kindely. But to finish this discoverie, we passed on further, where within an

[1] This is an error; the landing took place on May 14, 1607, and the voyage of exploration up the river began on May 21.

[2] This word is generally written "Arrohateck," and according to William Wallace Tooker, the distinguished anthropologist, was cognate with the Natick *ahahnetau*, "he laughs at him." Hence the name given by the settlers "Arrohatecks Joy." A farm, a little above Farrar's Island on the north side of the river, distant about twenty miles from Richmond, still retains the name Arrohateck.

[3] The chief at the Falls was Parahunt, son of Powhatan.

ile[1] we were intercepted with great craggy stones in the midst of the river, where the water falleth so rudely, and with such a violence, as not any boat can possibly passe, and so broad disperseth the streame, as there is not past five or sixe Foote at a low water, and to the shore scarce passage with a barge, the water floweth foure foote, and the freshes by reason of the Rockes have left markes of the inundations 8. or 9. foote: The South side is plaine low ground, and the north side is high mountaines the rockes being of a gravelly nature, interlaced with many vains of glistring spangles. That night we returned to Powhatan: the next day (being Whitsunday after dinner) we returned to the fals, leaving a mariner in pawn with the Indians for a guide of theirs; hee that they honoured for King followed us by the river. That afternoone we trifled in looking upon the Rockes and river (further he would not goe) so there we erected a crosse, and that night taking our man at Powhatan, Captaine Newport congratulated his kindenes with a Gown and a Hatchet: returning to Arseteche, and stayed there the next day to observe the height[2] therof, and so with many signes of love we departed. The next day the Queene of Agamatack[3] kindely intreated us, her people being no lesse contented then the rest, and from thence we went to another place (the name whereof I do not remember) where the people shewed us the manner of their diving for Mussels, in which they finde Pearles.

That night passing by Weanock[4] some twentie miles from

[1] "Within an ile" is probably intended for "within a mile." In the more particular description of Gabriel Archer, *A Relatyon of the Discovery of our River*, the distance of the Indian town Powhatan from the Falls is put at three miles. It stood on a hill, and in the river in front was an island, which serves to identify the site of the town with Marin Hill or Tree Hill on the north side of James River. Above the Falls, where Richmond now stands, was the territory of the Manakins, who were enemies of the chief Powhatan.

[2] They took the latitude of the place.

[3] Appomattox. The site of the village of Queen Opussoquionuske was Bermuda Hundred, near the mouth of the Appomattox River.

[4] The modern spelling of this name is Weyanoke. The chief town of this tribe was on the south side, at the head of Powell's Creek, though the country opposite on the north side was also subject to their sway. The name adheres to the north side instead of to the south.

our Fort, they according to their former churlish condition, seemed little to affect us, but as wee departed and lodged at the point of Weanocke, the people the next morning seemed kindely to content us, yet we might perceive many signes of a more Jealousie in them then before, and also the Hinde that the King of Arseteck had given us, altered his resolution in going to our Fort, and with many kinde circumstances left us there. This gave us some occasion to doubt some mischiefe at the Fort, yet Capt. Newport intended to have visited Paspahegh and Tappahanocke, but the instant change of the winde being faire for our return we repaired to the fort with all speed [1] where the first we heard was that 400. Indians the day before had assalted the fort, and supprised it, had not God (beyond al their expectations) by meanes of the shippes, at whom they shot with their Ordinances and Muskets, caused them to retire, they had entred the fort with our own men, which were then busied in setting Corne, their Armes beeing then in driefats [2] and few ready but certain Gentlemen of their own, in which conflict, most of the Counsel was hurt, a boy slaine in the Pinnas, and thirteene or fourteene more hurt. With all speede we pallisadoed our Fort: (each other day) for sixe or seaven daies we had alarums by ambuscadoes, and four or five cruelly wounded by being abroad: the Indians losse wee know not, but as they report three were slain and divers hurt.

Captaine Newport having set things in order, set saile for England the 22d of June, leaving provision for 13. or 14 weeks. The day before the Ships departure, the King of Pamaunke [3] sent the Indian that had met us before in our

[1] They reached the fort May 27.

[2] Dry-vats, *i.e.*, baskets or packing-cases.

[3] The Pamunkey country lay between the Pamunkey and Mattapony rivers. At Uttamussick, the Indians had three long arbor-like wigwams, where the medicine-men performed their conjurations and incantations. The king of the Pamunkeys was the celebrated Opechancanough, the second brother and second successor of Powhatan. In 1616 he was chosen by the Chickahominies to be their king. He died, at nearly one hundred years of age, in 1646.

discoverie, to assure us peace; our fort being then palisadoed round, and all our men in good health and comfort, albeit, that thro[u]gh some discontented humors, it did not so long continue, for the President and Captaine Gosnold, with the rest of the Counsell, being for the moste part discontented with one another, in so much, that things were neither carried with that discretion nor any busines effected in such good sort as wisdome would, nor our owne good and safetie required, whereby, and through the hard dealing of our President, the rest of the counsell beeing diverslie affected through his audacious commaund; and for Captaine Martin, albeit verie honest, and wishing the best good, yet so sicke and weake; and my selfe so disgrac'd through others mallice: through which disorder God (being angrie with us) plagued us with such famin and sicknes, that the living were scarce able to bury the dead: our want of sufficient and good victualls, with continuall watching, foure or five each night at three Bulwarkes, being the chiefe cause: onely of Sturgion wee had great store, whereon our men would so greedily surfet, as it cost manye their lives: the Sack, Aquavitie,[1] and other preservatives for our health, being kept onely in the Presidents hands, for his owne diet, and his few associates.[2] Shortly after Captaine Gosnold fell sicke, and within three weekes died, Captaine Ratcliffe being then also verie sicke and weake, and my selfe having also tasted of the extremitie therof, but by Gods assistance being well recovered, Kendall about this time, for divers reasons deposed from being of the Councell: and shortly after it pleased God (in our extremity) to move the Indians to bring us Corne, ere it was halfe ripe, to refresh us, when we rather expected when they would destroy us: about the tenth of

[1] Brandy.

[2] Wingfield had charge of the common store, but he denied vigorously that he feasted in the way suggested by Smith, who hated him. He dispensed the oil, vinegar, sack (sherry) and aqua vitae (brandy) with great care, and when the quantity was much reduced had the rest sealed up to be kept for emergencies, but "Lord, how they then longed for to supp up that litle remnant, for they had nowe emptied all their owne bottles and all other that they could smell out." Wingfield, *A Discourse of Virginia*.

September there was about 46. of our men dead, at which time Captaine Wingefield having ordred the affaires in such sort that he was generally hated of all, in which respect with one consent he was deposed from his presidencie, and Captaine Ratcliffe [1] according to his course was elected.

Our provision being now within twentie dayes spent, the Indians brought us great store both of Corne and bread ready made: and also there came such aboundance of Fowles into the Rivers, as greatly refreshed our weake estates, whereuppon many of our weake men were presently able to goe abroad. As yet we had no houses to cover us, our Tents were rotten and our Cabbins worse then nought: our best commoditie was Yron which we made into little chissels. The president and Captaine Martins sicknes, constrayned me to be Cape Marchant, and yet to spare no paines in making houses for the company; who notwithstanding our misery, little ceased their mallice, grudging, and muttering. As at this time were most of our chiefest men either sicke or discontented, the rest being in such dispaire, as they would rather starve and rot with idlenes, then be perswaded to do any thing for their owne reliefe without constraint: our victualles being now within eighteene dayes spent, and the Indians trade decreasing, I was sent to the mouth of the river, to Kegquouhtan an Indian Towne, to trade for Corne, and try the River for Fish, but our fishing we could not effect by reason of the stormy weather. The Indians thinking us neare famished, with carelesse kindnes, offred us little pieces of bread and small handfulls of beanes or wheat, for a hatchet or a piece of copper: In like maner I entertained their kindnes, and in like scorne offered them like commodities, but the Children, or any that shewed extraordinary kindnes,

[1] John Ratcliffe's true name appears to have been John Sicklemore, and his *alias* "Ratcliffe" was probably due to a second marriage of his mother to one Ratcliffe. He made no concealment of his *alias*, as Smith suggests in another paper. He was president till July, 1608, when he was removed and Matthew Scrivener became president. He went to England in January, 1609, and returned to Virginia in June, 1609, where he was betrayed and slain by the Indians in the winter of 1609–1610.

I liberally contented with free gifte, such trifles as wel contented them. Finding this colde comfort, I anchored before the Towne, and the next day returned to trade, but God (the absolute disposer of all heartes) altered their conceits, for now they were no lesse desirous of our commodities then we of their Corne: under colour to fetch fresh water, I sent a man to discover the Towne, their Corne, and force, to trie their intent, in that they desired me up to their houses: which well understanding, with foure shot I visited them. With fish, oysters, bread, and deere, they kindly traded with me and my men, beeing no lesse in doubt of my intent, then I of theirs; for well I might with twentie men have fraighted a Shippe with Corne. The Towne conteineth eighteene houses, pleasantly seated upon three acres of ground, uppon a plaine, halfe invironed with a great Bay of the great River, the other parte with a Baye of the other River falling into the great Baye, with a little Ile fit for a Castle in the mouth thereof,[1] the Towne adjoyning to the maine by a necke of Land of sixtie yardes. With sixteene bushells of Corne I returned towards our Forte: by the way I encountred with two Canowes of Indians, who came aboord me, being the inhabitants of Waroskoyack,[2] a kingdome on the south side of the river, which is in breadth 5. miles and 20 mile or neare from the mouth: With these I traded, who having but their hunting provision, requested me to returne to their Towne, where I should load my boat with corne: and with near thirtie bushells I returned to the fort, the very name wherof gave great comfort to our desparing company.

Time thus passing away, and having not above 14. daies victuals left, some motions were made about our presidents and Captaine Archers going for England, to procure a supply: in which meane time we had reasonably fitted us with houses. And our President and Captaine Martin being able to walk

[1] The island on which Fort Monroe now stands.

[2] Warascoyack was an Indian town situated on Pagan River in Isle of Wight County.

abroad, with much adoe it was concluded, that the pinnace and barge should goe towards Powhatan, to trade for corne: Lotts were cast who should go in her, the chance was mine; and while she was a rigging, I made a voiage to Topohanack,[1] where arriving, there was but certain women and children who fled from their houses, yet at last I drew them to draw neere; truck they durst not, corne they had plenty, and to spoile I had no commission: In my returne to Paspahegh, I traded with that churlish and trecherous nation: having loaded 10 or 12 bushels of corne, they offred to take our pieces and swords, yet by stelth, but [we] seeming to dislike it, they were ready to assault us: yet standing upon our guard, in coasting the shore, divers out of the woods would meet with us with corn and trade. But least we should be constrained, either to indure overmuch wrong or directly [to] fal to revenge, seeing them dog us from place to place, it being night, and our necessitie not fit for warres, we tooke occasion to returne with 10 bushells of corne: Captaine Martin after made 2 journies to that nation of Paspahegh, but eache time returned with 8. or 10. bushells.

All things being now ready for my journey to Powhatan, for the performance thereof, I had 8. men and my selfe for the barge, as well for discoverie as trading; the Pinnace, 5. Marriners, and 2. landmen to take in our ladings at convenient places. The 9 of November I set forward for the discovery of the country of Chikhamania,[2] leaving the pinnace the next tide to followe, and stay for my comming at Point weanock, 20 miles from our fort: the mouth of this river falleth into the great river at Paspahegh, 8 miles above our fort: That afternoone I stayed the eb in the bay of Paspahegh with the Indians: towards the evening certaine Indians haled me, one of them being of Chikahamania, offred to conduct me to his country.

[1] Quiyoughcohannock in Surry County is intended.

[2] According to William Wallace Tooker Chickahominy was not a place-name, but the designation of a people who contributed corn to the colonists, thus saving them from starvation. He gives its etymology as *Chick-aham-min-anaugh*; "coarse-pounded corn people," or in brief, "hominy people."

The Paspahegheans grudged therat: along we went by moone-light: at midnight he brought us before his Towne, desiring one of our men to go up with him, whom he kindely intertained, and returned back to the barge: The next morning I went up to the towne, and shewed them what copper and hatchets they shold have for corne, each family seeking to give me most content: so long they caused me to stay that 100 at least was expecting my comming by the river, with corne. What I liked, I bought; and least they should perceive my too great want, I went higher up the river: This place is called Manosquosick,[1] a quarter of a mile from the river, conteining thirtie or fortie houses, uppon an exceeding high land: at the foote of the hill towards the river, is a plaine wood, watered with many springes which fall twentie yardes right downe into the river. Right against the same is a great marsh, of 4. or 5. miles circuit, divided in 2 Ilands, by the parting of the river, abounding with fish and foule of all sorts. A mile from thence is a Towne called Oraniocke. I further discovered the Townes of Mansa, Apanaock, Werawahone, and Mamanahunt, at eche place kindely used: especially at the last, being the hart of the Country; where were assembled 200. people with such aboundance of corne, as having laded our barge, as also I might have laded a ship.

I returned to Paspahhegh, and considering the want of Corne at our Fort, it being night, with the ebb, by midnight I arived at our fort, where I found our Pinnis run aground: The next morning I unladed seaven hogsheds into our store. The next morning I returned againe: the second day I arived at Mamanahunt, wher the people having heard of my comming, were ready with 3 or 400. baskets litle and great, of which having laded my barge, with many signes of great kindnes I returned: At my departure they requested me to hear our pieces, being in the midst of the river; which in regard of the eccho seemed a peale of ordnance. Many birds and fowles

[1] This town was probably located at Barret's Ferry on the road to Richmond.

they see us dayly kil that much feared them. So desirous of trade wer they, that they would follow me with their canowes; and for anything, give it me, rather then returne it back. So I unladed again 7 or 8. hogsheads at our fort.

Having thus by Gods assistance gotten good store of corne, notwithstanding some bad spirits not content with Gods providence, still grew mutinous; in so much, that our president having occasion to chide the smith for his misdeamenour, he not only gave him bad language, but also offred to strike him with some of his tooles. For which rebellious act, the smith was by a Jury condemned to be hanged, but being uppon the ladder, continuing very obstinate as hoping upon a rescue, when he saw no other way but death with him, he became penitent, and declared a dangerous conspiracy: for which, Captaine Kendall, as principal, was by a Jury condemned, and shot to death. This conspiracy appeased, I set forward for the discovery of the River Checka Hamania. This third time I discovered the Townes of Matapamient, Morinogh, Ascacap, moysenock, Righkahauck, Nechanichock, Mattalunt, Attamuspincke, and divers others: their plenty of corne I found decreased, yet lading the barge, I returned to our fort.

Our store being now indifferently wel provided with corne, there was much adoe for to have the pinace goe for England, against which Captain Martin and my selfe stood chiefly against it: and in fine after many debatings *pro et contra,* it was resolved to stay a further resolution: This matter also quieted, I set forward to finish this discovery, which as yet I had neglected in regard of the necessitie we had to take in provision whilst it was to be had. 40. miles I passed up the river, which for the most part is a quarter of a mile broad, and 3. fatham and a half deep, exceeding osey, many great low marshes, and many high lands, especially about the midst at a place called Moysonicke,[1] a Peninsule of 4. miles circuit, betwixt two

[1] This description seems to agree with the bend of the Chickahominy at Lanexa on the Chesapeake and Ohio Railroad.

rivers joyned to the main by a neck of 40. or 50. yards, and 40. or 50 yards from the high water marke: On both sides in the very necke of the maine, are high hills and dales, yet much inhabited, the Ile declining in a plaine fertile corne field, the lower end a low marsh. More plentie of swannes, cranes, geese, duckes, and mallards, and divers sorts of fowles, none would desire: more plaine fertile planted ground, in such great proportions as there, I had not seene; of a light blacke sandy mould, the cliffes commonly red, white, and yellowe coloured sand, and under, red and white clay; fish [in] great plenty, and people aboundance: the most of their inhabitants, in view of the neck of Land, where a better seat for a towne cannot be desired:

At the end of forty miles, this river invironeth many low Ilands at each high water drowned for a mile, where it uniteth it selfe at a place called Apokant, the highest Towne inhabited. 10. miles higher, I discovered with the barge: in the mid way, a greate tree hindered my passage, which I cut in two. Heere the river became narrower, 8. 9 or 10. foote at a high water, and 6. or 7. at a lowe: the streame exceeding swift, and the bottom hard channell: the ground, most part a low plaine, sandy soyle. This occasioned me to suppose it might issue from some lake or some broad ford, for it could not be far to the head, but rather then I would endanger the barge.[1] Yet to have beene able to resolve this doubt, and to discharge the imputation of malicious tungs, that halfe suspected I durst not, for so long delaying: some of the company as desirous as my self, we resolved to hier a Canow, and returne with the barge to Apocant, there to leave the barge secure, and put our selves upon the adventure: the country onely a vast and wilde wildernes, and but onely that Towne: Within three or foure mile, we hired a Canow, and 2. Indians to row us the next day a fowling. Having made such provision for the barge as was

[1] The sense here seems incomplete; it should read "but rather then (than) I would endanger the barge by going up further, I resolved to take it back to Apocant and use a canoe for the rest of the trip up the river."

needfull, I left her there to ride, with expresse charge not any to go ashore til my returne.

Though some wise men may condemn this too bould attempt of too much indiscretion, yet if they well consider the friendship of the Indians in conducting me, the desolateness of the country, the probabilitie of some lacke,[1] and the malicious judges of my actions at home,[2] as also to have some matters of worth to incourage our adventurers in england, might well have caused any honest minde to have done the like, as well for his own discharge as for the publike good:

Having 2 Indians for my guide and 2 of our own company, I set forward, leaving 7 in the barge: Having discovered 20 miles further in this desart, the river stil kept his depth and bredth, but much more combred with trees: Here we went ashore (being some 12 miles higher then the barge had bene) to refresh our selves, during the boyling of our vituals: One of the Indians I tooke with me, to see the nature of the soile, and to crosse the boughts[3] of the river: the other Indian I left with Maister Robbinson and Thomas Emry, with their matches light, and order to discharge a peece, for my retreat, at the first sight of any Indian. But within a quarter of an houre I heard a loud cry, and a hollowing of Indians, but no warning peece. Supposing them surprised, and that the Indians had betraid us, presently I seazed him and bound his arme fast to my hand in a garter, with my pistoll ready bent to be revenged on him: he advised me to fly, and seemed ignorant of what was done. But as we went discoursing, I was struck with an arrow on the right thigh, but without harme: upon this occasion I espied 2. Indians drawing their bowes, which I prevented in discharging a french pistoll: By that I had charged againe, 3 or 4 more did the like: for the first fell downe and fled: At my discharge, they did the like. My hinde[4] I made my barricado, who offered not to strive. 20. or 30. arrowes were shot at me but short. 3 or 4 times I had discharged my pistoll ere the king of Pamaunck called Opec-

[1] *I.e.*, lake. [2] *I.e.*, Jamestown. [3] Windings. [4] Indian.

kankenough with 200 men, invironed me, eache drawing their bowe: which done they laid them upon the ground, yet without shot: My hinde treated betwixt them and me of conditions of peace; he discovered me to be[1] the Captaine: my request was to retire to the boate: they demaunded my armes, the rest they saide were slaine, onely me they would reserve: The Indian importuned me not to shoot. In retiring being in the midst of a low quagmire, and minding them more then my steps, I stept fast into the quagmire, and also the Indian in drawing me forth:[2]

Thus surprised, I resolved to trie their mercies: my armes I caste from me, till which none durst approch me. Being ceazed on me, they drew me out and led me to the King. I presented him with a compasse diall, describing by my best meanes the use therof: whereat he so amazedly admired, as he suffered me to proceed in a discourse of the roundnes of the earth, the course of the sunne, moone, starres and plannets. With kinde speeches and bread he requited me, conducting me where the Canow lay and John Robbinson slaine, with 20 or 30. arrowes in him. Emry I saw not.

I perceived by the aboundance of fires all over the woods.[3] At each place I expected when they would execute me, yet they used me with what kindnes they could: Approaching their Towne,[4] which was within 6 miles where I was taken, onely made as arbors and covered with mats, which they remove as occasion requires: all the women and children, being advertised of this accident, came foorth to meet them, the King[5] well guarded with 20 bowmen 5 flanck and rear, and each flanck before him a sword and a peece, and after him the

[1] *I.e.*, explained that I was.

[2] Smith's capture seems to have occurred in White Oak Swamp.

[3] The sense requires here "that they were a party hunting deer." The method pursued in this occupation was as follows: Two or three hundred Indians would assemble and surround with many fires some spot frequented by the deer. Then several Indians would be placed between every two fires, and the deer being driven by others would in their efforts to avoid the fires run into the greater danger of the hunters, who would fill them with arrows.

[4] Rasawrack.

[5] Opechancanough.

like, then a bowman, then I on each hand a boweman, the rest in file in the reare, which reare led foorth amongst the trees in a bishion, eache his bowe and a handfull of arrowes, a quiver at his back grimly painted: on eache flanck a sargeant, the one running alwaies towards the front, the other towards the reare, each a true pace and in exceeding good order. This being a good time continued, they caste themselves in a ring with a daunce, and so eache man departed to his lodging. The Captain conducting me to his lodging, a quarter of Venison and some ten pound of bread I had for supper: what I left was reserved for me, and sent with me to my lodging: Each morning 3. women presented me three great platters of fine bread, more venison then ten men could devour I had: my gowne, points[1] and garters, my compas and my tablet they gave me again. Though 8 ordinarily guarded me, I wanted not what they could devise to content me: and still our longer acquaintance increased our better affection:

Much they threatned to assault our forte, as they were solicited by the King of Paspahegh: who shewed at our fort great signes of sorrow for this mischance.[2] The King[3] tooke great delight in understanding the manner of our ships, and sayling the seas, the earth and skies, and of our God: what he knew of the dominions he spared not to acquaint me with, as of certaine men cloathed at a place called Ocanahonan, cloathed like me: the course of our river, and that within 4 or 5 daies journey of the falles, was a great turning of salt water: I desired he would send a messenger to Paspahegh,[4] with a letter I would write, by which they shold understand how kindly they used me, and that I was well, least they should revenge my death. This he granted and sent three men, in such weather as in reason were unpossible by any naked to be indured. Their cruell mindes towards the fort I had de-

[1] Lacings for fastening the clothing.

[2] *I.e.*, the mischance of Smith's capture.

[3] The king here meant is not Paspahegh, but Opechancanough, chief of the Pamunkey Indians.

[4] *I.e.*, to Jamestown, which was situated in the country of the Paspaheghs.

verted, in describing the ordinance and the mines in the fields, as also the revenge Captain Newport would take of them at his returne. Their intent, I incerted the fort, the people of Ocanahonum and the back sea: this report they after found divers Indians that confirmed:

The next day after my letter, came a salvage to my lodging, with his sword, to have slaine me: but being by my guard intercepted, with a bowe and arrow he offred to have effected his purpose: the cause I knew not, till the King understanding thereof came and told me of a man a dying, wounded with my pistoll: he tould me also of another I had slayne, yet the most concealed they had any hurte: This was the father of him I had slayne, whose fury to prevent, the King presently conducted me to another Kingdome, upon the top of the next northerly river, called Youghtanan.[1] Having feasted me, he further led me to another branch of the river, called Mattapament;[2] to two other hunting townes they led me: and to each of these Countries, a house of the great Emperour of Pewhakan, whom as yet I supposed to bee at the Fals; to him I tolde him I must goe, and so returne to Paspahegh. After this foure or five dayes marsh,[3] we returned to Rasawrack, the first towne they brought me too: where binding the Mats in bundels, they marched two dayes journey, and crossed the River of Youghtanan, where it was as broad as Thames: so conducting me to a place called Menapacute in Pamaunke, where the King inhabited.

The next day another King of that nation called Kekataugh, having received some kindnes of me at the Fort, kindly invited me to feast at his house, the people from all places flocked to see me, each shewing to content me. By this, the great King hath foure or five houses, each containing fourescore or an hundred foote in length, pleasantly seated upon an high sandy hill, from whence you may see westerly a goodly

[1] Now known as Pamunkey River, which joins the Mattapony River at West Point, forty miles from Chesapeake Bay, to form the York River.

[2] Sometimes written Mattapanient, which was contracted to Mattapony, by which name the river still goes.

[3] March.

low Country, the river before the which his crooked course causeth many great Marshes of exceeding good ground. An hundred houses, and many large plaines are here togither inhabited. More abundance of fish and fowle, and a pleasanter seat cannot be imagined. The King with fortie Bowmen to guard me, intreated me to discharge my Pistoll, which they there presented me, with a mark at six score [1] to strike therwith: but to spoil the practise, I broke the cocke, whereat they were much discontented, though a chaunce supposed.

From hence, this kind King conducted mee to a place called Topahanocke, a kingdome upon another River northward: [2] The cause of this was, that the yeare before, a shippe had beene in the River of Pamaunke, who having beene kindly entertained by Powhatan their Emperour, they returned thence, and discovered the River of Topahanocke: where being received with like kindnesse, yet he slue the King, and tooke of his people, and they supposed I were hee. But the people reported him a great [3] man that was Captaine, and using mee kindly, the next day we departed.

This River of Topahanock seemeth in breadth not much lesse then that we dwell upon. At the mouth of the River is a Countrey called Cuttata women: upwards is Marraugh tacum, Tapohanock, Appamatuck, and Nantaugs tacum: at top, Manahocks, the head issuing from many Mountaines. The next night I lodged at a hunting town of Powhatans, and the next day arrived at Waranacomoco [4] upon the river of Pamauncke, where the great king is resident. By the way we passed by the top of another little river, which

[1] "Yards" to be supplied.

[2] The river "northward" was the Rappahannock, sometimes written Tappahannock, which is still the name of a town on the south side, marking the site of the Indian village. The chief of the tribe at the arrival of the English had been the guest, as we have seen, of the Quiyoughcohannocks and was mistaken by the whites as a resident on the James River.

[3] Tall.

[4] The correct spelling is "werowocomoco," meaning "the house of the werowance," or capital of the Powhatan confederacy. It was located on the north side of York River at Portan Bay, about fourteen miles from West Point.

is betwixt the two, called Payankatank. The most of this Country though Desert, yet exceeding fertil; good timber, most hils and dales, in each valley a cristall spring.

Arriving at Weramocomoco, their Emperour proudly lying uppon a Bedstead a foote high, upon tenne or twelve Mattes, richly hung with manie Chaynes of great Pearles about his necke, and covered with a great Covering of Rahaughcums.[1] At heade[2] sat a woman, at his feete another; on each side sitting uppon a Matte uppon the ground, were raunged his chiefe men on each side the fire, tenne in a ranke, and behinde them as many yong women, each a great Chaine[3] of white Beades over their shoulders, their heades painted in redde: and with such a grave and Majesticall countenance, as drave me into admiration to see such state in a naked Salvage, hee kindly welcomed me with good wordes, and great Platters of sundrie Victuals, assuring mee his friendship, and my libertie within foure days. Hee much delighted in Opechan Conoughs relation of what I had described to him, and oft examined me upon the same. Hee asked mee the cause of our comming. I tolde him being in fight with the Spaniards our enemie, beeing overpowred, neare put to retreat, and by extreame weather put to this shore: where landing at Chesipiack, the people shot us, but at Kequoughtan they kindly used us: we by signes demaunded fresh water, they described us up the River was all fresh water: at Paspahegh also they kindly used us: our Pinnasse being leake, we were inforced to stay to mend her, till Captaine Newport my father came to conduct us away. He demaunded why we went further with our Boate. I tolde him, in that I would have occasion to talke of the backe Sea, that on the other side the maine, where was salt water. My father[4] had a childe slaine, whiche wee supposed Monocan his enemie:[5] whose death we intended to revenge.

After good deliberation, hee began to describe mee the Countreys beyonde the Falles, with many of the rest; con-

[1] Raccoon skins. [2] *I.e.*, at *his* head. [3] Each *with* a great chain.
[4] *I.e.*, Christopher Newport. [5] Supply "had done."

firming what not onely Opechancanoyes, and an Indian which had beene prisoner to Pewhatan had before tolde mee: but some called it five dayes, some sixe, some eight, where the sayde water dashed amongest many stones and rockes, each storm; which caused oft tymes the heade of the River to bee brackish: Anchanachuck he described to bee the people that had slaine my brother: whose death hee would revenge. Hee described also upon the same Sea, a mighty Nation called Pocoughtronack, a fierce Nation that did eate men, and warred with the people of Moyaoncer and Pataromerke,[1] Nations upon the toppe of the heade of the Bay, under his territories: where the yeare before they had slain an hundred. He signified their crownes were shaven, long haire in the necke, tied on a knot, Swords like Pollaxes.

Beyond them, he described people with short Coates, and Sleeves to the Elbowes, that passed that way in Shippes like ours. Many Kingdomes hee described mee, to the heade of the Bay, which seemed to bee a mightie River issuing from mightie Mountaines betwixt the two Seas: The people cloathed at Ocamahowan, he also confirmed; and the Southerly Countries also, as the rest that reported us to be within a day and a halfe of Mangoge, two dayes of Chawwonock, 6. from Roonock,[2] to the south part of the backe sea: He described a countrie called Anone, where they have abundance of Brasse, and houses walled as ours.

I requited his discourse (seeing what pride hee had in his great and spacious Dominions, seeing that all hee knewe were under his Territories) in describing to him the territories of Europe, which was subject to our great King whose subject I was, the innumerable multitude of his ships, I gave him to understand the noyse of Trumpets, and terrible manner of fighting were under captain Newport my father: whom I intituled the Meworames,[3] which they call the King of all the waters. At his greatnesse, he admired: and not a little

[1] Misprint for Patawomecke (Potomac).

[2] Chowanoac and Roanoke.

[3] A variation of werowance.

feared. He desired mee to forsake Paspahegh, and to live with him upon his River, a Countrie called Capa Howasicke.[1] Hee promised to give me Corne, Venison, or what I wanted to feede us: Hatchets and Copper wee should make him, and none should disturbe us. This request I promised to performe: and thus, having with all the kindnes hee could devise, sought to content me, hee sent me home, with 4. men: one that usually carried my Gowne and Knapsacke after me, two other loded with bread, and one to accompanie me.

This River of Pamaunke is not past twelve mile from that we dwell on, his course northwest and westerly as the other. Weraocomoco is upon salt water in bredth two myles, and so [2] keepeth his course without any tarrying some twenty miles; where at the parting of the fresh water and the salt, it divideth it selfe into two partes, the one part to Goughland, as broad as Thames, and navigable with a Boate threescore or fourescore miles, and with a Shippe fiftie: exceeding crooked, and manie low grounds and marishes, but inhabited with aboundance of warlike and tall people. The Countrey of Youghtomam, of no lesse worth, onely it is lower; but all the soyle, a fatte, fertill, sandie ground. Above Manapacumter, many high sandie mountaines. By the River is many Rockes, seeming, if not, of severall Mines. The other branch a little lesse in breadth, yet extendeth not neare so farre, nor so well inhabited, somewhat lower, and a white sandie, and a white clay soyle: here is their best *Terra Sigillata*. The mouth of the River, as I see in the discoverie therof with captain Newport, is halfe a mile broad, and within foure miles not above a Musket shot: the channell exceeding good and deepe, the River straight to the devisions. Kiskirk [3] the nearest Nation to the entrances.

[1] The country of "Cappahowasicke" was on the north side of York River, east of Portan Bay. A wharf in that region still preserves the name.

[2] After "so" supply "the river."

[3] A variation of "Kiskiack" or "Chiskiack," a tribe whose chief town was on the south side of York River about three miles above the present Yorktown. The old brick church in this region, standing before 1861, was known by the name of Cheesecake Church.

Their religion and Ceremonie I observed was thus: Three or foure dayes after my taking, seven of them in the house where I lay, each with a rattle, began at ten a clocke in the morning to sing about the fire, which they invironed with a Circle of meale, and after a foote or two from that, at the end of each song, layde downe two or three graines of wheate: continuing this order till they have included sixe or seven hundred in a halfe Circle; and after that, two or three more Circles in like maner, a hand bredth from other. That done, at each song, they put betwixt everie three, two, or five graines, a little sticke; so counting as an old woman her *Pater noster*.

One disguised with a great Skinne, his head hung round with little Skinnes of Weasels and other vermine, with a Crownet of feathers on his head, painted as ugly as the divell, at the end of each song will make many signes and demonstrations, with strange and vehement actions. great cakes of Deere suet, Deare, and Tobacco he casteth in the fire: till sixe a clocke in the Evening, their howling would continue ere they would depart. Each morning in the coldest frost, the principall, to the number of twentie or thirtie, assembled themselves in a round circle, a good distance from the towne: where they told me they there consulted where to hunt the next day: So fat they fed mee, that I much doubted they intended to have sacrificed mee to the Quiyoughquosicke, which is a superiour power they worship: a more uglier thing cannot be described. One they have for chief sacrifices, which also they call Quiyoughquosick. To cure the sick, a man, with a Rattle, and extreame howling, showting, singing, and such violent gestures and Anticke actions over the patient, will sucke out blood and flegme from the patient, out of their unable stomacke, or any diseased place, as no labour will more tire them. Tobacco, they offer the water in passing in fowle weather. The death of any they lament with great sorrow and weeping. Their Kings they burie betwixt two mattes within their houses, with all his beads, jewels, hatchets, and copper: the other in graves like ours. They acknowledge no resurrection.

Powhatan hath three brethren, and two sisters, each of his brethren succeeded[1] other. For the Crowne, their heyres inherite not, but the first heyres of the Sisters, and so successively the weomens heires. For the Kings have as many weomen as they will, his Subjects two, and most but one.

From Weramocomoco is but 12. miles, yet the Indians trifled away that day,[2] and would not goe to our Forte by any perswasions: but in certaine olde hunting houses of Paspahegh we lodged all night. The next morning [3] ere Sunne rise, we set forward for our Fort, where we arrived within an houre: where each man with the truest signes of joy they could expresse welcommed me, except M. Archer, and some 2. or 3. of his, who was then in my absence, sworne Counsellour, though not with the consent of Captaine Martin: Great blame and imputation was laide upon mee by them, for the losse of our two men which the Indians slew: insomuch that they purposed to depose me. But in the midst of my miseries, it pleased God to send Captaine Nuport: who arriving there the same night, so tripled our joy as for a while these plots against me were deferred; though with much malice against me, which captain Newport in short time did plainly see. Now was maister Scrivener, captaine Martin, and my selfe, called Counsellers.

Within five or sixe dayes after the arrivall of the Ship, by a mischaunce our Fort was burned, and the most of our apparell, lodging and private provision. Many of our old men diseased, and of our new for want of lodging perished. The Empereur Powhatan, each weeke once or twice, sent me many presents of Deare, bread, Raugroughcuns; halfe alwayes for my father [4] whom he much desired to see, and halfe for me: and so continually importuned by messengers and presents, that I would come to fetch the corne, and take the Countrie

[1] "Succeedeth" or "will succeed." Smith means to say that the chief authority passed from brother to brother, but never to their descendants. After the death of the youngest brother the eldest sister succeeded, and then her children, the boys first and girls next.

[2] January 1, 1608. [3] January 2, 1608. [4] Captain Newport.

their King had given me, as at last Captaine Newport resolved to go see him. Such acquaintance I had amongst the Indians, and such confidence they had in me, as neare the Fort they would not come till I came to them; every of them calling me by my name, would not sell any thing till I had first received their presents, and what they had that I liked, they deferred to my discretion: but after acquaintance, they usually came into the Fort at their pleasure: The President and the rest of the Councell, they knewe not; but Captaine Newports greatnesse I had so described, as they conceyved him the chiefe, the rest his children, Officers, and servants.

We had agreed with the king of Paspahegh, to conduct two of our men to a place called Panawicke [1] beyond Roonok, where he reported many men to be apparelled. Wee landed him at Warraskoyack, where [2] playing the villaine, and deluding vs for rewards, returned within three or foure dayes after, without going further. Captaine Newport, maister Scrivener, and my selfe, found the mouth of Pamauncks river, some 25. or 30. miles north ward from Cape Henricke, the chanell good as before expressed.

Arriving at Weramocomoca, being jealous of the intent of this politick salvage; to discover his intent the better, I with 20. shot armed in Jacks,[3] went a shore. The Bay where he dwelleth hath in it 3. cricks, and a mile and a halfe from the chanel all os.[4] Being conducted to the towne, I found my selfe mistaken in the creeke, for they al there were within lesse then a mile: the Emperors sonne called Naukaquawis, the captaine that tooke me, and diverse others of his chiefe men, conducted me to their kings habitation. But in the mid way I was intercepted by a great creek over which they had made a bridge of grained stakes and railes. The king of Kiskieck, and Namontack, who all the journey, the king had sent to guide us, had conducted us this passage, which caused

[1] The Pananuaioc of Hakluyt and of De Bry's map. See *Early English and French Voyages*, in this series, p. 238. [2] After "where" supply "he."

[3] *I.e.*, twenty armed men clad in jacks, — coats made of thick leather.

[4] Ooze or marsh.

me to suspect some mischiefe: the barge I had sent to meet me at the right landing, when I found my selfe first deceyved. And knowing by experience the most of their courages to proceede from others feare, though fewe lyked the passage, I intermingled the Kings sonne, our conductors, and his chiefe men amongst ours, and led forward, leaving halfe at the one ende to make a guard for the passage of the Front. The Indians seeing the weakenesse of the Bridge, came with a Canow, and tooke me in of the middest, with foure or five more: being landed, wee made a guard for the rest till all were passed. Two in a ranke we marched to the Emperors house. Before his house stood fortie or fiftie great Platters of fine bread. Being entred the house, with loude tunes they all made signes of great joy. This proude salvage, having his finest women, and the principall of his chiefe men assembled, sate in rankes as before is expressed: himself as upon a Throne at the upper ende of the house, with such a Majestie as I cannot expresse, nor yet have often seene, either in Pagan or Christian. With a kinde countenance hee bad mee welcome, and caused a place to bee made by himselfe to sit. I presented him a sute of red cloath, a white Greyhound, and a Hatte: as Jewels he esteemed them, and with a great Oration made by three of his Nobles, if there be any amongst Salvages, kindly accepted them, with a publike confirmation of a perpetuall league and friendship.

After that, he commanded the Queene of Apamatuc, a comely yong Salvage, to give me water, a Turkie cocke, and breade to eate: Being thus feasted, hee began his discourse to this purpose. Your kinde visitation doth much content mee, but where is your father whom I much desire to see, is he not with you. I told him, he remained aboord, but the next day he would come unto him. With a merrie countenance he asked me for certaine peeces [1] which I promised him, when I went to Paspahegh. I told according to my promise, that I proferred the man that went with me foure Demy Culverings,[2]

[1] Guns.

[2] A kind of small cannon.

in that he so desired a great Gunne: but they refused to take them. Whereat with a lowde laughter, he desired to give him some of lesse burden: as for the other I gave him them, being sure that none could carrie them. But where are these men you promised to come with you. I told him, without. Who thereupon gave order to have them brought in, two after two, ever maintaining the guard without. And as they presented themselves, ever with thankes he would salute me: and caused each of them to have foure or five pound of bread given them. This done, I asked him for the corne and ground he promised me. He told me I should have it: but he expected to have all these men lay their armes at his feet, as did his subjects. I tolde him that was a ceremonie our enemies desired, but never our Friends, as we presented ourselves unto him; yet that he should not doubt of our friendship. The next day my Father would give him a child of his, in full assurance of our loves, and not only that, but when he should thinke it convenient, wee would deliver under his subjection the Country of Manacam and Pocoughtaonack his enemies.

This so contented him, as immediatly with attentive silence, with a lowd oration he proclaimed me Awerowanes [1] of Powhaton, and that all his subjects should so esteeme us, and no man account us strangers nor Paspaheghans, but Powhatans, and that the Corne, weomen and Country, should be to us as to his owne people. This proffered kindnes for many reasons we contemned not, but with the best Languages and signes of thankes I could expresse, I tooke my leave.

The King rising from his seat, conducted me foorth, and caused each of my men to have as much more bread as hee could beare: giving me some in a basket, and as much he sent a board for a present to my Father. Victuals you must know is all there wealth, and the greatest kindnes they could shew us.

Arriving at the River, the Barge was fallen so low [2] with the ebbe, though I had given order and oft sent to prevent the

[1] A werowance, *i.e.*, a chief.

[2] *I.e.*, down the river.

same, yet the messengers deceived mee. The Skies being very thicke and rainie, the King understanding this mischance, sent his Sonne and Mamontacke, to conduct mee to a great house sufficient to lodge mee: where entring I saw it hung round with bowes and arrowes. The Indians used all diligence to make us fires, and give us content: the kings Orators presently entertained us with a kinde oration, with expresse charge that not any should steale, or take our bowes or arrowes, or offer any injury. Presently after he sent me a quarter of Venizon to stay my stomacke: In the evening hee sent for mee to come onely with two shot with me. The company I gave order to stand upon their guard, and to maintaine two sentries at the ports all night. To my supper he set before me meate for twenty men, and seeing I could not eate, hee caused it to be given to my men: for this is a generall custome, that what they give, not to take againe, but you must either eate it, give it away, or carry it with you. Two or three houres we spent in our auncient [1] discourses; which done, I was with a fire stick lighted to my lodging.

The next day the King conducting mee to the River, shewed me his Canowes, and described unto me how hee sent them over the Baye, for tribute Beades: and also what Countries paid him Beads, Copper, or Skins. But seeing Captaine Nuport, and Maister Scrivener, comming a shore, the King returned to his house, and I went to meete him.[2] With a trumpet before him, wee marched to the King: who after his old manner kindly received him, especially a Boy of thirteen yeares old, called Thomas Salvage, whom he gave him as his Sonne. He requited this kindnes with each of us a great basket of Beanes. And entertaining him with the former discourse, we passed away that day, and agreed to bargaine the next day and so returned to our Pinnis.

The next day comming a shore in like order, the King having kindly entertained us with a breakfast, questioned us in this manner: Why we came armed in that sort, seeing hee

[1] Ancient. [2] Newport.

was our friend, and had neither bowes nor arrowes; what did wee doubt? I told him it was the custome of our Country, not doubting of his kindnes any waies: wherewith though hee seemed satisfied, yet Captaine Nuport caused all our men to retire to the water side, which was some thirtie score [1] from thence.

But to prevent the worst, Maister Scrivener or I were either the one or other by the Barge: experience had well taught me to beleeve his friendship till convenient opportunity suffred him to betray us. But quickly this polititian had perceived my absence, and cunningly sent for me; I sent for Maister Scrivener to supply my place: the King would demand for him, I would againe releeve him. And they sought to satisfie our suspition with kind Language: and not being agreed to trade for corne, hee desired to see all our Hatchets and Copper together, for which he would give us corne. With that auncient tricke the Chickahamaniens had oft acquainted me: his offer I refused, offering first to see what hee would give for one piece. Hee seeming to despise the nature of a Merchant, did scorne to sell: but we freely should give him, and he liberally would requite us.

Captaine Nuport would not with lesse then twelve great Coppers try his kindnes, which he liberally requited with as much corne as at Chickahamania I had for one of lesse proportion. Our Hatchets hee would also have at his owne rate: for which kindnes hee much seemed to affect Captaine Nuport. Some few bunches of blew Beades I had, which he much desired, and seeing so few, he offred me a basket of two pecks, and that I drew to be three pecks at the least, and yet [2] seemed contented and desired more. I agreed with him, the next day, for two bushells: for the ebbe now constrained us to returne to our Boate, although he earnestly desired us to stay dinner which was a providing; and being ready he sent aboard after us, which was bread and venizon sufficient for fiftie or sixtie persons.

[1] *I.e.*, thirty score yards.

[2] After "yet" supply "he."

The next day hee sent his Sonne in the morning, not to bring a shore with us any pieces, least his weomen and children should feare. Captaine Nuports good beliefe would have satisfied that request. Yet twentie or twentie five short[1] we got ashore: the King importuning mee to leave my armes a board, much misliking my sword pistol and target. I told him the men that slew my Brother with the like tearmes had perswaded me, and being unarmed shot at us, and so betraide us.

He oft entreated Captaine Nuport that his men might leave their armes: which[2] still hee[3] commanded to the water side. This day we spent in trading for blew Beads: and having neare fraighted our Barge, Captaine Nuport returned with them that came abord, leaving me and Maister Scrivener a shore, to follow in Canowes. Into one I got with sixe of our men, which beeing lanched, a stones cast from the shore stuck fast in the Ose.[4] Master Scrivener seeing this example, with seven or eight more passed the dreadfull bridge, thinking to have found deeper water on the other creeke: but they were inforced to stay, with such entertainment as a salvage.[5] Being forced ashore with wind and raine, having in his Canow, as commonly they have, his house and houshold, instantly set up a house of mats, which succoured them from the storme.

The Indians seeing me pestred in the Ose, called to me: six or seven of the Kings chiefe men threw off their skins, and to the middle in Ose, came to bear me out on their heads. Their importunacie caused me better to like the Canow than their curtesie, excusing my deniall for feare to fall into the Ose: desiring them to bring me some wood, fire, and mats to cover me, and I would content them. Each presently gave his helpe to satisfie my request, which paines a horse would scarce have indured: yet a couple of bells richly contented them.

The Emperor sent his Seaman Mantivas in the evening

[1] Shot, *i.e.*, twenty or twenty-five men with guns were landed.

[2] Whom.

[3] *I.e.*, Newport.

[4] Ooze.

[5] After "salvage" supply "could offer, who."

with bread and victuall for me and my men: he no more scrupulous then the rest seemed to take a pride in shewing how litle he regarded that miserable cold and durty passage, though a dogge would scarce have indured it. This kindnes I found, when I litle expected lesse then a mischiefe: but the blacke night parting our companies, ere midnight the flood served to carry us aboard.

The next day we came ashore, the King [1] with a solemne discourse, causing all to depart but his principall men: and this was the effect. When as hee perceived that we had a desire to invade Monacum, against whom he was no professed enemy: yet thus farre he would assist us in his enterprise. First hee would send his spies, perfectly to understand their strength and ability to fight, with which he would acquaint us himselfe. Captaine Nuport would not be seene in it himselfe, being great Werowances. They [2] would stay at home: but I, Maister Scrivener, and two of his [3] Sonnes, and Opechankanough the King of Pamaunke should have 100. of his men to goe before as though they were hunting; they giving us notise where was the advantage, we should kill them: the weomen and young children he wished we should spare, and bring them to him. Only 100. or 150. of our men he held sufficient for this exploit. Our boats should stay at the falls, where we might hew timber, which we might convey, each man a piece, till we were past the stones; and there joyne them to passe our men by water. If any were shot, his men should bring them backe to our boats. This faire tale had almost made Captaine Nuport undertake by this meanes to discover the South sea: [4] which will not be without trecherie, if wee ground our intent upon his constancie.

This day we spent in trading, dancing, and much mirth.

[1] Spoke. [2] Powhatan and Newport. [3] Powhatan's.

[4] The belief was general that the South Sea lay only a short distance overland from Chesapeake Bay, which appears remarkable when it is recalled that Sir Francis Drake had many years before, in his circumnavigation of the globe, sailed along the western coast of North America. This impression can only be adequately explained by supposing that the knowledge of longitudes at that time was grossly defective.

The King of Pamaunke sent his messenger (as yet not knowing Captaine Nuport) to come unto him: who had long expected mee, desiring also my Father to visite him. The messenger stayed to conduct us: but Powhatan understanding that we had Hatchets lately come from Paspahegh, desired the next day to trade with us, and not to go further. This new tricke he cunningly put upon him, but onely to have what he listed, and to try whether we would go or stay. Opechankenoughs messenger returned,[1] that wee would not come. The next day his [2] Daughter came to entreat me, shewing her Father had hurt his legge, and much sorrowed he could not see me.

Captaine Nuport being not to bee perswaded to goe, in that Powhatan had desired us to stay: sent her away with the like answer. Yet the next day, upon better consideration, intreatie prevailed; and wee anchored at Cinquoateck, the first twaine [3] above the parting of the river, where dwelled two Kings of Pamaunke, Brothers to Powhatan; the one called Opitchapam, the other Katatough. To these I went a shore, who kindly intreated mee and Maister Scrivener, sending some presents aboard to Captaine Nuport. Whilst we were trucking with these Kings, Opechankanough his wife, weomen, and children came to meete me: with a naturall kind affection hee seemed to rejoyce to see me.

Captaine Nuport came a shore, with many kind discourses wee passed that forenoone: and after dinner, Captaine Nuport went about with the Pinnis to Menapacant, which is twenty miles by water, and not one by land.[4] Opechankanough conducted me and Maister Scrivener by land: where having built a feasting house a purpose to entertaine us, with a kind Oration, after their manner, and his best provision, kindly welcomed us. That day he would not trucke, but did his best

[1] After "returned" supply "answer."

[2] *I.e.*, "Opechancanough's."

[3] Town. Cinquoateck was situated about where West Point now is.

[4] After leaving West Point, the Pamunkey River makes a great bend, though the distance is overestimated by Smith.

to delight us with content: Captaine Nuport arrived towards evening; whom the King presented with sixe great platters of fine bread, and Pansarowmana. The next day till noone wee traded: the King feasted all the company; and the afternoone was spent in playing, dauncing, and delight. By no meanes hee would have us depart till, the next day, he had feasted us with venizon; for which he had sent, having spent his first and second provision in expecting our comming: The next day, he performed his promise, giving more to us three, then would have sufficed 30. and in that we carried not away what we left, hee sent it after us to the Pinnis. With what words or signes of love he could expresse, we departed.

Captaine Nuport in the Pinnis, leaving mee in the Barge to digge a rocke, where wee supposed a Mine, at Cinquaoteck: which done, ere midnight, I arrived at Weracomoco, where our Pinnis anchored, being 20. miles [1] from Cinquaotecke. The next day, we tooke leave of Powhatan: who, in regard of his kindness, gave him an Indian. He well affected to goe with him for England in steed of his Sonne:[2] the cause, I assure me, was to know our strength and Countries condition: The next day we arrived at Kiskiack. The people so scornefully entertained us, as with what signes of scorne and discontent we could, we departed: and returned to our Fort with 250. bushells of Corne.[3] Our president, being not wholy recovered of his sicknes, in discharging his Piece, brake and split his hand off, which he is not yet [4] well recovered. At Captaine Nuports arrivall,[5] wee were victualled for twelve weeks: and having furnished him of what hee thought good, hee set saile for England the tenth of April. Master Scrivener and my selfe, with our shallop, accompanied him to Cape Hendrick:[6] Powhatan having for a farrewell, sent him five or sixe mens loadings, with Turkeys for [the] swords which hee sent him. In our return to the fort, we discovered the river of Nausamd,[7] a proud

[1] About fourteen miles.

[2] *I.e.*, Thomas Savage, whom Newport gave to Powhatan, calling him his son.

[3] March 9, 1608.

[4] June 2, 1608.

[5] At Jamestown, March 9, 1608.

[6] Henry

[7] Nansemond.

warlike Nation, as well we may testifie, at our first arrivall at Chesiapiack: but that injury Captaine Nuport well revenged at his returne. Where some of them intising him to their Ambuscadoes by a daunce, hee perceiving their intent, with a volly of musket shot, slew one, and shot one or two more, as themselves confesse.

The King at our arivall sent for me to come unto him. I sent him word what commodities I had to exchange for wheat,[1] and if he would, as had the rest of his Neighbours, conclude a Peace, we were contented. At last he came downe before the Boate which rid at anchor some fortie yards from the shore. He signified to me to come a shore, and sent a Canow with foure or five of his men: two whereof I desired to come aboard and to stay, and I would send two to talke with their King a shore. To this hee agreed. The King wee presented with a piece of Copper, which he kindly excepted,[2] and sent for victualls to entertaine the messengers. Maister Scrivener and my selfe also, after that, went a shore. The King kindly feasted us, requesting us to stay to trade till the next day. Which having done, we returned to the Fort.

This river[3] is a musket shot broad, each side being should[4] bayes; a narrow channel, but three fadom:[5] his course for eighteene miles, almost directly South, and by West where beginneth the first inhabitants: for a mile it turneth directly East; towards the West, a great bay, and a white chaukie Iland convenient for a Fort: his next course South, where within a quarter of a mile, the river divideth in two, the neck a plaine high Corne field, the wester bought[6] a highe plaine likewise, the Northeast answerable in all respects. In these plaines are planted aboundance of houses and people; they may containe 1000. Acres of most excellent fertill ground: so sweete, so pleasant, so beautifull, and so strong a prospect,

[1] Indian corn. [2] Accepted.

[3] The Nansemond River opens into the south side of Hampton Roads and is navigable for vessels of 100 tons as far as Suffolk, about twenty miles from the mouth. William Wallace Tooker states the meaning of the word to be "a good fishing place." [4] Shoal. [5] Deep. [6] Bend.

for an invincible strong City, with so many commodities, that I know as yet I have not seene. This is within one daies journey of Chawwonocke, the river falleth into the Kings[1] river, within twelve miles of Cape-hendicke.[2]

At our Fort, the tooles we had, were so ordinarily stolen by the Indians, as necessity inforced us to correct their braving theeverie: for he that stole to day, durst come againe the next day. One amongst the rest, having stolen two swords, I got the Counsels consent to set in the bilboes.[3] The next day, with three more, he came, with their woodden swordes, in the midst of our men to steale. Their custome is to take any thing they can ceaze off: onely the people of Pamaunke wee have not found stealing, but what others can steale, their King receiveth. I bad them depart, but flourishing their swords, they seemed to defend what they could catch but out of our hands: his pride urged me to turne him from amongst us, whereat he offred to strike me with his sword; which I prevented, striking him first. The rest offring to revenge the blow, received such an incounter, and fled. The better to affright them, I pursued them with five or sixe shot, and so chased them out of the Iland.[4]

The beginner of this broyle, litle expecting by his carriage, we durst have resisted, having, even till that present, not beene contradicted, especially them of Paspahegh: these Indians within one houre, having by other Salvages then in the Fort, understood that I threatened to be revenged, came presently of themselves, and fell to working upon our wears which were then in hand by other Salvages: who seeing their pride so incountred, were so submissive, and willing to doe any thing as might be. And with trembling feare desired to be friends, within three daies after. From Nawsamond, which is 30. miles from us, the King sent us a Hatchet which they had stollen from us at our being there: the messenger, as is the custome, also wee well rewarded and contented.

[1] *I.e.*, Powhatan's river. [2] Cape Henry.

[3] The stocks. [4] Or rather the peninsula on which Jamestown stood.

The twenty of Aprill, being at worke, in hewing downe Trees, and setting Corne, an alarum caused us with all speede to take our armes, each expecting a new assault of the Salvages: but understanding it a Boate under saile, our doubts were presently satisfied with the happy sight of Maister Nelson, his many perrills of extreame stormes and tempests,[1] his ship well as his company could testifie, his care in sparing our provision was well: but the providence [2] thereof, as also of our stones, Hatchets and other tooles (onely ours excepted) which of all the rest was most necessary: which might inforce us to thinke either a seditious traitor to our action, or a most unconscionable deceiver of our treasurs.

This happy arrivall of Maister Nelson in the *Phenix*, having beene then about three monethes missing after Captaine Nuports arrivall, being to all our expectations lost: albeit that now at the last, having beene long crossed with tempestuous weather and contrary winds, his so unexpected comming did so ravish us with exceeding joy, that now we thought our selves as well fitted as our harts could wish, both with a competent number of men, as also for all other needfull provisions, till a further supply should come unto us.[3] Whereupon the first thing that was concluded was that my selfe and Maister Scrivener, should with 70. men goe with the best meanes we could provide, to discover beyond the Falls, as in our judgements conveniently we might. Six or seaven daies we spent only in trayning our men to march, fight, and scirmish in the woods. Their willing minds to this action so quickned their understanding in this exercise as, in all judgements, wee were better able to fight with Powhatans whole force, in our order of battle amongst the Trees (for Thicks there is few) [4] then the Fort

[1] Passed.

[2] The providing.

[3] The *Phoenix* set out with Newport as a part of the First Supply, but was separated from him by winds, which delayed her arrival three months.

[4] The frequent fires made by the Indians in hunting had cleared away the underbrush in Virginia so that it is said a coach with four horses could be driven through the thickest group of trees. Behind the stockade at Jamestown, however, there was a branch of a swamp which was covered with high grasses, affording a secure hiding-place to the stealthy savages.

was to repulse 400. at the first assault, with some tenne or twenty shot not knowing what to doe, nor how to use a Piece.

Our warrant being sealed, Maister Nelson refused to assiste us with the voluntary Marriners and himself, as he promised, unlesse we would stand bound to pay the hire for shippe and Marriners, for the time they stayed. And further there was some controversie, through the diversitie of Contrary opinions: some alleadging that how profitable, and to what good purpose soever our journey should portend, yet our commission commanding no certaine designe, we should be taxed for the most indiscreete men in the world, besides the wrong we should doe to Captaine Nuport, to whom only all discoveries did belong, and to no other:

The meanes for guides, besides the uncertaine[1] courses of the river from which we could not erre much, each night would fortifie us in two houres better then that they first called the Fort. Their Townes upon the river each within one dayes journey of other, besides our ordinary provision, might well be supposed to adde reliefe: for truck and dealing only, but in love and peace, as with the rest. If they assalted us, their Townes they cannot defend, nor their luggage so convey that we should not share: but admit the worst, 16. daies provision we had of Cheese Oatmeale and bisket; besides our randevous we could, and might, have hid in the ground. With sixe men, Captaine Martin would have undertaken it[2] himselfe, leaving the rest to defend the Fort and plant our Corne. Yet no reason could be reason to proceede forward, though we were going aboard to set saile. These discontents caused so many doubts to some, and discouragement to others, as our journey ended. Yet some of us procured petitions to set us forward, only with hope of our owne confusions.

Our next course was to turne husbandmen, to fell Trees and set Corne. Fiftie of our men we imployed in this service; the rest kept the Fort, to doe the command of the president

[1] Smith refers to the necks of land made by the windings of the river, which were easily defended.

[2] *I.e.*, the expedition.

and Captaine Martin. 30. dayes[1] the ship[2] lay expecting the triall of certain matters which for some cause I keepe private.[3]

The next exploit was an Indian having stolen an Axe, was so pursued by Maister Scrivener and them next him, as he threw it downe: and flying, drew his bow at any that durst incounter him. Within foure or five dayes after, Maister Scrivener and I, being a litle from the Fort, among the Corne, two Indians, each with a cudgell, and all newly painted with *Terrasigillata*, came circling about me as though they would have clubed me like a hare. I knew their faining love is towards me not without a deadly hatred: but to prevent the worst, I calling maister Scrivener retired to the Fort. The Indians seeing me suspect them, with good tearmes, asked me for some of their men whom they would beate; and went with me into our Fort. Finding one that lay ordinarily with us, only for a spie; they offered to beat him. I in perswading them to forbeare, they offered to beginne with me; being now foure: for two other arrayed in like manner, came in on the other side the Fort. Whereupon I caused to shut the Ports,[4] and apprehend them. The president and Counsell, being presently acquainted, remembring at the first assault, they came in like manner, and never else but against[5] some villanie, concluded to commit them to prison, and expect the event. Eight more we ceazed[6] at that present. An houre after came three or foure other strangers extraordinarily fitted with arrowes, skinnes, and shooting gloves: their jealousie and feare bewrayed their bad intent, as also their suspitious departure.

[1] *I.e.*, from May 4 to June 2, 1608. [2] *I.e.*, the *Phoenix*.

[3] There was a quarrel between Smith and Martin as to the character of the return cargo. Martin wished to fill the ship with an ore resembling gold, but Smith, who favored a cargo of cedar, finally prevailed. Martin returned in the ship. There is a broad hint in this paragraph that matters merely of a personal nature were to be suppressed for fear of further dissensions.

[4] The fort, which was triangular in shape, had three gates in the centre of each side. It enclosed a little more than an acre of land, and was defended by palisades made of large poles about eight feet high and stuck three or four feet into the ground. [5] *I.e.*, for. [6] Seized.

The next day, came first an Indian, then another, as Embassadors for their men. They desired to speake with me. Our discourse was, that what Spades, Shovells, swords, or tooles they had stolne to bring home: if not, the next day, they should hang. The next newes was, they had taken two of our men ranging in the woods (which mischiefe [1] no punishment will prevent but hanging): and these they would, should redeeme [2] their owne 16. or 18.; thus braving us to our doores.

We desired the president, and Captaine Martin, that afternoone to sally upon them, that they might but know what we durst do: and at night, mand our Barge, and burnt their Townes, and spoiled and destroyed what we could. But they brought our men, and freely delivered them. The president released one. The rest we brought well guarded, to Morning and Evening prayers. Our men all in armes, their trembling feare then caused them to[o] much sorrow, which till then scoffed and scorned at what we durst doe. The Counsell concluded, that I should terrifie them with some torture, to know if I could know their intent. The next day, I bound one in hold to the maine Mast: [3] and presenting sixe Muskets with match in the cockes, forced him to desire life. To answere my demaunds he could not: but one of his Comovodos [4] was of the counsell of Paspahegh, that could satisfie me: I releasing him out of sight, I affrighted the other, first with the rack, then with Muskets; which seeing, he desired me to stay, and hee would confesse. To this execution Maister Scrivener came, his discourse was to this effect. That Paspehegh, the Chickahamaniar, Youghtanum, Pamaunka, Mattapanient, and Kiskiack: these Nations were al together a hunting that tooke me. Paspahegh and Chicahamanya had entended to surprise us at worke, to have had our tools. Powhatan and al his would seeme friends, till Captaine Nuports returne, that he had againe his man, which he called Namontack: where, with

[1] *I.e.*, ranging. [2] *I.e.*, they held them as ransoms for their own men.
[3] *I.e.*, of the *Phoenix*.
[4] Perhaps a misprint for *camaradas*, Spanish for "comrades."

a great feast, hee would so enamor Captain Nuport and his men, as they should ceaze on him. And the like traps would be laied for the rest.

This trap for our tooles we suspected. The chiefe occasion was [that] foure daies before, Powhatan had sent the boy [1] he had to us, with many Turkies to Maister Scrivener and me: understanding I would go up unto his Countries to destroy them; and he doubted [2] it the more, in that I so ofte practised my men, whose shooting he heard to his owne lodging, that much feared his wives and children. We sent him word, we entended no such thing, but only to goe to Powhatan, to seeke stones to make Hatchets; except his men shot at us, as Paspahegh had told us they would: which if they did shoote but one arrowe, we would destroy them. And, least this mischiefe might happen, sent the boy [3] to acquaint him thus much; and request him to send us Weanock, one of his subjects for a guide.

The boy he returned backe with his Chest and apparell, which then we had given him: desiring another for him. The cause was, he was practising with the Chikahamanias, as the boy suspected some villanie, by their extraordinary resort and secret conference, from whence they would send him. The boy we keepe. Now we would send him many messengers and presents, the guide we desired he sent us: and withall requested us to returne him, either the boy or some other. But none he could have. And that day these Indians were apprehended, his sonne with others that had loaded at our Fort, returned, and being out of the Fort, rayled on me, to divers of our men, to be enemies to him, and to the Chikamanias. Not long after, Weanock that had bin with us for our guide, whom wee kept to have conducted us in another journy, with a false excuse returned: and secretly after him, Amocis the Paspaheyan, who alwaies they kept amongst us for a spie, whom, the better to avoide suspition, presently after they came to beate away: These presumptions induced me to take any

[1] Thomas Savage. [2] Suspected. [3] Thomas Savage.

occasion, not onely to try the honesty of Amocis the spie, but also the meaning of these cunning trickes of their Emperour of Powhatan; whose true meaning Captaine Martin most confidently pleaded.

The confession of Macanoe, which was the counseller of Paspahegh, first I, then Maister Scrivener, upon their severall examinations, found by them all confirmed, that Paspahegh and Chickahammania did hate us, and intended some mischiefe: and who they were that tooke me, the names of them that stole our tooles and swords, and that Powhatan received them they all agreed. Certaine vollies of shot we caused to be discharged, which caused each other to think that their fellowes had beene slaine.

Powhatan understanding we detained certaine Salvages, sent his Daughter, a child of tenne yeares old: which, not only for feature, countenance, and proportion, much exceedeth any of the rest of his people: but for wit and spirit, the only Nonpariel of his Country.[1] This hee sent by his most trustie messenger, called Rawhunt, as much exceeding in deformitie of person; but of a subtill wit and crafty understanding. He, with a long circumstance, told mee, how well Powhatan loved and respected mee; and in that I should not doubt any way of his kindnesse, he had sent his child, which he most esteemed, to see me; a Deare and bread besides, for a present: desiring me that the Boy [2] might come againe, which he loved exceedingly. His litle Daughter hee had taught this lesson also, not taking notice at all of the Indeans that had beene prisoners three daies, till that morning that she saw their fathers and friends come quietly, and in good tearmes to entreate their libertie.

Opechankanough sent also unto us, that for his sake, we would release two that were his friends: and for a token, sent me his shooting Glove and Bracer,[3] which [4] the day our men

[1] Smith was mistaken as to the age of Pocahontas, as she was about thirteen years old at this time.

[2] Thomas Savage.

[3] A bracer was a covering to the arm protecting it from the vibrations of the string of the bow.

[4] After "which" supply "he used."

was taken upon, separating himselfe from the rest a long time,[1] intreated to speake with me, where in token of peace, he had preferred me the same. Now all of them having found their peremptorie conditions but to increase our malice; which they seeing us begin to threaten to destroy them, as familiarly as before, without suspition or feare, came amongst us, to begge libertie for their men. In the afternoone, they being gone, we guarded them as before to the Church; and after prayer, gave them to Pocahuntas, the Kings Daughter, in regard of her fathers kindnesse in sending her. After having well fed them, as all the time of their imprisonment, we gave them their bowes, arrowes, or what else they had; and with[2] much content, sent them packing. Pocahuntas also we requited with such trifles as contented her, to tel that we had used the Paspaheyans very kindly in so releasing them.

The next day, we had suspition of some other practise for an Ambuscado; but perfectly wee could not discover it. Two daies after, a Paspaheyan came to shew us a glistering Minerall stone, and with signes demonstrating it to be in great aboundance like unto Rockes: with some dozen more, I was sent to seeke to digge some quantitie, and the Indean to conduct me. But suspecting this some trick to delude us, for to get some Copper of us; or with some ambuscado to betray us, seeing him falter in his tale, being two miles on our way, led[3] him ashore: where abusing us from place to place, and so seeking either to have drawne us with him into the woods, or to have given us the slippe, I shewed him Copper, which I promised to have given him, if he had performed his promise. But for his scoffing and abusing us, I gave him twentie lashes with a Rope; and his bowes and arrowes, bidding him shoote if he durst: and so let him goe.

In all this time, our men being all or the most part well recovered, and we not willing to trifle away more time then necessitie enforced us unto: we thought good, for the better

[1] After "time" supply "the messenger."

[2] With *their* much content.

[3] Before "led" supply "we."

content of the adventurers, in some reasonable sort to fraight home Maister Nelson, with Cedar wood. About which, our men going with willing minds, was[1] in very good time effected, and the ship sent for England. Wee now remaining being in good health, all our men wel contented, free from mutinies,[2] in love one with another, and as we hope in a continuall peace with the Indians: where we doubt not but by Gods gracious assistance, and the adventurers willing minds and speedie furtherance to so honorable an action, in after times to see our Nation to enjoy a Country, not onely exceeding pleasant for habitation, but also very profitable for comerce in generall; no doubt pleasing to almightie God, honourable to our gracious Soveraigne, and commodious generally to the whole Kingdome.

[1] Before "was" supply "it."

[2] Of the original council Wingfield and Archer left the colony with Newport in the *John and Francis;* Martin in the *Phoenix.* Gosnold had died in the first summer and Kendall was shot. President Ratcliffe and Smith were the only two remaining, though Matthew Scrivener, who arrived in the First Supply, shared the authority with them. The condition of peace described by Smith did not long prevail.

# DESCRIPTION OF VIRGINIA AND PROCEEDINGS OF THE COLONIE BY CAPTAIN JOHN SMITH, 1612

# INTRODUCTION

The first part of this work is evidently an expanded and revised text of that "Mappe of the Bay and Rivers, with an annexed Relation of the countries and Nations that inhabit them," which President John Smith sent home about November, 1608, to the council in London, as the result of his explorations in Chesapeake Bay in the previous summer. Smith doubtless furnished the manuscript to Dr. William Simmonds, who revised it, and it was published at the expense of T. Abbay, who went with Smith to Virginia. It is a remarkably faithful account of the topography of Virginia, and of the Indian inhabitants. The second part was the result of the combined pens of at least six gentlemen and soldiers, who were friends of Smith. It was compiled and added to by Richard Pots, one of the expedition, tested and revised by William Simmonds, D. D., and published by T. Abbay. Whenever prejudice has no occasion to exist, the narrative may be accepted as correct and faithful; but the acts and motives of Wingfield, Archer, and the leading men not of Smith's party, receive but scant justice or consideration. Men were good haters in Smith's day, and there was no such thing as moderation of expression when an enemy was aimed at.

This work was printed at Oxford, in 1612, and it is sometimes called the Oxford tract, but it is rather a book than a tract. In 1625 an abridgment of the first part was published in Samuel Purchas, *His Pilgrimes*, Vol. II. In 1884 it was included by Edward Arber in his collection of John Smith's *Works*.

L. G. T.

# A MAP OF VIRGINIA:

*With a Description of the Countrey, the Commodities, People, Government and Religion. Written by Captaine Smith, sometimes Governour of the Countrey.*

*Whereunto is annexed the proceedings of those Colonies, since their first departure from England, with the discourses, Orations, and relations of the Salvages, and the accidents that befell them in all their Journies and discoveries. Taken faithfully as they were written out of the writings of*

| | |
|---|---|
| *Doctor Russell,* | *Richard Wiefin,* |
| *Tho. Studley,* | *Will. Phettiplace,* |
| *Anas Todkill,* | *Nathaniel Powell,* |
| *Jeffra Abot,* | *Richard Pots,* |

*And the relations of divers other diligent observers there present then, and now many of them in England. By W. S.*

*At Oxford, Printed by Joseph Barnes.* 1612.[1]

## TO THE RIGHT HONOURABLE S[r]. EDWARD SEMER KNIGHT, BARON BEAUCHAMP, AND EARLE OF HARTFORD,

LIEUTENANT TO HIS MOST EXCELLENT MAJESTIE, IN THE COUNTIES OF SOMERSET AND WILTSHIRE, MY HONOURABLE GOOD LORD AND MAISTER.[2]

*My Honourable Lord:*

If Vertue be the soule of true Nobilitie as wise men say, then blessed is your Lordship, that is every way noble, as well in vertue,

[1] This italic heading is copied from the title page of the original. The map implied in the title and published in the pamphlet is printed in Purchas's *Pilgrimes* and other volumes. It exists in eight different stages of development. "W.S." is Dr. William Simmonds.

[2] This dedication, for a copy of which we are indebted to Mr. Victor H. Paltsits of the Lenox Library, apparently occurs only in a copy of Smith's *Map of Virginia* possessed by that library, a copy bound in vellum, with the arms of Lord Hertford on both sides, in gold. The dedication has never before been reprinted. Its inconsistency with the language of that which follows, " To the Hand," found in most copies, is obvious.

as birth, and riches. Though riches now, be the chiefest greatnes of the great: when great and little are born, and dye, there is no difference: Virtue onely makes men more then men: Vice, worse then brutes. And those are distinguished by deedes, not words; though both be good, deedes are best, and of all evils, ingratitude the worst. Therefore I beseech you, that not to seeme ungratefull, I may present your Honour with this rude discourse, of a new old subject. It is the best gift I can give to the best friend I have. It is the best service I ever did to serve so good a worke: Wherin having beene discouraged for doing any more, I have writ this little: yet my hands hath been my lands this fifteene yeares in Europ, Asia, Afric, or America.

In the harbour of your Lo:[1] favour, I hope I ever shall rest secure, notwithstanding all weathers; lamenting others, that they fall into such miseries, as I foreseeing have foretold, but could not prevent. No more: but dedicating my best abilities to the honour and service of your renowned Vertues, I ever rest

Your Lordships true and faithfull Servant,

JOHN SMITH.

## TO THE HAND

LEAST I should wrong any in dedicating this Booke to one: I have concluded it shal be particular to none. I found it only dedicated to a Hand, and to that hand I addresse it. Now for that this businesse is common to the world, this booke may best satisfie the world, because it was penned in the Land it treateth of. If it bee disliked of men, then I would recommend it to women, for being dearely bought, and farre sought, it should be good for Ladies. When all men rejected Christopher Collumbus, that ever renowned Queene Izabell of Spaine, could pawne her Jewels to supply his wants; whom all the wise men (as they thought themselves) of that age contemned. I need not say what was his worthinesse, her noblenesse, and their ignorance, that so scornefully did spit at his wants, seeing

[1] Lordship's

the whole world is enriched with his golden fortunes. Cannot this successfull example move the incredulous of this time to consider, to conceave, and apprehend Virginia, which might be, or breed us a second India? hath not England an Izabell, as well as Spaine, nor yet a Collumbus as well as Genua? yes surely it hath, whose desires are no lesse then was worthy Collumbus, their certainties more, their experiences no way wanting, only there wants but an Izabell, so it were not from Spaine.

T. A.

Because many doe desire to knowe the maner of their language, I have inserted these few words.

*Ka ka torawincs yowo.* What call you this.
*Nemarough.* a man.
*Crenepo.* a woman.
*Marowanchesso.* a boy.
*Yehawkans.* Houses.
*Matchcores.*[1] Skins, or garments.
*Mockasins.* Shooes.
*Tussan.* Beds.
*Pokatawer.* Fire.
*Attawp.* A bowe.
*Attonce.* Arrowes.
*Monacookes.* Swords.
*Aumoughhowgh.* A Target.
*Pawcussacks.* Gunnes.
*Tomahacks.* Axes.
*Tockahacks.* Pickaxes.
*Pamesacks.* Knives.
*Accowprets.* Sheares.
*Pawpecones.* Pipes.
*Mattassin.* Copper.
*Ussawassin.* Iron, Brasse, Silver, or any white metal.
*Musses.* Woods.
*Attasskuss.* Leaves, weeds, or grasse.
*Chepsin.* Land.
*Shacquohocan.* A stone.
*Wepenter.* a cookold.
*Suckahanna.* Water.
*Noughmass.* Fish.
*Copotone.* Sturgion.
*Weghshaughes.* Flesh.
*Sawwehone.* Bloud.
*Netoppew.* Friends.
*Marrapough.* Enimies.
*Maskapow.* The worst of the enimies.

[1] This word, by *Volksetymologie*, the white men made into "matchcoats."

*Mawchick chammay.* The best of friends.

*Casacunnakack, peya quagh acquintan uttasantasough.* In how many daies will there come hether any more English ships?

Their numbers.

*Necut.* 1.
*Ningh.* 2.
*Nuss.* 3.
*Yowgh.* 4.
*Paranske.* 5.
*Comotinch.* 6.
*Toppawoss.* 7.
*Nusswash.* 8.
*Kekatawgh.* 9.
*Kaskeke.* [10.]

They count no more but by tennes as followeth.

*Case,* how many.
*Ninghsapooeksku.* 20.
*Nussapooeksku.* 30.
*Yowghapooeksku.* 40.
*Parankestassapooeksku.* 50.
*Comatinchtassapooeksku.* 60.
*Toppawousstassapooeksku.* 70.
*Nussswashtassapooeksku.* 80.
*Kekataughtassapooeksku.* 90.
*Necuttoughtysinough.* 100.
*Necuttweunquaough.* 1000.
*Rawcosowghs.* Daies.
*Keskowghes.* Sunnes.
*Toppquough.* Nights.
*Nepawweshowghs.* Moones.
*Pawpaxsoughes.* Yeares.
*Pummahumps.* Starres.
*Osies.* Heavens.
*Okes.* Gods.
*Quiyoughcosucks.* Pettie Gods, and their affinities.
*Righcomoughes.* Deaths.
*Kekughes.* Lives.

*Mowchick woyawgh tawgh noeragh kaquere mecher.* I am verie hungrie? what shall I eate?

*Tawnor nehiegh Powhatan.* where dwels Powwhatan.

*Mache, nehiegh yowrowgh, orapaks.* Now he dwels a great way hence at orapaks.

*Uttapitchewayne anpechitchs nehawper werowacomoco.* You lie, he staide ever at werowocomoco.

*Kator nehiegh mattagh neer uttapitchewayne.* Truely he is there I do not lie.

*Spaughtynere keragh werowance mawmarinough kekaten wawgh*

*peyaquaugh.* Run you then to the king mawmarynough and bid him come hither.

*Utteke, e peya weyack wighwhip.* Get you gone, and come againe quickly.

*Kekaten pokahontas patiaquagh niugh tanks manotyens neer mowchick rawrenock audowgh.* Bid Pokahontas bring hither two little Baskets, and I wil give her white beads to make her a chaine.

## THE DESCRIPTION OF VIRGINIA BY CAPTAINE SMITH

VIRGINIA is a Country in America, that lyeth betweene the degrees of 34 and 44[1] of the north latitude. The bounds thereof on the East side are the great *Ocean.* On the South lyeth Florida: on the North nova Francia. As for the West thereof, the limits are unknowne. Of all this country wee purpose not to speake, but only of that part which was planted by the English men in the yeare of our Lord, 1606.[2] And this is under the degrees 37. 38. and 39. The temperature of this countrie doth agree well with English constitutions being once seasoned [3] to the country. Which appeared by this, that though by many occasions our people fell sicke; yet did they recover by very small meanes and continued in health, though there were other great causes, not only to have made them sicke, but even to end their daies, etc.

The sommer is hot as in Spaine; the winter colde as in Fraunce or England. The heat of sommer is in June, Julie, and

[1] In the charter granted April 10, 1606, Virginia is defined to be the country between 34 and 45 degrees north latitude.

[2] The ships left London, December 20, 1606.

[3] "Seasoned" was a term current in Virginia for one hundred years later. All who came soon fell sick of the malaria of the rivers and creeks, and such as survived were called "seasoned" inhabitants. The mortality of these early days fell especially upon the servants exposed in the tobacco fields, of whom four out of five perished during the first year after their arrival, and this continued to be the case down to Sir William Berkeley's day. The opening of the fields, and the use of Peruvian bark, introduced much healthier conditions.

August, but commonly the coole Breeses asswage the vehemencie of the heat. The chiefe of winter is halfe December, January, February, and halfe March. The colde is extreame sharpe, but here the proverbe is true that no extreame long continueth.

In the yeare 1607. was an extraordinary frost in most of Europe, and this frost was founde as extreame in Virginia. But the next yeare for 8. or 10. daies of ill weather, other 14 daies would be as Sommer.

The windes here are variable, but the like thunder and lightning to purifie the aire, I have seldome either seene or heard in Europe. From the Southwest came the greatest gustes with thunder and heat. The Northwest winde is commonly coole, and bringeth faire weather with it. From the Northe is the greatest cold, and from the East and South-East as from the Barmadas, fogs and raines.

Some times there are great droughts, other times much raine, yet great necessity of neither, by reason we see not but that all the variety of needfull fruits in Europe may be there in great plenty by the industry of men, as appeareth by those we there planted.

There is but one entraunce by sea into this country, and that is at the mouth of a very goodly Bay, the widenesse whereof is neare 18. or 20. miles. The cape on the South side is called Cape Henry [1] in honour of our most noble Prince. The shew of the land there, is a white hilly sand like unto the Downes, and along the shores great plentie of Pines and Firres.

The north Cape is called Cape Charles in honour of the worthy Duke of Yorke.[2] Within is a country that may have the prerogative over the most pleasant places of Europe, Asia, Africa, or America, for large and pleasant navigable rivers: heaven and earth never agreed better to frame a place for mans habitation being of our constitutions, were it fully manured and inhabited by industrious people. Here are mountaines,

[1] Henry, eldest son of James I., was born in 1594. He was a promising and amiable youth, but died in 1612 in the eighteenth year of his age.

[2] Prince Charles, afterwards King Charles I.

hils, plaines, valleyes, rivers and brookes all running most pleasantly into a faire Bay compassed but for the mouth with fruitfull and delightsome land. In the Bay and rivers are many Isles both great and small, some woody, some plaine, most of them low and not inhabited. This Bay lieth North and South in which the water floweth neare 200 miles and hath a channell for 140 miles, of depth betwixt 7 and 15 fadome, holding in breadth for the most part 10 or 14 miles. From the head of the Bay at the north, the land is mountanous, and so in a manner from thence by a Southwest line; So that the more Southward, the farther of[f] from the Bay are those mounetaines. From which, fall certaine brookes, which after come to five principall navigable rivers. These run from the Northwest into the South east, and so into the west side of the Bay, where the fall of every River is within 20 or 15 miles one of an other.

The mountaines are of diverse natures, for at the head of the Bay the rockes are of a composition like miln-stones. Some of marble, &c. And many peeces of christall we found as throwne downe by water from the mountaines. For in winter these mountaines are covered with much snow, and when it dissolveth the waters fall with such violence, that it causeth great inundations in the narrow valleyes which yet is scarce perceived being once in the rivers. These waters wash from the rocks such glistering tinctures that the ground in some places seemeth as guilded, where both the rocks and the earth are so splendent to behold, that better judgements then ours might have beene perswaded, they contained more then probabilities.[1] The vesture of the earth in most places doeth manifestly prove the nature of the soile to be lusty and very rich. The coulor of the earth we found in diverse places, resembleth *bole Armoniac, terra sigillata ad lemnia*, Fullers earth, marle, and divers other such appearances. But generally for the most part the earth is a black sandy mould, in some places a fat slimy clay, in other places a very barren gravell. But the best

[1] The "glistening tinctures" were, however, only particles of mica.

ground is knowne by the vesture it beareth, as by the greatnesse of trees or abundance of weedes, &c.

The country is not mountanous nor yet low but such pleasant plaine hils and fertle valleyes, one prettily crossing an other, and watered so conveniently with their sweete brookes and christall springs, as if art it selfe had devised them. By the rivers are many plaine marishes containing some 20, some 100, some 200 Acres, some more, some lesse. Other plaines there are fewe, but only where the Savages inhabit: but all overgrowne with trees and weedes being a plaine wildernes as God first made it.

On the west side of the Bay, wee said were 5. faire and delightfull navigable rivers, of which wee will nowe proceed to report. The first of those rivers and the next to the mouth of the Bay, hath his course from the West and by North. The name of this river they call Powhatan accor[ding] to the name of a principall country that lieth upon it. The mouth of this river is neere three miles in breadth, yet doe the shoules force the Channell so neere the land that a Sacre[1] will overshoot it at point blanck. This river is navigable 100 miles, the shouldes and soundings are here needlesse to bee expressed. It falleth from Rockes farre west in a country inhabited by a nation that they call Monacan. But where it commeth into our discoverie it is Powhatan. In the farthest place that was diligently observed, are falles, rockes, showles, &c., which makes it past navigation any higher. Thence in the running downeward, the river is enriched with many goodly brookes, which are maintained by an infinit number of small rundles and pleasant springs that disperse themselves for best service, as doe the vaines of a mans body. From the South there fals into this river, First the pleasant river of Apamatuck: next more to the East are the two rivers of Quiyoughcohanocke.[2] A little farther is a Bay wherein falleth 3 or 4 prettie brookes and creekes that halfe intrench the Inhabitants of Warraskoyac;

[1] A sacre, more often saker, was a small piece of artillery.

[2] Upper and Lower Chippokes Creeks in Prince George and Surry counties.

then the river of Nandsamund, and lastly the brooke of Chisapeack.[1] From the North side is the river of Chickahamania, the backe river[2] of James Towne; another by the Cedar Isle where we lived 10 weekes upon oisters, then a convenient harbour for fisher boats or smal boats at Kecoughtan, that so conveniently turneth it selfe into Bayes and Creeks that make that place very pleasant to inhabit, their corne-fields being girded therein in a manner as Peninsulaes. The most of these rivers are inhabited by severall nations, or rather families, of the name of the rivers. They have also in every of those places some Governour, as their king, which they call Werowances. In a Peninsula on the North side of this river are the English planted in a place by them called James Towne, in honour of the Kings most excellent Majestie: upon which side are also many places under the Werowances.

The first and next the rivers mouth, are the Kecoughtans, who besides their women and children, have not past 20. fighting men. The Paspaheghes, on whose land is seated the English Colony, some 40. miles from the Bay, have not passed 40. The river called Chickahamania neere 200. The Weanocks 100. The Arrowhatocks 30. The place called Powhatan, some 40. On the South side this river, the Appamatucks have 60 fighting men. The Quiyougcohanocks, 25. The Warraskoyacks 40. The Nandsamunds 200. The Chesapeacks are able to make 100. Of this last place the Bay beareth the name. In all these places is a severall commander, which they call Werowance, except the Chickhamanians, who are governed by the Priestes and their Assistants of their Elders called Caw-cawwassoughes.[3] In somer no place affordeth more plentie of Sturgeon, nor in winter more abundance of

[1] Elizabeth River, on which Norfolk and Portsmouth are now situated.

[2] Powhatan Creek came out of the woods at the head of Jamestown Peninsula, where, hindered from entering the main river by the neck of land connecting the peninsula with the mainland, it made a detour on the north of the island till it flowed into the river at the east end. That part of the creek bounding the island was called the "Back River."

[3] *Kakärusu,* "he speaks repeatedly." The white men often transmuted the word into *cockarouse.*

fowle, especially in the time of frost. There was once taken 52 Sturgeons at a draught, at another draught 68. From the later end of May till the end of June are taken few, but yong Sturgeons of 2 foot or a yard long. From thence till the midst of September, them of 2 or three yards long and fewe others. And in 4 or 5 houres with one nette were ordinarily taken 7 or 8: often more, seldome lesse. In the small rivers all the yeare there is good plentie of small fish, so that with hookes those that would take paines had sufficient.

Fourteene miles Northward from the river Powhatan, is the river Pamaunke, which is navigable 60 or 70 myles, but with Catches and small Barkes 30 or 40 myles farther. At the ordinary flowing of the salt water, it divideth it selfe into two gallant branches.[1] On the South side inhabit the people of Youghtanund, who have about 60 men for warres. On the North branch Mattapament, who have 30 men. Where this river is divided, the Country is called Pamaunke, and nourisheth neere 300 able men. About 25 miles [2] lower on the North side of this river is Werawocomoco, where their great King inhabited when Captain Smith was delivered him prisoner; yet there are not past 40 able men. But now he hath abandoned that, and liveth at Orapakes [3] by Youghtanund in the wildernesse. 10 or 12 myles lower, on the South side of this river is Chiskiack, which hath some 40 or 50 men. These, as also Apamatuck, Irrohatock, and Powhatan, are their great kings chiefe alliance and inhabitance. The rest (as they report) his Conquests.

Before we come to the third river that falleth from the mountaines, there is another river (some 30 myles navigable) that commeth from the Inland: the river is called Payankatanke, the Inhabitants are about some 40 serviceable men.

[1] Youghtamund (now called Pamunkey) and Mattapanient (Mattapony).

[2] This is a mistake. Werowocomoco was about fourteen miles from West Point. In the *True Relation*, Smith represents the distance from the parting of the river at West Point as twenty miles.

[3] Orapakes is believed to have been situated in White Oak Swamp. The word was a combination of *oro*, "solitary," and *paks* (*peaks*), "a little water place."

The third navigable river is called Toppahanock.[1] (This is navigable some 130 myles.) At the top of it inhabit the people called Mannahoackes amongst the mountaines, but they are above the place we describe.

Upon this river on the North side are seated a people called Cuttatawomen, with 30 fighting men. Higher on the river are the Moraughtacunds, with 80 able men. Beyond them Toppahanock with 100 men. Far above is another Cuttatawomen with 20 men. On the South, far within the river is Nautaughtacund having 150 men. This river also, as the two former, is replenished with fish and foule.

The fourth river is called Patawomeke and is 6 or 7 miles in breadth. It is navigable 140 miles, and fed as the rest with many sweet rivers and springs, which fall from the bordering hils. These hils many of them are planted, and yeelde no lesse plenty and variety of fruit then the river exceedeth with abundance of fish. This river is inhabited on both sides. First on the South side at the very entrance is Wighcocomoco and hath some 130 men: beyond them Sekacawone[2] with 30. The Onawmanient with 100. Then Patawomeke with 160 able men. Here doth the river divide it selfe into 3 or 4 convenient rivers; The greatest of the least is called Quiyough[3] [and] treadeth[4] north west, but the river it selfe turneth North east and is stil a navigable streame. On the westerne side of this bought is Tauxenent with 40 men. On the north of this river is Secowocomoco with 40 men. Some what further Potapaco with 20. In the East part of the bought of the river is Pamacacack with 60 men. After, Moyowances with 100. And lastly, Nacotchtanke with 80 able men. The river 10 miles above this place maketh his passage downe a low pleasant vally

[1] Rappahannock.

[2] Otherwise Chicacoan. A river in Northumberland County is still known as Coan.

[3] Quia or Aquia Creek. As the charter for Maryland, in 1632, declared that the southern boundary of Maryland should begin at the westernmost fountain of the Potomac River, Lord Baltimore first claimed this creek as his southern boundary, believing it to go farther westward, — a claim which, if acquiesced in, would have much curtailed the limits of Maryland.

[4] Trendeth.

overshaddowed in manie places with high rocky mountaines; from whence distill innumerable sweet and pleasant springs.

The fifth river is called Pawtuxunt, and is of a lesse proportion then the rest; but the channell is 16 or 18 fadome deepe in some places. Here are infinit skuls of divers kinds of fish more than elsewhere. Upon this river dwell the people called Acquintanacksuak, Pawtuxunt and Mattapanient. 200 men was the greatest strength that could bee there perceived. But they inhabit togither, and not so dispersed as the rest. These of al other were found the most civill to give intertainement.

Thirty leagues Northward is a river not inhabited, yet navigable; for the red earth or clay resembling bole Armoniack, the English called it Bolus.[1] At the end of the Bay where it is 6 or 7 miles in breadth, there fall into it 4 small rivers, 3 of them issuing from diverse bogges invironed with high mountaines.[2] There is one that commeth du north, 3 or 4. daies journy from the head of the Bay, and fals from rocks and mountaines. Upon this river inhabit a people called Sasquesahanock. They are seated 2 daies higher then was passage for the discoverers Barge, which was hardly 2 toons, and had in it but 12 men to perform this discovery, wherein they lay above the space of 12 weekes upon those great waters in those unknowne Countries, having nothing but a little meale or oatmeale and water to feed them; and scarse halfe sufficient of that for halfe that time, but that by the Savages and by the plentie of fish they found in all places, they made themselves provision as opportunitie served; yet had they not a marriner or any that had skill to trim their sayles, use their oares, or any businesse belonging to the Barge, but 2 or 3. The rest being Gentlemen or as ignorant in such toyle and labour: yet necessitie in a short time, by their Captaines diligence and example, taught them to become so perfect, that what they did by such small meanes, I leave to the censure of the Reader to judge by this discourse and the annexed Map. But to proceed, 60 of those Sasquesahanocks came to the discoverers with skins, Bowes, Arrowes,

[1] Now Gunpowder River.

[2] Hills, rather.

Targets, Beads, Swords, and Tobacco pipes for presents. Such great and well proportioned men, are seldome seene, for they seemed like Giants to the English, yea and to the neighbours: yet seemed of an honest and simple disposition, with much adoe restrained from adoring the discoverers as Gods. Those are the most strange people of all those Countries, both in language and attire; for their language it may well beseeme their proportions, sounding from them, as it were a great voice in a vault, or cave, as an Eccho. Their attire is the skinnes of Beares and Woolves, some have Cassacks made of Beares heades and skinnes that a mans necke goes through the skinnes neck, and the eares of the beare fastned to his shoulders behind, the nose and teeth hanging downe his breast, and at the end of the nose hung a Beares Pawe: the halfe sleeves comming to the elbowes were the neckes of Beares and the armes through the mouth, with pawes hanging at their noses. One had the head of a Woolfe hanging in a chaine for a Jewell; his Tobacco pipe 3 quarters of a yard long, prettily carved with a Bird, a Beare, a Deare, or some such devise at the great end, sufficient to beat out the braines of a man: with bowes, and arrowes, and clubs, sutable to their greatnesse and conditions. These are scarse knowne to Powhatan. They can make neere 600 able and mighty men, and are pallisadoed in their Townes to defend them from the Massawomekes [1] their mortall enimies. 5 of their chiefe Werowances came aboard the discoverers, and crossed the Bay in their Barge. The picture of the greatest of them is signified in the Mappe. The calfe of whose leg was 3 quarters of a yard about: and all the rest of his limbes so answerable to that proportion, that he seemed the goodliest man that ever we beheld. His haire, the one side was long, the other shore close with a ridge over his crown like a cocks combe. His arrowes were five quarters [2] long, headed with flints or splinters of stones, in forme like a heart, an inch broad, and an inch and a halfe or more long. These hee wore in a woolves skinne at his backe for his quiver,

[1] The Five Nations.

[2] After "quarters" supply "of a yard."

his bow in the one hand and his clubbe in the other, as is described.

On the East side the Bay is the river of Tockwhogh,[1] and upon it a people that can make 100 men, seated some 7 miles within the river: where they have a Fort very wel pallisadoed and mantelled with the barke of trees. Next to them is Ozinies with 60 men. More to the South of that East side of the Bay, the river of Rapahanock; neere unto which is the river of Kuskarawaock, upon which is seated a people with 200 men. After that is the river of Tants Wighcocomoco, and on it a people with 100 men. The people of those rivers are of little stature, of another language from the rest, and very rude. But they on the river of Acohanock with 40 men, and they of Accomack 80 men, doth equalize any of the Territories of Powhatan and speake his language; who over all those doth rule as king.

Southward they went to some parts of Chawonock and the Mangoags, to search [2] them there left by Sir Walter Raleigh; for those parts to the Towne of Chisapeack, hath formerly been discovered by Mr Heriots and Sir Raph Layne.

Amongst those people are thus many severall nations of sundry languages, that environ Powhatans Territories. The Chawonokes, the Mangoags, the Monacans, the Mannahokes, the Masawomekes, the Powhatans, the Sasquesahanocks, the Atquanachukes, the Tockwoghes, and the Kuscarawaokes. Al those not any one understandeth another but by Interpreters. Their severall habitations are more plainly described by this annexed Mappe, which will present to the eie, the way of the mountaines and current of the rivers, with their severall turnings, bays, shoules, Isles, Inlets, and creekes, the breadth of the waters, the distances of places and such like. In which Mappe observe this, that as far as you see the little Crosses on rivers, mountaines, or other places, have beene discovered; the rest was had by information of the Savages, and are set downe according to their instructions.

[1] The village marked the extreme northern extension of Powhatan's power.

[2] "Search for."

### *Of such things which are naturall in Virginia and how they use them.*

Virginia doth afford many excellent vegitables and living Creatures, yet grasse there is little or none but what groweth in lowe Marishes: for all the Countrey is overgrowne with trees, whose droppings continually turneth their grasse to weedes, by reason of the rancknesse of the ground; which would soone be amended by good husbandry. The wood that is most common is Oke and Walnut: many of their Okes are so tall and straight, that they will beare two foote and a halfe square of good timber for 20 yards long. Of this wood there is 2 or 3 severall kinds. The Acornes of one kind, whose barke is more white then the other, is somewhat sweetish; which being boyled halfe a day in severall waters, at last afford a sweete oyle, which they keep in goards to annoint their heads and joints. The fruit they eate, made in bread or otherwise. There is also some Elme, some black walnut tree, and some Ash: of Ash and Elme they make sope Ashes. If the trees be very great, the ashes will be good, and melt to hard lumps: but if they be small, it will be but powder, and not so good as the other. Of walnuts there is 2 or 3 kindes: there is a kinde of wood we called Cypres, because both the wood, the fruit, and leafe did most resemble it; and of those trees there are some neere 3 fadome about at the root, very straight, and 50, 60, or 80 foot without a braunch. By the dwelling of the Savages are some great Mulbery trees; and in some parts of the Countrey, they are found growing naturally in prettie groves. There was an assay made to make silke, and surely the wormes prospered excellent well, till the master workeman fell sicke: during which time, they were eaten with rats.

In some parts, were found some Chesnuts whose wild fruit equalize the best in France, Spaine, Germany, or Italy, to their tasts that had tasted them all. Plumbs there are of 3 sorts. The red and white are like our hedge plumbs:

but the other, which they call *Putchamins*,[1] grow as high as a Palmeta. The fruit is like a medler; it is first greene, then yellow, and red when it is ripe: if it be not ripe it will drawe a mans mouth awrie with much torment; but when it is ripe, it is as delicious as an Apricock.

They have Cherries, and those are much like a Damsen; but for their tastes and colour, we called them Cherries. We see some few Crabs, but very small and bitter. Of vines, great abundance in many parts, that climbe the toppes of the highest trees in some places, but these beare but fewe grapes. But by the rivers and Savage habitations where they are not overshadowed from the sunne, they are covered with fruit, though never pruined nor manured. Of those hedge grapes, wee made neere 20 gallons of wine, which was neare as good as your French Brittish wine, but certainely they would prove good were they well manured. There is another sort of grape neere as great as a Cherry, this they call *Messaminnes;* they bee fatte, and the juyce thicke: neither doth the tast so well please when they are made in wine. They have a small fruit growing on little trees, husked like a Chesnut, but the fruit most like a very small acorne. This they call *Chechinquamins*,[2] which they esteeme a great daintie. They have a berry much like our gooseberry, in greatnesse, colour, and tast; those they call *Rawcomenes*, and doe eat them raw or boyled. Of these naturall fruits they live a great part of the yeare, which they use in this manner. The walnuts, Chesnuts, Acornes, and *Chechinquamens* are dryed to keepe. When they need them, they breake them betweene two stones, yet some part of the walnut shels will cleave to the fruit. Then doe they dry them againe upon a mat over a hurdle. After, they put it into a morter of wood, and beat it very small: that done, they mix it with water, that the shels may sinke to the bottome. This water will be coloured as milke; which they cal *Pawcohiscora*, and keepe it for their use. The fruit like medlers, they call *Putchamins*, they cast uppon hurdles on a mat, and

[1] Persimmons.

[2] Chinquapins.

preserve them as Pruines. Of their Chesnuts and *Chechinquamens* boyled 4 houres, they make both broath and bread for their chiefe men, or at their greatest feasts. Besides those fruit trees, there is a white populer, and another tree like unto it, that yeeldeth a very cleere and an odoriferous Gumme like Turpentine, which some called Balsom. There are also Cedars and Saxafras trees. They also yeeld gummes in a small proportion of themselves. Wee tryed conclusions to extract it out of the wood, but nature afforded more then our arts.

In the watry valleyes groweth a berry, which they call *Ocoughtanamnis*, very much like unto Capers. These they dry in sommer. When they will eat them, they boile them neare halfe a day; for otherwise they differ not much from poyson. *Mattoume* groweth as our bents do in meddows. The seede is not much unlike to rie, though much smaller. This they use for a dainty bread buttered with deare suet.

During Somer there are either strawberries which ripen in April; or mulberries which ripen in May and June, Raspises, hurtes, or a fruit that the Inhabitants call *Maracocks*, which is a pleasant wholsome fruit much like a lemond. Many hearbes in the spring time there are commonly dispersed throughout the woods, good for brothes and sallets, as Violets, Purslin, Sorrell, &c. Besides many we used whose names we know not.

The chiefe roote they have for foode is called *Tockawhoughe*.[1] It groweth like a flagge in low muddy freshes. In one day a Savage will gather sufficient for a weeke. These rootes are much of the greatnes and taste of Potatoes. They use to cover a great many of them with oke leaves and ferne, and then cover all with earth in the manner of a colepit; over it, on each side, they continue a great fire 24 houres before they dare eat it. Raw it is no better then poison, and being roasted, except it be tender and the heat abated, or sliced and dried in the sun, mixed with sorrell and meale or such like, it will prickle and

[1] Tuckahoe. This name was also given to a kind of fungus found at the roots of certain trees.

torment the throat extreamely, and yet in sommer they use this ordinarily for bread.

They have an other roote which they call *wighsacan:* as thother feedeth the body, so this cureth their hurts and diseases. It is a small root which they bruise and apply to the wound. *Pocones* is a small roote that groweth in the mountaines, which being dryed and beate in powder turneth red: and this they use for swellings, aches, annointing their joints, painting their heads and garments. They account it very pretious and of much worth. *Musquaspenne* [1] is a roote of the bignesse of a finger, and as red as bloud. In drying, it will wither almost to nothing. This they use to paint their Mattes, Targets, and such like.

There is also Pellitory of Spaine, Sasafrage,[2] and divers other simples, which the Apothecaries gathered, and commended to be good and medicinable.

In the low Marshes, growe plots of Onyons containing an acre of ground or more in many places; but they are small, not past the bignesse of the Toppe of ones Thumbe.

Of beastes the chief are Deare, nothing differing from ours. In the deserts towards the heads of the rivers, ther are many, but amongst the rivers few. There is a beast they call *Arough-cun,*[3] much like a badger, but useth to live on trees as Squirrels doe. Their Squirrels some are neare as greate as our smallest sort of wilde rabbits; some blackish or blacke and white, but the most are gray.

A small beast they have, they call *Assapanick,* but we call them flying squirrels, because spreading their legs, and so stretching the largenesse of their skins that they have bin seene to fly 30 or 40 yards. An *Opassom* hath an head like a Swine, and a taile like a Rat, and is of the bignes of a Cat. Under her belly shee hath a bagge, wherein shee lodgeth, carrieth, and sucketh her young. *Mussascus* [4] is a beast of the forme and nature of our water Rats, but many of them smell exceeding strongly of muske. Their Hares no bigger then our Conies, and few of them to be found.

[1] Bloodroot. [2] Sassafras. [3] Raccoon. [4] Muskrat.

Their Beares are very little in comparison of those of Muscovia and Tartaria. The Beaver is as bigge as an ordinary water dogge, but his legges exceeding short. His fore feete like a dogs, his hinder feet like a Swans. His taile somewhat like the forme of a Racket bare without haire; which to eate, the Savages esteeme a great delicate. They have many Otters, which, as the Beavers, they take with snares, and esteeme the skinnes great ornaments; and of all those beasts they use to feede, when they catch them.

There is also a beast they call *Vetchunquoyes* in the forme of a wilde Cat. Their Foxes are like our silver haired Conies, of a small proportion, and not smelling like those in England. Their Dogges of that country are like their Wolves, and cannot barke but howle; and their wolves not much bigger then our English Foxes. Martins, Powlecats, weessels and Minkes we know they have, because we have seen many of their skinnes, though very seldome any of them alive. But one thing is strange, that we could never perceive their vermine destroy our hennes, egges, nor chickens, nor do any hurt: nor their flyes nor serpents anie waie pernitious; where [1] in the South parts of America, they are alwaies dangerous and often deadly.

Of birds, the Eagle is the greatest devourer. Hawkes there be of diverse sorts as our Falconers called them, Sparowhawkes, Lanarets, Goshawkes, Falcons and Osperayes; but they all pray most upon fish. Pattridges there are little bigger then our Quailes, wilde Turkies are as bigge as our tame. There are woosels or blackbirds with red shoulders, thrushes, and diverse sorts of small birds, some red, some blew, scarce so bigge as a wrenne, but few in Sommer. In winter there are great plenty of Swans, Craynes gray and white with blacke wings, Herons, Geese, Brants, Ducke, Wigeon, Dotterell, Oxeies, Parrats, and Pigeons. Of all those sorts great abundance, and some other strange kinds, to us unknowne by name. But in sommer not any, or a very few to be seene.

[1] Whereas.

Of fish we were best acquainted with Sturgeon, Grampus, Porpus, Seales, Stingraies whose tailes are very dangerous, Brettes, mullets, white Salmonds, Trowts, Soles, Plaice, Herrings, Conyfish, Rockfish, Eeles, Lampreyes, Catfish, Shades, Pearch of 3 sorts, Crabs, Shrimps, Crevises, Oysters, Cocles, and Muscles. But the most strange fish is a smal one so like the picture of S. George his Dragon, as possible can be, except his legs and wings: and the Todefish which will swell till it be like to brust, when it commeth into the aire.

Concerning the entrailes of the earth little can be saide for certainty. There wanted good Refiners: for these that tooke upon them to have skill this way, tooke up the washings from the mounetaines and some moskered shining stones and spangles which the waters brought down; flattering themselves in their own vaine conceits to have been supposed that they were not, by the meanes of that ore, if it proved as their arts and judgements expected. Only this is certaine, that many regions lying in the same latitude, afford mines very rich of diverse natures. The crust also of these rockes would easily perswade a man to beleeve there are other mines then yron and steele, if there were but meanes and men of experience that knew the mine from spare.

### *Of their Planted fruits in Virginia and how they use them.*

They divide the yeare into 5. seasons. Their winter some call *Popanow*, the spring *Cattapeuk*, the sommer *Cohattayough*, the earing of their Corne *Nepinough*, the harvest and fall of leafe *Taquitock*. From September untill the midst of November are the chiefe Feasts and sacrifice. Then have they plenty of fruits as well planted as naturall, as corne greene and ripe, fish, fowle, and wild beastes exceeding fat.

The greatest labour they take, is in planting their corne, for the country naturally is overgrowne with wood. To prepare the ground they bruise the barke of the trees neare the roote, then do they scortch the roots with fire that they grow no more. The next yeare with a crooked peece of wood, they beat up the woodes by the rootes; and in that[1] moulds, they plant their corne. Their manner is this. They make a hole in the earth with a sticke, and into it they put 4 graines of wheat and 2 of beanes. These holes they make 4 foote one from another. Their women and children do continually keepe it with weeding, and when it is growne midle high, they hill it about like a hop-yard.

In Aprill they begin to plant, but their chiefe plantation is in May, and so they continue till the midst of June. What they plant in Aprill they reape in August, for May in September, for June in October. Every stalke of their corne commonly beareth two eares, some 3, seldome any 4, many but one, and some none. Every eare ordinarily hath betwixt 200 and 500 graines. The stalke being green hath a sweet juice in it, somewhat like a suger Cane, which is the cause that when they gather their corne greene, they sucke the stalkes: for as wee gather greene pease, so doe they their corne being greene, which excelleth their old. They plant also pease they cal *Assentamens*, which are the same they cal in Italye, *Fagioli*. Their Beanes are the same the Turkes call *Garnanses*, but these they much esteeme for dainties.

Their corne they rost in the eare greene, and bruising it in a morter with a Polt,[2] lappe it in rowles in the leaves of their corne, and so boyle it for a daintie. They also reserve that corne late planted that will not ripe, by roasting it in hot ashes, the heat thereof drying it. In winter they esteeme it being boyled with beans for a rare dish, they call *Pausarowmena*. Their old wheat[3] they first steep a night in hot water, in the morning pounding it in a morter. They use a small basket for their Temmes,[4] then pound againe the great, and so separating by dashing their hand in the basket, receave the flower[5] in a platter made of wood scraped to that forme with burning and shels. Tempering this flower with water, they make it either in cakes, covering them with ashes till they bee baked, and then washing them in faire water, they

[1] Those. [2] Thump [3] Corn. [4] Hulls. [5] The meal.

drie presently with their owne heat: or else boyle them in water eating the broth with the bread which they call *Ponap.*[1] The grouts and peeces of the cornes remaining, by fanning in a Platter or in the wind away the branne, they boile 3 or 4 houres with water; which is an ordinary food they call *Ustatahamen*. But some more thrifty then cleanly, doe burne the core of the eare to powder which they call *Pungnough,* mingling that in their meale; but it never tasted well in bread, nor broth. Their fish and flesh they boyle either very tenderly, or broyle it so long on hurdles over the fire; or else, after the Spanish fashion, putting it on a spit, they turne first the one side, then the other, til it be as drie as their jerkin beefe in the west Indies, that they may keepe it a month or more without putrifying. The broth of fish or flesh they eate as commonly as the meat.

In May also amongst their corne, they plant Pumpeons, and a fruit like unto a muske millen, but lesse and worse; which they call *Macocks*. These increase exceedingly, and ripen in the beginning of July, and continue until September. They plant also *Maracocks* a wild fruit like a lemmon, which also increase infinitely: they begin to ripe in September and continue till the end of October. When all their fruits be gathered, little els they plant, and this is done by their women and children; neither doth this long suffice them: for neere 3 parts of the yeare, they only observe times and seasons, and live of what the Country naturally affordeth from hand to mouth, &c.

*The commodities in Virginia or that may be had by industrie.*

The mildnesse of the aire, the fertilitie of the soile, and the situation of the rivers are so propitious to the nature and use of man as no place is more convenient for pleasure, profit, and mans sustenance. Under that latitude or climat, here will live any beasts, as horses, goats, sheep, asses, hens, &c. as

[1] A misprint or mistake for *ponak,* plural of *pon,* whence our word "pone."

appeared by them that were carried thither. The waters, Isles, and shoales, are full of safe harbours for ships of warre or marchandize, for boats of all sortes, for transportation or fishing, &c. The Bay and rivers have much marchandable fish and places fit for Salt coats, building of ships, making of iron, &c.

Muscovia and Polonia doe yearely receave many thousands, for pitch, tarre, sope ashes, Rosen, Flax, Cordage, Sturgeon, masts, yards, wainscot, Firres, glasse, and such like; also Swethland[1] for iron and copper. France in like manner, for Wine, Canvas, and Salt, Spaine asmuch for Iron, Steele, Figges, Reasons, and Sackes. Italy with Silkes and Velvets, consumes our chiefe commodities. Holand maintaines it selfe by fishing and trading at our owne doores. All these temporize with other for necessities, but all as uncertaine as peace or warres: besides the charge, travell, and danger in transporting them, by seas, lands, stormes, and Pyrats. Then how much hath Virginia the prerogative of all those florishing kingdomes for the benefit of our land, whenas within one hundred miles all those are to bee had, either ready provided by nature, or else to bee prepared, were there but industrious men to labour. Only of Copper wee may doubt is wanting, but there is good probabilitie that both copper and better munerals are there to be had for their labor. Other Countries have it. So then here is a place a nurse for souldiers, a practise for marriners, a trade for marchants, a reward for the good, and that which is most of all, a businesse (most acceptable to God) to bring such poore infidels to the true knowledge of God and his holy Gospell.

## *Of the naturall Inhabitants of Virginia.*

The land is not populous, for the men be fewe; their far greater number is of women and children. Within 60 miles of James Towne there are about some 5000 people, but of able men fit for their warres scarse 1500. To nourish so many

[1] Sweden.

together they have yet no means, because they make so smal a benefit of their land, be it never so fertill. 6 or 700 have beene the most [that] hath beene seene together, when they gathered themselves to have surprised Captaine Smyth at Pamaunke, having but 15 to withstand the worst of their furie. As small as the proportion of ground that hath yet beene discovered, is in comparison of that yet unknowne. The people differ very much in stature, especially in language, as before is expressed. Some being very great as the Sesquesahamocks, others very little as the Wighcocomocoes: but generally tall and straight, of a comely proportion, and of a colour browne, when they are of any age, but they are borne white. Their haire is generally black; but few have any beards. The men weare halfe their heads shaven, the other halfe long. For Barbers they use their women, who with 2 shels will grate away the haire, of any fashion they please. The women are cut in many fashions agreeable to their yeares, but ever some part remaineth long. They are very strong, of an able body and full of agilitie, able to endure to lie in the woods under a tree by the fire, in the worst of winter, or in the weedes and grasse, in Ambuscado in the Sommer. They are inconstant in everie thing, but what feare constraineth them to keepe. Craftie, timerous, quicke of apprehension and very ingenuous. Some are of disposition fearefull, some bold, most cautelous, all Savage. Generally covetous of copper, beads, and such like trash. They are soone moved to anger, and so malitious, that they seldome forget an injury: they seldome steale one from another, least their conjurors should reveale it, and so they be pursued and punished. That they are thus feared is certaine, but that any can reveale their offences by conjuration I am doubtfull. Their women are carefull not to bee suspected of dishonesty without the leave of their husbands. Each houshold knoweth their owne lands and gardens, and most live of their owne labours. For their apparell, they are some time covered with the skinnes of wilde beasts, which in winter are dressed with the haire, but in sommer without. The better sort use large mantels of deare skins not much differing in fashion from the Irish mantels. Some imbrodered with white beads, some with copper, other painted after their manner. But the common sort have scarce to cover their nakednesse but with grasse, the leaves of trees, or such like. We have seen some use mantels made of Turky feathers, so prettily wrought and woven with threeds that nothing could bee discerned but the feathers, that was exceeding warme and very handsome. But the women are alwaies covered about their midles with a skin and very shamefast to be seene bare. They adorne themselves most with copper beads and paintings. Their women some have their legs, hands, brests and face cunningly imbrodered with diverse workes, as beasts, serpentes, artificially wrought into their flesh with blacke spots. In each eare commonly they have 3 great holes, whereat they hange chaines, bracelets, or copper. Some of their men weare in those holes, a smal greene and yellow coloured snake, neare halfe a yard in length, which crawling and lapping her selfe about his necke often times familiarly would kiss his lips. Others wear a dead Rat tied by the tail. Some on their heads weare the wing of a bird or some large feather, with a Rattell. Those Rattels are somewhat like the chape of a Rapier but lesse, which they take from the taile of a snake. Many have the whole skinne of a hawke or some strange fowle, stuffed with the wings abroad. Others a broad peece of copper, and some the hand of their enemy dryed. Their heads and shoulders are painted red with the roote *Pocone* braied to powder mixed with oyle; this they hold in somer to preserve them from the heate, and in winter from the cold. Many other formes of paintings they use, but he is the most gallant that is the most monstrous to behould.

Their buildings and habitations are for the most part by the rivers or not farre distant from some fresh spring. Their houses are built like our Arbors of small young springs[1] bowed and tyed, and so close covered with mats or the barkes of trees very handsomely, that notwithstanding either winde raine

[1] Sprigs.

or weather, they are as warme as stooves, but very smoaky, yet at the toppe of the house there is a hole made for the smoake to goe into right over the fire.

Against the fire they lie on little hurdles of Reedes covered with a mat, borne from the ground a foote and more by a hurdle of wood. On these round about the house, they lie heads and points one by thother against the fire: some covered with mats, some with skins, and some starke naked lie on the ground, from 6 to 20 in a house. Their houses are in the midst of their fields or gardens; which are smal plots of ground, some 20,[1] some 40, some 100. some 200. some more, some lesse. Some times from 2 to 100 of these houses togither, or but a little separated by groves of trees. Neare their habitations is little small wood, or old trees on the ground, by reason of their burning of them for fire. So that a man may gallop a horse amongst these woods any waie, but where the creekes or Rivers shall hinder.

Men women and children have their severall names according to the severall humor of their Parents. Their women (they say) are easilie delivered of childe, yet doe they love children verie dearly. To make them hardy, in the coldest mornings they wash them in the rivers, and by painting and ointments so tanne their skins, that after year or two, no weather will hurt them.

The men bestowe their times in fishing, hunting, wars, and such manlike exercises, scorning to be seene in any woman like exercise, which is the cause that the women be verie painefull and the men often idle. The women and children do the rest of the worke. They make mats, baskets, pots, morters, pound their corne, make their bread, prepare their victuals, plant their corne, gather their corne, beare al kind of burdens, and such like.

Their fire they kindle presently by chafing a dry pointed sticke in a hole of a little square peece of wood, that firing it selfe, will so fire mosse, leaves, or anie such like drie thing

[1] Twenty acres.

that will quickly burne. In March and Aprill they live much upon their fishing weares, and feed on fish, Turkies and squirrels. In May and June they plant their fieldes, and live most of Acornes, walnuts, and fish. But to mend their diet, some disperse themselves in small companies, and live upon fish, beasts, crabs, oysters, land Torteyses, strawberries, mulberries, and such like. In June, Julie, and August, they feed upon the rootes of *Tocknough*, berries, fish, and greene wheat. It is strange to see how their bodies alter with their diet; even as the deare and wild beastes, they seeme fat and leane, strong and weak. Powhatan their great king and some others that are provident, rost their fish and flesh upon hurdles as before is expressed, and keepe it till scarce times.

For fishing and hunting and warres they use much their bow and arrowes. They bring their bowes to the forme of ours by the scraping of a shell. Their arrowes are made, some of straight young sprigs, which they head with bone some 2 or 3 inches long. These they use to shoot at squirrels on trees. An other sort of arrowes they use, made of reeds. These are peeced with wood, headed with splinters of christall or some sharpe stone, the spurres of a Turkey, or the bill of some bird. For his knife, he hath the splinter of a reed to cut his feathers in forme. With this knife also, he will joint a Deare or any beast, shape his shooes, buskins, mantels, &c. To make the noch of his arrow hee hath the tooth of a Bever set in a sticke, wherewith he grateth it by degrees. His arrow head he quickly maketh with a little bone, which he ever weareth at his bracer, of any splint of a stone, or glasse in the forme of a hart, and these they glew to the end of their arrowes. With the sinewes of Deare, and the tops of Deares hornes boiled to a jelly, they make a glew that will not dissolve in cold water.

For their wars also they use Targets that are round and made of the barkes of trees, and a sworde of wood at their backs, but oftentimes they use for swords the horne of a Deare put through a peece of wood in forme of a Pickaxe. Some, a long stone sharpened at both ends used in the same manner.

This they were wont to use also for hatchets, but now by trucking they have plenty of the same forme, of yron. And those are their chiefe instruments and armes.

Their fishing is much in Boats. These they make of one tree by bowing [1] and scratching away the coles with stone and shels till they have made it in forme of a Trough. Some of them are an elne deepe, and 40 or 50 foot in length, and some will beare 40 men, but the most ordinary are smaller, and will beare 10, 20, or 30. according to their bignes. Insteed of oares, they use paddles and sticks, with which they will row faster then our Barges. Betwixt their hands and thighes, their women use to spin the barks of trees, deare sinews, or a kind of grasse they call *Pemmenaw*; of these they make a thred very even and readily. This thred serveth for many uses, as about their housing, apparell, as also they make nets for fishing, for the quantity as formally braded as ours. They make also with it lines for angles. Their hookes are either a bone grated, as they nock their arrows, in the forme of a crooked pinne or fishhook or of the splinter of a bone tied to the clift of a litle stick, and with the ende of the line, they tie on the bate. They use also long arrowes tyed in a line wherewith they shoote at fish in the rivers. But they of Accawmack use staves like unto Javelins headed with bone. With these they dart fish swimming in the water. They have also many artificiall weares in which they get abundance of fish.

In their hunting and fishing they take extreame paines; yet it being their ordinary exercise from their infancy, they esteeme it a pleasure and are very proud to be expert therein. And by their continuall ranging, and travel, they know all the advantages and places most frequented with Deare, Beasts, Fish, Foule, Rootes, and Berries. At their huntings they leave their habitations, and reduce themselves into companies, as the Tartars doe, and goe to the most desert places with their families, where they spend their time in hunting and fowling up towards the mountaines, by the heads of their rivers, where

[1] Burning.

there is plentie of game. For betwixt the rivers, the grounds are so narrowe, that little commeth there which they devoure not. It is a marvel they can so directly passe these deserts some 3 or 4 daies journey without habitation. Their hunting houses are like unto Arbours covered with mats. These their women beare after them, with Corne, Acornes, Morters, and all bag and baggage they use. When they come to the place of exercise, every man doth his best to shew his dexteritie, for by their excelling in those quallities, they get their wives. Forty yards will they shoot levell, or very neare the mark, and 120 is their best at Random. At their huntings in the deserts they are commonly 2 or 300 together. Having found the Deare, they environ them with many fires, and betwixt the fires they place themselves. And some take their stands in the midst. The Deare being thus feared by the fires and their voices, they chace them so long within that circle, that many times they kill 6, 8, 10, or 15 at a hunting. They use also to drive them into some narrowe point of land, when they find that advantage, and so force them into the river, where with their boats they have Ambuscadoes to kill them. When they have shot a Deare by land, they follow him like blood hounds by the blood and straine, and oftentimes so take them. Hares, Pattridges, Turkies, or Egges, fat or leane, young or old, they devoure all they can catch in their power. In one of these huntings, they found Captaine Smith in the discoverie of the head of the river of Chickahamania, where they slew his men, and tooke him prisoner in a Bogmire; where he saw those exercises, and gathered these observations.

One Savage hunting alone, useth the skinne of a Deare slit on the one side, and so put on his arme, through the neck, so that his hand comes to the head which is stuffed, and the hornes, head, eies, eares, and every part as arteficially counterfeited as they can devise. Thus shrowding his body in the skinne, by stalking he approacheth the Deare, creeping on the ground from one tree to another. If the Deare chance to find fault, or stande at gaze, hee turneth the head with his hand to his best advantage to seeme like a Deare, also gazing and licking himselfe. So watching his best advantage to approach, having shot him, hee chaseth him by his blood and straine till he get him.

When they intend any warres, the Werowances usually have the advice of their Priests and Conjurors, and their Allies and ancient friends, but chiefely the Priestes determine their resolution. Every Werowance, or some lustie fellow, they appoint Captaine over every nation. They seldome make warre for lands or goods, but for women and children, and principally for revenge. They have many enimies, namely all their westernely Countries beyond the mountaines, and the heads of the rivers. Upon the head of the Powhatans are the Monacans, whose chiefe habitation is at Russawmeake, unto whome the Mouhemenchughes, the Massinnacacks, the Monahassanuggs, and other nations, pay tributs. Upon the head of the river of Toppahanock is a people called Mannahoacks. To these are contributers the Tauxsnitanias, the Shackaconias, the Outponcas, the Tegoneaes, the Whonkentyaes, the Stegarakes, the Hassinnungas, and diverse others, all confederats with the Monacans, though many different in language, and be very barbarous, living for most part of wild beasts and fruits. Beyond the mountaines from whence is the head of the river Patawomeke, the Savages report, inhabit their most mortall enimies, the Massawomekes upon a great salt water, which by all likelyhood is either some part of Commada,[1] some great lake, or some inlet of some sea that falleth into the South sea. These Massawomekes are a great nation and very populous. For the heads of all those rivers, especially the Pattawomekes, the Pautuxuntes, the Sasquesahanocks, the Tockwoughes, are continually tormented by them: of whose crueltie, they generally complained, and very importunate they were with Captaine Smith and his company, to free them from these tormentors. To this purpose, they offered food, conduct, assistance, and continuall subjection. To which he concluded to effect. But the counsell then present, emulating

[1] Canada.

his successe, would not thinke it fit to spare him 40 men to be hazarded in those unknowne regions, having passed (as before was spoken of) but with 12, and so was lost that opportunitie. Seaven boats full of these Massawomeks the discoverers encountred at the head of the Bay; whose Targets, Baskets, Swords, Tobaccopipes, Platters, Bowes and Arrowes, and every thing shewed, they much exceeded them of our parts: and their dexteritie in their small boats made of the barkes of trees sowed with barke, and well luted with gumme, argueth that they are seated upon some great water.

Against all these enimies the Powhatans are constrained sometimes to fight. Their chiefe attempts are by Stratagems, trecheries, or surprisals. Yet the Werowances, women and children, they put not to death, but keepe them Captives. They have a method in warre, and for our pleasures, they shewd it us, and it was in this manner performed at Mattapanient.

Having painted and disguised themselves in the fiercest manner they could devise, they divided themselves into two Companies, neare a 100 in a company. The one company called Monacans, the other Powhatans. Either army had their Captaine. These as enimies tooke their stands a musket shot one from another; ranked themselves 15 abreast, and each ranke from another 4 or 5 yards, not in fyle, but in the opening betwixt their fyles, so as the Reare could shoot as conveniently as the Front. Having thus pitched the fields; from either part went a Messenger with these conditions, that whosoever were vanquished, such as escape, upon their submission in 2 daies after, should live, but their wives and children should be prize for the Conquerers. The messengers were no sooner returned, but they approached in their orders. On each flanke a Sarjeant, and in the Reare an office for leuitenant, all duly keeping their orders, yet leaping and singing after their accustomed tune, which they use only in warres. Upon the first flight of arrowes, they gave such horrible shouts and screeches, as though so many infernall helhounds could not have made them more terrible. When they had spent their arrowes, they joined together prettily, charging and retiring, every ranke seconding other. As they got advantage, they catched their enimies by the haire of the head, and downe he came that was taken. His enimie with his wooden sword seemed to beat out his braines, and still they crept to the Reare, to maintaine the skirmish. The Monacans decreasing, the Powhatans charged them in the forme of a halfe moone: they unwilling to be inclosed, fled all in a troope to their Ambuscadoes, on whome they led them very cunningly. The Monacans disperse themselves among the fresh men, whereupon the Powhatans retired with al speed to their seconds; which the Monacans seeing, took that advantage to retire againe to their owne battell, and so each returned to their owne quarter. All their actions, voices and gestures, both in charging and retiring, were so strained to the hight of their quallitie and nature, that the strangenes thereof made it seem very delightfull.

For their musicke they use a thicke cane, on which they pipe as on a Recorder.[1] For their warres, they have a great deepe platter of wood. They cover the mouth thereof with a skin, at each corner they tie a walnut, which meeting on the backside neere the bottome, with a small rope they twitch them togither till it be so tought and stiffe, that they may beat upon it as upon a drumme. But their chiefe instruments are Rattels made of small gourds or Pumpion shels. Of these they have Base, Tenor, Counter-tenor, Meane and Trible.[2] These mingled with their voices sometimes 20 or 30 togither, make such a terrible noise as would rather affright then delight any man. If any great commander arrive at the habitation of a Werowance, they spread a mat as the Turkes do a carpet, for him to sit upon. Upon an other right opposite they sit themselves. Then doe all with a tunable voice of showting bid him welcome. After this, doe 2. or more of their chiefest men make an oration, testifying their love. Which they do with such vehemency and so great passions, that they sweate till they drop, and are so out of breath they can scarce speake.

[1] A musical pipe. [2] Bass, tenor, high tenor, alto, and soprano.

So that a man would take them to be exceeding angry or starke mad. Such victuall as they have, they spend freely, and at night where his lodging is appointed, they set a woman fresh painted red with *Pocones* and oile, to be his bedfellow.

Their manner of trading is for copper, beades, and such like; for which they give such commodities as they have, as skins, fowle, fish, flesh, and their country corne. But their victuall is their chiefest riches.

Every spring they make themselves sicke with drinking the juice of a root they call *wighsacan*, and water, whereof they powre so great a quantity, that it purgeth them in a very violent maner; so that in 3 or 4 daies after, they scarce recover their former health. Sometimes they are troubled with dropsies, swellings, aches, and such like diseases; for cure wherof they build a stove in the form of a dovehouse with mats, so close that a fewe coales therein covered with a pot, will make the pacient sweate extreamely. For swellings also they use smal peeces of touchwood, in the forme of cloves, which pricking on the griefe, they burne close to the flesh, and from thence draw the corruption with their mouth. With this root *wighsacan* they ordinarily heal greene wounds: but to scarrifie a swelling or make incision, their best instruments are some splinted stone. Old ulcers or putrified hurtes are seldome seene cured amongst them. They have many professed Phisitions, who with their charmes and Rattels, with an infernall rowt of words and actions, will seeme to sucke their inwarde griefe from their navels or their grieved places; but of our Chirurgians they were so conceipted, that they beleeved any Plaister would heale any hurt.

### *Of their Religion.*

There is yet in Virginia no place discovered to bee so Savage in which the Savages have not a religion, Deare, and Bow and Arrowes. All thinges that were able to do them hurt beyond their prevention, they adore with their kinde of divine worship; as the fire, water, lightning, thunder, our ordinance, peeces, horses, &c. But their chiefe God they worship is the Divell. Him they call *Oke* and serve him more of feare than love. They say they have conference with him, and fashion themselves as neare to his shape as they can imagine. In their temples, they have his image evill favouredly carved, and then painted and adorned with chaines, copper, and beades, and covered with a skin, in such manner as the deformity may well suit with such a God. By him is commonly the sepulcher of their kings. Their bodies are first bowelled, then dryed upon hurdles till they bee verie dry, and so about the most of their jointes and necke they hang bracelets or chaines of copper, pearle, and such like, as they use to weare: their inwards they stuffe with copper beads and cover with a skin, hatchets, and such trash. Then lappe they them very carefully in white skins, and so rowle them in mats for their winding sheetes. And in the Tombe, which is an arch made of mats, they lay them orderly. What remaineth of this kinde of wealth their kings have, they set at their feet in baskets. These Temples and bodies are kept by their Priests.

For their ordinary burials, they digge a deep hole in the earth with sharpe stakes, and the corp[s]es being lapped in skins and mats with their jewels, they lay them upon sticks in the ground, and so cover them with earth. The buriall ended, the women being painted all their faces with black cole and oile, doe sit 24 howers in the houses mourning and lamenting by turnes, with such yelling and howling as may expresse their great passions.

In every Territory of a werowance is a Temple and a Priest 2 or 3 or more. Their principall Temple or place of superstition is at Uttamussack at Pamaunke, neare unto which is a house Temple or place of Powhatans.

Upon the top of certaine redde sandy hils in the woods, there are 3 great houses filled with images of their kings and Divels and Tombes of their Predecessors. Those houses are neare 60[1] foot in length, built arbor wise, after their building.

[1] In the *True Relation* Smith represents these houses as about 100 feet long.

This place they count so holy as that [none] but the Priestes and kings dare come into them: nor the Savages dare not go up the river in boats by it, but that they solemnly cast some peece of copper, white beads, or Pocones, into the river, for feare their *Oke* should be offended and revenged of them.

In this place commonly is resident 7 Priests. The chiefe differed from the rest in his ornaments: but inferior Priests could hardly be knowne from the common people, but that they had not so many holes in their eares to hang their jewels at. The ornaments of the chiefe Priest was certain attires for his head made thus. They tooke a dosen or 16 or more snake skins, and stuffed them with mosse; and of weesels and other vermine skins, a good many. All these they tie by their tailes, so as all their tailes meete in the toppe of their head, like a great Tassell. Round about this Tassell is as it were a crown of feathers; the skins hang round about his head necke and shoulders, and in a manner cover his face. The faces of all their Priests are painted as ugly as they can devise. In their hands, they had every one his Rattell, some base, some smaller.[1] Their devotion was most in songs which the chiefe Priest beginneth and the rest followed him: sometimes he maketh invocations with broken sentences, by starts and strange passions, and at every pause, the rest give a short groane.

It could not bee perceived that they keepe any day as more holy then other: but only in some great distresse, of want, feare of enimies, times of triumph and gathering togither their fruits, the whole country of men women and children come togither to solemnities. The manner of their devotion is sometimes to make a great fire in the house or fields, and all to sing and dance about it, with rattles and shouts togither, 4 or 5 houres. Sometimes they set a man in the midst, and about him they dance and sing, he all the while clapping his hands as if he would keepe time. And after their songs and dauncings ended, they goe to their Feasts.

[1] Lighter in sound.

They have also divers conjurations. One they made when Captaine Smith was their prisoner (as they reported) to know if any more of his countrymen would arive there, and what he there intended. The manner of it was thus. First they made a faire fire in a house. About this fire set 7 Priests setting him by them, and about the fire, they made a circle of meale. That done, the chiefe Priest attired as is expressed, began to shake his rattle, and the rest followed him in his song. At the end of the song, he laid downe 5 or 3 graines of wheat, and so continued counting his songs by the graines, till 3 times they incirculed the fire. Then they divide the graines by certaine numbers with little stickes, laying downe at the ende of every song a little sticke. In this manner, they sat 8, 10, or 12 houres without cease, with such strange stretching of their armes, and violent passions and gestures as might well seeme strange to him they so conjured, who but every houre expected his end. Not any meat they did eat till, late in the evening, they had finished this worke: and then they feasted him and themselves with much mirth. But 3 or 4 daies they continued this ceremony.

They have also certaine Altar stones they call *Pawcorances*: but these stand from their Temples, some by their houses, other in the woodes and wildernesses. Upon these, they offer blood, deare suet, and Tobacco. These they doe when they returne from the warres, from hunting, and upon many other occasions. They have also another superstition that they use in stormes, when the waters are rough in the rivers and sea coasts. Their Conjurers runne to the water sides, or passing in their boats, after many hellish outcries and invocations, they cast Tobacco, Copper, *Pocones*, and such trash into the water, to pacifie that God whome they thinke to be very angry in those stormes. Before their dinners and suppers, the better sort will take the first bit, and cast it in the fire, which is all the grace they are known to use.

In some part of the Country, they have yearely a sacrifice of children. Such a one was at Quiyoughcohanock, some 10 miles from James Towne, and thus performed. Fifteene of the properest young boyes, betweene 10 and 15 yeares of age, they painted white. Having brought them forth, the people spent the forenoone in dancing and singing about them with rattles. In the afternoone, they put those children to the roote of a tree. By them, all the men stood in a guard, every one having a Bastinado in his hand, made of reeds bound together. This [1] made a lane betweene them all along, through which there were appointed 5 young men to fetch these children. So every one of the five went through the guard, to fetch a child, each after other by turnes: the guard fearelessly beating them with their Bastinadoes, and they patiently enduring and receaving all, defending the children with their naked bodies from the unmercifull blowes they pay them soundly, though the children escape. All this while, the women weepe and crie out very passionately, providing mats, skinnes, mosse, and drie wood, as things fitting their childrens funerals. After the children were thus passed the guard, the guard tore down the tree, branches and boughs, with such violence, that they rent the body, and made wreathes for their heads, or bedecked their haire with the leaves. What else was done with the children was not seene; but they were all cast on a heape in a valley, as dead: where they made a great feast for al the company. The Werowance being demanded the meaning of this sacrifice, answered that the children were not al dead, but that the *Oke* or Divell did sucke the blood from their left breast,[2] who chanced to be his by lot, till they were dead. But the rest were kept in the wildernesse by the yong men till nine moneths were expired, during which time they must not converse with any: and of these, were made their Priests and Conjurers. This sacrifice they held to bee so necessarie, that if they should omit it, their *Oke* or Divel and all their other *Quiyoughcosughes* (which are their other Gods) would let them have no Deare, Turkies, Corne nor fish: and yet besides, hee would make great slaughter amongst them.

They thinke that their Werowances and Priestes, which they also esteeme *Quiyoughcosughes*, when they are dead,

[1] These.

[2] *I.e.*, from the left breast of those.

doe goe beyound the mountaines towardes the setting of the sun, and ever remaine there in forme of their Oke, with their heads painted with oile and *Pocones*, finely trimmed with feathers, and shal have beades, hatchets, copper, and tobacco, doing nothing but dance and sing with all their Predecessors. But the common people, they suppose shall not live after death.

To divert them from this blind idolatrie, many used their best indeavours, chiefly with the Werowances of Quiyoughcohanock, whose devotion, apprehension, and good disposition much exceeded any in those Countries: who though we could not as yet prevaile withall to forsake his false Gods, yet this he did beleeve, that our God as much exceeded theirs, as our Gunnes did their Bowes and Arrows, and many times did send to the President, at James towne, men with presents, intreating them to pray to his God for raine, for his Gods would not send him any. And in this lamentable ignorance doe these poore soules sacrifice themselves to the Divell, not knowing their Creator.

*Of the manner of the Virginians governement.*[1]

Although the countrie people be very barbarous; yet have they amongst them such governement, as that their Magistrats for good commanding, and their people for du subjection and obeying, excell many places that would be counted very civill.

The forme of their Common wealth is a monarchicall governement. One as Emperour ruleth over many kings or governours. Their chiefe ruler is called Powhatan, and taketh his name of the principall place of dwelling called Powhatan. But his proper name is Wahunsonacock. Some countries he hath, which have been his ancestors, and came unto him by inheritance, as the countrie called Powhatan, Arrohateck, Appamatuke, Pamaunke, Youghtanud, and Mattapanient. All the rest of his Territories expressed in the Map, they report

[1] See James Mooney, "The Powhatan Confederacy, Past and Present," in the *American Anthropologist*, n. s., IX. 129–152.

have beene his severall conquests. In all his ancient inheritances, hee hath houses built after their manner like arbours, some 30, some 40 yardes long, and at every house, provision for his entertainement, according to the time. At Werowcomoco, he was seated upon the North side of the river Pamaunke, some 14 miles from James Towne, where for the most part, hee was resident, but he tooke so little pleasure in our neare neighbourhood, that were able to visit him against his will in 6 or 7 houres, that he retired himself [1] to a place in the deserts at the top of the river Chickahamania betweene Youghtanund and Powhatan. His habitation there is called Orapacks, where he ordinarily now resideth. He is of parsonage a tall well proportioned man, with a sower looke, his head somwhat gray, his beard so thinne that it seemeth none at al. His age neare 60; of a very able and hardybody to endure any labour. About his person ordinarily attendeth a guard of 40 or 50 of the tallest men his Country doth afford. Every night upon the 4 quarters of his house are 4 Sentinels, each standing from other a flight shoot: and at every halfe houre, one from the Corps du guard doth hollowe, unto whom every Sentinell doth answer round from his stand. If any faile, they presently send forth an officer that beateth him extreamely.

A mile from Orapakes in a thicket of wood, hee hath a house, in which he keepeth his kind of Treasure, as skinnes, copper, pearle, and beades, which he storeth up against the time of his death and buriall. Here also is his store of red paint for ointment, and bowes and arrowes. This house is 50 or 60 yards in length, frequented only by Priestes. At the 4 corners of this house stand 4 Images as Sentinels, one of a Dragon, another a Beare, the 3 like a Leopard, and the fourth like a giantlike man: all made evill favordly, according to their best workmanship.

He hath as many women as he will: whereof when hee lieth on his bed, one sitteth at his head, and another at his feet, but when he sitteth, one sitteth on his right hand, and

[1] In January, 1609.

another on his left. As he is wearie of his women, hee bestoweth them on those that best deserve them at his hands. When he dineth or suppeth, one of his women, before and after meat, bringeth him water in a wo[o]den platter to wash his hands. Another waiteth with a bunch of feathers to wipe them insteed of a Towell, and the feathers when he hath wiped are dryed againe. His kingdome descendeth not to his sonnes nor children: but first to his brethren, whereof he hath 3. namely Opitchapan, Opechancanough, and Catataugh, and after their decease to his sisters. First to the eldest sister, then to the rest: and after them to the heires male and female of the eldest sister, but never to the heires of the males.

He nor any of his people understand any letters wherby to write or read, only the lawes whereby he ruleth is custome. Yet when he listeth, his will is a law and must bee obeyed: not only as a king, but as halfe a God they esteeme him. His inferiour kings whom they cal werowances are tyed to rule by customes, and have power of life and death as their command in that nature. But this word Werowance which we call and conster [1] for a king, is a common worde whereby they call all commanders: for they have but fewe words in their language and but few occasions to use anie officers more then one commander, which commonly they call werowances. They all knowe their severall landes, and habitations, and limits to fish, fowle, or hunt in, but they hold all of their great Werowances Powhatan, unto whome they pay tribute of skinnes, beades, copper, pearle, deare, turkies, wild beasts, and corne. What he commandeth they dare not disobey in the least thing. It is strange to see with what great feare and adoration all these people doe obay this Powhatan. For at his feet, they present whatsoever he commandeth, and at the least frowne of his browe, their greatest spirits will tremble with feare: and no marvell, for he is very terrible and tyrannous in punishing such as offend him. For example, hee caused certaine malefactors to be bound hand and foot, then having of many

[1] Construe, translate.

fires gathered great store of burning coles, they rake these coles round in the forme of a cockpit, and in the midst they cast the offenders to broyle to death. Sometimes he causeth the heads of them that offend him, to be laid upon the altar or sacrificing stone, and one with clubbes beates out their braines. When he would punish any notorious enimie or malefactor, he causeth him to be tied to a tree, and, with muscle shels or reeds, the executioner cutteth of[f] his joints one after another, ever casting what they cut of[f] into the fire; then doth he proceed with shels and reeds to case the skinne from his head and face; then doe they rip his belly, and so burne him with the tree and all. Thus themselves reported they executed George Cassen. Their ordinary correction is to beate them with cudgels. Wee have seene a man kneeling on his knees, and at Powhatans command, two men have beat him on the bare skin, till he hath fallen senselesse in a s[w]ound, and yet never cry nor complained.

In the yeare 1608, hee surprised the people of Payankatank, his neare neighbours and subjects. The occasion was to us unknowne, but the manner was thus. First he sent diverse of his men as to lodge amongst them that night, then the Ambuscadoes invironed al their houses, and at the houre appointed, they all fell to the spoile; 24 men they slewe, the long haire of the one side of their heades with the skinne cased off with shels or reeds, they brought away. They surprised also the women and the children and the Werowance. All these they present to Powhatan. The Werowance, women and children became his prisoners, and doe him service. The lockes of haire with their skinnes he hanged on a line unto two trees. And thus he made ostentation as of a great triumph at Werowocomoco, shewing them to the English men that then came unto him, at his appointment: they expecting provision; he, to betray them, supposed to halfe conquer them, by this spectacle of his terrible crueltie.

And this is as much as my memory can call to mind worthie of note; which I have purposely collected, to satisfie my friends of the true worth and qualitie of Virginia. Yet some bad natures will not sticke to slander the Countrey, that will slovenly spit at all things, especially in company where they can find none to contradict them. Who though they were scarse ever 10 miles from James Town, or at the most but at the falles; yet holding it a great disgrace that amongst so much action, their actions were nothing, exclaime of all things, though they never adventured to knowe any thing; nor ever did any thing but devoure the fruits of other mens labours. Being for most part of such tender educations and small experience in martiall accidents: because they found not English cities, nor such faire houses, nor at their owne wishes any of their accustomed dainties, with feather beds and downe pillowes, Tavernes and alehouses in every breathing place, neither such plenty of gold and silver and dissolute liberty as they expected, had little or no care of any thing, but to pamper their bellies, to fly away with our Pinnaces, or procure their means to returne for England. For the Country was to them a miserie, a ruine, a death, a hell, and their reports here, and their owne actions there according.[1]

Some other there were that had yearely stipends to pass to and againe for transportation: who to keepe the mystery of the businesse in themselves, though they had neither time nor meanes to knowe much of themselves; yet al mens actions or relations they so formally tuned to the temporizing times simplicitie, as they could make their ignorances seeme much more then al the true actors could by their experience. And those with their great words deluded the world with such strange promises as abused the businesse much worse then the rest. For the businesse being builded upon the foundation of their fained experience, the planters, the mony, tinne [time], and meanes have still miscaried: yet they ever return-

[1] Smith attributes the calamities of the colony to his enemies, but other causes purposely underestimated had more to do with the matter, — imported diseases, a climate singularly fatal to newcomers, the faction-breeding charter, Indian attack, and the unreasonable desire of the company in London for immediate profit. No better proof of the patriotism of the colonists could be afforded than the death-rate.

ing, and the Planters so farre absent, who could contradict their excuses? which, stil to maintain their vaineglory and estimation, from time to time they have used such diligence as made them passe for truthes, though nothing more false. And that the adventurers might be thus abused, let no man wonder; for the wisest living is soonest abused by him that hath a faire tongue and a dissembling heart.

There were many in Virginia meerely projecting verbal[1] and idle contemplatours, and those so devoted to pure idlenesse that though they had lived two or three yeares in Virginia lordly, necessitie it selfe could not compell them to passe the Peninsula, or Pallisadoes of James Towne; and those wittie spirits, what would they not affirme in the behalfe of our transporters, to get victuall from their ships, or obtaine their good words in England to get their passes? Thus from the clamors and the ignorance of false informers are sprung those disasters that spring in Virginia, and our ingenious verbalists were no lesse plague to us in Virginia, then the Locusts to the Egyptians. For the labour of 30 of the best only, preserved in Christianitie, by their industrie, the idle livers of neare 200 of the rest: who lived neer 10 months of such naturall meanes, as the Country naturally of it selfe afforded. Notwithstanding all this, and the worst furie of the Savages, the extremitie of sicknesse, mutinies, faction, ignorances, and want of victuall; in all that time I lost but 7 or 8 men: yet subjected the Savages to our desired obedience, and receaved contribution from 35 of their kings, to protect and assist them against any that should assalt them, in which order they continued true and faithful, and as subjects to his Majestie, so long after as I did govern there, untill I left the Country: Since, how they have revolted, the Countrie lost, and againe replanted, and the businesses hath succeeded from time to time, I referre you to the relations of them returned from Virginia, that have bin more diligent in such observations.

[1] Speculating and theoretical.

# THE PROCEEDINGS OF THE ENGLISH COLONIES IN VIRGINIA

*Since their first beginning from England in the yeare of our Lord 1606, till this present 1612, with all their accidents that befell them in their Journies and Discoveries.*

*Also the Salvages discourses, orations and relations of the Bordering neighbours, and how they became subject to the English.*

*Unfolding even the fundamentall causes from whence have sprang so many miseries to the undertakers, and scandals to the businesse: taken faithfully as they were written out of the writings of Thomas Studley the first provant maister, Anas Todkill, Walter Russell Doctor of Phisicke, Nathaniell Powell, William Phettyplace, Richard Wyffin, Thomas Abbay, Tho: Hope, Rich: Pots and the labours of divers other diligent observers, that were residents in Virginia. And perused and confirmed by diverse now resident in England that were actors in this busines. By W. S.*

*At Oxford, Printed by Joseph Barnes. 1612.*[1]

## TO THE READER

LONG hath the world longed, but to be truely satisfied what Virginia is, with the truth of those proceedings, from whence hath flowne so manie reports of worth, and yet few good effects of the charge, which hath caused suspition in many well willers that desire yet but to be truely satisfied therein. If any can

[1] This italic heading is taken from the title-page of the original. Part II. has a separate title-page and pagination, but was issued with the *Map and Description*. As to "W. S.," see p. 76, note 1.

resolve this doubt it is those that have lived residents in the land: not salers, or passengers, nor such mercinary contemplators, that only bedeck themselves with others plumes. This discourse is not from such, neither am I the author, for they are many, whose particular discourses are signed by their names. This solid treatise, first was compiled by Richard Pots, since passing the hands of many to peruse, chancing into my hands, (for that I know them honest men, and can partly well witnesse their relations true) I could do no lesse in charity to the world then reveale; nor in conscience, but approve. By the advise of many grave and understanding gentlemen, that have pressed it to the presse, it was thought fit to publish it, rather in it[s] owne rude phrase then other waies. For that nothing can so purge that famous action from the infamous scandal some ignorantly have conceited, as the plaine simple and naked truth. For defect whereof the businesse is still suspected, the truth unknowne, and the best deservers discouraged, and neglected, some by false reports, others by conjecture, and such power hath flattry to ingender of those, hatred and affection, that one is sufficient to beguile more then 500 can keepe from being deceived.

But this discourse is no Judge of mens manners, nor catalogue of their former courses; only a reporter of their actions in Virginia, not to disgrace any, accuse any, excuse any, nor flatter any; for which cause there is no wrong done but this, shortnesse in complaining, and so sparing in commending as only the reader may perceive the truth for his paines, and the action purged of foule slander; it can detract from none that intendeth there to adventure their fortunes; and to speake truly of the first planters, that brake the yce and beate the path, howsoever many difficulties obscured their indevours, he were worse then the worst of Ingrates, that would not spare [their] memory that have buried themselves in those forrain regions. From whose first adventures may spring more good blessings then are yet conceived. So I rest thine, that will read, peruse, and understand me. If you finde false orthography or broken

English, they are small faultes in souldiers, that not being able to write learnedly, onlie strive to speake truely, and be understood without an Interpreter.

T. ABBAY.

## THE PROCEEDINGS OF THE ENGLISH COLONY IN VIRGINIA

*taken faithfully out of the writings of Thomas Studly, Capemarchant, Anas Todkill, Doctor Russell, Nathaniell Powell, William Phetiplace, and Richard Pot*[s], *with the laboures of other discreet observers, during their residences.*

## CHAPTER I

It might wel be thought, a countrie so faire (as Virginia is) and a people so tractable,[1] would long ere this have beene quietly possessed, to the satisfaction of the adventurers, and the eternizing of the memorie of those that affected it. But because all the world doe see a defailement; this following Treatise shall give satisfaction to all indifferent readers, how the businesse hath beene carried, where no doubt they will easily understand and answer to their question, howe it came to passe there was no better speed and successe in those proceedings.

Captaine Bartholomew Gosnold, the first mover of this plantation, having many yeares solicited many of his friends, but found small assistants; at last prevailed with some Gentlemen, as Mr Edward-maria Wingfield, Captaine John Smith, and diverse others, who depended a yeare upon his projects, but nothing could be effected, till by their great charge and industrie it came to be apprehended by certaine of the Nobilitie, Gentrie, and Marchants, so that his Majestie by his letters patent, gave commission for establishing Councels, to direct

[1] When Smith represents the Indians of Virginia as "tractable," he subjects his opinion to question.

here, and to governe and to execute there. To effect this, was spent another yeare, and by that time, three ships [1] were provided, one of 100 Tonns, another of 40. and a Pinnace of 20. The transportation of the company was committed to Captaine Christopher Newport, a Marriner well practised for the westerne parts of America. But their orders for governement were put in a box, not to be opened, nor the governours knowne untill they arived in Virginia.

On the 19 of December, 1606. we set saile, but by unprosperous winds, were kept six weekes in the sight of England; all which time, Mr Hunt our Preacher, was so weake and sicke, that few expected his recoverie. Yet although he were but 10 or 12 miles from his habitation (the time we were in the Downes), and notwithstanding the stormie weather, nor the scandalous imputations (of some few, little better then Atheists, of the greatest ranke amongst us) suggested against him, all this could never force from him so much as a seeming desire to leave the busines, but preferred the service of God, in so good a voyage, before any affection to contest with his godlesse foes, whose disasterous designes (could they have prevailed) had even then overthrowne the businesse, so many discontents did then arise, had he not, with the water of patience, and his godly exhortations (but chiefly by his true devoted examples) quenched those flames of envie, and dissention.

Wee watred at the Canaries, wee traded with the Salvages at Dominica; three weekes we spent in refreshing our selvs amongst these west-India Iles; in Gwardalupa we found a bath so hot, as in it we boiled porck as well as over the fire. And at a little Ile called Monica, we tooke from the bushes with our hands, neare two hogsheads full of birds in 3 or 4 houres. In Mevis,[2] Mona, and the Virgin Iles, we spent some time, where with a lothsome beast like a Crocadil, called a Gwayn,[3] Tortoses, Pellicans, Parrots, and fishes, we daily feasted. Gone from thence in search of Virginia, the company was not a little

[1] The *Sarah Constant*, the *Goodspeed*, and the *Discovery*.

[2] Nevis.

[3] An iguana, a kind of large lizard.

discomforted, seeing the Marriners had three daies passed their reckoning, and found no land, so that Captaine Ratcliffe (Captaine of the Pinnace) rather desired to beare up the helme to returne for England, then make further search. But God, the guider of all good actions, forcing them by an extream storme to hul all night, did drive them by his providence to their desired port, beyond all their expectations, for never any of them had seene that coast. The first land they made, they called Cape Henry; where anchoring, Mr Wingfield, Gosnoll, and Newport, with 30 others, recreating themselves on shore, were assalted by 5 Salvages, who hurt 2 of the English very dangerously. That night [1] was the box opened, and the orders read, in which Bartholomew Gosnoll, Edward Wingfield, Christopher Newport, John Smith, John Ratliffe, John Martin, and George Kendall, were named to bee the Councell, and to choose a President amongst them for a yeare, who with the Councell should governe. Matters of moment were to be examined by a Jurie, but determined by the major part of the Councell in which the Precedent [2] had 2 voices. Untill the 13 of May, they sought a place to plant in, then the Councell was sworne, M. Wingfield was chosen Precident, and an oration made, whie Captaine Smith was not admitted of the Councell as the rest.

Now falleth every man to worke, the Councell contrive the Fort, the rest cut downe trees to make place to pitch their Tents; some provide clapbord to relade the ships, some make gardens, some nets, &c. The Salvages often visited us kindly. The Precidents overweening jealousie would admit no exercise at armes, or fortification but the boughs of trees cast together in the forme of a halfe moone by the extraordinary paines and diligence of Captaine Kendall. Newport, with Smith, and 20 others, were sent to discover the head of the river: by divers smal habitations they passed, in 6 daies they arrived at a towne called Powhatan, consisting of some 12 houses pleasantly seated on a hill; before it, 3 fertil Iles,

[1] April 26, 1607.

[2] President.

about it many of their cornefields. The place is very pleasant, and strong by nature. Of this place the Prince is called Powhatan, and his people Powhatans. To this place, the river is navigable, but higher within a mile, by reason of the Rockes and Iles, there is not passage for a smal boate: this they call the Falles. The people in al parts kindly intreated them, til being returned within 20 miles of James towne, they gave just cause of jealousie. But had God not blessed the discoverers otherwise then those at the fort, there had then beene an end of that plantation. For at the fort, where they arived the next day, they found 17 men hurt, and a boy slaine by the Salvages. And had it not chanced a crosse barre shot from the ships strooke down a bough from a tree amongst them, that caused them to retire, our men had all been slaine, being securely all at worke, and their armes in drie fats.

Hereupon the President was contented the Fort should be pallisadoed, the ordinance mounted, his men armed and exercised, for many were the assaults and Ambuscadoes of the Salvages, and our men by their disorderly stragling were often hurt, when the Salvages by the nimblenesse of their heeles well escaped. What toile wee had, with so smal a power to guard our workmen adaies, watch al night, resist our enimies and effect our businesse, to relade the ships, cut downe trees, and prepare the ground to plant our corne, &c., I referre to the readers consideration.

Six weekes being spent in this manner, Captaine Newport (who was hired only for our transportation) was to return with the ships. Now Captaine Smith, who all this time from their departure from the Canaries, was restrained[1] as a prisoner, upon the scandalous suggestions of some of the chiefe (envying his repute), who fained he intended to usurpe the governement, murder the Councell, and make himselfe king, that his confederats were dispearsed in all the three ships, and that divers of his confederats that revealed it, would affirme it: for this he

[1] Smith was under arrest from about March 24, 1607, when they reached Dominica, to June 20, when he was admitted to the council.

was committed. 13 weekes he remained thus suspected, and by that time the ships should returne, they pretended, out of their commisserations, to referre him to the Councell in England, to receave a check, rather then by particulating his designes, make him so odious to the world, as to touch his life, or utterly overthrowe his reputation. But he much scorned their charitie, and publikely defied the uttermost of their crueltie. Hee wisely prevented their pollicies, though he could not suppresse their envies; yet so wel he demeaned himselfe in this busines, as all the company did see his innocencie, and his adversaries malice, and those suborned to accuse him, accused his accusers of subornation. Many untruthes were alleaged against him, but being so apparently disproved begat a generall hatred in the harts of the company against such unjust commanders. Many were the mischiefes that daily sprong from their ignorant (yet ambitious) spirits; but the good doctrine and exhortation of our preacher Mr Hunt reconciled them, and caused Captaine Smith to be admitted of the Councell. The next day all receaved the Communion: the day following the Salvages voluntarily desired peace, and Captaine Newport returned for England with newes; leaving in Virginia, 100. the 15 of June 1607.[1]

The names of them that were the first planters, were these following.

| Councell. | | Gent. | |
|---|---|---|---|
| Mr Edward Maria Wingfield. | Councell. | Mr Robert Hunt Preacher. | |
| Captaine Bartholomew Gosnoll. | Councell. | Mr George Percie. | Gent. |
| Cap. John Smyth. | Councell. | Anthony Gosnoll. | Gent. |
| Cap. John Rat[c]liffe. | Councell. | Cap. Gabriell Archer. | Gent. |
| Cap. John Martin. | Councell. | Robert Ford. | Gent. |
| Cap. George Kendall. | Councell. | William Bruster. | Gent. |
| | | Dru Pickhouse. | Gent. |
| | | John Brookes. | Gent. |

[1] Smith here missed the time by a week. Newport left Virginia June 22, 1607.

Gent.:
Thomas Sands.
John Robinson.
Ustis Clovill.
Kellam Throgmorton.
Nathaniel Powell.
Robert Behethland.
Jeremy Alicock.
Thomas Studley.
Richard Crofts.
Nicholas Houlgrave.
Thomas Webbe.
John Waler.
William Tankard.
Francis Snarsbrough.
Edward Brookes.
Richard Dixon.
John Martin.
George Martin.
Anthony Gosnold.
Thomas Wotton, Sierg.
Thomas Gore.
Francis Midwinter.

Carpenters.:
William Laxon.
Edward Pising.
Tho. Emry.
Rob. Small.

Anas Todkill
John Capper

James Read, Blacksmith
Jonas Profit, Sailor
Tho. Couper, Barber.
John Herd, Bricklayer.
William Garret, Bricklayer.
Edward Brinto, Mason.
William Love, Taylor.
Nic. Skot, Drum.[1]

Labourers.:
John Laydon.
William Cassen.
George Cassen.
Tho. Cassen.
William Rods.
William White.
Ould Edward.
Henry Tavin.
George Golding.
John Dods.
William Johnson.
Will. Unger.

Will. Wilkinson, Surgeon.

Boyes.:
Samuell Collier.
Nat. Pecock.
James Brumfield.
Rich. Mutton.

with diverse others to the number of 105.[2]

[1] Drummer.

[2] A longer list, 82 names against 67 given here, is printed in Smith's *Generall Historie*, pp. 43, 44.

## CHAPTER II

*What happened till the first supply.*

Being thus left to our fortunes, it fortuned that, within tenne daies, scarse ten amongst us coulde either goe, or well stand, such extreame weaknes and sicknes oppressed us. And thereat none need mervaile, if they consider the cause and reason, which was this; whilest the ships staied, our allowance was somewhat bettered by a daily proportion of bisket which the sailers would pilfer to sell, give, or exchange with us, for mony, saxefras, furres, or love. But when they departed, there remained neither taverne, beere-house, nor place of relife but the common kettell. Had we beene as free from all sinnes as gluttony and drunkeness, we might have bin canonized for Saints. But our President would never have bin admitted, for ingrossing to his privat[1] Otemeale, sacke, oile, aquavitæ, beefe, egs, or what not, but the kettel; that indeede he allowed equally to be distributed, and that was halfe a pinte of wheat, and as much barly, boyled with water, for a man a day, and this having fryed some 26. weeks in the ships hold, contained as many wormes as graines, so that we might truely call it rather so much bran than corne. Our drinke was water, our lodgings, castles in the aire. With this lodging and diet, our extreame toile in bearing and planting pallisadoes, so strained and bruised us, and our continuall labour in the extremity of the heate had so weakned us, as were cause sufficient to have made us as miserable in our native country, or any other place in the world. From May to September, those that escaped lived upon Sturgion and sea-Crabs. 50. in this time we buried. The rest seeing the Presidents projects to escape these miseries in our Pinnas by flight (who all this time, had neither felt want nor sicknes), so moved our

[1] *I.e.*, to his own use. This charge President Wingfield indignantly denied.

dead spirits, as we deposed him;[1] and established Ratcliffe in his place: Gosnoll being dead,[2] Kendall deposed, Smith newly recovered; Martin and Ratliffe was, by his care, preserved and relieved. But now was all our provision spent, the Sturgeon gone, all helps abandoned, each houre expecting the fury of the Salvages; when God, the patron of all good indeavours, in that desperate extreamity, so changed the harts of the Salvages, that they brought such plenty of their fruits and provision, as no man wanted.

And now where some affirmed it was ill done of the Councel to send forth men so badly provided, this incontradictable reason will shew them plainely they are too ill advised to nourish such il conceipts. First, the fault of our going was our owne. What could bee thought fitting or necessary wee had, but what wee should finde, what we should want, where we shoulde bee, we were all ignorant, and supposing to make our passage in two monthes, with victuall to live, and the advantage of the spring to worke: we weare at sea 5. monthes, where we both spent our victuall and lost the opportunity of the time and season to plant.

Such actions have ever since the worlds beginning beene subject to such accidents, and every thing of worth is found full of difficulties, but nothing so difficult as to establish a common wealth so farre remote from men and meanes, and where mens mindes are so untoward as neither do well themselves, nor suffer others. But to proceed.

The new President, and Martin, being little beloved, of weake judgement in dangers and lesse industry in peace, committed the managing of all things abroad to captaine Smith: who, by his owne example, good words, and faire promises, set some to mow, others to binde thatch, some to build houses, others to thatch them, himselfe alwaies bearing the greatest taske for his own share, so that, in short time, he provided most of them lodgings, neglecting any for himselfe. This done, seeing the Salvages superfluity beginne to decrease,[3] (with

[1] September 10, 1607. [2] August 22, 1607. [3] After "decrease" supply "he."

some of his workemen) shipped himselfe in the shallop, to search the country for trade. The want of the language, knowledge to mannage his boat without sailers, the want of a sufficient power (knowing the multitude of the Salvages), apparell for his men, and other necessaries, were infinite impediments, yet no discouragement. Being but 6 or 7 in company, he went down the river to Kecoughtan, where at first they scorned him, as a starved man, yet he so dealt with them, that the next day they loaded his boat with corne. And in his returne, he discovered and kindly traded with the Weraskoyks.[1] In the meane time, those at the fort so glutted the Salvages with their commodities, as they became not regarded.

Smith perceiving (notwithstanding their late miserie) not any regarded but from hand to mouth, the company being well recovered, caused the Pinas to bee provided with things fitting to get provision for the yeare following. But in the interim, he made 3. or 4. journies, and discovered the people of Chickahamine. Yet what he carefully provided, the rest carelesly spent. Wingfield and Kendall living in disgrace, (seeing al things at randome in the absence of Smith, the companies dislike of their Presidents weaknes, and their small love to Martins never-mending sicknes) strengthened themselves with the sailers and other confederates, to regaine their former credit and authority, or at least such meanes abord the Pinas (being fitted to saile as Smith had appointed for trade), to alter her course, and to go for England. Smith unexpectedly returning[2] had the plot discovered to him. Much trouble he had to prevent it, till with store of fauken[3] and musket shot, he forced them stay or sinke in the river. Which action cost the life of captaine Kendall.[4] These brawles are so disgustfull, as some will say they were better forgotten, yet all men of good judgement will conclude, it were better their basenes should be manifest to the world, then the busines beare the scorne and shame of their excused disorders. The

[1] Warascoyacks. [2] November, 1607. [3] Falcon, a small cannon.
[4] Who was shot to death about December 1, 1607.

President and captaine Archer not long after intended also to have abandoned the country, which project also was curbed and suppressed by Smith. The Spanyard never more greedily desired gold then he victuall, which he found so plentiful in the river of Chickahamine, where hundreds of Salvages, in divers places, stood with baskets expecting his coming. And now the winter approaching, the rivers became so covered with swans, geese, duckes, and cranes, that we daily feasted with good bread, Virginia pease, pumpions, and putchamins, fish, fowle, and diverse sorts of wild beasts as fat as we could eat them: so that none of our Tuftaffaty[1] humorists desired to goe for England. But our comædies never endured long without a Tragedie. Some idle exceptions being muttered against Captaine Smith, for not discovering the head of Chickahamine river, and taxed by the Councell, to bee too slow in so worthie an attempt: the next voyage, hee proceeded so farre that with much labour, by cutting of trees in sunder, he made his passage. But when his Barge could passe no farther, he left her in a broad bay, out of danger of shot, commanding none should goe ashore till his returne; himselfe, with 2 English and two Salvages, went up higher in a Canowe. But hee was not long absent, but his men went ashore, whose want of government gave both occasion and opportunity to the Salvages, to surprise one George Casson, and much failed not to have cut of[f] the boat and all the rest. Smith little dreaming of that accident, being got to the marshes at the rivers head, 20 myles in the desert, had his 2 men slaine (as is supposed) sleeping by the Canowe, whilst himselfe by fowling sought them victuall. Who finding he was beset with 200 Salvages, 2 of them hee slew, stil defending himselfe with the aid of a Salvage his guid, whome hee bounde to his arme and used as his buckler, till at last slipping into a bogmire, they tooke him prisoner. When this newes came to the fort, much was their sorrow for his losse, fewe expecting what ensued. A month[2]

[1] Silken dressed.

[2] The exact period seems to have been from December 10 to January 2, a little more than three weeks.

those Barbarians kept him prisoner. Many strange triumphes and conjurations they made of him: yet hee so demeaned himselfe amongst them, as he not only diverted them from surprising the Fort, but procure his owne liberty, and got himselfe and his company such estimation amongst them, that those Salvages admired him as a demi-God. So returning safe to the Fort[1] once more staied the Pinnas her flight for England, which, til his returne, could not set saile, so extreame was the weather, and so great the frost

His relation of the plentie he had seene, especially at Werowocomoco, where inhabited Powhatan (that till that time was unknowne)[2] so revived againe their dead spirits as all mens feare was abandoned. Powhatan having sent with this Captaine, divers of his men loaded with provision, he had conditioned, and so appointed his trustie messengers to bring but 2 or 3 of our great ordenances; but the messengers being satisfied with the sight of one of them discharged, ran away amazed with feare, till meanes was used with guifts to assure them our loves. Thus you may see what difficulties stil crossed any good indeavour, and the good successe of the businesse, and being thus oft brought to the very period of destruction, yet you see by what strange meanes God hath still delivered it. As for the insufficiencie of them admitted in commission, that errour could not be prevented by their electors, there being no other choice, and all were strangers each to others education, quallities, or disposition. And if any deeme it a shame to our nation, to have any mention made of these enormities, let them peruse the histories of the Spanish discoveries and plantations, where they may see how many mutinies, discords, and dissentions have accompanied them and crossed their attempts; which being knowne to be particular mens offences, doth take away the generall scorne and contempt, mallice[3] and ignorance might else produce to the scandall and reproach of those whose actions and valiant resolution deserve

[1] January 2, 1608; "he once more staid," etc.

[2] *I.e.*, personally.

[3] Which malice, etc.

a worthie respect. Now whether it had beene better for Captaine Smith to have concluded with any of their severall projects to have abandoned the Countrie with some 10 or 12 of them [that] we cal the better sort; to have left Mr Hunt our preacher, Mr Anthony Gosnoll (a most honest worthy and industrious gentleman) with some 30 or 40 others, his countrie men, to the furie of the Salvages, famin, and all manner of mischiefes and inconveniences, or starved himselfe with them for company, for want of lodging, or but adventuring abroad to make them provision, or by his opposition, to preserve the action, and save all their lives, I leave to the censure of others to consider.

THOMAS STUDLEY.[1]

## CHAPTER III

*The arrivall of the first supply with their proceedings and returne.*

All this time, our cares were not so much to abandon the Countrie, but the Treasurer and Councell in England were as diligent and carefull to supplie us. Two tall ships they sent us, with neere 100 men, well furnished with all things could be imagined necessarie, both for them and us. The one commanded by Captaine Newport: the other, by Captaine Nelson, an honest man and an expert marriner, but such was the leewardnesse of his ship, that (though he were within sight of Cape Henry), by stormy contrarie windes, was forced so farre to sea as the West Indies was the next land,[2] for the repaire of his Masts, and reliefe of wood and water. But Captaine Newport got in, and arived at James towne[3] not long after the redemption of Captaine Smith; to whome the Salvages, every other day, brought such plentie of bread, fish, turkies, squirrels, deare, and other wild beasts: part they gave him

[1] As Studley died August 28, 1607, he could have been the authority for only the first page of the narrative. The rest was probably by Anas Todkill.

[2] After "land" supply "he made." The margin names the *Phenix* as Nelson's ship.

[3] January 2, 1608.

as presents from the king; the rest, hee as their market clarke, set the price how they should sell.

So he had inchanted those pore soules (being their prisoner) in demonstrating unto them the roundnesse of the world, the course of the moone and starres, the cause of the day and night, the largenes of the seas, the quallities of our ships shot and powder, the devision of the world, with the diversity of the people, their complexions customes and conditions. All which hee fained to be under the command of Captaine Newport, whom he tearmed to them his father; of whose arrival it chanced he so directly prophecied, as they esteemed him an oracle. By these fictions he not only saved his owne life, and obtained his liberty; but had them at that command, [that] he might command them what his listed. That God that created al these things, they knew he adored for his God; whom they would also tearme in their discourses, the God of captaine Smith. The President and Councel so much envied his estimation amongst the Salvages (though wee all in generall equally participated with him of the good therof) that they wrought it into their understandings, by their great bounty in giving 4. times more for their commodities then he appointed, that their greatnesse and authority as much exceed [ed] his, as their bounty and liberality. Now the arrivall of [t]his first supply so overjoyed us, that we could not devise too much to please the mariners. We gave them liberty to track [1] or trade at their pleasures. But in a short time, it followed that could not be had for a pound of copper, which before was sold for an ounce. Thus ambition and sufferance cut the throat of our trade, but confirmed their opinion of Newports greatnes; wherewith Smith had possessed Powhatan: especially by the great presents Newport often sent him, before he could prepare the Pinas to go and visit him. So that this Salvage also desired to see him. A great bruit there was to set him forwarde. When he went, he was accompanied with captaine Smith and Mr Scrivener (a very wise understanding gentleman newly ar-

[1] Truck.

rived, and admitted of the Councell), and 30. or 40. chosen men for that guarde. Arriving at Werowocomo[co], Newports conceipt of this great Salvage bred many doubts and suspitions of treacheries. Which Smith, to make appeare was needlesse, with 20. men well appointed, undertooke to encounter (with that number) the worst that could happen. There names were

| | |
|---|---|
| Nathaniell Powell. | John Taverner. |
| Robert Beheathland. | William Dier. |
| William Phettiplace. | Thomas Coe. |
| Richard Wyffin. | Thomas Hope. |
| Anthony Gosnoll. | Anas Todkell. |

with 10. others whose names I[1] have forgotten. These being kindly received a shore; with 2. or 300. Salvages were conducted to their towne. Powhatan strained himselfe to the uttermost of his greatnes, to entertain us, with great shouts of Joy, orations of protestations, and the most plenty of victuall hee could provide to feast us. Sitting upon his bed of mats, his pillow of leather imbroydred (after their rude manner) with pearle and white beades, his attire a faire Robe of skins as large as an Irish mantle, at his head and feet a handsome young woman: on each side his house sate 20. of his concubines, their heads and shoulders painted red, with a great chaine of white beades about their necks; before those sate his chiefest men, in like order, in his arbor-like house. With many pretty discourses to renue their olde acquaintaunce; the great kinge and our captaine spent the time till the ebbe left our Barge a ground, then renuing their feasts and mirth, we quartred that night with Powhatan: The next day Newport came a shore, and received as much content as those people could give him. A boy named Thomas Savage was then given unto Powhatan, who Newport called his son, for whom Powhatan gave him Namontacke his trusty servant, and one of a shrewd subtill capacity. 3. or 4. daies were spent in feasting, dancing, and trading, wherin Powhatan carried himselfe so prowdly, yet

[1] Evidently Anas Todkill.

discreetly (in his Salvage manner), as made us all admire his natural gifts, considering his education. As scorning to trade as his subjects did, he bespake Newport in this manner.

Captain Newport it is not agreable with my greatnes in this pedling manner to trade for trifles; and I esteeme you a great werowans. Therefore lay me down all your commodities togither, what I like I will take, and in recompence give you that I thinke fitting their value.

Captaine Smith being our interpreter, regarding Newport as his father, knowing best the disposition of Powhatan, told us his intent was but to cheat us; yet captaine Newport thought to out-brave this Salvage in ostentation of greatnes, and so to bewitch him with his bounty, as to have what he listed: but so it chanced, Powhatan having his desire, valued his corne at such a rate, as I thinke it better cheape in Spaine, for we had not 4. bushels for that we expected 20. hogsheads [for]. This bred some unkindnes betweene our two captaines, Newport seeking to please the humor of the unsatiable Salvage, Smith to cause the Salvage to please him, but smothering his distast to avoide the Salvages suspition, glaunced in the eies of Powhatan many Trifles; who fixed his humour upon a few blew beads. A long time he importunatly desired them, but Smith seemed so much the more to affect them: so that ere we departed, for a pound or two of blew beads, he brought over my king for 2 or 300 bushels of corne, yet parted good friends. The like entertainement we found of Opechanchynough, king of Pamaunke, whom also he in like manner fitted (at the like rates) with blew beads: and so we returned to the fort.[1] Where this New Supply being lodged with the rest, [had] accidently fired the quarters, and so the Towne, which being but thatched with reeds, the fire was so fierce as it burnt their pallizadoes (though 10. to 12 yardes distant), with their armes, bedding, apparell, and much private provision. Good Mr Hunt our preacher, lost

[1] On March 9, 1608.

all his library, and al that he had but the cloathes on his backe, yet [did] none ever see him repine at his losse. This hapned in the winter, in that extreame frost, 1607.[1] Now though we had victuall sufficient, I meane only of Oatmeale, meale, and corne, yet the ship staying there 14. weeks (when shee might as well have been gone in 14. daies), spent the beefe, porke, oile, aquavitæ, fish, butter and cheese, beere, and such like, as was provided to be landed us. When they departed, what their discretion could spare us, to make a feast or two with bisket, pork, beefe, fish, and oile, to relish our mouths; of each somewhat they left us, yet I must confess those that had either mony, spare clothes, credit to give bils of payment, gold rings, furres, or any such commodities, were ever welcome to this removing taverne. Such was our patience to obay such vile commanders, and buy our owne provision at 15 times the valew, suffering them feast, we bearing the charge, yet must not repine, but fast; and then leakage, ship-rats and other casualties occasioned the losse. But the vessell and remnants (for totals), we were glad to receive with all our hearts to make up the account, highly commending their providence for preserving that. For all this plentie, our ordinarie was but meale and water; so that this great charge little relieved our wants, whereby, with the extreamity of the bitter cold aire, more than halfe of us died, and tooke our deathes, in that piercing winter. I cannot deny but both Skrivener and Smith did their best to amend what was amisse, but with the President went the major part,[2] that their hornes were too short. But the worst mischiefe was our gilded refiners, with their golden promises, made all men their slaves in hope of recompence. There was no talke, no hope, nor worke, but dig gold, wash gold, refine gold, load gold. Such a brute of gold, as one mad fellow desired to bee buried in the sandes, least they should by their art make gold of his bones. Little need there was and lesse reason, the ship should stay, their wages run on, our victuall consume 14 weekes, that the Marriners might say, they

[1] 1607–1608.

[2] The majority of the council

built such a golden Church, that we can say, the raine washed neare to nothing in 14 daies. Were it that Captaine Smith would not applaud all those golden inventions, because they admitted him not to the sight of their trials, nor golden consultations I knowe not: but I heard him question with Captaine Martin and tell him, except he would shew him a more substantiall triall, hee was not inamored with their durtie skill. Breathing out these and many other passions, never any thing did more torment him, than to see all necessarie businesse neglected, to fraught such a drunken ship with so much gilded durt. Till then wee never accounted Captaine Newport a refiner, who being fit to set saile for England, and wee not having any use of Parliaments, plaies, petitions, admirals, recorders, interpreters, chronologers, courts of plea, nor Justices of peace, sent M. Wingfield, and Captaine Archer with him, for England, to seeke some place of better imploiment.

## CHAPTER IV

*The arival of the Phœnix, her returne, and other accidents.*

The authoritie nowe consisting in refining Captaine Martin and the still sickly President, the sale of the stores commodities maintained their estates as inheritable revenews. The spring approching, and the ship departed, M. Skrivener and Capt. Smith divided betwixt them the rebuilding our towne, the repairing our pallisadoes, the cutting downe trees, preparing our fields, planting our corne, and to rebuild our Church, and re-cover our store-house. Al men thus busie at their severall labours, M. Nelson arived [1] with his lost Phœnix, (lost I say, for that al men deemed him lost), landing safely his men. So well hee had mannaged his ill hap, causing the Indian Iles to feed his company, that his victuall (to [2] that was left us before) was sufficient for halfe a yeare. He had nothing but he freely imparted it, which honest dealing (being a marriner) caused

[1] April 20, 1608.

[2] Added to.

us admire him. Wee would not have wished so much as he did for us. Nowe to relade this ship with some good tidings, the President (yet not withstanding[1] with his dignitie to leave the fort), gave order to Captaine Smith and M. Skrivener to discover and search the commodities of Monacans countrie beyound the Falles. 60 able men was allotted their number, the which, within 6 daies exercise, Smith had so well trained to their armes and orders, that they little feared with whome they should encounter. Yet so unseasonable was the time, and so opposite was Captain Martin to every thing but only to fraught his ship also with his phantasticall gold, as Captaine Smith rather desired to relade her with Cedar, which was a present despatch, than either with durt, or the reports of an uncertaine discoverie. Whilst their conclusion was resolving, this hapned.

Powhatan to expresse his love to Newport, when he departed, presented him with 20 Turkies, conditionally to returne him 20 Swords, which immediately were sent him.[2] Now after his departure, hee presented Captaine Smith with the like luggage, but not finding his humour obaied, in sending him weapons, he caused his people with 20. devises to obtain them. At last, by ambuscadoes at our very ports, they would take them perforce, surprise us at work or any way, which was so long permitted that they became so insolent, there was no rule. The command from England was so straight not to offend them, as our authority bearers (keeping their houses) would rather be any thing then peace breakers. This charitable humor prevailed, till well it chaunced they medled with Captaine Smith, who, without farther deliberation, gave them such an incounter, as some he so hunted up and downe the Ile, some he so terrified with whipping beating and imprisonment, as for revenge, they surprised two of his forraging disorderly souldiers, and having assembled their forces, boldly threatned at our ports to force Smith to redeliver 7 Salvages which for their villanies he detained prisoners. But to try their furies, in

[1] *I.e.*, it not standing.

[2] "An ill example, to sell swords to Salvages," says the margin.

lesse then halfe an houre, he so hampered their insolencies, that they brought the 2. prisoners, desiring peace without any farther composition for their prisoners, who being threatned and examined their intents, and plotters of their villanies, confessed they were directed only by Powhatan, to obtaine him our owne weapons to cut our own throats, with the manner how, where, and when, which wee plainely found most true and apparant. Yet he sent his messengers and his dearest Daughter Pocahuntas to excuse him of the injuries done by his subjects, desiring their liberties, with the assuraunce of his love. After Smith had given the prisoners what correction hee thought fit, used them well a day or two after, and then delivered them [to] Pocahuntas, for whose sake only, he fained to save their lives and graunt them liberty. The patient Councel, that nothing would move to warre with the Salvages, would gladly have wrangled with captaine Smith for his cruelty, yet none was slaine to any mans knowledge, but it brought them [1] in such feare and obedience, as his very name would sufficiently affright them. The fraught of this ship being concluded to be Cedar, by the diligence of the Master, and captaine Smith, shee was quickly reladed; Mr Scrivener was neither Idle nor slow, to follow all things at the fort. The ship falling to the Cedar Ile, captaine Martin having made shift to be sicke neare a yeare, and now neither pepper, suger, cloves, mace, nor nugmets [2] ginger, nor sweet meates in the country: (to enjoy the credit of his supposed art) at his earnest request, was most willingly admitted to returne for England. Yet having beene there but a yeare, and not past halfe a year since the ague left him, that he might say somewhat he had seene, hee went twice by water to Paspahegh a place neere 7 miles from James towne, but lest the dew should distemper him, was ever forced to returne before night. Thus much I thought fit to expresse, he expresly commanding me to record his journies, I being his man, and he sometimes my master.

THOMAS STUDLY, ANAS TODKILL.

[1] The Indians.

[2] Nutmegs.

Their names that were landed in this supply:

Matthew Scrivener, appointed to be of the Councell.

|  | |
|---|---|
| Michaell Phetyplace. | Gent. |
| William Phetyplace. | Gent. |
| Ralfe Morton. | Gent. |
| William Cantrill. | Gent. |
| Richard Wyffin. | Gent. |
| Robert Barnes. | Gent. |
| George Hill. | Gent. |
| George Pretty. | Gent. |
| John Taverner. | Gent. |
| Robert Cutler. | Gent. |
| Michaell Sickelmore. | Gent. |
| Thomas Coo. | Gent. |
| Peter Pory. | Gent. |
| Richard Killingbeck. | Gent. |
| William Causey. | Gent. |
| Doctor Russell. | Gent. |
| Richard Worley. | Gent. |
| Richard Prodger. | Gent. |
| William Bayley. | Gent. |
| Richard Molynex. | Gent. |
| Richard Pots. | Gent. |
| Jefry Abots. | Gent. |
| John Harper. | Gent. |
| Timothy Leds. | Gent. |
| Edward Gurganay. | Gent. |
| George Forest. | Gent. |
| John Nickoles. | Gent. |
| William Gryvill. | Gent. |
| Daniel Stalling, Jueller. | |
| William Dawson, Refiner. | |
| Abraham Ransacke, Refiner. | |
| William Johnson, Goldsmith. | |
| Peter Keffer, a Gunner. | |
| Robert Alberton, a Perfumer. | |
| Richard Belfield, Goldsmith. | |
| Ramon Goodyson. | Labourers. |
| John Speareman. | Labourers. |
| William Spence. | Labourers. |
| Richard Brislow. | Labourers. |
| William Simons. | Labourers. |
| John Bouth. | Labourers. |
| William Burket. | Labourers. |
| Nicholas Ven. | Labourers. |
| William Perce. | Labourers. |
| Francis Perkins. | Labourers. |
| Francis Perkins. | Labourers. |
| William Bentley. | Labourers. |
| Richard Gradon. | Labourers. |
| Rowland Nelstrop. | Labourers. |
| Richard Salvage. | Labourers. |
| Thomas Salvage. | Labourers. |
| Richard Miler. | Labourers. |
| William May. | Labourers. |
| Vere. | Labourers. |
| Michaell. | Labourers. |
| Bishop Wyles. | Labourers. |
| John Powell. | Tailers. |
| Thomas Hope. | Tailers. |
| William Beckwith. | Tailers. |
| William Yonge. | Tailers. |
| Lawrence Towtales. | Tailers. |
| William Ward. | Tailers. |
| Christopher Rodes. | |
| James Watkings. | |
| Richard Fetherstone. | |
| James Burne. | |

Thomas Feld. }
John Harford. } Apothecaries.
Post Gittnat, a C[hir]urgion.
John Lewes, a Couper.
Robert Cotten, a Tobaco-pipe-maker.
Richard Dole, a blacke Smith and divers others, to the number of 120.

## CHAPTER V

*The accidents that happened in the Discoverie of the bay.*

The prodigality of the Presidents state went so deepe in the store, that Smith and Scrivener had a while tyed both Martin and him to the rules of proportion, but now Smith being to depart, the Presidents authorite so overswayed Mr Scriveners discretion, as our store, our time, our strength and labours, was idlely consumed to fulfill his phantasies. The second of June 1608. Smith left the fort, to performe his discoverie; with this company.

Walter Russell Doctour of Physicke.

Ralp Morton. }
Thomas Momford. }
William Cantrill. }
Richard Fetherstone. } Gent.
James Bourne. }
Michael Sicklemore. }

Anas Todkill. }
Robert Small. }
James Watkins. } Sould.
John Powell. }
James Read, blacke smith.
Richard Keale, fishmonger.
Jonas Profit, fisher.

These being in an open barge of two tunnes burthen, leaving the *Phenix* at Cape-Henry, we crossed the bay to the Easterne shore, and fell with the Iles called Smiths Iles.[1] The first people we saw were 2. grimme and stout Salvages

[1] In 1611 Sir Thomas Dale established a settlement under Lieutenant Craddock at Smith's Island near Cape Charles for the purpose of making salt out of sea-water. He called this settlement "Dale's Gift."

upon Cape-Charles, with long poles like Javelings, headed with bone. They boldly demanded what we were, and what we would, but after many circumtances, they in time seemed very kinde, and directed us to Acawmacke, the habitation of the Werowans, where we were kindly intreated. This king was the comliest proper civill Salvage wee incountred. His country is a pleasant fertill clay-soile. Hee told us of a straunge accident lately happened him, and it was: Two deade children, by the extreame passions of their parents, or some dreaming visions, phantasie, or affection moved them againe to revisit their dead carkases, whose benummed bodies reflected to the eies of the beholders such pleasant delightfull countenances, as though they had regained their vital spirits. This, as a miracle, drew many to behold them: all which, (being a great part of his people) not long after died, and not any one escaped. They spake the language of Powhatan wherein they made such descriptions of the bay, Iles, and rivers that often did us exceeding pleasure. Passing along the coast, searching every inlet and bay fit for harbours and habitations: seeing many Iles in the midst of the bay, we bore up for them, but ere wee could attaine them, such an extreame gust of wind, raine, thunder, and lightning happened, that with great daunger, we escaped the unmercifull raging of that ocean-like water. The next day, searching those inhabitable Iles (which we called Russels Isles) to provide fresh water, the defect whereof forced us to follow the next Easterne channell, which brought us to the river Wighcocomoco. The people at first with great furie seemed to assault us, yet at last with songs, daunces, and much mirth, became very tractable. But searching their habitations for water, wee could fill but 3,[1] and that such puddle that never til then wee ever knew the want of good water. We digged and search many places but ere the end of two daies, wee would have refused two barricoes of gold for one of that puddle water of Wighcocomoco. Being past these Isles, falling with a high land upon the maine, wee found a great pond of fresh water,

[1] *I.e.*, three barricoes.

but so exceeding hot, that we supposed it some bath. That place we called Point ployer. Being thus refreshed, in crossing over from the maine to other Iles, the wind and waters so much increased with thunder lightning and raine, that our fore-mast blew overbord, and such mightie waves overwrought us in that smal barge, that with great labour wee kept her from sinking, by freeing out the water. 2 daies we were inforced to inhabit these uninhabited Iles, which (for the extremitie of gusts, thunder, raine, stormes, and il weather) we called Limbo. Repairing our fore saile with our shirts, we set saile for the maine, and fel with a faire river on the East called Kuskarana-ocke. By it inhabit the people of Soraphanigh, Nause, Arsek, and Nautaquake, that much extolled a great nation called Massawomekes, in search of whome wee returned by Limbo. But finding this easterne shore shallow broken Iles, and the maine for most part without fresh water, we passed by the straights of Limbo, for the weasterne shore. So broad is the bay here, that we could scarse perceive the great high Cliffes on the other side. By them, wee ancored that night, and called them Richards Cliffes. 30 leagues we sailed more Northwards, not finding any inhabitants, yet the coast well watred, the mountaines very barren, the vallies very fertil, but the woods extreame thicke, full of Woolves, Beares, Deare, and other wild beasts. The first inlet we found, wee called Bolus, for that the clay (in many places) was like (if not) Bole-Armoni-acke. When we first set saile, some of our gallants doubted nothing, but that our Captaine would make too much hast home. But having lien not above 12 daies in this smal Barge, oft tired at their oares, their bread spoiled with wet, so much that it was rotten (yet so good were their stomacks that they could digest it), did with continuall complaints so importune him now to returne, as caused him bespeak them in this manner.

Gentlemen, if you would remember the memorable historie of Sir Ralfe Lane, how his company importuned him to proceed in the discoverie of Morattico, alleaging, they had yet a dog, that being boyled with Saxafras leaves, would richly feed them in their returnes; what shame would it be for you (that have beene so suspitious of my tendernesse) to force me returne with a months provision, scarce able to say where we have bin, nor yet heard of that wee were sent to seeke. You cannot say but I have shared with you of the worst[1] is past; and for what is to come, of lodging, diet, or whatsoever, I am contented you allot the worst part to my selfe. As for your feares, that I will lose my selfe in these unknowne large waters, or be swallowed up in some stormie gust, abandon those childish feares, for worse then is past cannot happen, and there is as much danger to returne, as to proceed forward. Regaine therefore your old spirits; for returne I wil not, (if God assist me) til I have seene the Massawomekes, found Patawomeck, or the head of this great water you conceit to be endlesse.

3 or 4 daies we expected [2] wind and weather, whose adverse extreamities added such discouragements to our discontents as 3 or 4 fel extreame sicke, whose pitiful complaints caused us to returne, leaving the bay some 10 miles broad at 9 or 10 fadome water.

The 16 of June, we fel with the river of Patawomeck. Feare being gon, and our men recovered, wee were all contente to take some paines to knowe the name of this 9 mile broad river. We could see no inhabitants for 30 myles saile. Then we were conducted by 2 Salvages up a little bayed creeke toward Onawmament, where all the woods were laid with Ambuscadoes to the number of 3 or 400 Salvages, but so strangely painted, grimed, and disguised, showting, yelling, and crying, as we rather supposed them so many divels. They made many bravadoes, but to appease their furie, our Captaine prepared (with a seeming willingnesse, as they) to encounter them. The grazing of the bullets upon the river, with the ecco of the woods so amazed them, as down went their bowes and arrowes; and exchanging hostage, James Watkins was sent 6. myles up the woods, to their kings habitation. Wee were kindly used by these Salvages, of whom we understood, they were commaunded to betray us, by Powhatans direction,

[1] After "worst" supply "**that.**"

[2] Experienced.

and hee so directed from the discontents of James towne. The like incounters we found at Patawomeck, Cecocawone, and divers other places; but at Moyaones, Nacothtant, and Taux, the people did their best to content us. The cause of this discovery was to search a glistering mettal, the Salvages told us they had from Patawomeck (the which Newport assured that he had tryed [1] to hold halfe silver), also to search what furres, metals, rivers, Rockes, nations, woods, fishings, fruits, victuals, and other commodities the land afforded, and whether the bay were endlesse, or how farre it extended. The mine we found 9 or 10 myles up in the country from the river, but it proved of no value.[2] Some Otters, Beavers, Martins, Luswarts, and sables we found and, in diverse places, that abundance of fish lying so thicke with their heads above the water, as for want of nets (our barge driving amongst them) we attempted to catch them with a frying pan; but we found it a bad instrument to catch fish with. Neither better fish, more plenty or variety, had any of us ever seene in any place, swimming in the water, then in the bay of Chesapeack, but there not to be caught with frying-pans. To expresse al our quarrels, treacheries and incounters amongst those Salvages, I should be too tedious; but in briefe, at al times we so incountred them and curbed their insolencies, as they concluded with presents to purchase peace, yet wee lost not a man. At our first meeting, our captaine ever observed this order, to demaunde their bowes and arrowes, swords, mantles, or furres, with some childe for hostage: whereby he could quickly perceive when they intended any villany.

Having finished this discovery, (though our victuall was neare spent) he intended to have seene his imprisonments acqaintance upon the river of Toppahannock. But our boate (by reason of the ebbe) chansing to ground upon a many shoules lying in the entrance, we spied many fishes lurking amongst the weedes on the sands. Our captaine sporting himselfe to catch them by nailing them to the ground with

[1] Tested.

[2] "Antimony," says the margin.

his sword, set us all a fishing in that manner. By this devise, we tooke more in an houre then we all could eat. But it chanced, the captaine taking a fish from his sword (not knowing her condition), being much of the fashion of a thornebacke with a longer taile whereon is a most poysoned sting of 2. or 3. inches long, which shee strooke an inch and halfe into the wrist of his arme. The which, in 4. houres, had so extreamly swolne his hand, arme, shoulder, and part of his body, as we al with much sorrow concluded[1] his funerall, and prepared his grave in an Ile hard by (as himselfe appointed), which then wee called Stingeray Ile, after the name of the fish. Yet by the helpe of a precious oile, Doctour Russel applyed, ere night his tormenting paine was so wel asswaged that he eate the fish to his supper: which gave no lesse joy and content to us, then ease to himselfe. Having neither Surgeon nor surgerie but that preservative oile, we presently set saile for James Towne. Passing the mouth of Pyankatanck and Pamaunke rivers, the next day we safely arrived at Kecoughtan. The simple Salvages seeing our captaine hurt, and another bloudy (which came by breaking his shin), our number of bowes, arrowes, swords, targets, mantles and furs, would needs imagine we had bin at warres. The truth of these accidents would not satisfie them; but impaciently they importuned us to know with whom wee fought. Finding their aptnes to beleeve, we failed not (as a great secret) to tel them any thing that might affright them, what spoile wee had got and made of the Masawomeekes. This rumor went faster up the river then our barge. That arrived at Weraskoyack, the 20 of Julie, where trimming her with painted streamers and such devises, we made the Fort jealious of a Spanish frigot; where we all safely arrived the 21. of July. There wee found the Last Supply al sicke; the rest, some lame, some bruised, al unable to do any thing but complain of the pride and unreasonable needlesse cruelty of their sillie President[2] that had riotously consumed the store; and to fulfill his follies, about building

[1] Anticipated.

[2] Ratcliffe.

him an unnecessarie pallas in the woodes, had brought them all to that miserie, that had not we arrived, they had as strangely tormented him with revenge. But the good newes of our discovery, and the good hope we had (by the Salvages relation) our Bay had stretched to the South sea, appeased their fury; but conditionally that Ratliffe should be deposed, and that captaine Smith would take upon him the governement. Their request being effected, hee substituted Mr Scrivener, his deare friend, in the Presidencie; equally distributing those private provisions the other[s] had ingrossed; appointing more honest officers to assist Scrivener (who the[n] lay extreamelie tormented with a callenture):[1] and in regard of the weaknes of the company, and heat of the yeare, they being unable to worke, he left them to live at ease, but imbarked himselfe to finish his discoverie.

Written by Walter Russell and Anas Todkill.

## CHAPTER VI

*What happened the second voyage to discover the Bay.*

The 20.[2] of July, Captaine Smith set forward to finish the discovery, with 12. men. Their names were

| | | | |
|---|---|---|---|
| Nathaniell Powell.<br>Thomas Momford.<br>Richard Fetherstone.<br>Michaell Sicklemore.<br>James Bourne. | Gent. | Anas Todkill.<br>Edward Pysing.<br>Richard Keale.<br>Anthony Bagnall.<br>James Watkins. | Sould. |
| | | William Ward.<br>Jonas Profit. | |

The winde beeing contrary, caused our stay 2 or 3 daies at Kecoughtan, the werowans feasting us with much mirth. His people were perswaded we went purposely to be revenged

[1] Fever.

[2] Or rather 24th.

of the Massawomeckes. In the evening, we firing 2. or 3. rackets, so terrified the poore Salvages, they supposed nothing impossible wee attempted, and desired to assist us. The first night, we anchored at Stingeray Ile, the next day, crossed Patawomecks river, and hasted for the river Bolus. Wee went not much farther, before wee might perceive the Bay to devide in 2. heads, and arriving there, we founde it devided in 4, all which we searched so far as we could saile them. 2. of them wee found uninhabited, but in crossing the bay to the other, wee incountered 7. or 8. Canowes-full of Massawomecks. We seeing them prepare to assault us, left our oares, and made way with our saile to incounter them, yet were we but five (with our captaine) could stand; [f]or within 2. daies after wee left Kecoughtan, the rest (being all of the Last Supply) were sicke almost to death (untill they were seasoned to the country). Having shut them under our tarpawling, we put their hats upon stickes by the barge side, to make us seeme many. And so we thinke the Indians supposed those hats to be men, for they fled with all possible speed to the shoare, and there stayed, staring at the sailing of our barge, till we anchored right against them. Long it was ere we could drawe them to come unto us. At last, they sent 2 of their company unarmed in a Canowe: the rest all followed to second them, if need required. These 2 being but each presented with a bell, brought aborde all their fellowes, presenting the captain with venison, beares flesh, fish, bowes, arrows, clubs, targets, and beare-skins. Wee understood them nothing at all but by signes, whereby they signified unto us they had been at warres with the Tockwoghs, the which they confirmed by shewing their green wounds. But the night parting us, we imagined they appointed the next morning to meete, but after that we never saw them.

Entring the River of Tockwogh, the Salvages all armed in a fleete of Boates round invironed us. It chanced one of them could speake the language of Powhatan, who perswaded the rest to a friendly parly. But when they see us furnished with the Massawomeckes weapons, and we faining the invention of Kecoughtan to have taken them perforce; they conducted us to their pallizadoed towne, mantelled with the barkes of trees, with Scaffolds like mounts, brested about with Barks very formally. Their men, women, and children, with dances, songs, fruits, fish, furres, and what they had, kindly entertained us, spreading mats for us to sit on, stretching their best abilities to expresse their loves.

Many hatchets, knives, and peeces of yron and brasse, we see, which they reported to have from the Sasquesahanockes, a mighty people, and mortall enimies with the Massawomeckes. The Sasquesahanocks inhabit upon the chiefe spring of these 4., two daies journey higher then our Barge could passe for rocks. Yet we prevailed with the interpreter to take with him an other interpreter to perswade the Sasquesahanocks to come to visit us, for their language are different. 3. or 4. daies we expected their returne. Then 60. of these giantlike-people came downe, with presents of venison, Tobacco pipes, Baskets, Targets, Bowes and Arrows. 5 of their Werowances came boldly abord us, to crosse the bay for Tockwogh, leaving their men and Canowes, the winde being so violent that they durst not passe.[1]

Our order was, dayly, to have prayer, with a psalm, at which solemnitie the poore Salvages much wondered. Our prayers being done, they were long busied with consultation till they had contrived their businesse. Then they began in most passionate manner, to hold up their hands to the sunne, with a most feareful song. Then imbracing the Captaine, they began to adore him in like manner: though he rebuked them, yet they proceeded til their song was finished. Which don, with a most strange furious action, and a hellish voice, began an oration of their loves. That ended, with a great painted beares skin, they covered our Captaine. Then one ready with a chaine of white beads (waighing at least 6 or 7 pound) hung it about his necke; the others had 18 mantles made of divers sorts of skinnes sowed together. All these, with many other toyes, they laid at his feet, stroking their

[1] *I.e.*, durst not attempt to cross in canoes.

ceremonious handes about his necke, for his creation to be their governour, promising their aids, victuals, or what they had, to be his, if he would stay with them, to defend and revenge them of the Massawomecks. But wee left them at Tockwogh, they much sorrowing for our departure, yet wee promised the next yeare againe to visit them. Many descriptions and discourses they made us of Atquanahucke, Massawomecke, and other people, signifying they inhabit the river of Cannida, and from the French to have their hatchets and such like tooles by trade.[1] These knowe no more of the territories of Powhatan then his name, and he as little of them.

Thus having sought all the inlets and rivers worth noting, we returned to discover the river of Pawtuxunt. These people we found very tractable, and more civill then any. Wee promised them, as also the Patawomecks, the next yeare to revenge them of the Massawomecks. Our purposes were crossed in the discoverie of the river of Toppahannock, for wee had much wrangling with that peevish nation; but at last, they became as tractable as the rest. It is an excellent, pleasant, well inhabited, fertill, and a goodly navigable river. Toward the head thereof, it pleased God to take one of our sicke (called M. Fetherstone), where in Fetherstons bay, we buried him, in the night, with a volly of shot. The rest (notwithstanding their ill diet, and bad lodging, crowded in so small a barge, in so many dangers, never resting but alwaies tossed to and againe) al well recovered their healthes. Then we discovered the river of Payankatank, and set saile for James Towne. But in crossing the bay in a faire calme, such a suddaine gust surprised us in the night, with thunder and raine, as wee were halfe imployed in freeing out water, never thinking to escape drowning; yet running before the winde, at last we made land by the flashes of fire from heaven, by which light only, we kept from the splitting shore, until it pleased God in that black darknes, to preserve us by that light to find Point com-

[1] In the previous month, July, 1608, Champlain had laid the foundations of Quebec. See *Voyages of Champlain*, in this series, pp. 131, 132.

fort. And arived safe at James Towne, the 7 of September, 1608: where wee found M. Skrivener and diverse others well recovered, many dead, some sicke; the late President prisoner for muteny; by the honest diligence of Master Skrivener, the harvest gathered; but the stores provision much spoiled with raine. Thus was that yeare (when nothing wanted) consumed and spent, and nothing done (such was the government of Captain Ratliffe) but only this discoverie: wherein to expresse all the dangers, accidents, and incounters, this small number passed in that small barge, with such watrie diet in these great waters and barbarous Countries (til then to any Christian utterly unknowne) I rather referre their merit to the censure[1] of the courteous and experienced reader, than I would be tedious, or partiall being a partie.

By Nathaniell Poell, and Anas Todkill.

## CHAPTER VII

*The Presidencie surrendred to Captaine Smith. The arrivall and returne of the second supply: and what happened.*

The 10. of September 1608. by the election of the Councel, and request of the company, Captaine Smith received the letters patents, and tooke upon him the place of President, which till then by no meanes he would accept, though hee were often importuned thereunto. Now the building of Ratcliffes pallas staide, as a thing needlesse: the church was repaired, the storehouse re-covered; building prepared for the supply we expected. The fort reduced to the forme of this figure,[2] the order of watch renued, the squadrons (each setting of the watch) trained. The whole company every Satturday exercised in a fielde prepared for that purpose; the boates trimmed for trade, which

[1] Judgment.

[2] "*Quere,*" says the margin, indicating that the drawing suggested in the manuscript had not reached the printer.

in their Journey encountred the second supply, that brought them back to discover the country of Monacan. How, or why Captaine Newport obtained such a private commission as not to returne without a lumpe of gold, a certainty of the south sea, or one of the lost company of Sir Walter Rawley, I know not, nor why he brought such a 5. pieced barge, not to beare us to that south sea, till we had borne her over the mountaines (which how farre they extend is yet unknowne). As for the coronation of Powhatan, and his presents of Bason, Ewer, Bed, Clothes, and such costly novelties, they had bin much better well spared, then so ill spent: for we had his favour much better onlie for a poore peece of Copper, till this stately kinde of soliciting made him so much overvalue himselfe, that he respected us as much as nothing at all. As for the hiring of the Poles and Dutch, to make pitch and tarre, glasse, milles, and sope-ashes, was most necessarie and well. But to send them and seaventy more without victuall, to worke, was not so well considered; yet this could not have hurt us, had they bin 200., though then we were 130 that wanted for our selves. For we had the Salvages in that Decorum, (their harvest beeing newly gathered) that we feared not to get victual sufficient, had we bin 500. Now was there no way to make us miserable but to neglect that time to make our provision, whilst it was to be had; the which was done to perfourme this strange discovery, but more strange coronation. To loose that time, spend that victuall we had, tire and starve our men, having no means to carry victuall, munition, the hurt or sicke, but their owne backs, how or by whom they were invented I know not. But Captaine Newport we only accounted the author, who to effect these projects, had so gilded all our hopes with great promises, that both company and Councel concluded [1] his resolution. I confesse we little understood then our estates, to conclude his conclusion against al the inconveniences the foreseeing President alleadged. There was added to the councell, one Captaine Waldo, and Captaine Winne, two ancient

[1] Adopted.

souldiers and valiant gentlemen, but ignorant of the busines, being newly arrived. Ratcliffe was also permitted to have his voice, and Mr Scrivener desirous to see strange countries. So that although Smith was President, yet the Councell had the authoritie, and ruled it as they listed. As for cleering Smiths objections, how pitch, and tarre, wanscot, clapbord, glasse, and sope ashes could be provided to relade the ship; or provision got to live withal when none was in the Country, and that which we had, spent before the ships departed: The answer was, Captaine Newport undertook to fraught the Pinnace with corne, in going and returning in his discoverie, and to refraught her againe from Werawocomoco; also promising a great proportion of victuall from his ship, inferring that Smiths propositions were only devises to hinder his journey, to effect it himselfe; and that the crueltie Smith had used to the Salvages in his absence, might occasion them to hinder his designes. For which, al workes were left, and 120 chosen men were appointed for his guard. And Smith, to make cleere these seeming suspicions, that the Salvages were not so desperat as was pretended by Captaine Newport, and how willing he was to further them to effect their projects, because the coronation would consume much time, undertooke their message to Powhatan (to intreat him to come to James Towne to receive his presents) accompanied only with Captaine Waldo, M. Andrew Buckler, Edward Brinton, and Samuel Collier. With these 4, hee went overland against Werawocomoco, there passed the river of Pamaunke in the Salvages Canowes, Powhatan being 30 myles of[f], who presently was sent for. In the meane time, his women entertained Smith in this manner.

In a faire plaine field, they made a fire, before which, he sitting uppon a mat, suddainly amongst the woods was heard such a hideous noise and shriking, that they betooke them to their armes, supposing Powhatan with all his power came to surprise them; but the beholders, which were many, men women and children, satisfied the Captaine there was no such matter, being presently presented with this anticke. 30 young women came naked out of the woods (only covered behind and before with a few greene leaves), their bodies al painted, some white, some red, some black, some partie colour, but every one different. Their leader had a faire paire of stagges hornes on her head, and an otter skinne at her girdle, another at her arme, a quiver of arrowes at her backe, and bow and arrowes in her hand. The next, in her hand a sword, another, a club, another a pot-stick, all hornd alike. The rest, every one with their severall devises. These feindes, with most hellish cries and shouts, rushing from amongst the trees, cast themselves in a ring about the fire, singing and dauncing with excellent ill varietie, oft falling into their infernall passions, and then solemnely againe to sing and daunce. Having spent neere an houre, in this maskarado; as they entered, in like manner departed. Having reaccomodated themselves, they solemnely invited Smith to their lodging, but no sooner was hee within the house, but all these Nimphes more tormented him than ever, with crowding, and pressing, and hanging upon him, most tediously crying, *love you not mee.* This salutation ended, the feast was set, consisting of fruit in baskets, fish and flesh in wooden platters, beans and pease there wanted not (for 20 hogges), nor any Salvage daintie their invention could devise; some attending, others singing and dancing about them. This mirth and banquet being ended, with firebrands (instead of torches) they conducted him to his lodging.

The next day, came Powhatan. Smith delivered his message of the presents sent him, and redelivered him Namontack, desiring him come to his Father Newport to accept those presents, and conclude their revenge against the Monacans. Whereunto the subtile Salvage thus replied

If your king have sent me presents, I also am a king, and this my land. 8 daies I will stay to receave them. Your father is to come to me, not I to him, nor yet to your fort, neither will I bite at such a baite. As for the Monacans, I can revenge my owne injuries, and as for Atquanuchuck, where you say your brother was slain, it is a contrary way from those parts you suppose it. But for any salt water beyond the mountaines, the relations you have had from my people are false.

Whereupon he began to draw plots upon the ground, according to his discourse, of all those regions. Many other discourses they had (yet both desirous to give each other content in Complementall courtesies), and so Captaine Smith returned with this answer.

Upon this Captaine Newport sent his presents by water, which is neare 100 miles, with 50 of the best shot himselfe went by land, which is but 12 miles, where he met with our 3 barges to transport him over. All things being fit for the day of his coronation, the presents were brought, his bason, ewer, bed and furniture set up, his scarlet cloake and apparel (with much adoe) put on him, (being perswaded by Namontacke they would doe him no hurt). But a fowle[1] trouble there was to make him kneele to receave his crowne. He, neither knowing the majestie nor meaning of a Crowne, nor bending of the knee, indured so many perswasions, examples, and instructions, as tired them all. At last, by leaning hard on his shoulders, he a little stooped, and Newport put the Crowne on his head; when, by the warning of a pistoll, the boates were prepared with such a volly of shot, that the king start up in a horrible feare, till he saw all was well. Then remembring himselfe, to congratulate their kindnesse, he gave his old shoes and his mantle to Captain Newport. But perceiving his purpose was to discover the Monacans, hee laboured to divert his resolution, refusing to lend him either men or guides more then Namontack. And so, after some complementall kindnesse on both sides, in requitall of his presents, he presented Newport with a heape of wheat eares, that might contain 7 or 8 bushels, and as much more we bought, ready dressed, in the town, wherewith we returned to the fort.

The ship having disburdened her selfe of 70 persons, with the first gentlewoman and woman servant that arrived in our Colony; Captaine Newport with al the Councell, and 120 chosen men, set forward for the discovery of Monacan, leaving the President at the fort with 80. (such as they were) to relade

[1] Great.

the shippe. Arriving at the falles, we marched by land some forty myles in 2 daies and a halfe, and so returned downe to the same path we went. Two townes wee discovered of the Monacans, the people neither using us well nor ill, yet for our securitie wee tooke one of their pettie Werowances, and lead him bound, to conduct us the way. And in our returne searched many places wee supposed mynes, about which we spent some time in refining, having one William Callicut a refiner, fitted for that purpose. From that crust of earth wee digged, hee perswaded us to beleeve he extracted some smal quantitie of silver (and not unlikely better stuffe might bee had for the digging). With this poore trial, we were contented to leave this faire, fertill, well watred countrie. Comming to the Falles, the Salvages fained there were diverse ships come into the Bay to kill them at James Towne. Trade they would not, and find their corn we could not, for they had hid it in the woods; and being thus deluded, we arrived at James Towne, halfe sicke, all complaining and tired with toile famine and discontent to have only but discovered our gilded hopes, and such fruitlesse certaineties, as the President foretold us.

No sooner were we landed, but the President dispersed many as were able, some for glasse, others for pitch, tarre, and sope ashes, leaving them with the fort,[1] to the Councels oversight. But 30 of us he conducted 5. myles from the fort to learn to make clapboard, cut downe trees, and ly in woods. Amongst the rest, he had chosen Gabriell Beadell, and John Russell the only two gallants of this last supply, and both proper gentlemen. Strange were these pleasures to their conditions; yet lodging, eating, drinking, working, or playing, they doing but as the President, all these things were carried so pleasantly, as within a weeke, they became Masters, making it their delight to heare the trees thunder as they fell. But the axes so oft blistered their tender fingers, that commonly every third blow had a lowd oath to drowne the eccho; for remedy of which sin, the President devised howe to have everie mans oathes numbered, and at night, for every oath

[1] *I.e.*, those who were at the fort.

to have a can of water powred downe his sleeve. With which, every offender was so washed (himselfe and all) that a man should scarse heare an oath in a weeke.

By this, let no man think that the President, or these gentlemen spent their times as common wood-hackers at felling of trees, or such like other labours, or that they were pressed to anything as hirelings or common slaves; for what they did (being but once a little inured), it seemed, and they conceited it, only as a pleasure and a recreation. Yet 30 or 40 of such voluntary Gentlemen would doe more in a day then 100 of the rest that must bee prest to it by compulsion.[1] Master Scrivener, Captaine Waldo, and Captaine Winne at the fort; every one in like manner, carefully regarded their charge. The President, returning from amongst the woodes, seeing the time consumed, and no provision gotten, (and the ship lay Idle, and would do nothing), presently imbarked himselfe in the discovery barge, giving order to the Councell, to send Mr Persey [2] after him, with the next barge that arrived at the fort. 2 barges he had himselfe, and 20 men. But arriving at Chickahamina, that dogged nation was too wel acquainted with our wants, refusing to trade with as much scorne and insolencie as they could expresse. The President perceiving it was Powhatans pollicy to starve us, told them he came not so much for their corne, as to revenge his imprisonment, and the death of his men murdered by them.[3] And so landing his men, and ready to charge them, they immediately fled. But then they sent their imbassadours, with corne, fish, fowl, or what they had, to make their peace; (their corne being that year bad) they complained extreamly of their owne wants, yet fraughted our boats with 100 bushels of corne, and in like manner Mr Persies, that not long after us arrived. They having done the best they could to content us, within 4. or 5. daies, we returned to James Towne.

[1] "One gentleman better than 20 lubbers," says the margin.

[2] George Percy, author of the *Observations* printed at the beginning of this volume.

[3] *I.e.*, on his trip up the Chickahominy in December, 1607.

Though this much contented the company (that then feared nothing but starving) yet some so envied his good successe, that they rather desired to starve, then his paines should prove so much more effectuall then theirs. Some projects there was, not only to have deposed him but to have kept him out of the fort, for that being President, he would leave his place and the fort without their consents; but their hornes were so much too short to effect it, as they themselves more narrowly escaped a greater mischiefe.

All this time our old taverne [1] made as much of all them that had either mony or ware as could bee desired; and by this time they were become so perfect on all sides (I meane Souldiers, Sailers, and Salvages,) as there was ten times more care to maintaine their damnable and private trade, then to provide for the Colony things that were necessary. Neither was it a small pollicy in the mariners, to report in England wee had such plenty, and bring us so many men without victuall, when they had so many private factors in the fort, that within 6. or 7. weekes after the ships returne, of 2. or 300. hatchets, chissels, mattocks, and pickaxes, scarce 20 could be found; for pike-heads, knives, shot, powder, or any thing (they could steale from their fellowes) was vendible. They knew as well (and as secretly) how to convay them to trade with the Salvages, for furres, baskets, mussaneekes,[2] young beastes, for such like commodities, as exchange them with the sailers, for butter, cheese, biefe, porke, aquavitæ, beere, bisket, and oatmeale, and then faine, all was sent them from their friends. And though Virginia afford no furs for the store, yet one mariner in one voyage hath got so many, as hee hath confessed to have solde in England for 30*l*.

Those are the Saint-seeming worthies of Virginia, that have notwithstanding all this, meate, drinke, and pay; but now they begin to grow weary, their trade being both perceived and prevented. None hath bin in Virginia (that hath not

[1] Referring to trade conducted despite the orders of the council.

[2] Squirrels.

observed any thing) which knowes not this to be true, and yet the scorne and shame was the poore souldiers, gentlemen, and carelesse governours, who were all thus bought and solde, the adventurers cousened,[1] and the action overthrowne by their false excuses, informations, and directions. By this let all the world Judge how this businesse coulde prosper, being thus abused by such pilfering occasions.

*The proceedings and accidents, with the second supply.*

Mr Scrivener was sent with the barges and Pinas to Werawocomoco, where he found the Salvages more ready to fight then trade, but his vigilancy was such, as prevented their projectes, and by the meanes of Namontack, got 3. or 4. hogsheads of corne, and as much Red paint, which (then) was esteemed an excellent die.

Captaine Newport being dispatched with the tryals of pitch, tarre, glasse, frankincense, and sope ashes, with that clapbord and wainscot [which] could bee provided, met with Mr Scrivener at point Comfort, and so returned for England, leaving us in all 200, with those hee brought us.

The names of those in this supply are these.

Captaine Peter Winne.
Captaine Richard Waldo. } were appointed to bee of the Councell.

| | | | |
|---|---|---|---|
| Mr Francis West. | Gent. | Henry Ley. | Gent. |
| Thomas Graves. | | Harmon Haryson. | |
| Rawley Chroshaw. | | Daniell Tucker. | |
| Gabriell Bedle. | | Hugh Wollystone. | |
| John Russell. | | John Hoult. | |
| John Bedle. | | Thomas Norton. | |
| William Russell. | | George Yarington. | |
| John Gudderington. | | George Burton. | |
| William Sambage. | | Henry Philpot. | |
| Henry Collings. | | Thomas Maxes. | |

[1] Cheated.

|  | |
|---|---|
| Michaell Lowicke.<br>Mr Hunt.<br>Thomas Forest.<br>William Dowman.<br>John Dauxe.<br>Thomas Abbay. | Gent. |
| Thomas Phelps.<br>John Part.<br>John Clarke.<br>Jefry Shortridge.<br>Dius Oconor.<br>Hugh Wynne.<br>Davi Uphu.<br>Thomas Bradley.<br>John Burras.<br>Thomas Lavander.<br>Henry Bell. | Tradesm.[1] |
| Master Powell.<br>Davi Ellys.<br>Thomas Gipson. | Tradesm. |
| Thomas Dowse.<br>Thomas Mallard.<br>William Taler.<br>Thomas Fox.<br>Nicholas Hancock.<br>Walker.<br>Williams.<br>Morrell.<br>Rose.<br>Scot.<br>Hardwin. | Labourers. |
| Milman.<br>Hellyard. | Boys. |

Mistresse Forest and Anne Buras her maide, 8. Dutchmen and Poles, with divers to the number of 70. persons.

Those poore conclusions so affrighted us all with famine, that the President provided for Nansamund, tooke with him Captaine Winne, and Mr Scrivener (then returning from Captaine Newport). These people also long denied him trade (excusing themselves to bee so commanded by Powhatan) til we were constrained to begin with them perforce, and then they would rather sell us some, then wee should take all. So loading our boats with 100 bushels, we parted friends, and came to James Towne; at which time, there was a marriage between John Laydon and Anne Burrowes, being the first marriage we had in Virginia.

Long he staied not, but fitting himselfe and captaine Waldo with 2. barges, from Chawopo, weanocke and all parts there, was found neither corne nor Salvage, but all fled

[1] *I.e.*, artisans.

(being jealous of our intents) till we discovered the river and people of Appametuck, where we found little. That they had we equally devided betwixt the Salvages and us, but gave them copper in consideration. Mr Persie and Mr Scrivener went also abroad, but could finde nothing.

The President seeing this proc[r]astinating of time, was no course to live, resolved with Captaine Waldo (who he knew to be sure in time of need), to surprise Powhatan and al his provision; but the unwillingnes of Captaine Winne, and Mr Scrivener (for some private respects), did their best to hinder their project. But the President, whom no perswasions could perswade to starve, being invited by Powhatan to come unto him, and if he would send him but men to build him a house, bring him a grinstone, 50. swords, some peeces, a cock and a hen, with copper and beads, he would loade his shippe with corne. The President not ignoraunt of his devises, yet unwilling to neglect any opportunity, presently sent 3. Dutchmen and 2. English (having no victuals to imploy them, all for want thereof being idle). Knowing there needed no better castel then that house, to surprize Powhatan, to effect this project, he took order with Captaine Waldo, to second him, if need required. Scrivener, he left his substitute, and set forth with the Pinnas, 2. barges, and six and forty men, which only were such as voluntarily offered themselves for his journy, the which (by reason of Mr Scriveners ill successe) was censured very desperate. They all knowing Smith would not returne empty howsoever, caused many of those that he had appointed to find excuses to stay behinde.

## CHAPTER VIII

### *Captaine Smiths journey to Pamaunke.*

The 29 of December, hee set forward for Werawocomoco: his company were these.

In the Discovery barge, himselfe.

| | | | |
|---|---|---|---|
| Robert Behethland. | Gent. | Anas Todkill. | Sould. |
| Nathaniell Powell. | | William Love. | |
| John Russell. | | William Bentley. | |
| Rawly Crashaw. | | Geoffery Shortridge. | |
| Michaell Sicklemore. | | Edward Pising. | |
| Richard Worlie. | | William Warde. | |

In the Pinnace.

Mr George Persie, brother to the Earle of Northumberland; Mr Frauncis West, brother to the Lord De-la-Ware.

William Phetiplace, Captaine of the Pinnas.

Jonas Profit, Master.

Robert Ford, clarcke of the councell.

| | | | |
|---|---|---|---|
| Michaell Phetiplace. | Gent. | Henry Powell. | Sould. |
| Geoffery Abbot, Serg. | | David Ellis. | |
| William Tankard. | | Thomas Gipson. | |
| George Yarington. | | John Prat. | |
| James Bourne. | | George Acrigge. | |
| George Burton. | | James Reade. | |
| Thomas Coe. | | Nicholas Hancocke. | |
| John Dods. | Sould. | James Watkins. | |
| Edward Brinton. | | Anthony Baggly, Serg. | |
| Nathaniel Peacocke. | | Thomas Lambert. | |
| | | Edward Pising, Serg. | |

4 Dutchmen and Richard Salvage were sent by land, to build the house for Powhatan against our arrivall.

This company being victualled but for 3. or 4. daies, lodged the first night at Weraskoyack, where the President tooke sufficient provision. This kind Salvage did his best to divert him from seeing Powhatan, but perceiving he could not prevaile, he advised in this manner, Captaine Smith, you shall finde Powhatan to use you kindly, but trust him not, and bee sure hee have no opportunitie to seaze on your armes, for hee hath sent for you only to cut your throats. The Captaine thanked him for his good counsell, yet the better to try his love, desired guides to Chowanoke, for he would sent a present to that king to bind him his friend. To performe this journey was sent Michael Sicklemore, a very honest, valiant, and painefull soldier: with him, two guids, and directions howe to search for the lost company of Sir Walter Rawley, and silke grasse. Then wee departed thence, the President assuring the king [of] his perpetuall love, and left with him Samuell Collier his page, to learne the language.

The next night being lodged at Kecoughtan, 6 or 7 daies the extreame wind, raine, frost, and snowe caused us to keepe Christmas amongst the Salvages, where wee were never more merrie, nor fedde on more plentie of good oysters, fish, flesh, wild foule, and good bread, nor never had better fires in England then in the drie warme smokie houses of Kecoughtan. But departing thence, when we found no houses, we were not curious [1] (in any weather) to lie, 3 or 4 nights together, upon any shore, under the trees, by a good fire. 148 fowles, the President, Anth. Bagly, and Edward Pising did kill at 3. shoots. At Kiskiack, the frost forced us 3 or 4 daies, also to suppresse the insolencie of those proud Salvages, to quarter in their houses and guard our barge, and cause them give us what wee wanted; yet were we but 12 with the President, and yet we never wanted harbour [2] where we found any houses.

The 12 of Januarie we arrived at Werawocomoco, where the river was frozen neare halfe a mile from the shore. But to neglect no time, the President with his barge, so farre had approached, by breaking the Ice, as the eb left him amongst those oozie shoules; yet, rather then to lie there frozen to death, by his owne example, hee taught them to march middle deepe, more then a flight shot, through this muddie froye [3] ooze. When the barge floted, he appointed 2 or 3 to returne her abord the Pinnace, where, for want of water, in melting the salt ice they made fresh water. But in this march, M. Russell (whome none could perswade to stay behind) being somewhat ill and exceeding heavie, so overtoiled himselfe, as

[1] Fastidious. [2] Shelter. [3] Frozen.

the rest had much adoe (ere he got a shore) to regain life into his dead benummed spirits. Quartering in the next houses we found, we sent to Powhatan for provision, who sent us plentie of bread, Turkies, and Venison. The next day, having feasted us after his ordinarie manner, he began to aske, when wee would bee gon, faining hee sent not for us, neither had hee any corne, and his people much lesse, yet for 40 swords he would procure us 40 bushels. The President, shewing him the men there present, that brought him the message and conditions, asked him, how it chaunced he became so forgetful; thereat, the king concluded the matter with a merry laughter, asking for our commodities, but none he liked without gunnes and swords, valuing a basket of corne more pretious then a basket of copper, saying he could eate his corne, but not his copper.

Captaine Smith seeing the intent of this subtil Salvage, began to deale with him after this manner.

Powhatan, though I had many courses to have made my provision; yet beleeving your promises to supply my wants, I neglected all, to satisfie your desire; and to testifie my love, I sent you my men for your building, neglecting my owne. What your people had, you have engrossed, forbidding them our trade, and nowe you thinke by consuming the time, wee shall consume for want, not having [wherewith] to fulfill your strange demandes. As for swords and gunnes, I told you long agoe, I had none to spare. And you shall knowe, those I have, can keepe me from want: yet steale, or wrong you, I will not, nor dissolve that friendship wee have mutually promised, except you constraine mee by your bad usage.

The king having attentively listned to this discourse, promised that both hee and his Country would spare him what they could; the which within 2 daies, they should receave. Yet, Captaine Smith, (saith the king)

some doubt I have of your comming hither, that makes me not so kindly seeke to relieve you as I would; for many do informe me, your comming is not for trade, but to invade my people and possesse my Country, who dare not come to bring you corne, seeing you thus armed with your men. To cheere us of this feare, leave abord your weapons, for here they are needlesse, we being all friends and for ever Powhatans.

With many such discourses, they spent the day, quartring that night in the kings houses. The next day, he reviewed his building, which hee little intended should proceed. For the Dutchmen finding his plenty, and knowing our want, and perceiving his preparation to surprise us, little thinking wee could escape both him, and famine, to obtaine his favour, revealed to him as much as they knew of our estates and projects, and how to prevent them. One of them being of so good a judgement, spirit, and resolution (and a hireling that was certaine of wages for his labour, and ever well used, both he and his countrimen) that the President knewe not whome better to trust, and, not knowing any fitter for that imploiment, had sent him as a spie, to discover Powhatans intent, then little doubting his honestie, nor could ever be certaine of his villany till neare halfe a yeare after.

Whilst we expected the comming in of the countrie, we wrangled out of the king 10 quarters of corne for a copper kettle; the which the President perceiving him much to effect, valued it at a much greater rate, but (in regard of his scarcety) hee would accept of as much more the next yeare, or else the country of Monacan. The King exceeding liberall of that hee had not, yeelded him Monacan. Wherewith each seeming well contented, Powhatan began to expostulate the difference betwixt peace and war, after this manner.

Captaine Smith, you may understand that I, having seene the death of all my people thrice, and not one living of those 3 generations but my selfe, I knowe the difference of peace and warre better then any in my Countrie. But now I am old, and ere long must die. My brethren, namely Opichapam, Opechankanough, and Kekataugh, my two sisters, and their two daughters, are distinctly each others successours. I wish their experiences no lesse then mine, and your love to them, no lesse then mine to you: but this brute from Nansamund, that you are come to destroy my Countrie, so much affrighteth all my people, as they dare not visit you. What will it availe you to take that perforce, you may quietly have with love, or to destroy them that provide you food? What can you get by war, when we can hide our provision and flie to the woodes, whereby you must famish, by wronging us your friends? And whie are you thus jealous of our loves, seeing us unarmed, and both doe, and are willing still to feed you with that you cannot get but by our labours? Think you I am so simple not to knowe it is better to eate good meate, lie well, and sleepe quietly with my women and children, laugh, and be merrie with you, have copper, hatchets, or what I want being your friend; then bee forced to flie from al, to lie cold in the woods, feed upon acorns roots and such trash, and be so hunted by you that I can neither rest eat nor sleepe, but my tired men must watch, and if a twig but breake, everie one crie, there comes Captaine Smith: then must I flie I knowe not whether, and thus with miserable feare end my miserable life, leaving my pleasures to such youths as you, which, through your rash unadvisednesse, may quickly as miserably ende, for want of that you never knowe how to find? Let this therefore assure you of our loves, and everie yeare our friendly trade shall furnish you with corne; and now also if you would come in friendly manner to see us, and not thus with your gunnes and swords, as to invade your foes.

To this subtil discourse, the President thus replied.

Seeing you will not rightly conceave of our words, wee strive to make you knowe our thoughts by our deeds. The vow I made you of my love, both my selfe and my men have kept. As for your promise I finde it everie daie violated by some of your subjects; yet wee finding your love and kindnesse, our custome is so far from being ungratefull, that for your sake only, wee have curbed our thirsting desire of revenge, else had they [1] knowne as wel the crueltie we use to our enimies as our true love and curtesie to our friendes. And I thinke your judgement sufficient to conceive, as well by the adventures we have undertaken, as by the advantage we have by our armes, of yours: that had wee intended you anie hurt, long ere this we coulde have effected it. Your people comming to me at James towne, are entertained with their bowes and arrowes without

[1] Your Indians.

exception; we esteeming it with you, as it is with us, to weare our armes as our apparell. As for the dangers of our enimies, in such warres consist our chiefest pleasure. For your riches we have no use. As for the hiding your provision, or by your flying to the woods; we shall [not] so unadvisedly starve as you conclude: your friendly care in that behalfe is needlesse, for we have a rule to finde beyond your knowledge.

Manie other discourses they had, til at last they began to trade. But the king seing his will would not bee admitted as a lawe, our guard dispersed, nor our men disarmed; he, sighing, breathed his mind once more, in this manner.

Captaine Smith, I never used anie of Werowances so kindlie as your selfe; yet from you, I receave the least kindnesse of anie. Captaine Newport gave me swords, copper, cloths, a bed, tooles, or what I desired; ever taking what I offered him: and would send awaie his gunnes when I intreated him. None doth denie to laie at my feet, or do, what I desire, but onelie you; of whom I can have nothing but what you regard not: and yet you wil have whatsoever you demand. Captain Newport you call father, and so you call me: but I see, for all us both, you will doe what you list, and wee must both seeke to content you. But if you intend so friendlie as you saie, sende hence your armes that I may beleeve you: for you see the love I beare you, doth cause mee thus nakedlie forget my selfe.

Smith (seeing this Salvage but trifled the time, to cut his throat) procured the Salvages to breake the ice, that his boat might come to fetch both him and his corne; and gave order for his men to come ashore, to have surprised the king: with whom also, he but trifled the time till his men landed; and to keepe him from suspition, entertained the time with this reply.

Powhatan, you must knowe as I have but one God, I honour but one king: and I live not here as your subject, but as your friend to pleasure you with what I can. By the gifts you bestowe on me, you gaine more then by trade: yet would you visite mee as I doe you, you should knowe it is not our customes to sell our curtesie as a vendible commoditie. Bring all your Country with you for your gard, I will not dislike of it as being over jealous. But to content you, to-morrow I will leave my armes, and trust to your promise. I call you father indeed, and as a father you shall see I will love you: but the smal care you had of such a child, caused my men perswade me to shift for my selfe.

By this time, Powhatan having knowledge his men were readie; whilst the ice was breaking, his luggage, women and children fledde. And to avoid suspition left 2 or 3 of his women talking with the Captaine, whilst he secretly fled, and his men as secretlie beset the house. Which being at the instant discovered to Captaine Smith; with his Pistol, Sword and Target, he made such a passage amongst those naked divels that they fled before him, some one waie, some another: so that without hurt, he obtained[1] the Corps du guard. When they perceived him so well escaped, and with his 8 men (for he had no more with him), to the uttermost of their skill, they sought by excuses to dissemble the matter. And Powhatan, to excuse his flight and the suddaine comming of this multitude, sent our Captaine a greate bracelet and a chaine of pearle, by an ancient Orator that bespoke us to this purpose (perceiving then from our Pinnace, a barge and men departing and comming unto us.)

Captaine Smith, our Werowans is fled, fearing your guns; and knowing when the ice was broken, there would come more men, sent those of his, to guard his corne from the pilfrie that might happen without your knowledge. Now though some bee hurt by your misprison; yet he is your friend, and so wil continue. And since the ice is open, hee would have you send awaie your corne; and if you would have his companie, send also your armes, which so affrighteth this people that they dare not come to you, as he hath promised they should.

Nowe having provided baskets for our men to carrie the corne, they kindlie offered their service to gard our armes,

[1] Reached.

that none should steale them. A great manie they were, of goodlie well appointed fellowes, as grim as divels: yet the verie sight of cocking our matches against them, and a few words, caused them to leave their bowes and arrowes to our guard, and beare downe our corne on their own backes. Wee needed not importune them to make quick despatch. But our own barge being left by the ebb, caused us to staie till the midnight tide carried us safe abord.[1] Having spent that halfe night with such mirth as though we never had suspected or intended anything; we left the Dutchman to build, Brinton to kil fowle for Powhatan as by his messengers he importunately desired; and left directions with our men to give Powhatan all the content they could, that we might injoy his company at our returne from Pamaunke.

## CHAPTER IX

*How we escaped surprising at Pamaunke.*

Wee had no sooner set saile, but Powhatan returned, and sent Adam and Francis (2. stout Dutch men) to the fort: who fained to Captaine Winne that al things were well, and that Captaine Smith had use for their armes: wherefore they requested newe (the which were given them). They told him their comming was for some extraordinary tooles and shift of apparell. By this colourable excuse, they obtained 6. or 7. more to their confederacie, such expert theefes that presently furnished them with a great many swords, pike-heads, peeces, shot, powder, and such like. They had Salvages at hand ready to carry it away. The next day, they returned unsuspected, leaving their confederates to follow; and, in the interim, to convay them a competencie of all things they could: for which service, they should live with Powhatan as his chiefe affected, free from those miseries that would happen the Col-

[1] *I.e.*, to the pinnace.

ony. Samuell their other consort, Powhatan kept for their pledge; whose diligence had provided him 300. of their kinde of hatchets; the rest, 50. swords, 8. peeces, and 8. pikes. Brinton and Richard Salvage seeing the Dutch-men so strangly diligent to accommodate the Salvages these weapons, attempted to have got to James Towne; but they were apprehended: Within 2. or 3. daies, we arrived at Pamaunke: the king[1] as many daies entertained us with feasting and much mirth. And the day he appointed to begin our trade, the President, with Mr Persie, Mr West, Mr Russell, Mr Beheathland, Mr Powell, Mr Crashaw, Mr Ford, and some others, to the number of 15., went up to Opechancanougs house (near a quarter of a mile from the river); where we[2] founde nothing but a lame fellow and a boy, and all the houses about, of all things abandoned. Not long we staide ere the king arrived, and after him, came divers of his people loaded with bowes and arrowes; but such pinching commodities, and those esteemed at such a value, as our Captaine beganne with him, in this manner.

Opechancanough, the great love you professe with your tongue, seemes meere deceipt by your actions. Last yeare, you kindly fraughted our ship; but now you have invited me to starve with hunger. You know my want; and I, your plenty: of which, by some meanes, I must have part. Remember it is fit for kings to keepe their promise. Here are my commodities, whereof take your choice: the rest I will proportion fit bargaines for your people.

The king seemed kindly to accept this offer; and the better to colour his project, sold us what they had to our own content: promising the next day, more company, better provided. The barges and Pinnas being committed to the charge of Mr Phetiplace: the President, with his old 15, marched up to the kings house; where we found 4 or 5 men newly come with great baskets. Not long after came the king, who, with a strained

[1] *I.e.*, Opechancanough.

[2] Probably Richard Wiffin, W. Phettiplace and Anas Todkill, who wrote this portion of the work and probably went along with the party to Pamunkey

cheerefulnes, held us with discourse, what paines he had taken to keepe his promise, till Mr Russell brought us in news that we were all betraied, for at least 6. or 700.[1] of well appointed Indians had invironed the house and beset the fields. The king conjecturing what Russell related, we could wel perceive how the extremity of his feare bewrayed his intent. Whereat, some of our companie seeming dismaide with the thought of such a multitude, the Captaine incouraged us after this manner.

Worthy countrymen, were the mischiefes of my seeming friends no more then the danger of these enemies, I little cared, were they as many more, if you dare do but as I. But this is my torment, that if I escape them, our malicious councell,[2] with their open-mouthed minions, will make mee such a peace-breaker (in their opinions) in England, as wil break my neck. I could wish those here, that make these seeme Saints, and me an oppressor. But this is the worst of all, wherin I pray, aide me with your opinions. Should wee begin with them and surprize this king, we cannot keep him and defend well our selves. If we should each kill our man, and so proceede with al in this house, the rest will all fly: then shall we get no more then the bodies that are slaine, and then starve for victuall. As for their fury, it is the least danger. For well you know, being alone assaulted with 2 or 300 of them, I made them compound to save my life; and we are now 16 and they but 700. at the most; and assure your selves God wil so assist us, that if you dare but to stand to discharge your peeces, the very smoake will bee sufficient to affright them. Yet howsoever, if there be occasion, let us fight like men, and not die like sheep: but first I will deale with them to bring it to passe, we may fight for something, and draw them to it by conditions. If you like this motion, promise me youle [3] be valiant.

The time not permitting any argument, all vowed to execute whatsoever he attempted, or die. Whereupon the captaine approaching the king, bespoke him in this manner.

[1] Probably this number is greatly exaggerated.

[2] The council at this time consisted of Scrivener, Winn, and Waldo, who are spoken of quite highly by Smith's friends. The council in London had given strict orders to keep on good terms with the savages.

[3] You will.

I see Opechancanough, your plot to murder me; but I feare it not. As yet your men and mine have done no harme but by our directions. Take therefore your arms, you see mine. My body shalbe as naked as yours, the Ile in your river is a fit place, if you be contented; and the conqueror, of us two, shalbe Lord and Master over all our men. Otherwaies drawe all your men into the field, if you have not enough, take time to fetch more; and bring what number you will, so everie one bring a basket of corne: against all which, I will stake the value in copper. You see I have but 15 men, and our game shalbe, the conqueror take all.

The king, being guarded with 50 or 60 of his chiefe men, seemed kindly to appease Smiths suspition of unkindnesse, by a great present at the dore, they intreated him to receive. This was to draw him without the dore, where the present was garded with at the least 200 men, and 30 lying under a greate tree that lay thwart as a Barricado, each his arrow nocked ready to shoot. Some, the President commanded to go and see what kinde of deceit this was, and to receive the present; but they refused to do it: yet divers offered, whom he would not permit: but commanding Mr Persie and Mr West to make good the house, tooke Mr Poell and Mr Beheathland to guard the dore; and in such a rage, snatched the king by his vambrace,[1] in the midst of his men, with his pistoll ready bent against his brest. Thus he led the trembling king, neare dead with feare, amongst all his people; who delivering the Captaine his bow and arrowes, all his men were easily intreated to cast downe their armes, little dreaming anie durst in that manner have used their king: who then, to escape himselfe, bestowed his presents in good sadnesse. And having caused all his multitude to approach disarmed, the President argued with them to this effect.

I see, you Pamaunkies, the great desire you have to cut my throat, and my long suffering your injuries have imboldened you to this presumption. The cause I have forborne your insolencies is

[1] *I.e.*, the leather covering from the elbow to the wrist protecting the arm from the bow; elsewhere called "bracer."

the promise I made you, before the God I serve, to be your friend, till you give me just cause to bee your enimie. If I keepe this vow, my God will keepe mee; you cannot hurt mee: if I breake it, he will destroie me. But if you shoot but one arrow to shed one drop of blood of any of my men, or steale the least of these beades or copper I spurne before me with my foot; you shall see, I wil not cease revenge, if once I begin, so long as I can heare where to find one of your nation that will not deny the name of Pamaunke. I am not now at Rasseneac [1] halfe drownd with mire, where you tooke me prisoner: yet then, for keeping your promise, and your good usage, and saving my life, I so affect you, that your denials of your treacherie doth half perswade me to mistake my selfe. But if I be the marke you aime at, here I stand, shoote hee that dare. You promised to fraught my ship ere I departed; and so you shall, or I meane to load her with your dead carkases. Yet if as friends you wil come and trade, I once more promise not to trouble you, except you give me the first occasion.

Upon this, awaie went their bowes and arrowes; and men, women, and children brought in their commodities. But 2 or three houres they so thronged about the President, and so overwearied him, as he retired himself to rest, leaving Mr. Beheathland and Mr Powel to accept their presents. But some Salvage perceiving him fast asleepe, and the guard carelessly dispersed, 40 or 50 of their choice men each with an English sword in his hand, began to enter the house; with 2 or 300 others that pressed to second them. The noise and hast they made in, did so shake the house as they awoke him from his sleep; and being halfe amazed with this suddaine sight, betooke him straight to his sword and target; Mr Crashaw and some other charging in like manner, they thronged faster back, then before forward. The house thus clensed, the king and his ancients, with a long oration came to excuse this intrusion. The rest of the day was spent with much kindnesse: the company againe renuing their presents of their best provision. And whatsoever we gave them, they seemed well contented with it.

[1] Rawsenac.

Now in the meane while, since our departure, this hapned at the fort. Mr Scrivener willing to crosse [1] the surprizing of Powhatan, 9 daies after the Presidents departure, would needs visit the Ile of hogges; [2] and took with him Captaine Waldo (though the President had appointed him to bee readie to second his occasions) with Mr Antony Gosnoll and eight others: but so violent was the wind (that extreame frozen time) that the boat sunke; but where, or how, none doth knowe, for they were all drowned. Onlie this was knowne, that the Skiffe was much overloaded, and would scarse have lived in that extreme tempest had she beene emptie: but by no perswasion could hee bee diverted, though both Waldo and 100 others doubted as it hapned. The Salvages were the first that found their bodies, which so much the more encouraged them to effect their projects. To advertise the President of this heavie newes, none could bee found would undertake it: but the journey was often refused of all in the fort, untill Mr Wiffin undertooke alone the performance thereof. Wherein he was encountred with many dangers and difficulties; and in all parts as hee passed, as also that night he lodged with Powhatan, perceived such preparation for warre that assure[d] him some mischiefe was intended: but with extraordinarie bribes and much trouble, in three daies travell, at length, he found us in the midst of these turmoiles. This unhappie newes, the President swore him to conceale from the rest; and so, dissembling his sorrow with the best countenance he could, when the night approached, went safely abord with all his companie.

Now so extreamely Powhatan had threatned the death of his men, if they did not, by some meanes, kill Captaine Smith, that the next day they appointed the Countrie should come to trade unarmed: yet unwilling to be treacherous but that they were constrained, hating fighting almost as ill as hanging; such feare they had of bad successe. The next morning, the sunne had not long appeared, but the fieldes appeared covered with people, and baskets to tempt us ashore. The President

[1] Counterwork. [2] Hog Island, about seven miles from Jamestown.

determined to keepe abord; but nothing was to bee had with out his presence, nor would they not indure the sight of a gun. Then the President, seeing many depart, and being unwilling to lose such a booty, so well contrived the Pinnace and his barges with Ambuscadoes; as only with Mr Persie, Mr West, and Mr Russell armed, he went ashore. Others unarmed, he appointed to receive what was brought. The Salvages flocked before him in heapes, and (the bancke serving as a trench for retreat) hee drewe them faire open to his ambuscadoes. For he not being to be perswaded to go to visit their king, the King[1] came to visit him, with 2 or 300 men, in the forme of two halfe-moons, with some 20 men and many women loaded with great painted baskets. But when they approached somewhat neare us, their women and children fled. For when they had environed and beset the fieldes in this manner, they thought their purpose sure; yet so trembled with fear as they were scarse able to nock their arrowes. Smith standing with his 3 men readie bent, beholding them till they were within danger of our ambuscado; who, upon the word, discovered themselves, he retiring to the banke: which the Salvages no sooner perceived, but away they fled, esteeming their heeles for their best advantage.

That night, we sent to the fort Mr Crashaw and Mr Foard; who, in the midway betweene Werawocomoco and the fort, met 4 or 5. of the Dutch mens confederates going to Powhatan: the which (to excuse[2] those gentlemens Suspition, of their running to the Salvages) returned to the fort, and there continued.

The Salvages hearing our barge depart in the night,[3] were so terriblie afraide that we sent for more men (we having so much threatned their ruine, and the rasing of their houses, boats, and canowes), that the next day the King sent our Captaine a chaine of pearle to alter his purpose and stay his men; promising, though they wanted themselves, to fraught our ship, and to bring it abord to avoid suspition: so that, 5 or 6

[1] Opechancanough. [2] Remove. [3] With Crowshaw and Ford.

daies after, from al parts of the countrie within 10 or 12 miles, in the extreame cold frost and snow, they brought us provision on their naked backes.

Yet notwithstanding this kindnesse and trade, had their art and poison bin sufficient, the President with Master West and some others had been poysoned. It made them sicke but expelled it selfe. Wecuttanow, a stout yong fellow, knowing hee was suspected for bringing this present of poison, with 40 or 50. of his choice companions, seeing the President with but a few men at Pontauncat, so prowdlie braved it, as though he expected to incounter a revenge. Which the President perceiving, in the midst of his companie, did not onlie beat, but spurned him like a dogge, as scorning to doe him any worse mischiefe: whereupon all of them fled into the woods, thinking they had done a great matter to have so well escaped; and the townsmen remaining presentlie fraughted our barge, to bee rid of our companies, framing manie excuses to excuse Wecuttanow, being son to their chiefe king but Powhatan,[1] and told us if we would shew them him that brought the poyson, they would deliver him to us to punish as wee pleased.

Men maie thinke it strange there should be this stir for a little corne: but had it been gold with more ease wee might have got it; and had it wanted,[2] the whole colonie had starved. We maie be thought verie patient to indure all those injuries. Yet onlie with fearing[3] them, we got what they had: whereas if we had taken revenge, then by their losse, we should have lost our selvs. We searched also the countries of Youghtanund and Mattapamient, where the people imparted what little they had with such complaints and tears from women and children, as he had bin too cruell to be a Christian that would not have bin satisfied and moved with compassion.[4] But had this happened in October, November, and December, when that unhappie discoverie of Monacan was made; wee

[1] *I.e.*, their chief next in power to Powhatan.

[2] Been lacking.

[3] Frightening.

[4] The Indians were improvident, and their grief was real.

might have fraughted a ship of 40 tuns, and twice as much might have bin had from the rivers of Toppahannock, Patawomeck, and Pawtuxunt. The maine occasion of our temporizing with the Salvages was to part friends, as we did, to give the lesse cause of suspition to Powhatan to fly: by whom we now returned, with a purpose to have surprised him and his provision. For effecting whereof, when we came against the towne, the President sent Mr Wiffin and Mr Coe a shore, to discover and make waie for his intended project. But they found that those damned Dutchman had caused Powhatan to abandon his new house and werawocomoco, and to carrie awaie all his corne and provision: and the people, they found, by their means, so ill affected, that had they not stood well upon their guard, they had hardlie escaped with their lives. So the President finding his intention thus frustrated, and that there was nothing now to be had, and therefore an unfit time to revenge their abuses, helde on his course for James Towne: we having in this Jornie (for 25l of copper, 50l of Iron and beads) kept 40 men 6. weekes;[1] and dailie feasted with bread, corne, flesh, fish, and fowle. Everie man having for his reward (and in consideration of his commodities) a months provision, no trade being allowed but for the store; and we delivered at James Towne to the Cape Marchant, 279 bushels of corne.

Those temporall[2] proceedings, to some maie seeme too charitable, to such a dailie daring trecherous people; to others unpleasant that we washed not the ground with their blouds, nor shewed such strange inventions in mangling, murdering, ransaking, and destroying (as did the Spaniards) the simple bodies of those ignorant soules; nor delightful, because not stuffed with relations of heaps and mines of gold and silver, nor such rare commodities as the Portugals and Spaniards found in the East and West Indies. The want wherof hath begot us, that were the first undertakers, no lesse scorne and contempt, than their noble conquests and valiant adventures (beautified with it), praise and honor. Too much, I confesse,

[1] From December 29, 1608, to about February 8, 1609. [2] Temporizing.

the world cannot attribute to their ever memorable merit. And to cleare us from the worlds blind ignorant censure, these fewe words may suffise to any reasonably understanding.

It was the Spaniards good hap to happen in those parts where were infinite numbers of people, whoe had manured the ground with that providence that it afforded victuall at all times; and time had brought them to that perfection they had the use of gold and silver, and the most of such commodities as their countries affoorded: so that what the Spaniard got was only the spoile and pillage of those countrie people, and not the labours of their owne hands. But had those fruitfull Countries beene as Salvage, as barbarous, as ill-peopled, as little planted laboured and manured, as Virginia; their proper labours, it is likely would have produced as small profit as ours. But had Virginia bin peopled, planted, manured, and adorned with such store of pretious Jewels and rich commodities as was the Indies: then, had we not gotten and done as much as by their examples might bee expected from us, the world might then have traduced us and our merits, and have made shame and infamy our recompence and reward.

But we chanced in a lande, even as God made it. Where we found only an idle, improvident, scattered people, ignorant of the knowledge of gold, or silver, or any commodities; and carelesse of anything but from hand to mouth, but for bables of no worth; nothing to encourage us but what accidentally wee found nature afforded. Which ere wee could bring to recompence our paines, defray our charges, and satisfie our adventurers; we were to discover the country, subdue the people, bring them to be tractable civil and industrious, and teach them trades that the fruits of their labours might make us recompence, or plant such colonies of our owne that must first make provision how to live of themselves ere they can bring to perfection the commodities of the countrie: which doubtless will be as commodious for England as the west Indies for Spaine, if it be rightly managed; notwithstanding all our home-bred opinions that will argue the contrarie, as formerly such like have done against the Spaniards and Portugals. But to conclude, against all rumor of opinion I only say this for those that the three first yeares began this plantation: notwithstanding al their factions, mutenies, and miseries, so gently corrected and well prevented, peruse the Spanish *Decades*, the relations of M. Hacklut;[1] and tell mee how many ever, with such smal meanes as a barge of 2 Tunnes, sometimes with 7. 8. 9, or but at most 15 men, did ever discover so many faire and navigable rivers, subject so many severall kings people and nations to obedience and contribution, with so little bloud shed.

And if in the search of those Countries, wee had hapned where wealth had beene, we had as surely had it, as obedience and contribution; but if wee have overskipped it, we will not envy them that shall chance to finde it. Yet can wee not but lament it was our ill fortunes to end, when wee had but only learned how to begin, and found the right course how to proceed.

By Richard Wiffin, William Phettiplace, and Anas Todkill.

## CHAPTER X

### *How the Salvages became subject to the English.*

When the shippes departed[2] al the provision of the store but that the President had gotten, was so rotten with the last somers rain, and eaten with rats and wormes as the hogs would scarsely eat it; yet it was the souldiers diet till our returnes: so that wee found nothing done, but victuall spent, and the most part of our tooles, and a good part of our armes conveyed to the Salvages. But now, casting up the store and finding sufficient till the next harvest, the feare of starving

[1] Hakluyt. "The Spanish Decades" means such works as the *Decades* of Peter Martyr and the general histories of Oviedo and Herrera, organized in decades of ten books each.

[2] November, 1608.

was abandoned: and the company divided into tennes, fifteenes, or as the businesse required, 4 houres each day was spent in worke, the rest in pastimes and merry exercise. But the untowardnesse of the greatest number caused the President to make a generall assembly; and then he advised them as followeth.

Countrimen, the long experience of our late miseries, I hope is sufficient to perswade every one to a present correction of himselfe; and thinke not that either my pains, or the adventurers purses, will ever maintaine you in idlenesse and sloth. I speake not this to you all; for diverse of you, I know, deserve both honor and reward better then is yet here to bee had; but the greater part must be more industrious, or starve. Howsoever you have bin heretofore tolerated by the authoritie of the Councell from that I have often commanded you: yet seeing nowe the authoritie resteth wholly in my selfe, you must obay this for a law, that he that will not worke, shall not eate, except by sicknesse he be disabled. For the labours of 30 or 40 honest and industrious men shall not bee consumed to maintaine 150 idle varlets. Now though you presume the authoritie here is but a shaddow, and that I dare not touch the lives of any but my own must answer it; the letters patents each week shall be read you, whose contents will tell you the contrary. I would wish you therefore, without contempt, seeke to observe these orders set downe; for there are now no more Councells to protect you, nor curbe my indeavours. Therefore hee that offendeth, let him assuredly expect his due punishment.

Hee made also a table [1] as a publike memoriall of every mans deserts, to encourage the good, and with shame to spurne on the rest to amendment. By this, many became very industrious: yet more by severe punishment performed their businesse; for all were so tasked, that there was no excuse could prevail to deceive him. Yet the Dutchmens consorts so closely still convai[e]d powder, shot, swords, and tooles; that though we could find the defect, we could not find by whom it was occasioned, till it was too late.

[1] Notice board.

All this time, the Dutchmen remaining with Powhatan, received them, instructing the Salvages their use. But their consorts not following them as they expected, to know the cause, they sent Francis their companion, a stout young fellow, disguised Salvage like, to the glasse-house,[1] a place in the woods neere a myle from James Towne, where was the randavus for all their unsuspected villany. 40 men, they procured of Powhatan to lie in Ambuscadoe for Captaine Smith; who no sooner heard of this Dutchman, but hee sent to apprehend him. Who found he was gon; yet to crosse[2] his returne to Powhatan, Captaine Smith presently dispatched 20 shot after him. And then returning but from the glasse-house alone, hee incountred the King of Paspaheigh, a most strong stout Salvage; whose perswasions not being able to perswade him to his ambush, seeing him only armed but with a fauchion,[3] attempted to have shot him. But the President prevented his shot by grapling with him; and the Salvage as well prevented him from drawing his fauchion, and perforce bore him into the river to have drowned him. Long they struggled in the water, from whence the king perceiving two of the Poles upon the sandes, would have fled: but the President held him by the haire and throat til the Poles came in. Then seeing howe pittifully the poore Salvage begged his life, they conducted him prisoner to the fort. The Dutchman ere long was also brought in, whose villany (though all this time it was suspected), yet he fained such a formall excuse that for want of language[4] Win had not rightly understood them: and for their dealings with Powhatan, that to save their lives, they were constrained to accommodate [him with] his armes; of whome he extreamely complained to have detained them perforce, and that hee made his escape with the hazard of his life, and meant not to have returned but only walked in the woods to gather walenuts. Yet for all this faire tale, there was so smal appearance of truth, hee went by the

[1] The glass-house was erected about this time on the mainland, at the west end of the connecting neck.

[2] Prevent.

[3] Falchion.

[4] He spoke Dutch or German (High Dutch).

heeles.[1] The king also he put in fetters, purposing to regaine the Dutch-men, by the saving his life. The poore Salvage did his best, by his daily messengers to Powhatan, but all returned [2] that the Dutchmen would not return: neither did Powhatan stay them; and bring them fiftie myles on their backes,[3] they were not able. Daily this kings wives children and people came to visit him with presents, which hee liberally bestowed to make his peace. Much trust they had in the Presidents promise: but the king finding his gard negligent, though fettered yet escaped. Captaine Win thinking to pursue him, found such troopes of Salvages to hinder his passages, as they exchanged many volies of shot for flights of arrowes. Captaine Smith hearing of this, in returning to the fort, tooke two Salvages prisoners: the one called Kemps, the other Kinsock; the two most exact villaines in the countrie. With those, Captaine Win and 50 chosen men attempted that night to have regained the king, and revenged his injurie. And so had done, if he had followed his directions, or bin advised by those two villaines (that would have betraied both their king and kindred for a peece of copper); but hee trifling away the night, the Salvages, the next morning by the rising of the sunne, braved him come a shore to fight. A good time both sides let flie at other; but wee heard of no hurt. Only they tooke two Canows, burnt the kings house; and so returned.

The President fearing those bravadoes would but incourage the Salvages, begun himself to trie his conclusions; whereby 6 or 7 Salvages were slaine, as many made prisoners; burnt their houses; tooke their boats with all their fishing weares, and planted them at James Towne for his owne use: and now resolved not to cease till he had revenged himselfe upon al that had injured him. But in his journey, passing by Paspaheigh towards Chickahamina, the Salvages did their best to draw him to their ambuscadoes: but seeing him regardlesly passe their Countrey, all shewed themselves in their bravest manner, to trie their valours. He could not but

[1] Was put in irons. [2] Answered. [3] Overland from Oropaks.

let flie, and ere he could land, the Salvages no sooner knewe him, but they threw downe their armes and desired peace. Their Orator was a stout young man called Ocanindge; whose worthie discourse deserveth to be remembered. And this it was.

Captaine Smith, my master is here present in this company, thinking it Captaine Win, and not you; and of him, hee intended to have beene revenged, having never offended him. If hee have offended you in escaping your imprisonment, the fishes swim, the fowles flie, and the very beastes strive to escape the snare and live: then blame not him being a man. Hee would entreat you remember your being a prisoner, what paines he tooke to save your life. If since he hath injured you, he was compelled to it; but, howsoever, you have revenged it with our too great losse. We perceive and well knowe you intend to destroy us, that are here to intreat and desire your friendship, and to enjoy our houses and plant our fields, of whose fruit you shall participate: otherwise you will have the worst by our absence. For we can plant any where, though with more labour; and we know you cannot live if you want our harvest and that reliefe wee bring you. If you promise us peace, we will beleeve you; if you proceed in reveng, we will abandon the Countrie.

Upon these tearmes the President promised them peace till they did us injury, upon condition they should bring in provision. So all departed good friends, and so continued till Smith left the Countrie.

Ariving at James Towne, complaint was made to the President that the Chickahaminos, who al this while continued trade and seemed our friendes, by colour thereof were the only theeves; and amongst other things, a pistol being stolne and the theefe fled, there were apprehended 2 proper young fellows that were brothers, knowne to be his confederats. Now to regain this pistoll, the one we imprisoned; the other was sent, to returne againe within 12 houres, or his brother to be hanged. Yet the President pittying the poore naked Salvage in the dungeon, sent him victuall and some charcole for fire. Ere midnight his brother returned with the pistoll: but the poore Salvage in the dungeon was so smothered with the smoke he had made, and so pittiously burnt that wee found him dead. The other most lamentably bewailed his death, and broke forth in such bitter agonies, that the President, to quiet him, told him that if hereafter they would not steal, he wold make him alive againe: but little thought hee could be recovered. Yet we doing our best with aquavitæ and vinegar, it pleased God to restore him againe to life: but so drunke and affrighted that he seemed lunaticke, not understanding any thing hee spoke or heard; the which as much grieved and tormented the other, as before to see him dead. Of which maladie, upon promise of their good behaviour afterward, the President promised to recover him; and so caused him to be laid by a fire to sleepe: who in the morning, having well slept, had recovered his perfect senses. And then being dressed of his burning, and each a peece of copper given them; they went away so well contented, that this was spread amongst all the Salvages for a miracle, that Captaine Smith could make a man alive that is dead. These and many other such pretty accidents so amazed and affrighted both Powhatan and all his people, that from all parts with presents they desired peace; returning many stolne things which wee neither demaunded nor thought of. And after that, those that were taken stealing, both Powhatan and his people have sent them backe to James Towne to receive their punishment; and all the countrie became absolutely as free for us, as for themselves.

## CHAPTER XI

*What was done in three monthes having victuall. The store devoured by rats. How we lived 3 monthes of such naturall fruits as the countrie afforded.*

Now wee so quietly followed our businesse that in 3 monthes, we made 3 or 4 Last[1] of pitch, and tarre, and sope ashes; produced a triall of glasse; made a well in the forte of excellent

[1] A last of pitch or tar is fourteen barrels; of ashes, twelve.

sweete water, which till then was wanting; built some 20 houses; re-covered our Church; provided nets and weares for fishing; and to stop the disorders of our disorderly theeves and the Salvages, built a blocke house in the necke of our Ile,[1] kept by a garrison, to entertaine the Salvages trade, and none to passe or repasse, Salvage nor Christian, without the Presidents order; 30 or 40 acres of ground, we digged and planted; of 3 sowes, in one yeare increased 60 and od pigges; and neere 500 chickens brought up themselves, without having any meate [2] given them: but the hogges were transported to Hog Ile, where also we built a blocke house, with a garrison, to give us notice of any shipping; and for their exercise, they made clapbord, wainscot, and cut downe trees against the ships comming. We built also a fort for a retreat, neare a convenient river, upon a high commanding hill, very hard to be assaulted, and easie to be defended:[3] but ere it was halfe finished, this defect caused a stay. In searching our casked corne, wee found it halfe rotten: and the rest so consumed with the many thousand rats, increased first from the ships, that we knewe not how to keepe that little wee had. This did drive us all to our wits ende; for there was nothing in the countrie but what nature afforded.[4] Untill this time Kemps and Tassore were fettered prisoners, and daily wrought; and taught us how to order and plant our fields: whom now, for want of victuall, we set at libertie; but so wel were they used, that they little desired it. And to express their loves, for 16 daies continuance, the Countrie brought us (when least) 100 a daie of squirrils, Turkies, Deare, and other wilde beastes. But this want of corne occasioned the end of all our workes, it being worke sufficient to provide victuall. 60 or 80 with Ensigne Laxon were sent downe the river to live upon oysters: and 20 with

[1] Jamestown Peninsula.

[2] Food.

[3] A mile up Gray's Creek (formerly Rolfe's Creek), opposite to Jamestown, is a bluff still called Smith's Fort, protected by water on three sides. It appears under this name in the land-grants as early as 1635.

[4] This condition of things was not very creditable to Smith's circumspection.

lieftenant Percie to trie for fishing at point Comfort, but in 6 weekes, they would not agree once to cast out their net. Mr West, with as many, went up to the falles; but nothing could bee found but a fewe berries and acornes. Of that in the store, every one had their equall proportion. Till this present, by the hazard and endeavour of some 30 or 40, this whole number had ever been fed. Wee had more Sturgeon then could be devoured by dogge and man; of which, the industrious by drying and pownding, mingled with caviare, sorrel and other wholsome hearbs, would make bread and good meate. Others would gather as much Tockwough roots in a day as would make them bread a weeke. So that of those wilde fruites, fish, and berries these lived very well, in regard of such a diet. But such was the most strange condition of some 150, that had they not beene forced nolens volens perforce to gather and prepare their victuall, they would all have starved, and have eaten one another. Of those wild fruites, the Salvages often brought us: and for that the President would not fulfill the unreasonable desire of those distracted lubberly gluttons, to sell not only our kettles, howes, tooles, and Iron, nay swords, peeces, and the very ordenance and houses (might they have prevailed but to have beene but idle) for those salvage fruits, they would have imparted all to the Salvages. Especially for one basket of corne they heard of to bee at Powhatans, 50 myles from our fort: though he bought neere halfe of it to satisfie their humours; yet to have had the other halfe, they would have sold their soules, though not sufficient to have kept them a weeke. Thousands were their exclamations, suggestions, and devises to force him to those base inventions, to have made it an occasion to abandon the Countrie. Want perforce constrained him to indure their exclaiming follies, till he found out the author, one Dyer, a most craftie knave, and his ancient maligner; whom he worthely punished: and with the rest, he argued the case, in this manner,

Fellow souldiers, I did little thinke any so false to report, or so many so simple to be perswaded, that I either intend to starve you; or that Powhatan at this present hath corne for himselfe, much lesse for you: or that I would not have it, if I knewe where it were to be had. Neither did I thinke any so malitious as nowe I see a great many: yet it shall not so much passionate me, but I will doe my best for my worst maligner. But dreame no longer of this vaine hope from Powhatan; nor that I wil longer forbeare to force you from your Idlenesse, and punish you if you raile. You cannot deny but that by the hazard of my life, many a time I have saved yours; when (might your owne wils have prevailed) you would have starved, and will doe still whether I will or no. But I protest by that God that made me, since necessitie hath not power to force you to gather for your selvs those fruits the earth doth yeeld; you shall not only gather for your selves, but for those that are sicke. As yet I never had more from the store then the worst of you, and all my English extraordinarie provision [1] that I have, you shall see mee devide among the sick.

And this Salvage trash you so scornfully repine at, being put in your mouthes, your stomacks can digest it; and therefore I will take a course you shall provide it. The sicke shal not starve, but equally share of all our labours; and every one that gathereth not every day as much as I doe, the next daie, shall be set beyond the river, and for ever bee banished from the fort: and live there or starve.

This order, many murmured, was very cruell. But it caused the most part so well bestir themselves that of 200 men (except they were drowned), there died not past 7 or 8. As for Captaine Win and Mr Ley, they died ere this want happened: and the rest died not for want of such as preserved the rest. Many were billitted among the Salvages, whereby we knewe all their passages, fieldes, and habitations; how to gather and use their fruits as well as themselves.

So well those poore Salvages used us, that were thus Billited, as divers of the souldiers ran away, to search [2] Kemps our old prisoner. Glad was this Salvage to have such an occasion to testifie his love, for insteed of entertaining them and such things as they had stolne, with all the great offers and promises they made them (to revenge their injuries upon

[1] Private provisions. [2] Search for.

Captaine Smith): First, he made himselfe sport, in shewing his countrymen, by them, how he was used; feeding them with this law, who would not worke must not eat, till they were neere starved; continuallie threatning to beate them to death. Neither could they get from him, til perforce he brought them to our Captaine, that so we contented him, and punished them; as manie others that intended also to have followed them, were rather contented to labour at home then adventure to live Idle among the Salvages; of whom there was more hope to make better christians and good subjects, then the one halfe of those that counterfeited themselves both. For so afeard were all those kings and the better sorte of their people to displease us, that some of the baser sort that we have extreamlie hurt and punished for their villanies, would hire us, that we should not tell it to their kings or countrymen, who would also repunish them, and yet returne them to James Towne to content the President, by that testimonie of their loves.

Mr Sicklemore well returned from Chawonock, but found little hope and lesse certainetie of them [that] were left by Sir Walter Rawley.[1] So that Nathaniell Powell and Anas Todkill were also, by the Quiyoughquohanocks, conducted to the Mangoages to search them there. But nothing could we learne but they were all dead. This honest, proper, good promis-keeping king, of all the rest, did ever best affect us, and though to his false Gods he was yet very zealous; yet he would confesse, our God as much exceeded his, as our guns did his bowe and arrowes: often sending our President manie presents to praie to his God for raine, or his corne would perish; for his Gods were angrie all this time. To reclaime the Dutchmen, and one Bentley an other fugitive, we imploied one William Volda (a Switzer by birth), with pardons and promises to regaine them. Litle we then suspected this double villanie of anie villain, who plainly taught us, in the most trust was the greatest treason. For this wicked hypocrit, by the seeming hate he bore to the lewd condition of his cursed countrimen,

[1] In 1587. See p. 17, note 2.

having this opportunitie, by his imploiment to regaine them, conveighed them everie thing they desired to effect their project to destroie the colonie. With much devotion they expected the Spanyard, to whom they intended to have done good service. But to begin with the first oportunitie, they seeing necessitie thus inforced us to disperse our selves, importuned Powhatan to lend them but his forces, and they would not onlie destroie our hogs, fire our towne, and betraie our Pinnas: but bring to his service and subjection the most part of our companies. With this plot they had acquainted manie discontents; and manie were agreed to their divelish practise. But Thomas Douese and Thomas Mallard, whose christian harts much relenting at such an unchristian act, voluntarily revealed it to Captaine Smith: who did his best it might be concealed, perswading Douese and Malard to proceed in the confederacie, onlie to bring the irreclamable Dutch men and inconstant Salvages in such a maner amongst his ambuscadoes as he had prepared, as not manie of them shoulde ever have returned from out our peni[n]sula. But this brute comming to the ears of the impatient multitude, they so importuned the President to cut of[f] those Dutchmen, as amongst manie that offered to cut their throates before the face of Powhatan, Master Wiffin and Jefra Abot were sent to stab or shoot them. But these Dutch men made such excuses, accusing Volday (whom they supposed had revealed their project), as Abbot would not; yet Wiffin would, perceiving it but deceipt. The king understanding of this their imploiment, sent presentlie his messengers to Captaine Smith to signifie it was not his fault to detaine them, nor hinder his men from executing his command; nor did he, nor would he maintaine them or anie, to occasion his displeasure. But ere this busines was brought to a point, God having seene our misery sufficient, sent in Captaine Argall [1] to fish for Sturgion, with a ship well furnished with wine and bisket; which, though it was not sent us, such

[1] The celebrated Captain Samuel Argall, navigator, destroyer (1613) of the French settlements on Mt. Desert and at Port Royal, deputy-governor of Virginia 1617–1619, and a member from 1622 of the Council for New England.

were our occasions we tooke it at a price: but left him sufficient to returne for England. Still dissembling Valdo his villany; but certainlie hee had not escaped, had the President continued.

By this you may see, for all those crosses, treacheries, and dissentions; howe he wrastled and overcame (without bloud shed) all that hapned: also what good was done, how few died, what food the country naturally affordeth; what small cause there is men should starve, or be murdered by the Salvages, that have discretion to manage this [1] courage and industry. The 2. first years though by his adventures he had oft brought the Salvages to a tractable trade, yet you see how the envious authority ever crossed him, and frustrated his best endeavours. Yet this wrought in him that experience and estimation among the Salvages, as otherwaies it had bin impossible he had ever effected that he did. Though the many miserable yet generous and worthy adventures he had long and oft indured as wel in some parts of Africa and America, as in the most partes of Europe and Asia, by land or sea, had taught him much: yet, in this case, he was againe to learne his Lecture [2] by experience; which with thus much a doe having obtained, it was his ill chance to end when hee had but onlie learned how to begin. And though hee left these unknowne difficulties (made easie and familiar) to his unlawfull successors; whoe onlie by living in James Towne, presumed to know more then al the world could direct them; though they had all his souldiers, with their triple power, and twise triple better meanes: by what they have done in his absence, the world doth see; and what they would have done in his presence, had he not prevented their indiscretions — it doth justlie approve what cause he had to send them for England. But they have made it more plaine since their returne: having his absolute authoritie freely in their power, with all the advantages and opportunity that his labours had effected. As I am sorry their actions have made it so manifest, so am I unwilling to say what reason doth compell me to make apparant the truth, least I should seeme partial, reasonlesse, or malitious.

[1] Manage *with*. [2] Lesson.

## CHAPTER XII

### *The Arival of the third supply.*

To redresse those jarres and ill proceedings, the Councell in England altered the governement: and devolved the authoritie to the Lord De-la-ware. Who for his deputie, sent Sir Thomas Gates and Sir George Somers.[1] With 9 ships and 500 persons, they set saile from England in May 1609. A small catch perished at sea in a *Herycano*. The Admiral,[2] with 150 men, with the two knights and their new commission, their bils of loading with al manner of directions, and the most part of their provision, arived not. With the other 7, as Captaines, arived Ratliffe (whose right name was Sickelmore), Martin, and Archer: who as they had been troublesome at sea, beganne againe to marre all ashore. For though, as is said, they were formerly deposed and sent for England: yet now returning againe, graced by the title of *Captaines of the passengers*, seeing the admirall wanting, and great probabilitie of her losse, strengthned themselves with those newe companies, so railing and exclaiming against Captaine Smith, that they mortally hated him ere ever they see his face. Who understanding by his scouts, the arivall of such a fleet, little dreaming of any such supply, supposing them Spaniards, hee so determined and ordered his affaires as wee little feared their arivall, nor the successe of our incounter: nor were the Salvages any way negligent or unwilling to aide and assist

[1] This is an error. Sir Thomas Gates was given the first commission as governor of Virginia. Lord Delaware was second governor, though the office was given him for life. Sir Thomas Gates, a soldier in the Elizabethan and Low-Country wars, was one of the original incorporators of the Virginia Company, and is named first in the charter; governor, 1609–1610, 1611–1614; a member of the Council of New England established in 1620. Sir George Somers had commanded important naval expeditions in the last years of Queen Elizabeth, and had been a member of Parliament under King James.

[2] Admiral in the sense of flagship; the *Sea Venture,* wrecked on the Bermuda Islands.

us with their best power. Had it so beene, wee had beene happy. For we would not have trusted them but as our foes; whereas receiving those as our countriemen and friends, they did their best to murder our President, to surprise the store, the fort, and our lodgings; to usurp the governement, and make us all their servants, and slaves to our owne merit. To 1000 mischiefes these lewd Captaines led this lewd company, wherein were many unruly gallants packed thether by their friends to escape il destinies: and those would dispose and determine of the governement, sometimes one, the next day another, to day the old commission, to morrow the new, the next day by neither. In fine, they would rule all or ruine all. Yet in charitie, we must endure them thus to destroy us; or by correcting their follies, have brought the worlds censure upon us, to have beene guiltie of their bloods. Happy had we bin had they never arrived, and we for ever abandoned and (as we were) left to our fortunes: for on earth was never more confusion or miserie then their factions occasioned.

The President seeing the desire those braves had to rule, seeing how his authoritie was so unexpectedly changed, would willingly have left all and have returned for England: but seeing there was smal hope this newe commission would arive, longer hee would not suffer those factious spirits to proceed. It would bee too tedious, too strange, and almost incredible, should I particularly relate the infinite dangers, plots, and practises hee daily escaped amongst this factious crue; the chiefe whereof he quickly laid by the heeles, til his leasure better served to doe them justice. And to take away al occasions of further mischiefe, Mr Persie had his request granted, to returne for England: and Mr West[1] with 120 went to plant at the falles; Martin with neare as many to Nansamund; with their due proportions of all provisions, according to their numbers.

Now the Presidents yeare being neere expired, he made Martin President: who knowing his own insufficiencie, and

[1] Francis West, afterward deputy-governor of Virginia, a younger brother of Lord Delaware.

the companies scorne, and conceit of his unworthinesse, within 3 houres, resigned it againe to Captane Smith: and at Nansamund thus proceeded. The people being contributers used him kindly. Yet such was his jealous feare and cowardize, in the midst of his mirth, hee did surprize this poore naked king, with his monuments, houses, and the Ile he inhabited; and there fortified himselfe, but so apparantly distracted with fear as imboldned the Salvages to assalt him, kill his men, redeeme their king, gather and carrie away more then 1000 bushels of corne, hee not once daring to intercept them: but sent to the President, then at the Falles, for 30 good shotte, which from James towne immediatly were sent him. But hee so well imploid them, as they did just nothing; but returned, complaining of his childishnesse, that with them fled from his company, and so left them to their fortunes.

Master West having seated his men at the Falles, presently returned to revisit James Towne. The President met him by the way, as he followed him to the falles: where he found this company so inconsiderately seated in a place, not only subject to the rivers inundation, but round invironed with many intollerable inconveniences.

For remedy whereof, he sent presently to Powhatan, to sell him the place called Powhatan, promising to defend him against the Monacans, and these should be his conditions: with his people, to resigne him the fort and houses and all that countrie for a proportion of copper. That all stealing offenders should bee sent him, there to receive their punishment. That every house as a custome [1] should pay him a bushell of corne for an inch square of copper, and a proportion of *Pocones* as a yearely tribute to King James for their protection, as a dutie: what else they could spare, to barter at their best discreation.

But both this excellent place and those good conditions did those furies [2] refuse, contemning both him, his kind care, and authoritie. The worst they could to shew their spite, they

[1] Tax.

[2] West's men.

did. I doe more then wonder to thinke how only with 5 men, he either durst, or would adventure as he did (knowing how greedy they were of his blood) to land amongst them, and commit to imprisonment the greatest spirits amongst them, till by their multitudes, being 120, they forced him to retire. Yet in that retreate, hee surprised one of the boates, wherewith hee returned to their shippe wherein was their provisions, which also hee tooke. And well it chaunced hee found the marriners so tractable and constant, or there had beene small possibility he had ever escaped. Notwithstanding there were many of the best, I meane of the most worthy in Judgement, reason, or experience, that from their first landing, hearing the generall good report of his old souldiers, and seeing with their eies his actions so wel managed with discretion (as Captaine Wood, Captaine Web, Captaine Mone, Captaine Phitz-James, Mr Partridge, Mr White, Mr Powell, and divers others): when they perceived the malice and condition of Ratliffe, Martin, and Archer, left their factions, and ever rested his faithfull friends. But the worst was, the poore Salvages that dailie brought in their contribution to the President. That disorderlie company so tormented those poore naked soules, by stealing their corne, robbing their gardens, beating them, breaking their houses, and keeping some prisoners, that they dailie complained to Captaine Smith he had brought them for protectors worst enimies then the Monocans themselves: which though till then, for his love, they had indured, they desired pardon, if hereafter they defended themselves, since he would not correct them, as they had long expected he would. So much they importuned him to punish their misdemeanores, as they offered, if hee would conduct them, to fight for him against them. But having spent 9. daies in seeking to reclaime them, shewing them how much they did abuse themselves with their great guilded hopes of seas, mines, commodities, or victories they so madly conceived; then, seing nothing would prevaile with them, he set saile for James Towne. Now no sooner was the ship under saile, but the Salvages assaulted those 120 in their fort, finding some stragling abroad in the woods, they slew manie; and so affrighted the rest as their prisoners escaped, and they scarse retired, with the swords and cloaks of these they had slaine. But ere we [1] had sailed a league, our shippe grounding, gave us once more libertie to summon them to a parlie. Where we found them all so strangelie amazed with this poore simple assault as they submitted themselves upon anie tearmes to the Presidents mercie: who presentlie put by the heels [2] 6 or 7 of the chiefe offenders. The rest he seated gallantlie at Powhatan in their Salvage fort, they built and pretilie fortified with poles and barkes of trees sufficient to have defended them from all the Salvages in Virginia, drie houses for lodgings, 300 acres of grounde readie to plant; and no place so strong, so pleasant and delightful in Virginia, for which we called it Nonsuch. The Salvages also he presentlie appeased, redelivering to every one their former losses. Thus al were friends, new officers appointed to command, and the President againe readie to depart. But at that instant arrived Mr West, whose good nature, with the perswasions and compassion of [3] those mutinous prisoners, was so much abused, that to regaine their old hopes, new turboiles [4] arose. For the rest, being possessed of al their victuall, ammunition and everie thing; they grow to that height in their former factions, as there the President left them to their fortunes: they returning againe to the open aire at West Fort, abandoning Nonsuch; and he to James Towne with his best expedition. But this hapned him in that Journie: [5]

Sleeping in his boat, for the ship was returned 2 daies before, accidentallie one fired his powder bag; which tore his flesh from his bodie and thighes 9. or 10. inches square, in a most pittifull manner: but to quench the tormenting fire, frying him in his cloaths, he leaped over board into the deepe river, where ere they could recover him, he was neere drownd. In this estat, without either Chirurgeon or chirurgery, he was to

[1] Richard Pott and William Phettiplace. [2] Put in irons.

[3] By the persuasions of, and through his compassion for.

[4] Dissensions. [5] About the beginning of September, 1609.

go neare 100. miles.[1] Ariving at James Towne, causing[2] all things to bee prepared for peace or warres,[3] to obtain provision. Whilest those things were providing, Martin, Ratliffe, and Archer being to have their trials, their guiltie consciences fearing a just reward for their deserts, seeing the President unable to stand, and neare bereft of his senses by reason of his torment; they had plotted to have murdered him in his bed. But his hart did faile him,[4] that should have given fire to that mercilesse pistol. So, not finding that course to be the best, they joined togither to usurp the governement, thereby to escape their punishment, and excuse themselves by accusing him. The President had notice of their projects, the which to withstand, though his old souldiers importuned him but permit them to take of[f] their heads that would resist his commaund; yet he would not permit them: but sent for the masters of the ships, and tooke order with them, for his returne for England.

Seeing there was neither chirurgeon nor chirurgery in the fort to cure his hurt, and the ships to depart the next daie; his commission to be suppressed, he knew not why; himselfe and souldiers to be rewarded, he knew not how; and a new commission graunted, they knew not to whom, the which so disabled that authority he had, as made them presume so oft to those mutinies and factions as they did. Besides so grievous were his wounds and so cruell his torment few expected he could live; nor was hee able to follow his businesse, to regaine what they had lost, suppresse those factions, and range the countries for provision as he intended, and well he knew in those affaires his own actions and presence were as requisit as his experience and directions, which now could not be: he went presently abord, resolving there to appoint them governours, and to take order for the mutiners and their confederates. Who seeing him gone, perswaded Master Persie to stay, and be their President: and within lesse then an howre was this mutation begun and concluded. For when the company

[1] The distance by water from Powhatan to Jamestown was about 68 miles.
[2] He caused. [3] After "warres" supply "and." [4] Coe or Dyer.

understood Smith would leave them, and see the rest in Armes called Presidents and councellors; divers began to fawne on those new commanders, that now bent all their wits to get him resigne them his commission. Who, after many salt and bitter repulses, that their confusion should not be attributed to him (for leaving the country without government and authority), having taken order to bee free from danger of their malice, he was not unwilling they should steale it from him, but never consented to deliver it to any. But had that unhappy blast not hapned, he would quickly have quallified the heate of those humors and factions, had the ships but once left them and us to our fortunes; and have made that provision from among the Salvages as we neither feared Spanyard, Salvage, nor famine: nor would have left Virginia, nor our lawfull authoritie, but at as deare a price as we had bought it, and paid for it.

What shall I say? but thus we lost him that, in all his proceedings, made Justice his first guid, and experience his second; ever hating basenesse, sloth, pride, and indignitie more then any dangers; that never allowed more for himselfe then his souldiers with him; that upon no danger, would send them where he would not lead them himselfe; that would never see us want what he either had, or could by any meanes get us; that would rather want then borrow, or starve then not pay; that loved actions more than wordes, and hated falshood and cousnage worse then death; whose adventures were our lives, and whose losse our deathes. Leaving us [1] thus, with 3 ships, 7 boates, commodities ready to trade, the harvest newly gathered, 10 weekes provision in the store, 490 and odde persons, 24 peeces of ordinances, 300 muskets snaphanches and fire lockes,[2] shot powder and match sufficient; curats, pikes, swords, and moryons more then men; the Salvages their language and habitations wel knowne to 100 well trained and expert souldiers, nets for fishing, tooles of all sortes

[1] About October 4, 1609.

[2] A snaphance was fired by flint and steel, a firelock by means of a match. Curat, below, means a cuirass; a morion was a steel cap.

to worke, apparell to supply our wants, 6 mares and a horse, 5 or 600 swine, as many hens and chicken, some goates, some sheep. What was brought or bread there remained.[1] But they regarded nothing but from hand to mouth, to consume that we had; tooke care for nothing, but to perfit[2] some colourable complaints aganst Captaine Smith. For effecting whereof, 3 weekes longer they stayed the 6 ships till they could produce them. That time and charge might much better have beene spent; but it suted well with the rest of their discreations.

Now all those Smith had either whipped, punished, or any way disgraced, had free power and liberty to say or sweare any thing; and from a whole armefull of their examinations this was concluded.

The mutiners at the Falles complained he caused the Salvages assalt them, for that hee would not revenge their losse (they being but 120, and he 5 men and himselfe): and this they proved by the oath of one hee had oft whipped for perjurie and pilfering. The dutchmen that he had appointed to bee stabd for their treacheries, swore he sent to poison them with rats baine. The prudent Councel that he would not submit himselfe to their stolne authoritie. Coe and Dyer that should have murdered him, were highly preferred for swearing they heard one say, he heard Powhatan say, that he heard a man say, if the king would not send that corne he had, he should not long enjoy his copper crowne, nor those robes he had sent him: yet those also swore hee might have had corne for tooles but would not. (The truth was, Smith had no such ingins[3] as the King demanded, nor Powhatan any corne. Yet this argued he would starve them.) Others complained hee would not let them rest in the fort (to starve), but force them to the oyster banks, to live or starve (as he lived himselfe). For though hee had of his owne private provisions sent from

[1] As many of these articles had been brought in by the newcomers, Smith was not entitled to the full credit. According to his own statement the colony was "at its wit's end," by the rats, and quartered all about among the Indians, when the newcomers arrived.

[2] Perfect. [3] Engines, *i.e.* tools.

England, sufficient; yet hee gave it all away to the weake and sicke: causing the most untoward (by doing as he did) to gather their food from the unknowne parts of the rivers and woods, that they lived (though hardly), that otherwaies would have starved ere they would have left their beds, or at most the sight of James Towne, to have got their own victuall. Some propheticall spirit calculated hee had the Salvages in such subjection, hee would have made himselfe a king, by marrying Pocahontas, Powhatans daughter. (It is true she was the very Nonparell of his kingdome, and at most not past 13 or 14 yeares of age. Very oft shee came to our fort, with what shee could get for Captaine Smith; that ever loved and used all the Countrie well, but her especially he ever much respected: and she so well requited it, that when her father intended to have surprized him, shee by stealth in the darke night came through the wild woods and told him of it. But her marriage could no way have intitled him by any right to the kingdome, nor was it ever suspected hee had ever such a thought; or more regarded her, or any of them, than in honest reason and discreation he might. If he would, he might have married her, or have done what him listed; for there was none that could have hindred his determination.) Some that knewe not any thing to say, the Councel instructed and advised what to sweare. So diligent they were in this businesse, that what any could remember hee had ever done or said in mirth, or passion, by some circumstantiall oath it was applied to their fittest use. Yet not past 8 or 9 could say much, and that nothing but circumstances which all men did knowe was most false and untrue. Many got their passes by promising in England to say much against him. I have presumed to say this much in his behalfe, for that I never heard such foule slanders so certainely beleeved and urged for truthes by many a hundred that doe still not spare to spread them, say them, and sweare them; that I thinke doe scarse know him though they meet him: nor have they ether cause or reason but their wills, or zeale to rumor or opinion. For the honorable and better sort of our Virginian adventurers, I think they understand it as I have writ it. For instead of accusing him, I have never heard any give him a better report, then many of those witnesses themselves that were sent home only to testifie against him. RICHARD POTS, W. P[HETTIPLACE].

When the ships departed, Davis arived in a smal Pinnace with some 16 proper men more: to those were added a company from James Towne under the command of Captaine Ratliffe, to inhabit Point comfort.[1] Martin and Mr West having lost their boates, and neere halfe their men amongst the Salvages, were returned to James Towne; for the Salvages no sooner understood of Captaine Smiths losse, but they all revolted, and did murder and spoile all they could incounter. Now were we all constrained to live only of that which Smith had only for his owne company, for the rest had consumed their proportions. And now have we 20 Presidents with all their appurtenances; for Mr Persie was so sicke he could not goe nor stand. But ere all was consumed, Mr West and Ratliffe, each with a pinnace, and 30 or 40 men wel appointed, sought abroad to trade: how they carried the businesse I knowe not, but Ratliffe and his men were most[ly] slaine by Powhatan; those that escaped returned neare starved in the Pinnace. And Mr West finding little better successe, set saile for England. Now wee all found the want of Captaine Smith, yea his greatest maligners could then curse his losse. Now for corne, provision, and contribution from the Salvages; wee had nothing but mortal wounds with clubs and arrowes. As for our hogs, hens, goats, sheep, horse, or what lived; our commanders and officers did daily consume them: some small proportions (sometimes) we tasted, till all was devoured. Then swords, arrowes, peeces, or any thing we traded to the Salvages; whose bloody fingers were so imbrued in our bloods, that what by their crueltie, our Governours indiscreation, and the losse of our ships; of 500, within 6 months after [2] there remained not many more then 60. most miserable and poore creatures. It were

[1] Ratcliffe built a fort at Point Comfort after the ships departed in October, 1609, which was called "Algernourne Fort."

[2] From October, 1609, to May, 1610.

to[o] vild to say what we endured: but the occasion was only our owne, for want of providence, industrie, and governement; and not the barrennesse and defect of the countrie, as is generally supposed. For till then, in 3 yeares (for the numbers were landed us)[1] we had never landed sufficient provision for 6 months: such a glutton is the sea, and such good fellowes the marriners, wee as little tasted of those great proportions for their provisions, as they of our miseries; that notwithstanding ever swaid and over-ruled the businesse. Though we did live as is said, 3 yeares chiefly of what this good countrie naturally affordeth: yet now had we beene in Paradice it selfe (with those governours) it would not have beene much better with us: yet was there some amongst us, who had they had the governement, would surely have kept us from those extremities of miseries, that in 10 daies more would have supplanted us all by death.

But God that would not it should bee unplanted, sent Sir Thomas Gates and Sir George Sommers, with a 150 men, most happily perserved by the Ber[m]ondoes to preserve us. Strange it is to say how miraculously they were preserved, in a leaking ship, in those extreme stormes and tempests in such overgrowne seas 3 daies and 3 nights by bayling out water. And having given themselvs to death, how happily when least expected, that worthy Captaine Sir George Somers having l[a]ine all that time cuning[2] the ship before those swalowing waves, discovered those broken Iles:[3] where how plentifully they lived with fish and flesh, what a paradice this is to inhabit, what industrie they used to build their 2 ships, how happily they did transport them to James Towne in Virginia,[4] I refer you to their owne printed relations.

But when those noble knights did see our miseries (being strangers to the country) and could understand no more of the cause but by their conjecture of our clamors and complaints, of accusing or excusing one another: they imbarked us with themselves, with the best means they could, and abandoning James Towne, set saile for England.

[1] *I.e.*, in consideration of the numbers of new colonists that were landed to us.

[2] Directing the steering.

[3] The Bermudas.

[4] Where they arrived May 23, 1610.

But yet God would not so have it, for ere wee left the river; we met the Lord de-la-ware, then governour for the countrie, with 3 ships exceeding well furnished with al necessaries fitting: who againe returned them to the abandoned James Towne, the 9 of June, 1610. accompanied with Sir Ferdinando Wainman, and divers other gentlemen of sort.[1] Sir George Somers and Captaine Argall he presentlie dispatcheth to require the Bermondas to furnish them with provision: Sir Thomas Gates for England to helpe forward their supplies; himselfe neglected not the best was in his power for the furtherance of the busines and regaining what was lost. But even in the beginning of his proceedings, his Lordship had such an incounter with a scurvy sicknesse, that made him unable to weld [2] the state of his bodie, much lesse the affaires of the colonie, so that after 8. monthes sicknesse, he was forced to save his life by his returne for England.

In this time Argall not finding the Bermondas, having lost Sir George Somers at sea, fell on the coast of Sagadahock;[3] where refreshing himselfe, found a convenient fishing for Cod. With a tast whereof, hee returned to James towne, from whence the Lord De-la-ware sent him to trade in the river of Patawomecke. Where finding an English boy [4] those people had preserved from the furie of Powhatan, by his acquaintance, had such good usage of those kind Salvages, that they fraughted his ship with corne; wherewith he returned to James Towne: and so for England, with the Lord Governour. Yet before his returne, the adventurers had sent Sir Thomas Dale [5] with

[1] Quality. [2] Wield, *i.e.*, to manage. [3] Maine.

[4] Henry Spelman, son of Sir Henry Spelman, the antiquary; given to Powhatan by Smith in August, 1609. After several years of life among the savages and of service to the colony as interpreter, he was killed by the Anacostan Indians in 1623.

[5] Sir Thomas Dale was a soldier in the service of the United Netherlands in the period 1588–1595, an attendant upon Prince Henry in Scotland, 1595–1603, and again in the Dutch military service, 1603–1611. After his six years of distinguished service to Virginia, 1611–1617, he sailed early in 1618 to the East in command of the East India Company's fleet. After valiant exploits, he died at Masulipatam in August, 1619.

3 ships, men and cattell, and all other provisions necessarie for a yeare: all which arived the 10 of May, 1611.

Againe, to second him with all possible expedition, there was prepared for Sir Thomas Gates, 6 tall ships with 300 men, and 100 kyne, with other cattell, with munition and all manner of provision could bee thought needfull, and they arived about the 1 of August next after, safely at James towne.

Sir George Somers all this time was supposed lost: but thus it hapned. Missing the Bermondas, hee fell also, as did Argall, with Sagadahock: where being refreshed, would not content himselfe with that repulse, but returned againe in the search; and there safely arived.[1] But overtoiling himselfe, on a surfeit died. And this Cedar ship built by his owne directions, and partly with his owne hands, that had not in her any iron but only one bolt in her keele, yet well endured thus tossed to and againe in this mightie Ocean, til with his dead bo[die] she arived in England at line:[2] and at Whitchurch in Dorsetshire, his body by his friends was honourably buried, with many volies of shot, and the rights of a souldier. And upon his Tombe was bestowed this Epitaph

*Hei mihi Virginia, quod tam cito præterit æstas,*
*Autumnus sequitur, sæviet inde et hyems.*
*At ver perpetuum nascetur, et Anglia læta,*
*Decerpit flores, Floryda terra tuos.*

Alas Virginia Somer so soone past,
Autume succeeds and stormy winters blast,
Yet Englands joyfull spring with Aprill shewres,
O Floryda, shall bring thy sweetest flowers.

Since, there was a ship fraughted with provision and 40 men, and another since then, with the like number and provision, to stay in the Countrie 12 months with Captaine Argall.

The Lord governour himselfe doth confidently determine to goe with the next, or as presently as he may, in his owne

[1] At the Bermudas. [2] At last.

person, with sundry other knights and gentlemen, with ships and men so farre as their meanes will extend to furnish. As for all their particular actions since the returne of Captaine Smith; for that they have beene printed from time to time, and published to the world, I cease farther to trouble you with any repetition of things so well knowne, more then are necessary. To conclude the historie, leaving this assurance to all posteritie, howe unprosperously things may succeed, by what changes or chances soever; the action is honorable and worthie to bee approved, the defect whereof hath only beene in the managing the businesse: which I hope now experience hath taught them to amend, or those examples may make others to beware, for the land is as good as this booke doth report it.

Captaine Smith I returne you the fruit of my labours, as Mr Croshaw [1] requested me, which I bestowed in reading the discourses, and hearing the relations of such which have walked and observed the land of Virginia with you. The pains I took was great: yet did the nature of the argument, and hopes I conceaved of the expedition, give me exceeding content. I cannot finde there is any thing, but what they all affirme, or cannot contradict: the land is good: as there is no citties, so no sonnes of Anak: al is open for labor of a good and wise inhabitant: and my prayer shall ever be, that so faire a land, may bee inhabited by those that professe and love the Gospell.

Your friend,

W. S.

[1] Raleigh Croshaw.

# THE RELATION OF THE LORD DE-LA-WARE, 1611

# INTRODUCTION

THE author of this letter, Thomas West, third Lord Delaware, was born July 9, 1577, and was son of Thomas West, second Lord Delaware, and Anne, daughter of Sir Francis Knollys by Katherine Cary, first cousin to Queen Elizabeth and sister of Henry Cary, first Lord Hunsdon. He was a master of arts of the university of Oxford, and was knighted by Essex at Dublin, Ireland, July 12, 1599. He served with distinction in the Low Countries, was implicated in the Essex Rebellion, February 8, 1601, was imprisoned and pardoned. His father, the second lord, died March 24, 1602, and he succeeded as third Lord Delaware and also as member of the privy council of Queen Elizabeth, and on her death became a privy councillor to James I. In 1609 he was a member of the superior council of the Virginia Company, and on February 28, 1610, was appointed governor and captain-general of the Virginia colony for life. He arrived at Jamestown June 10, 1610, and re-established the colony, which he found deserting the settlement. After a stay of a year he was compelled to leave on account of his health, and went first to the West Indies and then to England. He remained in the latter country till 1618; in his absence the government in Virginia was administered by deputy-governors — Gates, Dale, Yeardey, and Argall. In the latter year he was sent again to Virginia to rescue the government from the hands of Samuel Argall, who had incurred the strong censure of the London Company, but on his way over he died, June 7, 1618. He married Cecily, daughter of Sir Thomas Sherley. His son and successor was Henry, fourth Lord Delaware, who married Isabella, daughter of Sir Thomas

Edmonds, the ambassador. Governor Delaware had three brothers, Francis West, John West and Nathaniel West, who all lived in Virginia, and the first two of whom were deputy-governors at different times; William West, a nephew, was killed by Indians at the Falls of James River, Virginia, in 1611.

The *Relation* was entered for publication at Stationers' Hall on July 6, 1611. It was again printed by Purchas in his *Pilgrimes*, IV. 1762–1764, and Captain Smith gives some extracts from it in his *Generall Historie* (1624), p. 109. It was reprinted (fifty copies) in 1859, and again by Mr. Griswold (twenty copies) in 1868. In 1890 Alexander Brown printed it anew in his *Genesis of the United States*. At a sale in 1883, an original fetched $133. Originals are now preserved in this country in the Library of Congress, the Lenox and John Carter Brown libraries. Probably the chief value of the narrative proceeds from the strong defence it unconsciously affords of the character of the Virginia colonists. Here was Delaware given absolute power by a new charter established under the idea that the calamities in Virginia were due to the inveterate disposition of the Virginia colonists to quarrels and shiftlessness — a man toughened in war and given all the advantages of good living and the best medical attention. And yet what a doleful complaint he makes of the ague, the dysentery, and the scurvy, which in short order bombarded him out of the colony. The London Company and its servants — Smith, Delaware, Gates, Dale, and others — "boomed" the company's management and the natural advantages of Virginia, and very unjustly threw the responsibility on the poor colonists, who suffered untold horrors from starvation and disease.

L. G. T.

# THE RELATION OF THE LORD DE-LA-WARE, 1611

*The Relation of the Right Honourable the Lord De-La-Warre, Lord Governour and Captaine Generall of the Colonie, planted in Virginea. London: Printed by William Hall, for William Welbie, dwelling in Pauls Churchyeard at the Signe of the Swan. 1611.*[1]

*A Short Relation made by the Lord De-La-Warre, to the Lords and others of the Counsell of Virginia, touching his unexpected returne home, and afterwards delivered to the generall Assembly of the said Company, at a Court holden the twenty five of June, 1611. Published by authority of the said Counsell.*

*My Lords*, etc.

BEING now by accident returned from my Charge at Virginea, contrary either to my owne desire, or other men's expectations, who spare not to censure me, in point of duty, and to discourse and question the reason, though they apprehend not the true cause of my returne, I am forced, (out of a willingnesse to satisfie every man) to deliver unto your Lordships, and the rest of this Assembly, briefely (but truely), in what state I have lived, ever since my arrival to the Colonie; what hath beene the just occasion of my sudden departure thence; and in what termes I have left the same: The rather because I perceive, that since my comming into England, such a coldnesse and irresolution is bred in many of the Adventurers[2] that

[1] This italic heading is copied from the title-page of the original.

[2] The adventurers were those in England who subscribed to the stock of the London Company, the face value of whose shares was £12. 6s.

some of them seeke to withdraw those paiments, which they have subscribed towards the Charge of the Plantation, and by which that Action must bee supported and maintained; making this my returne the colour of their needlesse backwardnes and unjust protraction. Which, that you may the better understand, I must informe your Lordships, that presently after my arrival in James Towne, I was welcommed by a hote and violent Ague, which held mee a time, till by the advice of my Physition, Doctor Laurence Bohun,[1] (by blood letting) I was recovered, as in my first Letters by Sir Thomas Gates I have informed you. That disease had not long left me, til (within three weekes after I had gotten a little strength) I began to be distempered with other greevous sicknesses, which successively and severally assailed me: for besides a relapse into the former disease, which with much more violence held me more than a moneth, and brought me to great weakenesse, the Flux[2] surprised me, and kept me many daies: then the Crampe assaulted my weak body, with strong paines; and afterwards the Gout (with which I had heeretofore beene sometime troubled) afflicted mee in such sort, that making my body through weakenesse unable to stirre, or to use any maner of exercise, drew upon me the disease called the Scurvy; which though in others it be a sicknesse of slothfulnesse, yet was in me an effect of weaknesse, which never left me, till I was upon the point to leave the world.

These severall maladies and calamities, I am the more desirous to particularise unto Your Lordships (although they were too notorious to the whole Colonie) lest any man should misdeeme that under the general name and common excuse of sicknes, I went about to cloke either sloth, or feare, or anie other base apprehension, unworthy the high and generall charge which you had entrusted to my Fidelitie.

[1] He was "brought up among the most learned Surgeons and Physitions in the Netherlands." He was killed in 1621 in a sea-battle with the Spaniards, "wherein Dr. Bohun behaved most gallantly." See an account of the battle in the fourth book of Smith's *Generall Historie, post*, p. 340.

[2] Dysentery.

In these extremities I resolved to consult my friends, who (finding Nature spent in me, and my body almost consumed, my paines likewise daily encreasing) gave me advise to preferre a hopefull recovery, before an assured ruine, which must necessarily have ensued, had I lived, but twenty dayes longer, in Virginia: wanting at that instant, both food and Physicke, fit to remedy such extraordinary diseases, and restore that strength so desperately decayed.

Whereupon, after a long consultation held, I resolved by generall consent and perswasion, to ship my self for Mevis, an Island in the West Indies, famous for wholesome Bathes, there to try what help the Heavenly Providence would afford me, by the benefit of the hot Bathe: But God, who guideth all things, according to his good will and pleasure, so provided, that after wee had sailed an hundred Leagues, we met with Southerly windes which forced me to change my purpose (my body being altogether unable to endure the tediousnesse of a long voyage) and so sterne my course for the Western Islands,[1] which I no sooner recovered, then I found help for my health, and my sicknesse asswaged, by meanes of fresh diet, and especially of Orenges and Lemonds, an undoubted remedy and medicine for that disease, which lastly, and so long, had afflicted me: which ease as soone as I found, I resolved (although my body remained still feeble and weake), to returne backe to my charge in Virginia againe, but I was advised not to hazard my selfe before I had perfectly recovered my strength, which by Counsell I was perswaded to seeke in the naturall Ayre of my Countrey, and so I came for England. In which Accident,[2] I doubt not but men of reason, and of judgement will imagine, there would more danger and prejudice have hapned by my death there, then I hope can doe by my returne.

In the next place, I am to give accompt in what estate I left the Collony for government in my absence. It may please your Lordships therefore to understand that upon my departure thence, I made choise of Captaine George Pearcie, (a

[1] Azores.

[2] State of affairs.

gentleman of honour and resolution, and of no small experience in that place) to remaine Deputie Governour, untill the comming of the Marshall, Sir Thomas Dale, whose Commission was likewise to be determined, upon the arrivall of Sir Thomas Gates, according to the intent and order of your Lordships, and the Councill here.

The number of men I left there were upward of two hundred, the most in health, and provided of at least tenne moneths victuals,[1] in their store-house, (which is daily issued unto them) besides other helps in the Countrey, lately found out by Captaine Argoll, by trading with pettie kings in those parts, who for a small returne of a piece of Iron, Copper, &c. have consented to trucke great quantities of Corne, and willingly imbrace the intercourse of Traffique, shewing unto our people certaine signs of amitie and affection.

And for the better strengthening and securing of the Collony, in the time of my weaknesse there, I tooke order for the building of three severall Forts,[2] two of which are seated neere Poynt Comfort, to which adjoyneth a large Circuit of ground, open, and fit for Corne: the thirde Fort is at the Falles, upon an Island invironed also with Corne ground. These are not all manned, for I wanted the Commoditie of Boates, having but two, and one Bardge, in all the Countrey, which hath beene cause that our fishing hath beene (in some sort) hindered, for want of those provisions, which easily will be remedied when wee can gaine sufficient men to be imployed about those businesses, which in Virginia I found not: But since meeting with Sir Thomas Gates at the Cowes neere Portsmouth (to whom I gave a perticular accompt of all my proceedings, and of the present estate of the Collony as I left it) I understood those wants are supplyed in his Fleete.

[1] According to the *Breife Declaration* the people at Delaware's departure were provided with only three months' victuals and that at short allowance. One hundred and fifty had died during his stay, which was more than half the number of the settlers.

[2] Forts Henry and Charles on the east of Hampton River, and Fort West at the Falls.

The countrey is wonderfull fertile and very rich, and makes good whatsoever heretofore hath beene reported of it, the Cattell already there, are much encreased, and thrive exceedingly with the pasture of that Countrey: The Kine all this last Winter, though the ground was covered most with Snow, and the season sharpe, lived without other feeding than the grasse they found, with which they prospered well, and many of them readie to fall with Calve; Milke being a great nourishment and refreshing to our people, serving also (in occasion) as well for Physicke as for Food, so that it is no way to be doubted, but when it shall please God that Sir Thomas Dale, and Sir Thomas Gates, shall arrive in Virginia with their extraordinary supply of one hundred Kine, and two hundred Swine, besides store of all manner of other provisions for the sustenance and maintenance of the Collony, there will appeare that successe in the Action as shall give no man cause to distrust that hath already adventured, but encourage every good minde to further so worthy a worke, as will redound both to the Glory of God, to the Credit of our Nation, and to the Comfort of all those that have beene Instruments in the furthering of it.

The last discovery, during my continuall sicknesse, was by Captaine Argoll, who hath found a trade with Patomack (a King as great as Powhatan, who still remaines our enemie, though not able to doe us hurt). This is a goodly River called Patomack, upon the borders whereof there are growne the goodliest Trees for Masts, that may be found elsewhere in the World: Hempe better then English, growing wilde in aboundance: Mines of Antimonie and Leade.

There is also found without our Bay to the Northward an excellent fishing Bancke for Codde, and Ling as good as can be eaten, and of a kinde that will keepe a whole yeare, in Shippes hould, with little care; a tryall [1] whereof I now have brought over with mee. Other Islands there are upon our Coasts, that doe promise rich merchandise, and will further exceedingly

[1] Sample.

the establishing of the Plantation, by supply of many helpes, and will speedily afford a returne of many worthie Commodities.

I have left much ground in part manured to receive Corne, having caused it the last Winter to be sowed for rootes [1] with which our people were greatly releeved.

There are many Vines planted in divers places, and doe prosper well, there is no want of any thing, if the action can be upheld with constancy and resolution.

Lastly concerning my selfe, and my Course, though the World may imagine that this Countrey and Climate will (by that which I have suffered beyond any other of that Plantation) ill agree with the state of my body, yet I am so farre from shrinking or giving over this honourable enterprise, as that I am willing and ready to lay all I am worth upon the adventure of the Action, rather then so Honourable a worke should faile, and to returne with all the convenient expedition I may, beseeching your Lordships, and the rest, not onely to excuse my former wants, happened by the Almighty hand: but to second my resolutions with your friendly indeavours: that both the State may receive Honour, your selves Profit, and I future Comfort, by being imployed (though but as a weake Instrument) in so great an Action.

And thus having plainely, truely, and briefely, delivered the cause of my returne, with the state of our affayres, as wee now stand, I hope every worthy and indifferent hearer will by comparing my present resolution of returne, with the necessitie of my comming home, rest satisfied with this true and short Declaration.

**Finis.**

# LETTER OF DON DIEGO DE MOLINA, 1613

# INTRODUCTION

THE history of early Virginia has not only its domestic phases, but it is also interwoven to some extent with that of Spain and France. English colonization had its origin in rivalry with Spain; and the early proceedings of the Jamestown colony were beset with Spanish intrigue, and embarrassed by apprehensions of Spanish interference. In 1611 a Spanish caravel, sent by the king of Spain to spy out the conditions of things among the English in Virginia, appeared in James River. Three persons went ashore at Point Comfort to ask for a pilot — Don Diego de Molina, Marco Antonio, and Francisco Lembri. They were arrested and kept prisoners in Virginia. After several months Antonio died; and, in 1616, to satisfy the complaints of the Spanish, the two surviving spies were embarked with Dale for Europe. On the way over, Dale found out that Lembri was an Englishman, and was therefore a traitor as well as a spy, and hung him. Restored to his own country, Molina is reported, in 1618, as inciting the king of Spain to send troops to Virginia, "because of a silver mine there, from which he shows a piece to justify the truth thereof." The letter below must have been addressed to Don Alonzo de Velasco, who was Spanish ambassador at London from 1610 to 1613. It was translated for Dr. Alexander Brown and published in the *Genesis of the United States*, pp. 646–652. Our text is, however, a fresh translation from the Spanish. The original holographic letter is in the archives of Spain at Simancas.[1] Smith gives some account of the episode in his *Generall Historie*, Book IV.; see p. 320, *infra*.

L. G. T.

[1] Secretaría de Estado, *legajo* 2590, folio 47. Dr. Brown's transcript is in the Lenox Library.

# LETTER OF DON DIEGO DE MOLINA, 1613

The person who will give this to Your Lordship is very trustworthy and Your Lordship can give credence to everything he will say, so I will not be prolix in this but will tell in it what is most important. Although with my capture and the extraordinary occurrences following it His Majesty will have opened his eyes and seen this new Algiers of America, which is coming into existence here, I do not wonder that in all this time he has not remedied it because to effect the release would require an expedition, particularly as he lacks full information for making a decision. However I believe that with the aid of Your Lordship's intelligence and with the coming of the caravel[1] to Spain, His Majesty will have been able to determine what is most important and that that is to stop the progress of a hydra in its infancy, because it is clear that its intention is to grow and encompass the destruction of all the West, as well by sea as by land and that great results will follow I do not doubt, because the advantages of this place make it very suitable for a gathering-place of all the pirates of Europe, where they will be well received. For this nation has great thoughts of an alliance with them. And this nation by itself will be very powerful because as soon as an abundance of wheat shall have been planted and there shall be enough cattle, there will not be a man of any sort whatever who will not alone or in company with others fit out a ship to come here and join the rest, because as Your Lordship knows this Kingdom abounds in poor people who abhor peace — and of necessity because in

[1] *I.e.*, the caravel from which Molina had incautiously gone ashore at Point Comfort.

peace they perish — and the rich are so greedy and selfish that they even cherish a desire for the Indies and the gold and silver there — notwithstanding that there will not be much lack of these here, for they have discovered some mines which are considered good, although they have not yet been able to derive profit from them. But when once the preliminary steps are taken there are many indications that they will find a large number in the mountains. So the Indians say and they offer to show the locations that they know and they say that near the sources of the rivers, as they come down from the mountain, there is a great quantity of grains of silver and gold, but, as they do not set any value on these but only on copper which they esteem highly, they do not gather them.

As yet these men have not been able to go to discover these although they greatly desire it, nor to pass over this range to New Mexico and from there to the South Sea where they expect to establish great colonies and fit out fleets with which to become lords of that sea as well as of this, by colonizing certain islands among those to the east of the channel of Bahama and even to conquer others, as Puerto Rico, Santo Domingo and Cuba.[1] And although this would be difficult at the least, we have already seen signs of these purposes in the colonizing of Bermuda where they are said to have strong fortifications, because the lay of the land is such that a few can defend themselves against a great number and prevent disembarking and landing.[2] The depth as I have understood is not enough for ships of a hundred tons, but I believe that they make it out less than it is, for that island has already been described in the relation of Captain Diego Ramirez who was stranded there, and it seems to me that larger vessels can enter. I do not recall it well but the description is in the house of Don Rodrigo de Aguiar of the Council of the Indies and the

[1] This expectation came true in the course of years. The Bahama Islands belong to England, Porto Rico belongs to the United States, — a product of the Virginia settlement, — and Cuba is under American influence.

[2] The present English fortress at Bermuda is considered one of the strongest in the world.

register is in Seville in the house of the licentiate Antonio Moreno, cosmographer of the Council. But above all this captain will give enough information of the island, and it is very important for the military actions which may have to take place in it. Its fertility is great, there is abundance of fish and game, and pork as much as they can want, and so they get along very well in that colony because they have little need of England, for they are likewise rich in amber and pearl of which in a very few months it is said they have sent to that kingdom more than fifty thousand ducats in value, reckoning the ounce at a moderate price. Four days ago a vessel arrived here that brought them men and provisions and they do not cease talking of the excellence of that island and its advantages.

The soil in this place is very fertile for all species, only not for those which require much heat, because it is cold. There is much game and fish, but as they have not begun to get profit from the mines, but only from timber, the merchants have not been able to maintain this colony with as much liberality as was needed and so the people have suffered much want, living on miserable rations of oats or maize and dressing poorly. For which reason, if today three hundred men should come, this same year would destroy more than one hundred and fifty, and there is not a year when half do not die. Last year there were seven hundred people and not three hundred and fifty remain, because little food and much labor on public works kills them and, more than all, the discontent in which they live seeing themselves treated as slaves with cruelty.[1] Wherefore many have gone over to the Indians, at whose hands some have been killed, while others have gone out to sea, being sent to fish, and those who remain have become violent and are desirous that a fleet should come from Spain to take them out of their misery. Wherefore they cry to God of the injury that they receive and they appeal to His Majesty in whom they

[1] This is a strong confirmation of the terrible indictment by the colonists of the cruel experiences under Gates and Dale. See the *Breife Declaration*, and the *Tragicall Relation*, *post*.

have great confidence, and should a fleet come to give them passage to that kingdom, not a single person would take up arms.[1] Sooner would they forfeit their respect and obedience to their rulers who think to maintain this place till death.

And although it is understood there that the merchants [2] are deserting this colony, this is false for it is a strategem with which they think to render His Majesty careless, giving him to understand that this affair will settle itself, and that thus he will not need to go to the expense of any fleet whatever to come here. With eight hundred or one thousand soldiers he could reduce this place with great ease, or even with five hundred, because there is no expectation of aid from England for resistance and the forts which they have are of boards and so weak that a kick would break them down, and once arrived at the ramparts those without would have the advantage over those within because its beams and loopholes are common to both parts — a fortification without skill and made by unskilled men. Nor are they efficient soldiers, although the rulers and captains make a great profession of this because of the time they have served in Flanders on the side of Holland, where some have companies and castles. The men are poorly drilled and not prepared for military action.

However they have placed their hope on one of two settlements, one which they have founded twenty leagues up the river in a bend on a rugged peninsula [3] with a narrow entrance by land and they are persuaded that there they can defend themselves against the whole world. I have not seen it but I know that it is similar to the others and that one night the Indians entered it and ran all over the place without meeting any resistance, shooting their arrows through all the doors, so that I do not feel that there would be any difficulty in taking it or the one in Bermuda, particularly if my advice be taken in both matters as that of a man who has been here two years and has considered the case with care. I am awaiting His

[1] Probably the wish was father to the thought.

[2] The Virginia Company.

[3] Jamestown Peninsula, which is not over ten leagues up the river.

Majesty's decision and am desirous of being of some service and I do not make much of my imprisonment nor of the hardships which I have suffered in it, with hunger, want and illness, because one who does a labor of love holds lightly all his afflictions. The ensign Marco Antonio Perez died fifteen months ago, more from hunger than illness, but assuredly with the patience of a saint and the spirit of a good soldier. I have not fared very ill, but tolerably so, because since I arrived I have been in favor with these people and they have shown me friendship as far as their own wretchedness would allow, but with genuine good-will. The sailor who came with me is said to be English and a pilot. He declares that he is from Aragon and in truth no one would take him for a foreigner.[1]

This country is located in thirty-seven and a third degrees, in which is also the bay which they call Santa Maria.[2] Five rivers empty into this, very wide and of great depth — this one at its entrance nine fathoms and five and six within. The others measure seven, eight and twelve; the bay is eight leagues at its mouth but in places it is very wide, even thirty leagues.[3] There is much oak timber and facilities for making ships, trees for them according to their wish — very dark walnut which they esteem highly and many other kinds of trees.

The bearer is a very honorable Venetian gentleman, who having fallen into some great and serious errors is now returned to his first religion and he says that God has made me his instrument in this, for which I give thanks. He wishes to go to Spain to do penance for his sins. If I get my liberty I think of helping him in everything as far as I shall be able. I beseech Your Lordship to do me the favor of making him some present, for I hold it certain that it will be a kindness very acceptable to our Lord to see in Your Lordship indications that charity has not died out in Spain. And so Your Lordship ought to have charity and practise it in the case of a man who goes

[1] Francis Lembri, who was proven to be an Englishman and hung by Dale as a traitor, when returning to England in 1616. [2] Chesapeake Bay.

[3] The widest portion of the bay is not over thirteen leagues, or forty miles.

from here poor and sick and cannot make use of his abilities, and if I have to stay here long I am no less in need of Your Lordship's help (as you will learn from the report of this man, who will tell you how I am faring). Your Lordship might aid me by sending some shipstores such as are brought here for certain private individuals and in particular cloth and linen for clothing ourselves (this man and me) because we go naked or so ragged that it amounts to the same, without changing our shirts in a month, because, as the soldier says, my shirts are an odd number and do not come to three. I trust in God who will surely help me since He is beginning to give me my health which for eleven months has failed me. I have not sufficient opportunity to write to His Majesty. Your Lordship will be able to do this giving him notice of everything I am telling. May God guard Your Lordship as I desire. From Virginia, May 28 (according to Spanish reckoning), 1613.

If Your Lordship had the key to my cipher, I should write in it. But this letter is sewed between the soles of a shoe, so that I trust in God that I shall not have done wrong in writing in this way. When I first came here I wrote His Majesty a letter which had need of some interpretation and directed it with others to Your Lordship. I do not know whether you have received them.

I thought to be able to make a description of this country but the publicity of my position does not give me opportunity for it, but that which is most to the point is that the bay runs northeast by east and at four leagues distance from its mouth is this river from the south, nine fathoms in depth. At the entrance is a fort [1] or, to speak more exactly, a weak structure of boards ten hands high with twenty-five soldiers and four iron pieces. Half a league off is another [2] smaller with fifteen

[1] The fort at Point Comfort called "Algernourne Fort," first established in 1608 by President Percy. The Spanish here has a play upon words which cannot be translated, "a fort [*fuerte*, strong] or rather a weak."

[2] Fort Charles on Strawberry Bank in Elizabeth City, first established in 1611.

soldiers, without artillery. There is another[1] smaller than either half a league inland from here for a defence against the Indians. This has fifteen more soldiers. Twenty leagues off is this colony[2] with one hundred and fifty persons and six pieces; another twenty leagues further up is another[3] colony strongly located — to which they will all betake themselves if occasion arises, because on this they place their hopes — where are one hundred more persons and among them as here there are women, children and field laborers, which leaves not quite two hundred active men and those poorly disciplined.

[1] Fort Henry, on the east side of Hampton River, a musket shot to the west of Fort Charles.

[2] Jamestown.

[3] At Henrico, where Dutch Gap cuts the bend of the river. Some few scattered bricks still give evidence of this early settlement.

# LETTER OF FATHER PIERRE BIARD, 1614

## INTRODUCTION

Although Spanish interference was greatly feared by the English colonists at Jamestown, Spain was much reduced from its former estate and in no condition to make war upon England. Danger from France, though more removed, was far more real. In 1604 the Sieur de Monts established a French colony on the island of St. Croix in the St. Croix River. The next year the colony was removed to Port Royal (Annapolis). After three years spent in the country, during which time the New England coast was explored as far as Martha's Vineyard, the colonists returned to France. The design, however, was not abandoned. Poutrincourt returned in 1610 and re-established his colony at Port Royal. In 1611 two Jesuit priests, Biard and Massé, came over under the patronage of Madame de Guercheville, and in 1613, being joined by two other Jesuit priests, Quentin and du Thet, they planted a Jesuit station on the island of Mount Desert. The English had not recognized the claims of the French to any part of North America, and Sir Thomas Dale sent Captain Samuel Argall twice from Virginia, and burned all their settlements, — at Mount Desert Island, Isle de Ste. Croix, and Port Royal. The vigorous action of Argall probably saved New England to English colonization. The letter below was first published in a French translation by Father Auguste Carayon, S.J., in a work entitled *Première Mission des Jésuites au Canada* (Paris, 1864). The Latin original is preserved in the archives of the Society of Jesus. An English translation from the French was published by Dr. Alexander Brown in his *Genesis of the United States*, pp. 700–706. The translation printed below is however from the Latin and is taken, with permission, from Dr. R. G. Thwaites's *Jesuit Relations*, III. 5–19.

L. G. T.

# LETTER OF FATHER PIERRE BIARD, 1614

TO THE VERY REVEREND FATHER CLAUDE ACQUAVIVA, GENERAL OF THE SOCIETY OF JESUS, AT ROME, MAY 26, 1614

*Very Reverend Father in Christ:*

The peace of Christ be with you.

BOTH affection and duty urge me, fresh from such multiplied and mighty perils, from which I have been rescued by the surpassing favor of the Lord and by the prayers of your Paternity, to send you my greetings; and, in so far as it is possible, I throw myself at your knees and embrace you, assuredly with the utmost gratitude and devotion. And indeed I am bound, as it were, to contemplate myself, both to do penance, as I hope, and to express my gratitude; so great are the perils out of which I now marvel to see myself delivered. But, as it may at this time be wearisome to weave a long story of all these things, and as it is probable that Your Paternity has already learned many of them from Father Enemond Massé, I shall pass over all the rest, and confine myself for the present to this one matter: in what manner, after our violent capture by the English in New France, we were taken from place to place, and at last restored to this our native land.

There were, as Your Paternity knows, only four of our society in New France in the last year, 1613. Then, too, we first began to build in a convenient place a new settlement, a new colony,[1] etc. But most unexpectedly, by some hazard or other (for a hazard it certainly was, and not a premeditated plan),[2] some English from Virginia were driven upon our shores, who attacked our ships with the utmost fury, at a time

[1] At Mt. Desert Island.

[2] This appears to be an error.

when nearly all its defenders were occupied on land. Resistance was nevertheless made for a time, but we were soon obliged to surrender. In the struggle, two of the French were killed, four were wounded; and in addition our brother Gilbert Duthet received a mortal wound. He made a most Christian end, the following day, under my ministration.

Our ships having been captured and everything pillaged, it was a great concession to us, — that is, to us priests and Jesuits, — that we were not killed. And yet this sparing of our lives, if considered in itself only, would have been worse than any death. For what were we to do in an absolutely desert and barren region, despoiled and destitute of everything? The savages, indeed, used to come to us stealthily and by night; and with great generosity and devotion commiserated our misfortune, and promised us whatever they could. Truly the condition of things was such that either death itself, or a more calamitous misfortune, everywhere threatened us. There were in all thirty of us in these distressing circumstances. One consideration rendered the English less severe, namely, that one of our boats had escaped, in spite of their watchfulness; and as they had no doubt that it would bear witness to the violence done us, they were obliged to spare our lives, for they feared reprisals and dreaded our king. Therefore they finally offered (a great favor, forsooth) to leave for our thirty survivors a single boat, in which we might coast along the seashore, on the chance of finding some French vessel to take us back to our own country. It was shown that this boat could not hold over fifteen men; but nothing further could be obtained, even from among our own boats. To be brief: in this perplexity each of us took counsel as he could. Father Enemond Massé embarked with fourteen companions in the boat I have mentioned, and the Lord favored him, as Your Paternity has already learned. I went to the English captain and obtained a promise from him that I and Father Jacques Quentin, my companion, and also John Dixon — who had been admitted into the Society — and one servant, should be transported to the neighboring islands where the English usually fish, and that we should there be recommended to these English fishermen; so that, having been carried by them to England, we might easily return thence into France. I obtained, as I say, a promise to this effect, but there was no good faith in this promise. For they carried us off, together with the Frenchmen who remained, fifteen in all, straight to their own country, Virginia, distant from the place in which we had been captured at least two hundred and fifty leagues. In Virginia however a new peril arose; for the governor there[1] wished to hang us all, and especially the Jesuits. But the captain who had taken us resisted, alleging his promise to us. Finally this promise, or their fear of our king, prevailed.

After this episode the captain who had taken us was commissioned to return to that part of New France where he had plundered us, and to plunder any French ships he might find, and burn all the houses and settlements. There remained two French settlements there, that of Sainte Croix and that of Port Royal, where I had remained for two years. Three ships were equipped for this expedition, — two which they had taken from us, and a third and larger one, the man-of-war, as they call it, which had taken us. So eight of us Frenchmen were taken in this vessel, in view of any opportunity that might arise of sending us back to our own country. These vessels returned first to the place[2] where we had been captured, and all the crosses that we had set up they overthrew. But not unavenged! On the same spot, before our departure, they hanged one of their number whom they had apprehended in some plot. Thus one cross took the place of many.

Here a new peril arose. The English, as I have previously stated, wished to go to the settlement of Sainte Croix, although it had at this time no inhabitants. Some salt, however, had been left there. No one except myself knew the way; and the English knew that I had been there formerly. They accordingly demand that I lead them. I do all I can to evade and refuse

[1] Sir Thomas Gates was governor, but Sir Thomas Dale, who was marshal, had charge of the prisoners and threatened to hang them.

[2] St. Sauveur, on Mt. Desert Island.

this proposal; but it avails me nothing. They perceive clearly that I am unwilling to obey. At this the captain grows very angry, and my peril becomes imminent; when suddenly they find the place without my help, and plunder and burn it. They moreover on this occasion captured a savage, who guided them to Port Royal. Although this had delivered me from one great danger, it nevertheless involved me in another greater one. For after they had plundered and burnt Port Royal (which by some inexplicable chance they had found abandoned by its inhabitants), some Frenchman, one of those very men who had deserted Port Royal, brought an accusation against me, which was nothing less than this: that I was a genuine, native Spaniard; and that, on account of certain crimes committed in France, I dared not return there. Hereupon the captain, already incensed against me, having found a fine pretext for his wrath, asked his followers whether they did not think it would be just to cast me forth on the shore and abandon me there. The opinion of the majority prevailed, who thought it better to take me back to Virginia, and there to return me to that unlucky tree which, in accordance with law and justice, I had escaped. Thus I escaped death for the moment: and so we soon after started on our return voyage to Virginia. But two days later so fearful a tempest arose that the ships were separated, and none of us knew what became of the others. The captain of our ship, after he had endured the storm for three weeks, and had begun to run short of various necessaries, particularly of fresh water, concluding that there was no hope of getting back to Virginia for a long time, decided to run to the Portuguese islands called Terceras [Azores]. Through this decision I, who appeared to have escaped from the death by hanging that awaited me, again found myself in a greater peril; greater I may truly call it, since I had here companions in my danger. The sixteen Englishmen, on approaching these islands, began to reflect that they were lost if we priests and Jesuits appeared, for we would be set at liberty on the instant by these Portuguese Catholics, and they, on the contrary, would be punished as pirates and persecutors of priests. This anxiety troubled them. But what were they to do? Should they throw us overboard, or would it suffice to conceal us? In this embarrassment and uncertainty, the captain sent for me, and laid the matter before me. I said to him that death itself was not a greater evil, in my estimation, than to be the occasion of misfortune to others. I promised, in case he chose to conceal us, that I would lend myself to this scheme in good faith. With what idea did God inspire him, to make him believe me? I know not, truly; but this I know — that if he had foreseen the dangers into which he subsequently fell, he would not have trusted me. Accordingly he hid us in the hold of the vessel; during three weeks we did not behold the sun; but the captain encountered so many difficulties in the port of the island of Faal,[1] and the vessel was visited so frequently during this space of three weeks, that it seems marvellous that we escaped detection. But this also God purposed for the greater glory of the Society; for the English clearly saw that if we had wished to show ourselves, and to expose them, it would frequently have been in our power to do so. They themselves afterwards, when in England, often eulogized our good faith in the presence of their ministers, and to the admiration even of the enemies of truth. Escaping from these perils, our captors decided to return to England rather than to Virginia, which was so much farther distant, and which was to be reached only by a long voyage, for which they lacked all the necessaries. Accordingly we set sail for England. Our voyage was a long one, and was marked by many vicissitudes: finally, losing our bearings in the fog and the cloudy weather, we deviated from the right course and were carried to Wales, not far from Ireland. In Wales our captain, having landed near the town of Pembroke to lay in provisions, was seized and detained as a pirate, because of certain appearances pointing that way. He, however, to recover his liberty, denied being a pirate; and, as a proof of his innocence, he adduced the fact that he had in his vessel

[1] Fayal.

two Jesuits from whose own lips they could learn the truth, if they pleased to summon them. Oh skillful hand of divine Providence! Winter was then fully upon us, and in the ship we were in want of everything. Thus, had we not been provided for, we should have died of cold and hardships. But what need of a long story? The Jesuits are at once summoned, and, gazed at by all, are led into the town. We are ordered to give our evidence. We, of course, attest what was perfectly true, — that our captain was a royal officer and not a pirate, and that what he had done to us had been done in obedience to orders, rather than from his own free will. Accordingly, our captain was set at liberty; and in company with him we were detained in the town, and very well used, while awaiting orders from London. These were long delayed; and in the interval we frequently engaged in arguments with the ministers, and more frequently still with others, for nearly every one was permitted to have access to us, although we were not allowed to go out. In every other respect, as I have said, we were very kindly treated. Finally we received orders to sail from Pembroke to London. But the voyage proved a long one. Protracted delays intervened; to avoid a long enumeration of these, let it suffice to say that by order of the English king we were landed at Dover, and thence sent to Calais in France. At Calais we were hospitably received by the governor and the dean of the city, and rested three days; thence we came to Amiens, where we now are.

We remained in captivity during nine months and a half. We were in the ship all the time, except when we landed at Pembroke, as related. There were three months during which we daily received only about two ounces of bread, and a small quantity of salt fish, with water that was nearly always fetid; so that we marvel at not having fallen sick. Few of the English escaped illness, and some of them even died as the result. But God doubtless watched over us in answer to the prayer of Your Paternity and of all our Society; may He grant in his goodness that it result to his own greater glory and in my salvation and better life. This I hope for, through the prayers and the blessing of Your Paternity, which, with all possible humility and affection, I solicit on my knees. May the Lord Jesus ever watch over Your Paternity and may our Father with utmost goodness and favor increasingly bestow upon you his Most Holy grace.

Your Paternity's

Obedient son and unworthy servant,

PIERRE BIARD.

*Amiens*, May 26, 1614.

# LETTER OF JOHN ROLFE, 1614

# INTRODUCTION

John Rolfe, the author of this letter, came of an ancient family of Heacham, in the county of Norfolk, England, and was the son of John Rolfe and Dorothea Mason. He was baptized in the church at Heacham, May 6, 1585. In 1609 he went to Bermuda in the Third Supply with Sir Thomas Gates. While there, a wife, to whom he had been married in England, bore him a daughter, who was christened Bermuda, but soon died. The parents reached Virginia in May, 1610, where the mother died. Rolfe was the first Englishman to introduce the cultivation of tobacco in Virginia (1612). Not long after, Pocahontas was captured by Samuel Argall and brought to Jamestown. Rolfe fell in love with her and married her about April 5, 1614. Two months later he was made recorder of the colony; he remained in this office till 1619. He and his Indian bride went with Sir Thomas Dale, in 1616, to England, where Pocahontas was introduced at court by Lady Delaware and her portrait was engraved by Simon de Passe. While in England, he sent a description of Virginia to King James and to Sir Robert Rich. In the spring of 1617 he and Pocahontas made ready to return, with Samuel Argall as deputy-governor, when Pocahontas sickened and died at Gravesend, March 21, 1617. After his return Rolfe married Jane, daughter of Captain William Peirce, and had a grant of land in Mulberry Island. It was singular that this son-in-law of Powhatan should meet his death at the hands of the savages in the massacre of 1622. He left behind by Pocahontas one son,

Thomas Rolfe, who came to Virginia, where his descendants are still represented. This letter to Sir Thomas Dale, the deputy-governor, was published by Ralph Hamor in his tract entitled *A True Discourse of the Present Estate of Virginia and the Successe of the Affaires there till the 18 of June, 1614* (London, 1615), pp. 61–68.

L. G. T.

# LETTER OF JOHN ROLFE, 1614

*The coppie of the Gentle-mans letters to Sir Thomas Dale, that after maried Powhatans daughter, containing the reasons moving him thereunto.*

*Honourable Sir, and most worthy Governor:*

WHEN your leasure shall best serve you to peruse these lines, I trust in God, the beginning will not strike you into a greater admiration,[1] then the end will give you good content. It is a matter of no small moment, concerning my own particular, which here I impart unto you, and which toucheth mee so neerely, as the tendernesse of my salvation. Howbeit I freely subject my selfe to your grave and mature judgement, deliberation, approbation and determination; assuring my selfe of your zealous admonitions, and godly comforts, either perswading me to desist, or incouraging me to persist therin, with a religious feare and godly care, for which (from the very instant, that this began to roote it selfe within the secret bosome of my brest) my daily and earnest praiers have bin, still are, and ever shall be produced forth with as sincere a godly zeale as I possibly may to be directed, aided and governed in all my thoughts, words and deedes, to the glory of God, and for my eternal consolation. To persevere wherein I never had more neede, nor (till now) could ever imagine to have bin moved with the like occasion.

But (my case standing as it doth) what better worldly refuge can I here seeke, then [than] to shelter my selfe under the safety of your favourable protection? And did not my ease proceede from an unspotted conscience, I should not dare to offer to your view and approved judgement, these passions of

[1] Surprise, or wonder.

my troubled soule, so full of feare and trembling is hypocrisie and dissimulation. But knowing my owne innocency and godly fervor, in the whole prosecution hereof, I doubt not of your benigne acceptance, and clement construction. As for malicious depravers, and turbulent spirits, to whom nothing is tastful, but what pleaseth their unsavory pallat, I passe not for them being well assured in my perswasion (by the often triall and proving of my selfe, in my holiest meditations and praiers) that I am called hereunto by the spirit of God; and it shall be sufficient for me to be protected by your selfe in all vertuous and pious indevours. And for my more happie proceeding herein, my daily oblations [1] shall ever be addressed to bring to passe so good effects, that your selfe, and all the world may truely say: This is the worke of God, and it is marvelous in our eies.

But to avoid tedious preambles, and to come neerer the matter: first suffer me with your patence, to sweepe and make cleane the way wherein I walke, from all suspicions and doubts, which may be covered therein, and faithfully to reveale unto you, what should move me hereunto.

Let therefore this my well advised protestation, which here I make betweene God and my own conscience, be a sufficient witnesse, at the dreadfull day of judgement (when the secret of all mens harts shall be opened) to condemne me herein, if my chiefest intent and purpose be not, to strive with all my power of body and minde, in the undertaking of so mightie a matter, no way led (so farre forth as mans weakenesse may permit) with the unbridled desire of carnall affection: but for the good of this plantation, for the honour of our countrie, for the glory of God, for my owne salvation, and for the converting to the true knowledge of God and Jesus Christ, an unbeleeving creature, namely Pokahuntas. To whom my hartie and best thoughts are, and have a long time bin so intangled, and inthralled in so intricate a laborinth, that I was even awearied to unwinde my selfe thereout. But almighty God, who never

[1] Prayers.

faileth his, that truely invocate his holy name hath opened the gate, and led me by the hand that I might plainely see and discerne the safe paths wherein to treade.

To you therefore (most noble Sir) the patron and Father of us in this countrey doe I utter the effects of this my setled and long continued affection (which hath made a mightie warre in my meditations) and here I doe truely relate, to what issue this dangerous combate is come unto, wherein I have not onely examined, but throughly tried and pared my thoughts even to the quicke, before I could finde any fit wholesome and apt applications to cure so daungerous an ulcer. I never failed to offer my daily and faithfull praiers to God, for his sacred and holy assistance. I forgot not to set before mine eies the frailty of mankinde, his prones[1] to evill, his indulgencie of wicked thoughts, with many other imperfections wherein man is daily insnared, and oftentimes overthrowne, and them compared to my present estate. Nor was I ignorant of the heavie displeasure which almightie God conceived against the sonnes of Levie and Israel for marrying strange wives, nor of the inconveniences which may thereby arise, with other the like good motions which made me looke about warily and with good circumspection, into the grounds and principall agitations, which thus should provoke me to be in love with one whose education hath bin rude, her manners barbarous, her generation accursed, and so discrepant in all nurtriture from my selfe, that oftentimes with feare and trembling, I have ended my private controversie with this: surely these are wicked instigations, hatched by him who seeketh and delighteth in mans destruction; and so with fervent praiers to be ever preserved from such diabolical assaults (as I tooke those to be) I have taken some rest.

Thus when I had thought I had obtained my peace and quietnesse, beholde another, but more gracious tentation hath made breaches into my holiest and strongest meditations; with which I have bin put to a new triall, in a straighter manner

[1] Proneness.

then the former: for besides the many passions and sufferings which I have daily, hourely, yea and in my sleepe indured, even awaking mee to astonishment, taxing mee with remisnesse, and carelesnesse, refusing and neglecting to performe the duetie of a good Christian, pulling me by the eare, and crying: why dost not thou indevour to make her a Christian? And these have happened to my greater wonder, even when she hath bin furthest seperated from me, which in common reason (were it not an undoubted worke of God) might breede forgetfulnesse of a farre more worthie creature. Besides, I say the holy spirit of God hath often demaunded of me, why I was created? If not for transitory pleasures and worldly vanities, but to labour in the Lords vineyard, there to sow and plant, to nourish and increase the fruites thereof, daily adding with the good husband in the Gospell, somewhat to the tallent, that in the end the fruites may be reaped, to the comfort of the laborer in this life, and his salvation in the world to come? And if this be, as undoubtedly this is, the service Jesus Christ requireth of his best servant: wo unto him that hath these instruments of pietie put into his hands, and wilfully despiseth to worke with them. Likewise, adding hereunto her great apparance of love to me, her desire to be taught and instructed in the knowledge of God, her capablenesse of understanding, her aptnesse and willingnesse to receive anie good impression, and also the spirituall, besides her owne incitements stirring me up hereunto.

What should I doe? shall I be of so untoward a disposition, as to refuse to leade the blind into the right way? Shall I be so unnaturall, as not to give bread to the hungrie? or uncharitable, as not to cover the naked? Shall I despise to actuate these pious dueties of a Christian? Shall the base feare of displeasing the world, overpower and with holde mee from revealing unto man these spirituall workes of the Lord, which in my meditations and praiers, I have daily made knowne unto him? God forbid. I assuredly trust hee hath thus delt with me for my eternall felicitie, and for his glorie: and I hope so to be guided by his heavenly graice, that in the end by my faithfull paines, and christianlike labour, I shall attaine to that blessed promise, Pronounced by that holy Prophet Daniell unto the righteous that bring many unto the knowledge of God. Namely, that they shall shine like the starres forever and ever. A sweeter comfort cannot be to a true Christian, nor a greater incouragement for him to labour all the daies of his life, in the performance thereof, nor a greater gaine of consolation, to be desired at the hower of death, and in the day of judgement.

Againe by my reading, and conference with honest and religious persons, have I received no small encouragement, besides *serena mea conscientia,* the cleerenesse of my conscience, clean from the filth of impurity, *quæ est instar muri ahenei,* which is unto me, as a brasen wall. If I should set down at large, the perturbations and godly motions, which have striven within mee, I should but make a tedious and unnecessary volume. But I doubt not these shall be sufficient both to certifie you of my tru intents, in discharging of my dutie to God, and to your selfe, to whose gracious providence I humbly submit my selfe, for his glory, your honour, our Countreys good, the benefit of this Plantation, and for the converting of one unregenerate, to regeneration; which I beseech God to graunt, for his deere Sonne Christ Jesus his sake.

Now if the vulgar sort, who square [1] all mens actions by the base rule of their own filthinesse, shall taxe or taunt me in this my godly labour: let them know, it is not any hungry appetite, to gorge my selfe with incontinency; sure (if I would, and were so sensually inclined) I might satisfie such desire, though not without a seared conscience, yet with Christians more pleasing to the eie, and lesse fearefull in the offence unlawfully committed. Nor am I in so desperate an estate, that I regard not what becommeth of mee; nor am I out of hope but one day to see my Country, nor so void of friends, nor mean in birth, but there to obtain a mach [2] to my great content: nor have I ignorantly passed over my hopes there, or regardlesly

[1] Measure.

[2] Match.

seek to loose the love of my friends, by taking this course: I know them all, and have not rashly overslipped any.

But shal it please God thus to dispose of me (which I earnestly desire to fulfill my ends before sette down) I will heartely accept of it as a godly taxe appointed me, and I will never cease, (God assisting me) untill I have accomplished, and brought to perfection so holy a worke, in which I will daily pray God to blesse me, to mine, and her eternall happines. And thus desiring no longer to live, to enjoy the blessings of God, then [than] this my resolution doth tend to such godly ends, as are by me before declared: not doubting of your favourable acceptance, I take my leave, beseeching Almighty God to raine downe upon you, such plenitude of his heavenly graces, as your heart can wish and desire, and so I rest,

At your commaund most willing
to be disposed off
JOHN ROLFE.

# PROCEEDINGS OF THE VIRGINIA ASSEMBLY, 1619

# INTRODUCTION

During the period of Gates's administration the constitution of the Virginia Company was altered by a third charter (1612) which transferred all important business from the treasurer and council in London to a quarterly meeting of the whole body — treasurer, council, and stockholders. On the question of governing the colony the company soon divided, however, into the "court party" in favor of continuing martial law, at the head of which was Sir Robert Rich, afterwards Earl of Warwick; and the "country" or "patriot party" in favor of ending the system of servitude, led by Sir Edwin Sandys, Henry Wriothesley, Earl of Southampton, and Nicholas Ferrar, jr. Of the two the country party was more numerous, and when the period of the joint partnership expired, November 30, 1616, steps were taken by them to introduce free institutions.

On November 18, 1618, the company ratified the "great charter of priviledges, orders and Lawes," and directed it to the governor and council of estate in Virginia. The same day they adopted a commission for establishing a governor, a council of state and a General Assembly, thereby giving to America its first experience of a plantation with a written constitution for internal affairs.

On April 17, 1619, Sir George Yeardley arrived at Jamestown as governor and captain-general to put the new system into operation. Martial law and communism were abolished; lands were assigned to the settlers; four corporations were created; and the settlements were invited to send delegates to Jamestown to coöperate with the company in making laws.

Accordingly, July 30, 1619, the first legislative assembly that ever convened on the American continent met in the church at Jamestown. It consisted of the governor, six councillors, and twenty burgesses — two from each of ten settlements.

Captain John Martin's delegates were not seated, because of a clause in his patent excepting his plantation from colonial authority. The secretary of the colony, John Pory, who was a member by virtue of his being a member of the council, was elected speaker. He had served several years in Parliament, and was, therefore, familiar with the forms and proceedings of deliberative assemblies. The assembly after a prayer from Rev. Richard Buck, of Jamestown, sat six days and did much business.

When Hening published his collection of the statutes of Virginia (1809), he was unable to find any copy of the proceedings of this the first and most interesting of the assemblies of Virginia. In 1853, however, Conway Robinson reported to the Virginia Historical Society that, on a recent visit to London, he had seen the original in the State Paper Office of England. In 1857, George Bancroft had a copy made, and published it that year in the *Collections of the New York Historical Society*, (second series, III. 329–358). Subsequently a second copy was obtained from London by Col. Angus McDonald when sent to England to obtain papers necessary to protect the interests of Virginia against Maryland in regard to the boundary line. Still another copy was obtained, when Hon. D. C. De Jarnette went upon a similar errand. In 1874 De Jarnette's copy was printed by order of the Virginia State Senate as *Colonial Records of Virginia, Senate Document Extra*, and the copy below is made from this publication. The original record, which was written by the speaker, John Pory, is in the Public Record Office, State Papers, Domestic, James I., vol. I., no. 45.

L. G. T.

# PROCEEDINGS OF THE VIRGINIA ASSEMBLY, 1619

*A Reporte of the manner of proceeding in the General assembly convented at James citty in Virginia, July* 30, 1619, *consisting of the Governor, the Counsell of Estate and two Burgesses elected out of eache Incorporation and Plantation, and being dissolved the 4th of August next ensuing.*

FIRST. Sir George Yeardley,[1] Knight, Governor and Captaine general of Virginia, having sent his sumons all over the Country, as well to invite those of the Counsell of Estate that were absent as also for the election of Burgesses, there were chosen and appeared.

For James citty [2]
Captaine William Powell,
Ensigne William Spense.
For Charles citty [3]
Samuel Sharpe,
Samuel Jordan.
For the citty of Henricus [4]
Thomas Dowse,
John Polentine.

[1] Sir George Yeardley, who had been a soldier in the Low Country wars, sailed for Virginia as captain of Sir Thomas Gates's company in 1609. He was wrecked with Gates on the Bermuda Islands and reaching Virginia was deputy-governor from the departure of Dale in April, 1616, to the arrival of Argall in May, 1617. After Lord Delaware's death he was appointed to succeed him as governor and captain-general. He convened the first legislative assembly in America. He served till November 18, 1621. In March, 1626, he was reappointed governor, and continued in that office till his death in November, 1627.

[2] The immediate district of Jamestown.

[3] The region of City Point.

[4] Or Henrico; on Farrar's Island.

For Kiccowtan [1]
Captaine William Tucker,
William Capp.
For Martin Brandon [2]-Capt. John Martin's Plantation
Mr. Thomas Davis,
Mr. Robert Stacy.
For Smythe's hundred [3]
Captain Thomas Graves,
Mr. Walter Shelley.
For Martin's hundred [4]
Mr. John Boys,
John Jackson.
For Argall's guiffe [5]
Mr. Pawlett,
Mr. Gourgaing.
For Flowerdieu hundred [6]
Ensigne Roffingham,
Mr. Jefferson.
For Captain Lawne's plantation [7]
Captain Christopher Lawne,
Ensigne Washer.
For Captaine Warde's plantation [8]
Captaine Warde,
Lieutenant Gibbes.

[1] Elizabeth City.

[2] Brandon, on the south side of James River. This was one of the private plantations, resembling manors.

[3] Afterward Southampton Hundred, running along the north side of the James, from Weyanoke to the Chickahominy. This hundred, and some of those subsequently mentioned, were the property of different small associations subordinate to the Virginia Company. On hundreds, see p. 266, note 2.

[4] In the east end of the present James City County, some miles below Jamestown.

[5] Argall's Gift lay about a mile north of Jamestown. See p. 275, note 1.

[6] On the south side of the river, half way from Brandon to City Point.

[7] At Lawne's Creek in Isle of Wight County.

[8] On the south side of James River, above Brandon, where Ward's Creek still preserves the name.

The most convenient place we could finde to sitt in was the Quire [1] of the Churche Where Sir George Yeardley, the Governor, being sett downe in his accustomed place, those of the Counsel of Estate sate nexte him on both hands excepte onely the Secretary then appointed Speaker, who sate right before him, John Twine, clerke of the General assembly, being placed nexte the Speaker, and Thomas Pierse, the Sergeant, standing at the barre, to be ready for any service the Assembly shoulde comaund him. But forasmuche as men's affaires doe little prosper where God's service is neglected, all the Burgesses tooke their places in the Quire till a prayer was said by Mr. Bucke,[2] the Minister, that it would please God to guide and sanctifie all our proceedings to his owne glory and the good of this Plantation. Prayer being ended, to the intente that as we had begun at God Almighty, so we might proceed with awful and due respecte towards the Lieutenant,[3] our most gratious and dread Soveraigne, all the Burgesses were intreatted to retyre themselves into the body of the Churche, which being done, before they were fully admitted, they were called in order and by name, and so every man (none staggering at it) tooke the oathe of Supremacy, and entred the Assembly. At Captaine Warde the Speaker tooke exception, as at one that without any Comission or authority had seatted himselfe either upon the Companies, and then his Plantation would not be lawfull, or on Captain Martin's lande, and so he was but a limbe or member of him, and there could be but two Burgesses for all.[4] So Captaine Warde was comanded to absent himselfe till such time as the Assembly had agreed what was fitt for him to doe. After muche debate, they resolved on this order following:

[1] Choir.

[2] Rev. Richard Buck was educated at Oxford and came to Virginia in 1610 with Sir Thomas Gates. He married John Rolfe to Pocahontas in Jamestown, April 5, 1614. In 1618 Rolfe writes that "he was a verie good preacher." He died before February, 1624.

[3] King James I.

[4] The whole plantation.

*An order concluded by the General assembly concerning Captaine Warde, July 30th, 1619, at the opening of the said Assembly.*

At the reading of the names of the Burgesses, Exception was taken against Captaine Warde as having planted here in Virginia without any authority or comission from the Tresurer, Counsell and Company in Englande. But considering he had bene at so great chardge and paines to augmente this Colony, and adventured his owne person in the action, and since that time had brought home a good quantity of fishe, to relieve the Colony by waye of trade, and above all, because the Comission for authorising the General Assembly admitteth of two Burgesses out of every plantation without restrainte or exception, Upon all these considerations, the Assembly was contented to admitt of him and his Lieutenant (as members of their body and Burgesses) into their society. Provided, that the said Captaine Warde with all expedition, that is to saye between this and the nexte general assembly (all lawful impediments excepted), should procure from the Tresurer, Counsell and Company in England a comission lawfully to establish and plant himselfe and his Company as the Chieffs of other Plantations have done. And in case he doe neglect this he is to stande to the censure of the nexte general assembly. To this Captaine Warde, in the presence of us all, having given his consente and undertaken to performe the same was, together with his Lieutenant, by voices of the whole Assembly first admitted to take the oath of Supremacy, and then to make up their number and to sitt amongst them.

This being done, the Governor himselfe alledged that before we proceeded any further it behooved us to examine whither it were fitt, that Captaine Martin's[1] Burgesses shoulde have any place in the Assembly, forasmuche as he hath a clause in his Patente which doth not onely exempte him from that equality and uniformity of lawes and orders which the

[1] Captain John Martin was one of the original Council of Virginia, being the only member still resident in Virginia at this time. When Jamestown was abandoned in 1610, he was the only one of the colonists to protest against it. He was living as late as 1627.

great charter saith are to extende over the whole Colony, but also from diverse such lawes as we must be enforced to make in the General Assembly. That clause is as followeth: Item. That it shall and may be lawfull to and for the said Captain John Martin, his heyers, executours and assignes to governe and comaunde all suche person or persons as at this time he shall carry over with him, or that shalbe sente him hereafter, free from any comaunde of the Colony, excepte it be in ayding and assisting the same against any forren or domestical enemy.

Upon the motion of the Governor, discussed the same time in the assembly, ensued this order following:

*An order of the General Assembly touching a clause in Captain Martin's Patent at James Citty, July 30, 1619.*

After all the Burgesses had taken the oath of Supremacy and were admitted into the house and all sett downe in their places, a Copie of Captain Martin's Patent was produced by the Governor out of a Clause whereof it appeared that when the general assembly had made some kinde of lawes requisite for the whole Colony, he and his Burgesses and people might deride the whole company and chuse whether they would obay the same or no. It was therefore ordered in Courte that the foresaid two Burgesses should withdraw themselves out of the assembly till suche time as Captaine Martin had made his personall appearance before them. At what time, if upon their motion, if he would be contente to quitte and give over that parte of his Patente, and contrary thereunto woulde submitte himselfe to the general forme of governemente as all others did, that then his Burgesses should be readmitted, otherwise they were to be utterly excluded as being spies rather than loyal Burgesses, because they had offered themselves to be assistant at the making of lawes which both themselves and those whom they represented might chuse whether they would obaye or not.

Then came there in a complainte against Captain Martin, that having sente his Shallop to trade for corne into the baye, under the commaunde of one Ensigne Harrison, the saide Ensigne should affirme to one Thomas Davis, of Paspaheighe, Gent. (as the said Thomas Davis deposed upon oathe,) that they had made a harde voiage, had they not mett with a Canoa coming out of a creeke where their shallop could not goe. For the Indians refusing to sell their Corne, those of the shallop entered the Canoa with their armes and tooke it by force, measuring out the corne with a baskett they had into the Shallop and (as the said Ensigne Harrison saith) giving them satisfaction in copper beades and other trucking stuffe.

Hitherto Mr. Davys upon his oath.

Furthermore it was signified from Opochancano to the Governour that those people had complained to him to procure them justice. For which considerations and because suche outrages as this might breede danger and loss of life to others of the Colony which should have leave to trade in the baye hereafter, and for prevention of the like violences against the Indians in time to come, this order following was agreed on by the general assembly:

*A second order against Captain Martin, at James citty, July 30, 1619.*

It was also ordered by the Assembly the same day in case Captaine Martin and the ging [1] of his shallop would not thoroughly answere an accusation of an outrage committed gainst a certaine Conoa of Indians in the baye, that then it was thought reason (his Patent notwithstanding, the authority whereof he had in that case abused) he should from henceforth take leave of the Governour as other men, and should putt in security, that his people shall comitte no such outrage any more.

Upon this a letter or warrant was drawen in the name of the whole assembly to sumon Captaine Martin to appeare before them in the forme following:

*By the Governour and general assembly of Virginia.*

Captaine Martine, we are to request you upon sight hereof, with all convenient speed to repair hither to James citty to treatt

[1] Gang, or crew.

and conferre wth us about some matters of especial importance which concerns both us and the whole Colony [and] yourself. And of this we praye you not to faile. James citty, July 30, 1619.

*To our very loving friend, Captain John Martin, Esquire, Master of the ordinance.*

These obstacles removed, the Speaker, who for a long time has bene extreame sickly, and therefore not able to passe through long harangues, delivered in briefe to the whole assembly the occasions of their meeting. Which done he read unto them the commission for establishing the Counsell of Estate and the general Assembly, wherein their duties were described to the life.

Having thus prepared them he read over unto them the greate Charter, or commission of privileges, orders and laws,[1] sent by [2] Sir George Yeardley out of Englande. Which for the more ease of the Committies, having divided into fower books, he read the former two the same forenoon for expeditions sake, a second time over, and so they were referred to the perusall of twoe Committies, which did reciprocally consider of either, and accordingly brought in their opinions. But some may here objecte to what ende we should presume to referre that to the examination of Committies which the Counsell and Company in England had already resolved to be perfect, and did expect nothing but our assente thereunto. To this we answere, that we did it not to the ende to correcte or controll anything therein contained, but onely in case we should finde ought [3] not perfectly squaring with the state of this Colony or any lawe which did presse or binde too harde, that we might by waye of humble petition, seeke to have it redressed, especially because this great Charter is to bind us and our heyers for ever.

[1] This "greate Charter" was addressed to Sir George Yeardley. A copy is preserved in the Department of Manuscripts, Library of Congress, Washington. It is presented with several omissions in the *Virginia Magazine of History*, II. 154–165.

[2] With.

[3] Anything.

*The names of the Committies for perusing the first booke of the fower:*

1. Captain William Powell,
2. Ensigne Rosingham,
3. Captaine Warde,
4. Captaine Tucker,
5. Mr. Shelley,
6 Thomas Douse,
7. Samuel Jordan,
8. Mr. Boys.

*The names of the Committies for perusing the second booke:*

1. Captaine Lawne,
2. Captaine Graves,
3. Ensigne Spense,
4. Samuel Sharpe,
5. William Cap,
6. Mr. Pawlett,
7. Mr. Jefferson,
8. Mr. Jackson.

These Committies thus appointed, we brake up the first forenoon's assembly.

After dinner the Governour and those that were not of the Committies sate a second time, while the said Committies were employed in the perusall of those twoe bookes. And whereas the Speaker had propounded fower severall objects for the Assembly to consider on: namely, first the great charter of orders, lawes and privileges; Secondly, which of the instructions given by the Counsel in England to my Lo: La: warre,[1] Captain Argall or Sir George Yeardley, might conveniently putt on the habite of lawes; Thirdly, what lawes might issue out of the private conceipte of any of the Burgesses, or any other of the Colony; and lastly, what petitions were fitt to be sente home for England. It pleased the Governour for expedition sake to have the second objecte of the fower to be examined and prepared by himselfe and the Non-Committies. Wherein after having spente some three howers conference, the twoe Committies brought in their opinions concerning the twoe former bookes, (the second of which beginneth at these wordes of the charter: And forasmuche as our intente is to establish one

[1] Lord De-la-Warre or Delaware.

equall and uniforme kinde of government over all Virginia &c.,) which the whole Assembly, because it was late, deferred to treatt of till the next morning.

*Satturday, July 31.*

The nexte daye, therefore, out of the opinions of the said Committies, it was agreed, these Petitions ensuing should be framed, to be presented to the Treasurer, Counsel and Company in England. Upon the Committies perusall of the first book, the Generall Assembly doe become most humble suitors to their lo$^{ps}$ [1] and to the rest of that honble Counsell and renowned Company, that albeit they have bene pleased to allotte unto the Governo$^{r}$ to themselves, together with the Counsell of Estate here, and to the officers of Incorporations, certain lande [2] portions of lande to be layde out within the limites of the same, yet that they woulde vouchsafe also, that groundes as heretofore had bene granted by patent to the antient Planters by former Governours that had from the Company received comission so to doe, might not nowe after so muche labour and coste, and so many yeares habitation be taken from them. And to the ende that no man might doe or suffer any wrong in this kinde, that they woulde favour us so muche (if they meane to graunte this our petition) as to sende us notice, what comission or authority for graunting of landes they have given to eache particular Governour in times paste.

The second petition of the General assembly framed by the Committies out of the second book is. That the Treasurer and Company in England would be pleased with as muche convenient speed as may be to sende men hither to occupie their landes belonging to the fower Incorporations, as well for their owne behoofe and proffitt as for the maintenance of the Counsel of Estate, who are nowe to their extream hindrance often drawen far from their private busines and likewise that they will have a care to sende tenants to the ministers of the fower Incorporations to manure their gleab, to the intente that

[1] Lordships.

[2] Doubtless an error for *large*.

all allowance they have allotted them of 200 G.[1] a yeare may be more easily raised.

The thirde Petition humbly presented by this General Assembly to the Treasurer, Counsell and Company is, that it may plainly be expressed in the great Comission (as indeed it is not) that the antient Planters of both sortes, viz., suche as before Sir Thomas Dales' depart[2] were come hither upon their owne chardges, and suche also as were brought hither upon the Companie's coste, maye have their second, third and more divisions successively in as lardge and free manner as any other Planters. Also that they wilbe pleased to allowe to the male children, of them and of all others begotten in Virginia, being the onely hope of a posterity, a single share a piece, and shares for their issues or for themselves, because that in a newe plantation it is not knowen whether man or woman be more necessary.

Their fourth Petition is to beseech the Treasurer, Counsell and Company that they would be pleased to appoint a Sub-Treasurer here to collecte their rents, to the ende that the Inhabitants of this Colony be not tyed to an impossibility of paying the same yearly to the Treasurer in England, and that they would enjoine the said Sub-Treasurer not precisely according to the letter of the Charter to exacte mony of us (whereof we have none at all, as we have no minte), but the true value of the rente in comodity.[3]

The fifte Petition is to beseeche the Treasurer, Counsell and Company that, towards the erecting of the University and Colledge, they will sende, when they shall thinke it most convenient, workmen of all sortes, fitt for that purpose.[4]

[1] An error doubtless for £, as shown in the "Greate Charter," *Virginia Magazine*, II. 158.

[2] Departure.

[3] This refers to the quit-rent of twelve pence annually for every fifty acres of land granted to every settler "after midsummer day during the next seven years." The prayer of the petition is to pay "comodity," chiefly tobacco.

[4] In response to this petition workmen were sent over, lands were laid out at Henrico, and a rector was elected for said "University and Colledge"; but the Indians in March, 1622, killed nearly all the people at the settlement and destroyed the enterprise.

The sixte and laste is, they wilbe pleased to change the savage name of Kiccowtan, and to give that Incorporation a new name.[1]

These are the general Petitions drawen by the Comitties out of the two former bookes which the whole general assembly in maner and forme above sett downe doe most humbly offer up and present to the honourable construction of the Treasurer, Counsell and Company in England.

These petitions thus concluded on, those twoe Comitties broughte me a reporte what they had observed in the two latter bookes, which was nothing else but that the perfection of them was suche as that they could finde nothing therein subject to exception, only the Governors particular opinion to my selfe in private hathe bene as touching a clause in the thirde booke, that in these doubtfull times between us and the Indians, it would behoove us not to make as lardge distances between Plantation as ten miles, but for our more strength ande security to drawe nearer together. At the same time, there remaining no farther scruple in the mindes of the Assembly touching the said great Charter of lawes, orders and priviledges, the Speaker putt the same to the question, and so it had both the general assent and the applause of the whole assembly, who, as they professed themselves in the first place most submissively thankful to almighty god, therefore so they commaunded the Speaker to returne (as nowe he doth) their due and humble thankes to the Treasurer Counsell and company for so many priviledges and favours as well in their owne names as in the names of the whole Colony whom they represented.

This being dispatched we fell once more debating of suche instructions given by the Counsell in England to several Governors as might be converted into lawes, the last whereof was the Establishment of the price of Tobacco, namely, of the best at 3*d*[2] and the second at 18*d* the pounde. At the reading of this the Assembly thought good to send for Mr. Abraham Persey, the Cape marchant,[3] to publishe this instruction to

[1] It was given the name of Elizabeth City.

[2] An error for 3*s*.

[3] Keeper of the public stores.

him, and to demaunde of him if he knewe of any impediment why it might not be admitted of? His answere was that he had not as yet received any suche order from the Adventurers of the[1] in England. And notwithstanding he sawe the authority was good, yet was he unwilling to yield, till suche time as the Governor and Assembly had layd their commandment upon him, out of the authority of the foresaid Instructions as followeth:

*By the General Assembly.*

We will and require you, Mr. Abraham Persey, Cape Marchant, from this daye forwarde to take notice, that, according to an article in the Instructions confirmed by the Treasurer, Counsell and Company in Englande at a general quarter courte, both by voices and under their hands and the Comon seall, and given to Sir George Yeardley, knight, this present governour, Decemb. 3, 1618, that you are bounde to accepte of the Tobacco of the Colony, either for commodities or upon billes, at three shillings the beste and the second sorte at 18*d* the punde, and this shalbe your sufficient dischardge.

*James citty out of the said General*
*Assembly, July 31, 1619.*

At the same the Instructions convertible into lawes were referred to the consideration of the above named Committies, viz., the general Instructions to the first Committie and the particular Instructions to the second, to be returned by them into the assembly on Munday morning.

*Sunday, Aug. 1.*

Mr. Shelley,[2] one of the Burgesses, deceased.

*Munday, Aug. 2.*

Captain John Martin (according to the sumons sent him on Fryday, July 30,) made his personall appearance at the

[1] Supply "Magazine," which appears in the Bancroft and McDonald copies.
[2] Walter Shelley of Smyth's Hundred, the country on the north side of the river between Weyanoke and Chickahominy River.

barre, whenas the Speaker having first read unto him the orders of the Assembly that concerned him, he pleaded lardgely for himself to them both and indevoured to answere some other thinges that were objected against his Patente. In fine, being demanded out of the former order whether he would quitte that clause of his Patent which (quite otherwise then Sir William Throckmorton's, Captain Christopher Lawnes and other men's patentes) exempteth himselffe and his people from all services of the Colonie excepte onely in case of warre against a forren or domesticall enemie, His answere was negative, that he would not infringe any parte of his Patente. Whereupon it was resolved by the Assembly that his Burgesses should have no admittance.

To the second order his answere was affirmative, namely, that (his Patent notwithstanding) whensoever he should send in to the baye to trade, he would be contente to putt in security to the Governour for the good behaviour of his people towardes the Indians.

It was at the same time further ordered by the Assembly that the Speaker, in their names, should (as he nowe doth) humbly demaunde of the Treasurer, Counsell and Company an exposition of this one clause in Captaine Martin's Patente namely, where it is saide That he is to enjoye his landes in as lardge and ample manner, to all intentes and purposes, as any lord of any manours in England dothe holde his grounde out of which some have collected that he might by the same graunte protecte men from paying their debts and from diverse other dangers of lawe. The least the Assembly can alledge against this clause is, that it is obscure, and that it is a thing impossible for us here to knowe the Prerogatives of all manours in Englande. The Assembly therefore humbly beseeches their lo[pps] and the rest of that Honble house that in case they shall finde any thing in this or in any other parte of his graunte wherby that clause towards the conclusion of the great charter, (viz., that all grauntes aswell of the one sorte as of the other respectively, be made with equall favour, and graunts of like liberties and imunities as neer as may be, to the ende that all complainte of partiality and indifferency may be avoided,) might in any sorte be contradicted or the uniformity and equality of lawes and orders extending over the whole Colony might be impeached, That they would be pleased to remove any such hindrance as may diverte out of the true course the free and publique current of Justice.

Upon the same ground and reason their lo$^{ps}$, together with the rest of the Counsell and Company, are humbly besought by this general assembly that if in that other clause which exempteth Captaine Martin and his people from all services of the Colony etc., they shall finde any resistance [to] that equality and uniformity of lawes and orders intended nowe by them to be established over the whole Colony, that they would be pleased to reforme it.

In fine, wheras Captaine Martin, for those ten shares allowed him for his personal adventure and for his adventure of £70 besides, doth claim 500 acres a share, that the Treasurer, Counsell and Company woulde vouchsafe to give notice to the Governour here, what kinde of shares they meante he should have when they gave him his Patent.[1]

The premisses about Captaine Martin thus resolved, the Committies appointed to consider what instructions are fitt to be converted into lawes, brought in their opinions, and first of some of the general instructions.

*Here begin the lawes drawen out of the Instructions given by his Ma$^{ties}$ Counsell of Virginia in England to my lo: la warre, Captain Argall and Sir George Yeardley, knight.*

By this present General Assembly be it enacted that no injury or oppression be wrought by the English against the Indians whereby the present peace might be disturbed and antient quarrells might be revived. And farther be it ordained that the Chicohomini are not to be excepted out of this lawe; un-

[1] The question of Captain Martin's patent came up in England, and he was finally forced to take a new patent submitting to the authority of the colony.

till either that suche order come out of Englande or that they doe provoke us by some newe injury.

Against Idlenes, Gaming, drunkenes and excesse in apparell the Assembly hath enacted as followeth:

First, in detestation of Idlenes be it enacted, that if any man be founde to live as an Idler or renagate, though a freedman, it shalbe lawful for that Incorporation or Plantation to which he belongeth to appoint him a Mr[1] to serve for wages, till he shewe apparant signes of amendment.

Against gaming at dice and Cardes be it ordained by this present assembly that the winner or winners shall lose all his or their winninges and both winners and loosers shall forfaite ten shillings a man, one ten shillings whereof to go to the discoverer, and the rest to charitable and pious uses in the Incorporation where the faulte is comitted.

Against drunkenness be it also decreed that if any private person be found culpable thereof, for the first time he is to be reprooved privately by the Minister, the second time publiquely, the thirde time to lye in boltes 12 howers in the house of the Provost Marshall and to paye his fee, and if he still continue in that vice, to undergo suche severe punishment as the Governor and Counsell of Estate shall thinke fitt to be inflicted on him. But if any officer offende in this crime, the first time he shall receive reprooff from the Governour, the second time he shall openly be reprooved in the churche by the minister, and the third time he shall first be comitted and then degraded. Provided it be understood that the Governor hath alwayes power to restore him when he shall in his discretion thinke fitte.

Against excesse in apparell that every man be cessed in the churche for all publique contributions, if he be unmarried according to his owne apparell, if he be married, according to his owne and his wives, or either of their apparell.

As touching the instruction of drawing some of the better disposed of the Indians to converse with our people and to

[1] Master.

live and labour amongst them, the Assembly who knowe well their dispositions thinke it fitte to enjoin, least to counsell those of the Colony, neither utterly to reject them nor yet to drawe them to come in. But in case they will of themselves come voluntarily to places well peopled, there to doe service in killing of Deere, fishing, beatting of Corne and other workes, that then five or six may be admitted into every such place, and no more, and that with the consente of the Governour. Provided that good guarde in the night be kept upon them for generally (though some amongst many may proove good) they are a most trecherous people and quickly gone when they have done a villany. And it were fitt a house were builte for them to lodge in aparte by themselves, and lone inhabitants by no meanes to entertain them.

Be it enacted by this present assembly that for laying a surer foundation of the conversion of the Indians to Christian Religion, eache towne, citty, Borrough, and particular plantation do obtaine unto themselves by just means a certine number of the natives' children to be educated by them in true religion and civile course of life — of which children the most towardly boyes in witt and graces of nature to be brought up by them in the first elements of litterature, so to be fitted for the Colledge intended for them that from thence they may be sente to that worke of conversion.

As touching the busines of planting corne this present Assembly doth ordain that yeare by yeare all and every householder and householders have in store for every servant he or they shall keep, and also for his or their owne persons, whether they have any Servants or no, one spare barrell of corne, to be delivered out yearly, either upon sale or exchange as need shall require. For the neglecte of which duty he shalbe subjecte to the censure of the Governor and Counsell of Estate. Provided always that the first yeare of every newe man this lawe shall not be of force.

About the plantation of Mulbery trees, be it enacted that every man as he is seatted upon his division, doe for seven yeares together, every yeare plante and maintaine in growte six Mulberry trees at the least, and as many more as he shall think conveniente and as his vurtue and Industry shall move him to plante, and that all suche persons as shall neglecte the yearly planting and maintaining of that small proportion shalbe subjecte to the censure of the Governour and the Counsell of Estate.

Be it farther enacted as concerning Silke-flaxe, that those men that are upon their division or setled habitation doe this next yeare plante and dresse 100 plantes, which being founde a comodity, may farther be increased. And whosoever do faill in the performance of this shalbe subject to the punishment of the Governour and Counsell of Estate.

For hempe also both English and Indian and for English flax and Anniseeds, we do require and enjoine all householders of this Colony that have any of those seeds to make tryal thereof the nexte season.

Moreover be it enacted by this present Assembly, that every householder doe yearly plante and maintaine ten vines untill they have attained to the art and experience of dressing a Vineyard either by their owne industry or by the Instruction of some Vigneron. And that upon what penalty soever the Governor and Counsell of Estate shall thinke fitt to impose upon the neglecters of this acte.

Be it also enacted that all necessary tradesmen, or so many as need shall require, suche as are come over since the departure of Sir Thomas Dale, or that shall hereafter come, shall worke at their trades for any other man, each one being payde according to the quality of his trade and worke, to be estimated, if he shall not be contented, by the Governor and officers of the place where he worketh.

Be it further ordained by this General Assembly, and we doe by these presents enacte, that all contractes made in England between the owners of the lande and their Tenants and Servantes which they shall sende hither, may be caused to be duely performed, and that the offenders be punished as the Governour and Counsell of Estate shall thinke just and convenient.

Be it established also by this present Assembly that no crafty or advantagious means be suffered to be put in practise for the inticing awaye the Tenants or Servants of any particular plantation from the place where they are seatted. And that it shalbe the duty of the Governor and Counsell of Estate most severely to punish both the seducers and the seduced, and to returne these latter into their former places.

Be it further enacted that the orders for the Magazin lately made be exactly kepte, and that the Magazin [1] be preserved from wrong and sinister practises, and that according to the orders of courte in Englande all Tobacco and sasafras be brought by the Planters to the Cape marchant till suche time as all the goods nowe or heretofore sent for the Magazin be taken off their hands at the prices agreed on. That by this meanes the same going for Englande with one hande the price thereof may be upheld the better. And to that ende that all the whole Colony may take notice of the last order of Courte made in Englande and all those whom it concerneth may knowe howe to observe it, we holde it fitt to publishe it here for a lawe among the rest of our lawes. The which order is as followeth:

Upon the 26 of October, 1618, it was ordered that the Magazin should continue during the terme formerly prefixed and that certaine abuses now complained of should be reformed and that for preventing of all Impositions save the allowance of 25 in the hundred proffitt, the Governor shall have an invoice as well as the Cape Marchant, that if any abuse in the sale of the goods be offered, wee upon Intelligence and due examination thereof, shall see it correctede. And for incouragement of particular hundreds,[2] as Smythe's hundred, Martin's hundred, Lawnes' hundred, and the like, it is agreed that what comodoties are reaped upon anie of these General [3] Colonies,

[1] The company's storehouse.

[2] Hundred was the Anglo-Saxon word for a community occupying a larger territory than a town or for a subdivision of the county. The application was revived in Virginia, and the hundred might embrace several boroughs.

[3] Bancroft's and McDonald's copies render this word "severall," which is evidently right.

it shalbe lawefull for them to returne the same to their owne adventurers. Provided that the same comodity be of their owne growing, without trading with any other, in one entyre lumpe and not dispersed and that at the determination of the jointe stocke, the goods then remaining in the Magazin shalbe bought by the said particular Colonies before any other goods which shall be sente by private men. And it was moreover ordered that if the lady la warre, the Lady Dale, Captain Bargrave and the rest, would unite themselves into a settled Colony they might be capable of the same priviledges that are graunted to any of the foresaid hundreds. Hitherto the order.

All the general Assembly by voices concluded not only the acceptance and observation of this order, but of the Instruction also to Sir George Yeardley next preceding the same. Provided first, that the Cape Marchant do accepte of the Tobacco of all and everie the Planters here in Virginia, either for Goods or upon billes of Exchange at three shillings the pounde the beste, and 18*d* the second sorte. Provided also that the billes be only payde in Englande. Provided, in the third place, that if any other besides the Magazin have at any time any necessary comodity which the Magazine dothe wante, it shall and may be lawfull for any of the Colony to buye the said necessary comodity of the said party, but upon the termes of the Magazin viz: allowing no more gaine then 25 in the hundred, and that with the leave of the Governour. Provided lastly, that it may be lawfull for the Governor to give leave to any Mariner, or any other person that shall have any suche necessary comodity wanting to the Magazin to carrie home for Englande so muche Tobacco or other naturall comodities of the Country as his Customers shall pay him for the said necessary comodity or comodities. And to the ende we may not only persuade and incite men, but inforce them also thoroughly and loyally to aire their Tobacco before they bring it to the Magazine, be it enacted, and by these presents we doe enacte, that if upon the Judgement of fower sufficient men of any incorporation where the Magazine shall reside, (having first taken their oaths to give true sentence, twoe whereof to be chosen by the Cape Marchant and twoe by the Incorporation), any Tobacco whatsoever shall not proove vendible at the second price, that it shall there imediately be burnt before the owner's face. Hitherto suche lawes as were drawen out of the Instructions.

*Tuesday, Aug. 3, 1619.*

This morning a thirde sorte of lawes (suche as might proceed out of every man's private conceipt) were read and referred by halves to the same comitties which were from the beginning.

This done, Captaine William Powell presented to the Assembly a pettiton to have justice against a lewde and trecherous servante of his who by false accusation given up in writing to the Governor sought not only to gett him deposed from his government of James citty and utterly (according to the Proclamation) to be degraded from the place and title of a Captaine,[1] but to take his life from him also. And so out of the said Petition sprang this order following:

Captaine William Powell presented a pettition to the generall Assembly against one Thomas Garnett, a servant of his, not onely for extreame neglect of his business to the great loss and prejudice of the said Captaine, and for openly and impudently abusing his house, in sight both of Master and Mistress, through wantonnes with a woman servant of theirs, a widdowe, but also for falsely accusing him to the Governor both of Drunkennes and Thefte, and besides for bringing all his fellow servants to testifie on his side, wherein they justly failed him. It was thought fitt by the general assembly (the Governour himself giving sentence), that he should stand fower dayes with his eares nayled to the Pillory, viz: Wednesday, Aug. 4th, and so likewise Thursday, fryday, and Satturday next following, and every of those dayes should be publiquely whipped. Now, as touching the neglecte of his worke, what satisfaction ought to be made to his Mr [2] for that is referred to the Governour and Counsell of Estate.

[1] In 1617 Governor Samuel Argall made Powell captain of the governor's guard, and commander of Jamestown, the fort, and the blockhouses.

[2] Master.

The same morning the lawes abovewritten, drawen out of the instructions, were read, and one by one thoroughly examined, and then passed once again the general consente of the whole Assembly.

This afternoon the comitties brought in a reporte, what they had done as concerning the thirde sorte of lawes, the discussing whereof spente the residue of that daye. Excepte onely the consideration of a pettiton of Mr. John Rolfes againste Captaine John Martine for writing a letter to him wherein (as Mr. Rolfe alledgeth) he taxeth him both unseemly and amisse of certaine thinges wherein he was never faulty, and besides, casteth some aspersion upon the present government, which is the most temperate and juste that ever was in this country, too milde indeed, for many of this Colony, whom unwoonted liberty hath made insolente and not to know themselves. This Petition of Mr. Rolfes' was thought fitt to be referred to the Counsell of State.

*Wednesday, Aug. 4th.*

This daye (by reason of extream heat, both paste and likely to ensue and by that meanes of the alteration of the healthes of diverse of the general Assembly) the Governour, who himself also was not well, resolved should be the last of this first session; so in the morning the Speaker (as he was required by the Assembly) redd over all the lawes and orders that had formerly passed the house, to give the same yett one reviewe more, and to see whether there were any thing to be amended or that might be excepted againste. This being done, the third sorte of lawes which I am nowe coming to sett downe, were read over [and] thoroughly discussed, which, together with the former, did now passe the laste and finall consente of the General Assembly.

*A thirde sorte of lawes, suche as may issue out of every man's private conceipte.*

It shalbe free for every man to trade with the Indians, servants onely excepted, upon paine of whipping, unless the

Mr. will redeeme it off with the payment of an Angell,[1] one-fourth parte whereof to go to the Provost Marshall one fourth parte to the discoverer, and the other moyty [2] to the publique uses of the Incorporation.

That no man doe sell or give any of the greatter howes [3] to the Indians, or any English dog of quality, as a mastive, greyhound, bloodhounde, lande or water spaniel, or any other dog or bitche whatsoever, of the Englishe race, upon paine of forfaiting 5s sterling to the publique uses of the Incorporation where he dwelleth.

That no man do sell or give any Indians any piece shott or poulder, or any other armes, offensive or defensive upon paine of being held a Traytour to the Colony, and of being hanged as soon as the facte is proved, without all redemption.[4]

That no man may go above twenty miles from his dwelling-place, nor upon any voiage whatsoever shalbe absent from thence for the space of seven dayes together without first having made the Governor or comaunder of the same place acquainted therwith, upon paine of paying twenty shillings to the publique uses of the same Incorporation where the party delinquent dwelleth.

That no man shall purposely goe to any Indian townes, habitations or places or resortes without leave from the Governor or comaunder of that place wher he liveth, upon paine of paying 40*s* to publique uses as aforesaid.

That no man living in this Colony, but shall between this and the first of January nexte ensueing come or sende to the Secretary of Estate to enter his own and all his servants' names, and for what terme or upon what conditions they are to serve, upon penalty of paying 40*s* to the said Secretary of Estate. Also, whatsoever M^rs [5] or people doe come over to this plantation that within one month of their arrivall (notice being first given them of this very lawe) they shall likewise resorte

[1] An English coin bearing the figure of the archangel Michael, worth from 8*s.* 6*d.* to 10*s.*

[2] Half.

[3] Hoes.

[4] As long as the Indians had to depend on their bows and arrows, they were comparatively harmless.

[5] *I.e.*, masters.

to the Secretary of Estate and shall certifie him upon what termes or conditions they be come hither, to the ende that he may recorde their grauntes and comissions, and for how long time and upon what conditions their servants (in case they have any) are to serve them, and that upon paine of the penalty nexte above mentioned.

All Ministers in the Colony shall once a year, namely, in the moneth of Marche, bring to the Secretary of Estate a true account of all Christenings, burials and marriages, upon paine, if they faill, to be censured for their negligence by the Governor and Counsell of Estate; likewise, where there be no ministers, that the comanders of the place doe supply the same duty.

No man, without leave of the Governor, shall kill any Neatt[1] cattle whatsoever, young or olde, especially kine, Heyfurs or cow-calves, and shalbe careful to perserve their steers and oxen, and to bring them to the plough and such profitable uses, and without having obtained leave as aforesaid, shall not kill them, upon penalty of forfaiting the value of the beast so killed.

Whosoever shall take any of his neighbors' boates, oares, or canoas without leave from the owner shalbe helde and esteemed as a felon and so proceeded againste; tho hee that shall take away by violence or stelth any canoas or other thinges from the Indians shall make valuable restitution to the said Indians, and shall forfaict, if he be a freeholder, five pound; if a servant, 40*s*, or endure a whipping; and anything under the value of 13*d* shall be accounted Petty larcency.

All ministers shall duely read divine service, and exercise their ministerial function according to the Ecclesiastical lawes and orders of the churche of Englande, and every Sunday in the afternoon shall Catechize suche as are not yet ripe to come to the Com.[2] And whosoever of them shalbe found negligent or faulty in this kinde shalbe subject to the censure of the Governor and Counsell of Estate.

The Ministers and Churchwardens shall seeke to presente all ungodly disorders, the comitters wherofe if, upon goode

[1] Cattle as distinguished from horses, sheep, goats, etc. [2] Communion.

admontions and milde reprooff, they will not forbeare the said skandalous offenses, as suspicions of whordomes, dishonest company keeping with weomen and suche like, they are to be presented and punished accordingly.

If any person after two warnings, doe not amende his or her life in point of evident suspicion of Incontincy or of the comission of any other enormous sinnes, that then he or shee be presented by the Churchwardens and suspended for a time from the churche by the minister. In which Interim if the same person do not amende and humbly submit him or herself to the churche, he is then fully to be excomunicate and soon after a writt or warrant to be sent from the Governor for the apprehending of his person ande seizing on all his goods. Provided alwayes, that all the ministers doe meet once a quarter, namely, at the feast of St. Michael the Arkangell, of the nativity of our saviour, of the Annuntiation of the blessed Virgine, and about midsomer,[1] at James citty or any other place where the Governor shall reside, to determine whom it is fitt to excomunicate, and that they first presente their opinion to the Governor ere they proceed to the acte of excomunication.

For the reformation of swearing, every freeman and Mr.[2] of a family after thrise admontion shall give 5*s* or the value upon present demaunde, to the use of the church where he dwelleth; and every servant after the like admontion, excepte his Mr. discharge the fine, shalbe subject to whipping. Provided, that the payment of the fine notwithstanding, the said servant shall acknowledge his faulte publiquely in the Churche.

No man whatsoever, coming by water from above, as from Henrico, Charles citty, or any place from the westwarde of James citty, and being bound for Kiccowtan,[3] or any other parte on this side, the same shall presume to pass by, either by day or by night, without touching firste here at James citty to knowe whether the Governor will comande him any service. And the like shall they performe that come from Kicawtan

[1] September 29, December 25, March 25, and June 24.

[2] Master.

[3] Kecoughtan, *i.e.*, Elizabeth City

ward, or from any place between this and that, to go upwarde, upon paine of forfaiting ten pound sterling a time to the Governor. Provided, that if a servant having had instructions from his Master to observe this lawe, doe notwithstanding, transgresse the same, that then the said servant shalbe punished at the Governor's discretion; otherwise, that the master himselfe shall undergo the foresaid penalty.

No man shall trade into the baye, either in shallop, pinnace, or ship, without the Governor's license, and without putting in security that neither himself nor his Company shall force or wrong the Indians, upon paine that, doing otherwise, they shalbe censured at their returne by the Governor and Counsell of Estate.[1]

All persons whatsoever upon the Sabaoth daye shall frequente divine service and sermons both forenoon and afternoon, and all suche as beare armes shall bring their pieces swordes, poulder and shotte. And every one that shall transgresse this lawe shall forfaicte three shillinges a time to the use of the churche, all lawful and necessary impediments excepted. But if a servant in this case shall wilfully neglecte his Mr's comande he shall suffer bodily punishmente.

No maide or woman servant, either now resident in the Colonie or hereafter to come, shall contract herselfe in marriage without either the consente of her parents, or of her Mr or Mris, or of the magistrate and minister of the place both together. And whatsoever minister shall marry or contracte any suche persons without some of the foresaid consentes shalbe subjecte to the severe censure of the Governor and Counsell of Estate.

Be it enacted by this present assembly that whatsoever servant hath heretofore or shall hereafter contracte himselfe in England, either by way of Indenture or otherwise, to serve any Master here in Virginia and shall afterward, against his said former contracte depart from his Mr without leave, or,

[1] "The trade into the bay" was trade with the Indian tribes in furs, skins, and Indian baskets.

being once imbarked shall abandon the ship he is appointed to come in, and so, being lefte behinde, shall putt himselfe into the service of any other man that will bring him hither, that then at the same servant's arrival here, he shall first serve out his time with that Mr that brought him hither and afterward also shall serve out his time with his former Mr according to his covenant.

*Here ende the lawes.*

All these lawes being thus concluded and consented to as aforesaid Captaine Henry Spellman[1] was called to the barre to answere to certaine misdemeanors layde to his chardge by Robert Poole, interpretour, upon his oath (whose examination the Governor sente into England in the *Prosperus*), of which accusations of Poole some he acknowledged for true, but the greattest part he denyed. Whereupon the General Assembly having throughly[2] heard and considered his speaches, did constitute this order following against him:

*Aug. 4th, 1619.*

This day Captaine Henry Spelman was convented before the General Assembly and was examined by a relation upon oath of one Robert Poole, Interpreter, what conference had passed between the said Spelman and Opochancano at Poole's meeting with him in Opochancano's courte. Poole chardgeth him he spake very unreverently and maliciously against this present Governor, whereby the honour and dignity of his place and person, and so of the whole Colonie, might be brought into contempte, by which meanes what mischiefs might ensue from the Indians by disturbance of the peace or otherwise, may easily be conjectured. Some thinges of this relation Spelman confessed, but the most parte he denyed, excepte onely one matter of importance, and that was that he hade informed Opochancano that within a yeare there would come a Governor greatter then this that nowe is in place. By which and by other re-

[1] See p. 202, note 4.

[2] Thoroughly.

portes it seemeth he hath alienated the minde of Opochancano from this present Governour, and brought him in much disesteem, both with Opochancano and the Indians, and the whole Colony in danger of their slippery designes.

The general assembly upon Poole's testimony onely not willing to putt Spelman to the rigour and extremity of the lawe which might, perhaps both speedily and deservedly, have taken his life from him (upon the witness of one whom he muche excepted against) were pleased, for the present, to censure him rather out of that his confession above written then out of any other prooffe. Several and sharpe punishments were pronounced against him by diverse of the Assembly, But in fine the whole courte by voices united did encline to the most favorable, which was that for this misdemeanour he should first be degraded of his title of Captaine, at the head of the troupe, and should be condemned to performe seven years service to the Colony in the nature of Interpreter to the Governour.

This sentence being read to Spelman he, as one that had in him more of the Savage then of the Christian, muttered certaine wordes to himselfe neither shewing any remorse for his offenses, nor yet any thankfulness to the Assembly for theire sofavourable censure, which he at one time or another (God's grace not wholly abandoning him) might with some one service have been able to have redeemed.

This day also did the Inhabitants of Paspaheigh, alias Argall's towne,[1] present a petition to the general assembly to give them an absolute discharge from certain bondes wherein they stand bound to Captain Samuell Argall for the payment of 600$^{lb}$ and to Captain William Powell, at Captaine Argall's appointment, for the payment of 50$^{lb}$ more. To Captaine Argall for 15 skore acres of wooddy ground, called by the name of Argal's towne or Paspaheigh; to Captaine Powell in respect

[1] Argall's Town or Gift was situated on the north side of the river a mile from Jamestown in the old fields, where once stood the chief village of the Paspaheghs, but from which they had removed to Sandy Point not long before the coming of the white men. Argall's Town was established by Argall in 1617.

of his paines in clearing the grounde and building the houses, for which Captaine Argal ought to have given him satisfaction. Nowe, the general assembly being doubtful whether they have any power and authority to discharge the said bondes, doe by these presents (at the Instance of the said Inhabitants of Paspaheigh, alias Martin's hundred people) become most humble sutours to the Treasurer, Counsell and Company in England that they wilbe pleased to gett the said bondes for 600$^{lb}$ to be cancelled; forasmuche as in their great comission they have expressly and by name appointed that place of Paspaheigh for parte of the Governour's lande. And wheras Captain William Powell is payde his 50 which Captain Argall enjoined the saide Inhabitantes to presente him with, as parte of the bargaine, the general assembly, at their intreaty, do become sutours on their behalfe, that Captaine Argall, by the Counsell and Company in England, may be compelled either to restore the said 50$^{lb}$ from thence, or else that restitution thereof be made here out of the goods of the said Captaine Argall.

The last acte of the Generall Assembly was a contribution to gratifie their officers, as followeth:

*Aug. 4th, 1619.*

It is fully agreed at this general Assembly that in regard of the great paines and labour of the Speaker of this Assembly (who not onely first formed the same Assembly and to their great ease and expedition reduced all matters to be treatted of into a ready method, but also his indisposition notwithstanding wrote or dictated all orders and other expedients and is yet to write severall bookes for all the Generall Incorporations and plantations both of the great charter, and of all the lawes) and likewise in respecte of the diligence of the Clerke and sergeant, officers thereto belonging, That every man and manservant of above 16 yeares of age shall pay into the handes and Custody of the Burgesses of every Incorporation and plantation one pound of the best Tobacco, to be distributed to the

Speaker and likewise to the Clerke and sergeant of the Assembly, according to their degrees and rankes, the whole bulke whereof to be delivered into the Speaker's handes, to be divided accordingly. And in regarde the Provost Marshall of James citty hath also given some attendance upon the said General Assembly, he is also to have a share out of the same. And this is to begin to be gathered the 24th of February nexte.

In conclusion, the whole Assembly comaunded the Speaker (as nowe he doth) to present their humble excuse to the Treasurer Counsell and Company in England for being constrained by the intemperature of the weather and the falling sick of diverse of the Burgesses to breake up so abruptly — before they had so much as putt their lawes to the ingrossing. This they wholly comited to the fidelity of their speaker, who therin (his conscience telles him) hath done the parte of an honest man, otherwise he would be easily founde out by the Burgesses themselves, who with all expedition are to have so many bookes of the same lawes as there be both Incorporations and Plantations in the Colony.

In the seconde place, the Assembly doth most humbly crave pardon that in so shorte a space they could bring their matter to no more perfection, being for the present enforced to sende home titles rather then lawes, Propositions rather then resolutions, Attemptes then Acchievements, hoping their courtesy will accepte our poor endevour, and their wisedome wilbe ready to supporte the weakness of this little flocke.

Thirdly, the General Assembly doth humbly beseech the said Treasurer, Counsell and Company, that albeit it belongeth to them onely to allowe or to abrogate any lawes which we shall here make, and that it is their right so to doe, yet that it would please them not to take it in ill parte if these lawes which we have now brought to light, do passe currant and be of force till suche time as we may knowe their farther pleasure out of Englande: for otherwise this people (who nowe at length have gotten the raines of former servitude into their owne swindge) would in shorte time growe so insolent, as they would shake off all government, and there would be no living among them.[1]

Their last humble suite is, that the said Counsell and Company would be pleased, so soon as they shall finde it convenient, to make good their promise sett downe at the conclusion of their commission for establishing the Counsel of Estate and the General Assembly, namely, that they will give us power to allowe or disallowe of their orders of Courte, as his Majesty hath given them power to allowe or to reject our lawes.

In sume Sir George Yeardley, the Governour prorogued the said General Assembly till the firste of Marche, which is to fall out this present yeare of 1619,[2] and in the mean season dissolved the same.

[1] In after days the acts of the Assembly passed as laws, until they were vetoed by the king.

[2] *I.e.*, till March 1, 1620, of new style.

# LETTER OF JOHN PORY, 1619

# INTRODUCTION

John Pory was born about 1570, studied at the university of Cambridge, and about 1597 became a disciple of Richard Hakluyt in "cosmographie and foreign histories." In 1600 he translated, edited, and published *A Geographical Historie of Africa, written in Arabicke and Italian by John Leo, a More, borne in Granada and brought up in Barbarie.* From 1605 to 1611 he was a member of Parliament for Bridgewater, and on April 19, 1610, he was made a master of arts at Cambridge. The next seven years were spent chiefly in travel in Europe and in the East, where he was attached to several embassies. In January, 1619, he sailed to Virginia as secretary of state with Sir George Yeardley, and was speaker of the first General Assembly which met at Jamestown, July 30, 1619, where his experience in Parliament was very useful to the members. From the adjournment of the assembly to August 22, 1622, he remained in Virginia, prosecuting voyages of discovery, writing letters, and otherwise making himself useful. He then sailed for England, and, stopping at the Plymouth settlement on Cape Cod Bay, relieved the famished colonists by a timely supply of provisions. In October, 1623, he was sent to Virginia as one of the commissioners to inquire into the real condition of affairs. They made their report in February, 1624. On July 15, 1624, Pory was made by the King one of the Virginia commission. He died at his house at Sutton St. Edmunds in Lincolnshire, in 1636. He was at times intemperate in his habits, but William Bradford was proud of his friendship, and his life on the whole was valuable and praiseworthy. The following letter is in the Public Record Office, London, and was published in the *Collections of the Massachusetts Historical Society*, fourth series, IX. 4–30. Sir Dudley Carleton was an able diplomatist, and at this time English ambassador to the Netherlands.

L. G. T.

# LETTER OF JOHN PORY, 1619

## SECRETARY OF VIRGINIA, TO SIR DUDLEY CARLETON

*Right Honourable, and my singular good Lorde:*

Having mett with so fitt a messenger as this man of warre of Flushing,[1] I could not but imparte with your lordship (to whom I am so everlastingly bounde) these poore fruites of our labours here; wherein though your worship will espie many errours and imperfections, and matters of lowe esteeme; yet withall you wilbe contente to observe the very principle and rudiments of our Infant-Commonwealth; which though nowe contemptible, your worship may live to see a flourishing Estate: maugre both Spaniards and Indians. The occasion of this ship's coming hither was an accidental consortship in the West Indies with the *Tresurer*, an English man of warre also, licensed by a Commission from the Duke of Savoye to take Spaniards as lawfull prize. This ship, the *Treasurer*, wente out of England in Aprill was twelvemoneth, about a moneth, I thinke, before any peace was concluded between the king of Spaine and that prince. Hither shee came to Captaine Argall, then governour of this Colony, being parte-owner of her. Hee more for love of gaine, the root of all evill, then for any true love he bore to this Plantation, victualled and manned her

[1] This Dutch man-of-war is the one which in August, 1619, sold to the settlers at Jamestown the first Africans imported into this country. The ship had cruised in the West Indies in company with the *Treasurer* sent out by Captain Argall under a commission from the Duke of Savoy, then at war with Spain. Both came to Jamestown freighted with slaves. On its way to Jamestown the Dutch or Flemish man-of-war touched at the Bermudas, where Kerby, the captain, presented fourteen negroes to Governor Kendall in return for supplies. The *Treasurer* reached the Bermudas towards the close of 1619 with twenty-nine slaves.

anewe, and sent her with the same Commission to raunge the Indies. The evente thereof (we may misdoubte) will prove some attempte of the Spaniard upon us, either by waye of revenge, or by way of prevention; least we might in time make this place *sedem belli* against the West Indies. But our Governour being a Soldier truly bred in that university of warre, the Lowe Countries, purposeth at a place or two upon the river fortifiable to provide for them, animating in the meane while this warlike people (then whom for their small number no prince can be served with better) by his example to prepare their courages.

Both those of our nation and the Indians also have this Torride sommer bene visited with great sickness and mortality; which our good God (his name be blessed for it) hath recompensed with a marvelous plenty, suche as hath not bene since our first coming into the lande. For my selfe I was partly at land and partly at sea vexed with a calenture of some 4 or 5 moneths. But (praised be God) I am nowe as healthfull as ever I was in my life. Here (as your lordship cannot be ignorant) I am, for faulte of a better, Secretary of Estate, the first that ever was chosen and appointed by Commission from the Counsell and Company in England, under their handes and common seale. By my fees I must maintaine my selfe; which the Governour telles me, may this yeere amounte to a matter of 300*l* sterling; whereof fifty I doe owe to himselfe, and I pray God the remainder may amounte to a hundred more. As yet I have gotten nothing, save onely (if I may speak it without boasting) a general reputation of integrity, for having spoken freely to all matters, according to my conscience; and as neare as I could discerne, done every man right.

As touching the quality of this country, three thinges there bee which in fewe yeares may bring this Colony to perfection; the English plough, Vineyards, and Cattle. For the first, there be many grounds here cleared by the Indians to our handes, which being much worne out,[1] will beare no more of

[1] These were called "old fields."

their corne, which requireth an extrordinary deale of sappe and substance to nourish it; but of our graine of all sortes it will beare great abundance. We have had this yeare a plentifull cropp of English wheat, though the last harvest 1618 was onely shed upon the stubble, and so selfe-sowne, with out any other manurance. In July last so soon as we had reaped this selfe-sowen wheate, we sett Indian corne upon the same grounde, which is come up in great abundance; and so by this meanes we are to enjoye two crops in one yeare from off one and the same fielde. The greatest labour we have yet bestowed upon English wheate, hath bene upon newe broken up groundes, one ploughing onely and one harrowing, far shorte of the Tilthe used in Christendome, which when we shall have ability enough to performe, we shall produce miracles out of this earthe.

Vines here are in suche abundance, as where soever a man treads, they are ready to embrace his foote. I have tasted here of a great black grape as big as a Damascin,[1] that hath a true Muscatell-taste;[2] the vine whereof now spending itselfe to the topps of high trees, if it were reduced into a vineyard, and there domesticated, would yield incomparable fruite. The like or a better taste have I founde in a lesser sorte of black grapes.[3] White grapes[4] also of great excellency I have hearde to be in the country; but they are very rare, nor did I ever see or taste of them. For cattle, they do mightily increase here, both kine, hogges and goates, and are much greater in stature, then the race of them first brought out of England. No lesse are our horses and mares likely to multiply, which proove of a delicate shape, and of as good spirite and metall.

All our riches for the present doe consiste in Tobacco, wherein one man by his owne labour hath in one yeare raised to himselfe to the value of 200*l* sterling; and another by the meanes of sixe servants hath cleared at one crop a thousand

[1] Damson.

[2] The muscadine, the fruit of which grows in clusters of three or four berries.

[3] The frost grape.

[4] Probably the scopenong, which is found near the North Carolina line.

pound English.[1] These be true, yet indeed rare examples, yet possible to be done by others. Our principall wealth (I should have said) consisteth in servants: But they are chardgeable to be furnished with armes, apparell and bedding and for their transportation and casual,[2] both at sea, and for their first yeare commonly at lande also: But if they escape, they prove very hardy, and sound able men.[3]

Nowe that your lordship may knowe, that we are not the veriest beggers in the worlde, our cowekeeper here of James citty on Sundays goes accowtered all in freshe flaming silke; and a wife of one that in England had professed the black arte, not of a scholler, but of a collier of Croydon, weares her rough bever hatt with a faire perle hatband, and a silken suite thereto correspondent. But to leave the Populace, and to come higher; the Governour here, who at his first coming, besides a great deale of worth in his person, brought onely his sword with him, was at his late being in London, together with his lady, out of his meer gettings here, able to disburse very near three thousand pounde to furnishe himselfe for his voiage. And once within seven yeares, I am persuaded (*absit invidia verbo*) that the Governors place here may be as profittable as the lord Deputies of Irland.

All this notwithstanding, I may say of myselfe, that when I was the last yeare with your lordship at Middleborough, *si mens non laeva fuisset*, I might have gone to the Hagh with you, and founde myselfe there nowe in far better company, which indeed is the soule of this life, and might have bene deeply ingrafted into your lordship's service, which since I have a thousand time affected in vaine. And therefore seeing I have missed that singular happiness, I must for what remaines,

[1] One thousand pounds at that time was equivalent to $20,000 in present values.

[2] Contingent expenses.

[3] After their first year emigrants became in a measure acclimated or "seasoned." A thousand people were in Virginia at Easter, 1619, and to this number 3570 were added during the next three years, yet only 1240 were resident in the colony on Good Friday, March 22, 1622, a day when the horrors of an Indian massacre reduced the number to 894. The mortality from sickness fell heaviest, of course, on the servant class.

depende upon Gods providence, who my hope is, wilbe so merciful towards me, as once more before I dye, to vouchsafe me the sight of your countenance, wherein, I speak unfainedly, I shall enjoye as much happines as in any other thing I can imagine in this worlde.

At my first coming hither the solitary uncouthnes of this place, compared with those partes of Christendome or Turky where I had bene; and likewise my being sequestred from all occurrents and passages which are so rife there, did not a little vexe me. And yet in these five moneths of my continuance here, there have come at one time or another eleven saile of ships into this river; but fraighted more with ignorance, then with any other marchandize.[1] At length being hardned to this custome of abstinence from curiosity, I am resolved wholly to minde my busines here, and nexte after my penne, to have some good book alwayes in store, being in solitude the best and choicest company. Besides among these Christall rivers, and oderiferous woods I doe escape muche expense, envye, contempte, vanity, and vexation of minde. Yet good my lorde, have a little compassion upon me, and be pleased to sende me what pampletts and relations of the Interim since I was with you, as your lordship shall thinke good, directing the same (if you please) in a boxe to Mr. Ralfe Yeardley, Apothecary (brother to Sir George Yeardley our governour), dwelling at the signe of the Hartychoke in great Woodstreet,[2] to be sente to me by the first, together with his brothers thinges. This pacquett I delivered to one Marmaduke Rayner, an Englishman, who goes intertained as Pilott in this Flemishe

[1] The original settlers and the first two supplies were largely composed of gentlemen, who nearly all perished of diseases and lack of food. Then martial law was tried, and workmen were imported, but they did not do as well as the gentlemen, and nearly all died. The culture of tobacco immensely increased the supply of servants, but they continued to die very quickly, even after free institutions were introduced. About 1642 tobacco had fallen from 3*s.* 6*d.* a pound to 1*d.*, and after that time the emigration was of the best material in England, who sought rest from the turmoil of civil war. See Tyler, *England in America*, pp. 109, 115.

[2] London.

man of warre. If he come to your lordship, as he hathe promised, he wilbe the fittest messenger. All possible happines I wishe to your lordship and to my most honoured lady, and though remote in place, yet neare in affection, doe reste

Your lordships ever most humbly at your commande

Jo. Pory.

*James Citty in Virginia, Sept. 30, 1619.*

# THE GENERALL HISTORIE OF VIRGINIA BY CAPTAIN JOHN SMITH, 1624; THE FOURTH BOOKE

# INTRODUCTION

THE *Generall Historie of Virginia, New England and the Summer Isles,* compiled by Captain John Smith, was first printed at London in 1624, with an engraved title-page, profusely decorated. Smith had projected it as early as April 12, 1621, and attempted to interest the Virginia Company in the publication. In 1626, 1627, and 1632 what purported to be new editions were issued, but they had the same text with fresh title-pages only. In 1812 J. Pinkerton included the *Generall Historie* in his *General Collection of Voyages.* In 1819 it was reprinted at Richmond, Virginia, by Rev. John Holt Rice, along with the *True Travels* of 1630. In 1884 the *Generall Historie* was included in the complete *Works* of Captain John Smith, published at London by Edward Arber. In 1907 it was again reprinted, in Glasgow. It is divided into six books. The first book tells of the early voyages to, and attempts at, English settlement in America; the second is a reprint, with variations, of the first part of the *Map of Virginia* (1612); the third is a reprint, with variations, of the second part of the *Map of Virginia;* the fourth takes up the history of the Virginia colony from the departure for England of Captain Smith about October 4, 1609, to the dissolution of the Virginia Company in May, 1624; the fifth book gives the history of the Bermuda Islands from 1593 to 1624; and the sixth book gives a history of New England, which consists of a reprint of his *A Description of New England* (1616) and *New England's Trials* (1620), with some additional matter. Though Smith had proposed to the Virginia Company in 1621 the publication of such a work as the *Generall Historie,* it was never adopted or authorized by them.

The fourth book may be described as a compilation of extracts from the narratives of other men interspersed with the comments of Smith. It cannot be called history in the true sense for two reasons: first, because the journals of the Virginia Company — the most important source of information during the last five years — were never consulted; and second, because of the extreme partisan character of the writers. The "narratives" are written from the standpoint of that faction in the Virginia Company which was in favor of martial law, and Smith's comments are chiefly directed to his own glorification. Nevertheless, the errors that exist are to be found mainly in the coloring given to events and the prejudiced estimates placed upon men and conditions. Cautiously taken, therefore, the book is a valuable statement of events which occurred after Smith's departure from the colony. The fault is not so much that Smith misstates, as that he errs in his reasoning. A marked instance is his account of the "Starving Time." Thus, he claims credit for the condition of the colony at the time of his departure to England, in October, 1609, and enthusiastically tells of the great number of settlers and supplies which he left behind, contrasting this state of affairs with the desolation at the end of the "Starving Time." Now as a matter of fact, Smith's right to credit expired with the coming of the Third Supply in August, at which time the colony was reduced to a very low state, being billeted out in small companies among the savages. The numbers and supplies on hand in October were chiefly brought by the newcomers, whose presence was very objectionable to Smith. After all, the supplies were wholly insufficient for the support of such a multitude of men as were unloaded at Jamestown from the fleet of Sir Thomas Gates.

Another instance of Smith's false reasoning may be found in his comments on the revocation of the charter of the Virginia Company. He states that the company in carrying out "their owne conceits consumed more than £200,000 and neere eight thousand men's lives," and, referring to the administration of Sir Edwin Sandys and the Earl of Southampton, attributes the result to want of "good order and government." The simple facts are that the misfortunes of the colony, under these two eminent statesmen, were due to climatic diseases and an Indian massacre, for neither of which they were responsible.

**L. G. T.**

# THE GENERALL HISTORIE OF VIRGINIA BY CAPTAIN JOHN SMITH, 1624; THE FOURTH BOOKE

*To make plaine the True Proceedings of the Historie for* 1609. *we must follow the examinations of Doctor Simons, and two learned Orations published by the Companie;*[1] *with the relation of the Right Honourable the Lord De la Ware.*

*What happened in the first government after the alteration, in the time of Captaine George Piercie their Governor.*

THE day before Captaine Smith returned[2] for England with the ships, Captaine Davis arrived in a small Pinace, with some sixteene proper men more: To these were added a company from James towne, under the command of Captaine John Sickelmore alias Ratliffe, to inhabit Point Comfort. Captaine Martin and Captaine West, having lost their boats and neere halfe their men among the Salvages, were returned to James towne; for the Salvages no sooner understood Smith was gone, but they all revolted, and did spoile and murther all they incountered.

Now wee were all constrained to live onely on that Smith had onely for his owne Companie,[3] for the rest had consumed their proportions. And now they had twentie Presidents with all their appurtenances: Master Piercie, our new President, was so sicke hee could neither goe nor stand. But ere all was consumed, Captaine West and Captaine Sickel-

[1] "The examinations of Doctor Simons" (or Simmonds) may mean the portions of Book III. immediately preceding. "Two learned Orations published by the Companie" most probably refers to *Nova Britannia* (London, 1609) and *A True and Sincere Declaration* (London, 1610).

[2] About October 4, 1609.

[3] *I.e.*, the portion of the settlers retained at Jamestown.

more, each with a small ship and thirtie or fortie men well appointed, sought abroad to trade. Sickelmore upon the confidence of Powhatan, with about thirtie others as carelesse as himselfe, were all slaine; onely Jeffrey Shortridge escaped; and Pokahontas the Kings daughter saved a boy called Henry Spilman, that lived many yeeres after, by her meanes, amongst the Patawomekes. Powhatan still, as he found meanes, cut off their Boats, denied them trade: so that Captaine West set saile for England. Now we all found the losse of Captaine Smith, yea his greatest maligners could now curse his losse: as for corne provision and contribution from the Salvages, we had nothing but mortall wounds, with clubs and arrowes; as for our Hogs, Hens, Goats, Sheepe, Horse, or what lived, our commanders, officers and Salvages daily consumed them, some small proportions sometimes we tasted, till all was devoured; then swords, armes, pieces, or any thing, wee traded with the Salvages, whose cruell fingers were so oft imbrewed in our blouds, that what by their crueltie, our Governours indiscretion, and the losse of our ships, of five hundred within six moneths after Captaine Smiths departure, there remained not past sixtie men, women and children, most miserable and poore creatures; and those were preserved for the most part, by roots, herbes, acornes, walnuts, berries, now and then a little fish: they that had startch in these extremities, made no small use of it; yea, even the very skinnes of our horses. Nay, so great was our famine, that a Salvage we slew and buried, the poorer sort tooke him up againe and eat him; and so did divers one another boyled and stewed with roots and herbs: And one amongst the rest did kill his wife, powdered [1] her, and had eaten part of her before it was knowne; for which hee was executed, as hee well deserved: now whether shee was better roasted, boyled or carbonado'd, I know not; but of such a dish as powdered wife I never heard of. This was that time, which still to this day [2] we called the starving time; it were too vile to say, and scarce to be beleeved,

[1] Salted. [2] 1624.

what we endured: but the occasion was our owne, for want of providence industrie and government, and not the barrennesse and defect of the Countrie, as is generally supposed; for till then in three yeeres, for the numbers were landed us, we had never from England provision sufficient for six moneths, though it seemed by the bils of loading sufficient was sent us, such a glutton is the Sea, and such good fellowes the Mariners; we as little tasted of the great proportion sent us, as they of our want and miseries, yet notwithstanding they ever overswayed and ruled the businesse, though we endured all that is said, and chiefly lived on what this good Countrie naturally afforded. Yet had wee beene even in Paradice it selfe with these Governours, it would not have beene much better withe us; yet there was amongst us, who had they had the government as Captaine Smith appointed, but that they could not maintaine it, would surely have kept us from those extremities of miseries. This in ten daies more, would have supplanted us all with death.

But God that would not this Countrie should be unplanted, sent Sir Thomas Gates, and Sir George Sommers with one hundred and fiftie people most happily preserved by the Bermudas to preserve us: strange it is to say how miraculously they were preserved in a leaking ship, as at large you may reade in the insuing Historie of those Ilands.[1]

### *The government resigned to Sir Thomas Gates* 1610.

When these two Noble Knights did see our miseries, being but strangers in that Countrie, and could understand no more of the cause, but by conjecture of our clamours and complaints, of accusing and excusing one another: They embarked us with themselves, with the best meanes they could, and abandoning James towne,[2] set saile for England: whereby you may see the event of the government of the former Commanders [3]

[1] The history of the Bermudas or Somers Islands to 1624 is contained in the fifth book of the *Generall Historie*. Gates and Somers arrived May 23, 1610. [2] June 7, 1610. [3] Ratcliffe, Martin, and Archer.

left to themselves; although they had lived there many yeeres, as formerly hath beene spoken (who hindred now their proceedings, Captaine Smith being gone).

At noone they fell to the Ile of Hogs, and the next morning to Mulberypoint, at what time they descried the Long-boat of the Lord la Ware; for God would not have it so abandoned. For this honourable Lord, then Governour of the Countrie, met them with three ships exceedingly well furnished with all necessaries fitting; who againe returned them to the abandoned James towne.[1]

Out of the observations of WILLIAM SIMMONS Doctor of Divinitie.[2]

*The government devolved to the Lord la Ware.*

His Lordship arrived the ninth of June 1610. accompanied with Sir Ferdinando Waynman, Captaine Houlcroft, Captaine Lawson, and divers other Gentlemen of sort; the tenth he came up with his fleet, went on shore, heard a Sermon, read his Commission, and entred into consultation for the good of the Colonie: in which secret counsell we will a little leave them, that we may duly observe the revealed counsell of God. Hee that shall but turne up his eie, and behold the spangled canopie of heaven, or shall but cast downe his eie, and consider the embroydered carpet of the earth, and withall shall marke how the heavens heare the earth, and the earth the Corne and Oile, and they relieve the necessities of man, that man will acknowledge Gods infinite providence. But hee that shall further observe, how God inclineth all casuall events to worke the necessary helpe of his Saints, must needs adore the Lords infinite goodnesse. Never had any people more just cause, to cast themselves at the very foot-stoole of God, and

[1] An account of these transactions, by Delaware and his council, in the form of a letter, dated July 7, 1610, is printed in Brown's *Genesis*, pp. 404–413, and in Neill's *Virginia Company of London*, pp. 36–49.

[2] *I.e.*, what precedes is derived from *The Proceedings of the English Colony in Virginia*, by W. S. Its text is followed closely; see pp. 198–204, above.

to reverence his mercie, than this distressed Colonie; for if God had not sent Sir Thomas Gates from the Bermudas, within foure daies they had almost beene famished; if God had not directed the heart of that noble Knight to save the Fort from fiering at their shipping,[1] for many were very importunate to have burnt it, they had beene destitute of a present harbour and succour: if they had abandoned the Fort any longer time, and had not so soone returned, questionlesse the Indians would have destroied the Fort, which had beene the meanes of our safeties amongst them and a terror. If they had set saile sooner, and had lanched into the vast Ocean; who would have promised they should have incountered the Fleet of the Lord la Ware: especially when they made for Newfound land, as they intended; a course contrarie to our Navie approaching. If the Lord la Ware had not brought with him a yeeres provision, what comfort would those poore soules have received, to have beene relanded to a second distruction? This was the arme of the Lord of Hosts, who would have his people passe the red Sea and Wildernesse, and then to possesse the land of Canaan: It was divinely spoken of Heathen Socrates, If God for man be carefull, why should man bee over-distrustfull? for he hath so tempered the contrary qualities of the Elements,

That neither cold things want heat, nor moist things dry,
Nor sad things spirits, to quicken them thereby,
Yet make they music all content of contrarietie,
Which conquer'd, knits them in such links together,
They doe produce even all this whatsoever.

The Lord Governour, after mature deliberation, delivered some few words to the Companie, laying just blame upon them, for their haughtie vanities and sluggish idlenesse, earnestly intreating them to amend those desperate follies lest hee should be compelled to draw the sword of Justice and to cut off such delinquents, which he had rather draw

[1] From being set on fire at their embarkation.

to the shedding of his vitall bloud, to protect them from injuries; heartning them with relation of that store hee had brought with him, constituting officers of all conditions, to rule over them, allotting every man his particular place, to watch vigilantly, and worke painfully. This Oration and direction being received with a generall applause, you might shortly behold the idle and restie diseases of a divided multitude, by the unitie and authoritie of this government to be substantially cured. Those that knew not the way to goodnesse before, but cherished singularitie and faction, can now chalke out the path of all respective dutie and service: every man endevoureth to outstrip other in diligence: the French preparing to plant the Vines,[1] the English labouring in the Woods and grounds; every man knoweth his charge, and dischargeth the same with alacritie. Neither let any man be discouraged, by the relation of their daily labour (as though the sap of their bodies should bee spent for other mens profit) the setled times of working, to effect all themselves, or as the Adventurers need desire, required no more paines than from six of the clocke in the morning, untill ten, and from two in the afternoone, till foure; at both which times they are provided of spirituall and corporall reliefe. First, they enter into the Church, and make their praiers unto God; next they returne to their houses and receive their proportion of food. Nor should it bee conceived that this businesse excludeth Gentlemen, whose breeding never knew what a daies labour meant: for though they cannot digge, use the Spade, nor practice the Axe, yet may the staied spirits of any condition, finde how to imploy the force of knowledge, the exercise of counsell, the operation and power of their best breeding and qualities. The houses which are built, are as warme and defensive against wind and weather, as if they were tiled and slated, being covered above with strong boards, and some matted round with Indian mats. Our forces are now such as are able to tame the furie and trecherie of the Salvages: Our

[1] This was the first attempt at cultivating grapes in Virginia.

Forts assure the Inhabitants, and frustrate all assaylants. And to leave no discouragement in the heart of any, who personally shall enter into this great action, I will communicate a double comfort; first, Sir George Sommers, that worthy Admirall hath undertaken a dangerous adventure for the good of the Colonie.

Upon the 15. of June, accompanied with Captaine Samuel Argall, hee returned in two Pinaces unto the Bermudas, promising (if by any meanes God will open a way to that Iland of Rocks) that he would soone returne with six moneths provision of flesh; with much crosse weather at last hee there safely arrived, but Captaine Argall was forced backe againe to James towne: whom the Lord De la Ware not long after sent to the River of Patawomeke, to trade for Corne; where finding an English boy, one Henry Spilman,[1] a young Gentleman well descended, by those people preserved from the furie of Powhatan, by his acquaintance had such good usage of those kinde Salvages, that they fraughted his ship with Corne, wherewith he returned to James towne.

The other comfort is, that the Lord la Ware hath built two new Forts, the one called Fort Henry, the other Fort Charles, in honour of our most noble Prince, and his hopefull brother, upon a pleasant plaine, and neare a little Rivilet they call Southampton River; they stand in a wholsome aire, having plentie of Springs of sweet water, they command a great circuit of ground, containing Wood, Pasture and Marsh, with apt places for Vines, Corne and Gardens; in which Forts it is resolved, that all those that come out of England, shall be at their first landing quartered, that the wearisomnesse of the Sea may bee refreshed in this pleasing part of the Countrie. And Sir Thomas Gates hee sent for England.[2] But to correct some injuries of the Paspahegs, he sent Captaine Pearcie, Master Stacy, and fiftie or threescore shot: where the Salvages flying, they burnt their houses, tooke the Queene and her children prisoners, whom not long after they slew.

[1] See p. 202, note 4, *ante*.

[2] On July 15, 1610.

The fertilitie of the soile, the temperature of the climate, the forme of government, the condition of our people, their daily invocating of the Name of God being thus expressed; why should the successe, by the rules of mortall judgement, bee disparaged? why should not the rich harvest of our hopes be seasonably expected? I dare say, that the resolution of Cæsar in France, the designes of Alexander, the discoveries of Hernando Cortes in the West, and of Emanuel King of Portugal in the East, were not encouraged upon so firme grounds of state and possibilitie.

But his Lordship being at the fal[l]es, the Salvages assaulted his troopes and slew three or foure of his men. Not long after, his Honour growing very sicke, he returned for England the 28. of March; in the ship were about five and fiftie men, but ere we arrived at Fyall, fortie of us were neare sicke to death, of the Scurvie, Callenture, and other diseases: the Governour, being an English-man, kindly used us, but small reliefe we could get but Oranges, of which we had plenty; whereby within eight daies wee recovered, and all were well and strong by that[1] they came into England.

Written by WILLIAM BOX.

The Counsell of Virginia finding the smalnesse of that returne which they hoped should have defrayed the charge of a new supply, entred into a deep consultation, whether it were fit to enter into a new Contribution, or in time to send for them home and give over the action, and therefore they adjured Sir Thomas Gates to deale plainly with them, who with a solemne and a sacred oath replyed, That all things before reported were true: and that all men know that wee stand at the devotion of politicke Princes and States, who for their proper utilitie, devise all courses to grind our Merchants, and by all pretences to confiscate their goods, and to draw from us all manner of gaine by their inquisitive inventions; when in Virginia, a few yeeres labour by planting

[1] By the time.

and husbandry, will furnish all our defects with honour and securitie.

Out of a Declaration published by the COUNSELL, 1610.[1]

*The government surrendered to Sir Thomas Dale, who arrived in Virginia the tenth of May, 1611, out of Master Hamors*[2] *Booke.*

Before the Lord la Ware arrived in England, the Councell and Companie had dispatched away Sir Thomas Dale with three ships, men, and cattell, and all other provisions necessarie for a yeere; all which arrived well the tenth of May 1611: where he found them growing againe to their former estate of penurie, being so improvident as not to put Corne in the ground for their bread; but trusted to the store, then furnished but with three moneths provision.[3] His first care therefore was to imploy all hands about setting of Corne, at the two Forts at Kecoughtan, Henry and Charles; whereby, the season then not fully past, though about the end of May, wee had an indifferent crop of good Corne.

This businesse taken order for, and the care and trust of it committed to his under-Officers, to James towne he hastened, where most of the companie were at their daily and usuall works, bowling in the streets:[4] these hee imployed

[1] *A True Declaration of the Estate of the Colony of Virginia* (London, 1610), pp. 21–23. That tract is reprinted in Force's *Historical Tracts*, Vol. III. Next, Smith prints an abridgment of Delaware's *Relation* (1611). It is here omitted, that tract having been printed entire on p. 205–214, above.

[2] Ralph Hamor was recorder or secretary of state 1611 to 1614, and his narrative, *A True Discourse of the Present Estate of Virginia* (London, 1615), praises the administration of which he was part, at the expense of the colony. The abstract of it continues from this point to p. 316, except for the two interpolations noted in subsequent foot-notes. But the order followed is not precisely Hamor's. It is: pp. 26–33, 4–18, 37–46 of Hamor's tract.

[3] More than half the emigrants died during Delaware's stay in the colony, and the rest were probably too weak to do anything.

[4] Dale arrived at Jamestown, Sunday, May 19, and found some who were well enough bowling in the street — one of the usual pastimes thought in England proper for the day. His report on the state of affairs he found in

about necessarie workes, as felling of Timber, repayring their houses ready to fall on their heads, and providing pales, posts and railes, to impale his purposed new towne, which by reason of his ignorance, being but newly arrived, hee had not resolved where to seat. Therefore to better his knowledge, with one hundred men he spent some time in viewing the River of Nansamund, in despight of the Indians then our enemies; then our owne River to the Fal[l]es, where upon a high land, environed with the maine River, some twelve miles from the Fal[l]es, by Arsahattock, he resolved to plant his new towne.

It was no small trouble to reduce his people so timely to good order, being of so ill a condition, as may well witnesse his severitie and strict imprinted booke of Articles, then needfull with all extremitie to be executed; now much mitigated: so as if his Lawes had not beene so strictly executed, I see not how the utter subversion of the Colonie should have beene prevented, witnesse Webbes and Prices designe the first yeere, since that of Abbots and others, more dangerous than the former.[1] Here I entreat your patience for an Apologie, though not a pardon. This Jeffrey Abbots, how ever this Author censures him, and the Governor executes him; I know he had long served both in Ireland and Netherlands. Here hee was a Sargeant of my Companie, and I never saw in Virginia a more sufficient Souldier, lesse turbulent, a better wit, more hardy or industrious, nor any more forward to cut off them that sought to abandon the Countrie, or wrong the Colonie; how ingratefully those deserts might bee rewarded, envied or neglected, or his farre inferiors preferred to over-top him, I know not: but such occasions might move a Saint, much more a man, to an unadvised passionate impatience, but how ever, it seemes he hath beene punished for his offences, that was never rewarded for his deserts. And even this Sum-

Virginia at his arrival, written May 26, may be seen in Brown's *Genesis of the United States*, pp. 488–494.

[1] This is a disingenuous perversion of cause and effect. Dale's tyranny forced the men to run away, and afterwards, like other tyrants, he justified his harsh rule by its natural consequences. The remarks which follow, down to the mention of Cole's and Kitchins's plot, are Smith's, not Hamor's.

mer Cole and Kitchins plot[1] with three more, bending their course to Ocanahowan, five daies journey from us, where they report are Spaniards inhabiting. These were cut off by the Salvages, hired by us to hunt them home to receive their deserts. So as Sir Thomas Dale hath not beene so tyrannous nor severe by the halfe, as there was occasion, and just cause for it; and though the manner was not usuall, wee were rather to have regard to those, whom we would have terrified and made fearefull to commit the like offences, than to the offenders justly condemned: for amongst them so hardned in evill, the feare of a cruell painfull and unusuall death more restraines them, than death it selfe. This much I have proceeded of his endevours, untill the comming of Sir Thomas Gates, in preparing himselfe to proceed as he intended.

Now in England againe, to second this noble Knight, the Counsell and Companie with all possible expedition prepared for Sir Thomas Gates six tall ships, with three hundred men, and one hundred Kine and other Cattell, with munition and all other manner of provision that could be thought needfull; and about the first or second of August, 1611. arrived safely at James towne.

## *The government returned againe to Sir Thomas Gates, 1611.*

These worthy Knights being met, after their welcoming salutations, Sir Thomas Dale acquainted him what he had done, and what he intended: which designe Sir Thomas Gates well approving, furnished him with three hundred and fiftie men, such as himselfe made choice of. In the beginning of September, 1611. hee set saile, and arrived where hee intended to build his new towne: within ten or twelve daies he had inironed it with a pale, and in honour of our noble Prince

[1] Edward Cole, Kitchins, and others had been acting as the guard to Molina, a Spanish spy, and were persuaded by him to attempt to reach the Spanish settlements in Florida; and, it being now a time of peace, they had travelled "some five days' journey to Ocanahoen," when they were "cut off" by the Indians, and brought back to Jamestown, where they were tried and six of them condemned and executed. Brown, *First Republic*, pp. 158, 211.

Henry, called it Henrico. The next worke he did, was building at each corner of the Towne a high commanding Watch-house, a Church, and Store-houses: which finished, hee began to thinke upon convenient houses for himselfe and men, which, with all possible speed hee could, he effected, to the great content of his companie, and all the Colonie.

This towne is situated upon a necke of a plaine rising land, three parts invironed with the maine River, the necke of land well impaled, makes it like an Ile; it hath three streets of well framed houses, a handsome Church, and the foundation of a better laid (to bee built of Bricke), besides Store-houses, Watch-houses, and such like. Upon the verge of the River there are five houses, wherein live the honester sort of people, as Farmers in England,[1] and they keepe continuall centinell for the townes securitie. About two miles from the towne, into the Maine, is another pale, neere two miles in length, from River to River, guarded with severall Commanders, with a good quantitie of Corne-ground impailed, sufficiently secured to maintaine more than I suppose will come this three yeeres.

On the other side of the River, for the securitie of the towne, is intended to be impaled for the securitie of our Hogs, about two miles and a halfe, by the name of Hope in Faith, and Coxendale, secured by five of our manner of Forts, which are but Palisadoes, called Charitie Fort, Mount Malado (a guest house for sicke people) a high seat and wholsome aire, Elisabeth Fort, and Fort Patience: And here hath Master Whitaker[2] chosen his Parsonage, impaled a faire framed Parsonage, and one hundred acres called Rocke hall, but these are not halfe finished.

About Christmas following, in this same yeere 1611. in regard of the injurie done us by them of Apamatuck, Sir Thomas Dale, without the losse of any, except some few Salvages, tooke it and their Corne, being but five miles by land from Henrico: and considering how commodious it might be for us, resolved to possesse and plant it, and at the

[1] Hamor says, "as in Farmes in England."

[2] Alexander Whitaker, son of William Whitaker, a celebrated Puritan divine. He was minister in Virginia from 1611 to his death in 1617.

instant called it the new Bermudas; whereunto hee hath laid out and annexed to the belonging freedome and corporation for ever, many miles of Champian[1] and Woodland ground in severall hundreds, as the upper and nether hundreds, Rochdale hundred, West Sherly hundred, and Digs his hundred. In the nether hundred he first began to plant, for there is the most Corne-ground, and with a pale of two miles, cut over from River to River, whereby we have secured eight English miles in compasse: upon which circuit, within halfe a mile of each other, are many faire houses already built; besides particular mens houses neere to the number of fiftie. Rochdale, by a crosse pale welnigh foure miles long, is also planted with houses along the pale, in which hundred our Hogs and Cattell have twentie miles circuit to graze in securely. The building of the Citie[2] is referred till our harvest be in, which he intends to make a retreat against any forraigne enemie.

About fiftie miles from these is James towne, upon a fertill *peninsula*, which although formerly scandaled for an unhealthfull aire, wee finde it as healthfull as any other part of the Countrie; it hath two rowes of houses of framed timber, and some of them two stories and a garret higher, three large Store-houses joined together in length, and hee hath newly strongly impaled the towne. This Ile, and much ground about it, is much inhabited. To Kecoughtan we accounted it fortie miles, where they live well with halfe that allowance the rest have from the store, because of the extraordinarie quantitie of Fish, Fowle and Deere; as you may reade at large in the Discoveries of Captaine Smith. And thus I have truly related unto you the present estate of that small part of Virginia wee frequent and possesse.

Since there was a ship fraughted with provision,[3] and fortie men; and another since then with the like number and pro-

[1] Champaign, open lands.

[2] Bermuda City, subsequently Charles City, and now City Point, at the east of the mouth of the Appomattox River, across from Bermuda Hundred.

[3] At this point the margin, under date 1612, notes, "Sir Thomas Smith, Treasurer," or head of the company, as he had been since the grant of the first charter in 1606. The third charter was granted in March, 1612.

vision, to stay twelve moneths in the Countrie, with Captaine Argall, which was sent not long after. After hee had recreated and refreshed his Companie, hee was sent to the River Patawomeake, to trade for Corne: the Salvages about us having small quarter, but friends and foes as they found advantage and opportunitie. But to conclude our peace, thus it happened. Captaine Argall, having entred into a great acquaintance with Japazaws, an old friend of Captaine Smiths, and so to all our Nation, ever since hee discovered the Countrie, heard by him there was Pocahontas, whom Captaine Smiths Relations intituleth the Numparell[1] of Virginia, and though she had beene many times a preserver of him and the whole Colonie, yet till this accident shee was never seene at James towne since his departure.[2] Being at Patawomeke, as it seemes, thinking her selfe unknowne, was easily by her friend Japazaws perswaded to goe abroad with him and his wife to see the ship: for Captaine Argall had promised him a Copper Kettle to bring her but to him, promising no way to hurt her, but keepe her till they could conclude a peace with her father; the Salvage for this Copper Kettle would have done any thing, it seemed by the Relation. For though she had seene and beene in many ships, yet hee caused his wife to faine how desirous she was to see one, that hee offered to beat her for her importunitie, till she wept. But at last he told her, if Pocahontas would goe with her, hee was content: and thus they betraied the poore innocent Pocahontas aboord, where they were all kindly feasted in the Cabbin. Japazaws treading oft on the Captaines foot, to remember he had done his part; the Captaine when he saw his time, perswaded Pocahontas to the Gun-roome, faining to have some conference with Japazaws, which was onely that she should not perceive hee was any way guiltie of her captivitie: so sending for her againe, hee told her before her friends, she must goe with him, and compound peace betwixt her Countrie and us, before she ever should see Powhatan; whereat the old Jew and his wife began to howle and crie as

[1] Nonpareil. See pp. 69, 199, above. [2] In the autumn of 1609.

fast as Pocahontas, that upon the Captaines faire perswasions, by degrees pacifying her selfe, and Japazaws and his wife, with the Kettle and other toies, went merrily on shore; and shee to James towne. A messenger forthwith was sent to her father, that his daughter Pocahontas he loved so dearely, he must ransome with our men, swords, peeces, tooles, &c. hee trecherously had stolne.

This unwelcome newes much troubled Powhatan, because hee loved both his daughter and our commodities well, yet it was three moneths after [1] ere hee returned us any answer: then by the perswasion of the Councell, he returned seven of our men, with each of them an unserviceable Musket, and sent us word, that when wee would deliver his daughter, hee would make us satisfaction for all injuries done us, and give us five hundred bushels of Corne, and for ever be friends with us. That he sent, we received in part of payment, and returned him this answer: That his daughter should be well used; but we could not beleeve the rest of our armes were either lost or stolne from him, and therefore till hee sent them, we would keepe his daughter.

This answer, it seemed, much displeased him, for we heard no more from him for a longtime after: when with Captaine Argals ship, and some other vessels belonging to the Colonie; Sir Thomas Dale, with a hundred and fiftie men well appointed, went up into his owne River,[2] to his chiefe habitation, with his daughter. With many scornfull bravado's they affronted us, proudly demanding Why wee came thither; our reply was, Wee had brought his daughter, and to receive the ransome for her that was promised, or to have it perforce. They nothing dismayed thereat, told us, We were welcome if wee came to fight, for they were provided for us: but advised us, if wee loved our lives to retire; else they would use us as they had done Captaine Ratcliffe: We told them, Wee would presently have a better answer; but we were no sooner within shot of the shore than they let flie their Arrowes among us in the ship.

[1] July, 1613. [2] York River.

Being thus justly provoked, wee presently manned our Boats, went on shore, burned all their houses, and spoiled all they had we could finde; and so the next day proceeded higher up the River, where they demanded Why wee burnt their houses, and wee, Why they shot at us: They replyed, it was some stragling Salvage, with many other excuses, they intended no hurt, but were our friends: We told them, Wee came not to hurt them, but visit them as friends also. Upon this we concluded a peace, and forthwith they dispatched messengers to Powhatan; whose answer, they told us, wee must expect foure and twentie houres ere the messengers could returne: Then they told us, our men were runne away for feare we would hang them, yet Powhatans men were runne after them; as for our Swords and Peeces, they should be brought us the next day, which was only but to delay time; for the next day they came not. Then we went higher, to a house of Powhatans, called Matchot,[1] where we saw about foure hundred men well appointed; here they dared us to come on shore, which wee did; no shew of feare they made at all, nor offered to resist our landing, but walking boldly up and downe amongst us, demanded to conferre with our Captaine, of his comming in that manner, and to have truce till they could but once more send to their King to know his pleasure, which if it were not agreeable to their expectation, then they would fight with us, and defend their owne as they could. Which was but onely to deferre the time, to carrie away their provision; yet wee promised them truce till the next day at noone, and then if they would fight with us, they should know when we would begin by our Drums and Trumpets.

Upon this promise, two of Powhatans sonnes came unto us to see their sister: at whose sight, seeing her well, though they heard to the contrarie, they much rejoiced, promising they would perswade her father to redeeme her, and for ever be friends with us. And upon this, the two brethren went

[1] Matchot was an Indian village situated according to Smith's map on the south side of the Pamunkey River, but from the description in Hamor's *True Discourse*, it appears to have been on the north side.

aboord with us; and we sent Master John Rolfe and Master Sparkes to Powhatan, to acquaint him with the businesse: kindly they were entertained, but not admitted the presence of Powhatan, but they spoke with Opechancanough, his brother and successor; hee promised to doe the best he could to Powhatan, all might be well. So it being Aprill, and time to prepare our ground and set our Corne, we returned to James Towne, promising the forbearance of their performing their promise, till the next harvest.

Long before this, Master John Rolfe, an honest Gentleman, and of good behaviour, had beene in love with Pocahontas, and she with him: which thing at that instant I made knowne to Sir Thomas Dale by a letter from him, wherein hee intreated his advice, and she acquainted her brother with it, which resolution Sir Thomas Dale well approved: the bru[i]te of this mariage came soone to the knowledge of Powhatan, a thing acceptable to him, as appeared by his sudden consent, for within ten daies he sent Opachisco, an old Uncle of hers, and two of his sons, to see the manner of the mariage, and to doe in that behalfe what they were requested, for the confirmation thereof, as his deputie; which was accordingly done about the first of Aprill.[1] And ever since wee have had friendly trade and commerce, as well with Powhatan himselfe, as all his subjects.

Besides this, by the meanes of Powhatan, we became in league with our next neighbours, the Chicahamanias, a lustie and a daring people, free of themselves. These people, so soone as they heard of o[u]r peace with Powhatan, sent two messengers with presents to Sir Thomas Dale, and offered them his[2] service, excusing all former injuries, hereafter they would ever be King James his subjects, and relinquish the name of Chickahamania, to be called Tassautessus, as they call us; and Sir Thomas Dale there Governour, as the Kings Deputie; onely they desired to be governed by their owne Lawes, which

[1] More correctly, "about the fifth of April" (1614). See Rolfe's letter on pp. 235–244, above.

[2] Offered him their service.

is eight of their Elders as his substitutes. This offer he kindly accepted, and appointed the day hee would come to visit them.

When the appointed day came, Sir Thomas Dale and Captaine Argall with fiftie men well appointed, went to Chickahamania, where wee found the people expecting our comming; they used us kindly, and the next morning sate in counsell, to conclude their peace upon these conditions:

First, they should for ever bee called Englishmen, and bee true subjects to King James and his Deputies.

Secondly, neither to kill nor detaine any of our men, nor cattell, but bring them home.

Thirdly, to bee alwaies ready to furnish us with three hundred men, against the Spaniards or any.

Fourthly, they shall not enter our townes, but send word they are new Englishmen.

Fiftly, that every fighting man, at the beginning of harvest, shall bring to our store two bushels of Corne, for tribute, for which they shall receive so many Hatchets.

Lastly, the eight chiefe men should see all this performed, or receive the punishment themselves: for their diligence they should have a red coat, a copper chaine, and King James his picture, and be accounted his Noblemen.

All this they concluded with a generall assent, and a great shout to confirme it: then one of the old men began an Oration, bending his speech first to the old men, then to the young, and then to the women and children, to make them understand how strictly they were to observe these conditions, and we would defend them from the furie of Powhatan, or any enemie whatsoever, and furnish them with Copper, Beads, and Hatchets: but all this was rather for feare Powhatan and we, being so linked together, would bring them againe to his subjection; the which to prevent, they did rather chuse to be protected by us, than tormented by him, whom they held a Tyrant. And thus wee returned againe to James towne.

When our people were fed out of the common store, and laboured jointly together, glad was he could slip from his labour, or slumber over his taske he cared not how, nay, the most honest among them would hardly take so much true paines in a weeke, as now for themselves they will doe in a day: neither cared they for the increase, presuming that howsoever the harvest prospered, the generall store must maintaine them, so that wee reaped not so much Corne from the labours of thirtie, as now three or foure doe provide for themselves. To prevent which, Sir Thomas Dale hath allotted every man three Acres of cleare ground, in the nature of Farmes, except the Bermudas:[1] who are exempted, but for one moneths service in the yeere, which must neither bee in seed-time, nor harvest; for which doing, no other dutie they pay yeerely to the store, but two barrels and a halfe of Corne.[2] From all those Farmers (whereof the first was William Spence, an honest, valiant, and an industrious man, and hath continued from 1607. to this present) from those is expected such a contribution to the store, as wee shall neither want for our selves, nor to entertaine our supplies; for the rest, they are to worke eleven moneths for the store, and hath one moneth onely allowed them to get provision to keepe them for twelve, except two bushels of Corne they have out of the store. If those can live so, why should any feare starving; and it were much better to denie them passage that would not, ere they come, bee content to ingage themselves to those conditions: for onely from the slothfull and idle drones, and none else, hath sprung the manifold imputations, Virginia innocently hath undergone; and therefore I would deter such from comming here, that cannot well brooke labour, except they will undergoe much punishment and penurie, if they escape the skurvie: but for the industrious, there is reward sufficient, and if any thinke there is nothing but bread, I referre you to his[3] relations that discovered the Countrie first.

[1] Bermuda Hundred and Bermuda City at the mouth of the Appomattox River, or Upper and Nether Bermuda Hundreds.

[2] The remainder of this paragraph is not derived from Hamor.

[3] Smith's.

*The government left to Sir Thomas Dale, upon Sir Thomas Gates returne for England.*

Sir Thomas Dale understanding there was a plantation of Frenchmen in the north part of Virginia, about the degrees of 45. sent Captaine Argall to Port Royall and Sancta Crux; where finding the Frenchmen abroad dispersed in the Woods, surprized their Ship and Pinnace, which was but newly come from France, wherein was much good apparel and other provision, which he brought to James towne: but the men escaped, and lived among the Salvages of those Countries.

It pleased Sir Thomas Dale, before my returne to England, because I would be able to speake somewhat of my owne knowledge, to give mee leave to visit Powhatan and his Court: being provided, I had Thomas Salvage with mee, for my Interpreter; with him and two Salvages for guides, I went from the Bermuda in the morning, and came to Matchot the next night, where the King lay upon the River of Pamaunke. His entertainment was strange to me, the boy he knew well, and told him; My child, I gave you leave, being my boy, to goe see your friends, and these foure yeeres [1] I have not seene you, nor heard of my owne man Namontack I sent to England,[2] though many ships since have beene returned thence. Having done with him, hee began with mee, and demanded for the chaine of pearle he sent his brother Sir Thomas Dale at his first arrivall, which was a token betwixt them, when ever hee should send a messenger from himselfe to him, he should weare that chaine about his necke, since the peace was concluded, otherwaies he was to binde him and send him home.

It is true Sir Thomas Dale had sent him such word, and gave his Page order to give it me, but he forgot it, and till this present I never heard of it, yet I replyed I did know there was such an order, but that was when upon a sudden he should

[1] 1610–1614.

[2] Namontack, who was slain by another Indian, Matchumps, in the Bermuda Islands, when shipwrecked with Gates, in 1609.

have occasion to send an Englishman without an Indian Guide; but if his owne people should conduct his messenger, as two of his did me who knew my message, it was sufficient; with which answer he was contented, and so conducted us to his house, where was a guard of two hundred Bow-men that alwaies attend his person. The first thing he did, he offered me a pipe of Tobacco, then asked mee how his brother Sir Thomas Dale did, and his daughter, and unknowne sonne, and how they lived, loved and liked; I told him his brother was well, and his daughter so contented, she would not live againe with him; whereat he laughed, and demanded the cause of my comming: I told him my message was private, and I was to deliver it onely to himselfe and Papaschicher, one of my guides that was acquainted with it; instantly he commanded all out of the house, but onely his two Queenes, that alwaies sit by him, and bade me speake on.

I told him, by my Interpreter, Sir Thomas Dale hath sent you two pieces of Copper, five strings of white and blue Beads, five woodden Combes, ten Fish-hookes, a paire of Knives, and that when you would send for it, hee would give you a Grindstone; all this pleased him: but then I told him his brother Dale, hearing of the fame of his youngest daughter, desiring in any case he would send her by me unto him, in testimonie of his love, as well for that he intended to marry [1] her, as the desire her sister had to see her, because being now one people, and hee desirous for ever to dwell in his Countrie, he conceived there could not be a truer assurance of peace and friendship, than in such a naturall band of an united union. I needed not entreat his answer by his oft interrupting mee in my speech, and presently with much gravitie he thus replyed.

I gladly accept your salute of love and peace, which while I live, I shall exactly keepe; his pledges thereof I receive with no lesse thanks, although they are not so ample as formerly he had received: but for my daughter, I have sold her within

[1] A curious proposal of Dale's, as he had a wife and several children living in England.

this few daies to a great Werowance, for two bushels of Rawrenoke,[1] three daies journie from me. I replyed, I knew his greatnesse in restoring the Rawrenoke, might call her againe to gratifie his brother, and the rather, because she was but twelve yeeres old, assuring him, besides the band of peace, hee should have for her, three times the worth of the Rawrenoke, in Beads, Copper, Hatchets, &c. His answer was, he loved his daughter as his life, and though hee had many children, hee delighted in none so much as shee, whom if he should not often behold, he could not possibly live, which she living with us he could not do, having resolved upon no termes to put himselfe into our hands, or come amongst us; therefore desired me to urge him no further, but returne his brother this answer: That I desire no firmer assurance of his friendship than the promise hee hath made, from me he hath a pledge, one of my daughters, which so long as she lives shall be sufficient, when she dies, he shall have another: I hold it not a brotherly part to desire to bereave me of my two children at once. Farther, tell him though he had no pledge at all, hee need not distrust any injurie from me or my people; there have beene too many of his men and mine slaine, and by my occasion there shall never be more, (I which have power to performe it, have said it) although I should have just cause, for I am now old, and would gladly end my daies in peace; if you offer me injurie, my countrie is large enough to goe from you: Thus much I hope will satisfie my brother. Now because you are wearie, and I sleepie, wee will thus end. So commanding us victuall and lodging, we rested that night, and the next morning he came to visit us, and kindly conducted us to the best cheere hee had.

While I here remained, by chance came an Englishman, whom there had beene surprized three yeeres agoe[2] at Fort Henry, growne so like, both in complexion and habit like a Salvage, I knew him not, but by his tongue: hee desired mee to procure his libertie, which I intended, and so farre urged Powhatan, that he grew discontented, and told mee, You have

[1] Roanoke shells. [2] 1611. The margin reads, "William Parker recovered."

one of my daughters, and I am content: but you cannot see one of your men with mee, but you must have him away, or breake friendship; if you must needs have him, you shall goe home without guides, and if any evill befall you, thanke your selves.

I told him I would, but if I returned not well, hee must expect a revenge; and his brother might have just cause to suspect him. So in passion he left me till supper, and then gave me such as hee had with a cheerefull countenance: About midnight he awaked us, and promised in the morning my returne with Parker; but I must remember his brother to send him ten great pieces of Copper, a Shaving-knife, a Frowe,[1] a Grind-stone, a Net, Fish-hookes, and such toies; which lest I should forget, he caused me write in a table-booke he had; how ever he got it, it was a faire one, I desired hee would give it me; he told me, no, it did him much good in shewing to strangers, yet in the morning when we departed, having furnished us well with provision, he gave each of us a Bucks skin as well dressed as could be, and sent two more to his sonne and daughter: And so we returned to James towne.

Written by Master Ralph Hamor and John Rolph.

I have read the substance of this relation, in a Letter written by Sir Thomas Dale, another by Master Whitaker, and a third by Master John Rolfe; how carefull they were to instruct her in Christianity, and how capable and desirous shee was thereof, after she had beene some time thus tutored, shee never had desire to goe to her father, nor could well endure the society of her owne nation: the true affection she constantly bare her husband was much, and the strange apparitions and violent passions he endured for her love, as he deeply protested, was wonderful, and she openly renounced her countries idolatry, confessed the faith of Christ, and was baptized. But either the coldnesse of the adventurers, or the bad usage of that was collected, or both, caused this worthy Knight[2] to write thus.

[1] A wedge-shaped tool for splitting rails or staves.

[2] Sir Thomas Dale. What follows is an abridgment of his letter printed in Hamor, pp. 51–59.

Oh why should so many Princes and Noblemen ingage themselves, and thereby intermedling herein, have caused a number of soules transport themselves, and be transported hither? Why should they, I say, relinquish this so glorious an action: for if their ends be to build God a Church, they ought to persevere; if otherwise, yet their honour ingageth them to be constant; howsoever they stand affected, here is enough to content them. These are the things have animated me to stay a little season from them, I am bound in conscience to returne unto; leaving all contenting pleasures and mundall delights, to reside here with much turmoile, which I will rather doe than see Gods glory diminished, my King and Country dishonoured, and these poore soules I have in charge revived, which would quickly happen if I should leave them; so few I have with me fit to command or manage the businesse.

Master Whitaker their Preacher complaineth, and much museth, that so few of our English Ministers, that were so hot against the surplice and subscription come hether, where neither is spoken of. Doe they not wilfully hide their talents, or keepe themselves at home, for feare of losing a few pleasures; be there not any among them of Moses his minde, and of the Apostles, that forsooke all to follow Christ, but I refer them to the Judge of all hearts, and to the King that shall reward every one according to his talent.

From Virginia, June 18. 1614.[1]

The businesse being brought to this perfection, Captaine Argall returned for England, in the latter end of June, 1614. ariving in England, and bringing this good tidings to the Councell and company by the assistances of Sir Thomas Gates, that also had returned from Virginia but the March before; it was presently concluded, that to supply this good successe with all expedition, the standing Lottery should be drawne with all diligent conveniency, and that posterity may remember upon occasion to use the like according to the declaration, I thinke it not amisse to remember thus much.

[1] This is from Rev. Alexander Whitaker's letter printed in Hamor, pp. 59–61.

### *The Contents of the declaration of the Lottery published by the Counsell.*[1]

It is apparent to the world, by how many former Proclamations, we manifested our intents, to have drawn out the great standing Lottery long before this, which not falling out as we desired, and others expected whose monies are adventured therein, we thought good therefore for the avoiding all unjust and sinister constructions, to resolve the doubts of all indifferent minded, in three speciall points for their better satisfaction.

But ere I goe any farther, let us remember there was a running Lottery used a long time in Saint Pauls Churchyard, where this stood, that brought into the Treasury good summes of mony dayly, though the Lot was but small.

Now for the points, the first is, for as much as the Adventurers came in so slackly for the yeere past, without prejudice to the generality; in losing the blankes and prises, we were forced to petition to the honourable Lords, who out of their noble care to further this Plantation, have recommended their Letsenters [2] to the Countries, Cities, and good townes in England, which we hope by adding in their voluntary Adventurers, will sufficiently supply us.

The second for satisfaction to all honest well affected minds, is, that though this expectation answer not our hopes, yet wee have not failed in our Christian care, the good of that Colony, to whom we have lately sent two sundry supplies, and were they but now supplied with more hands, wee should soone resolve the division of the Country by Lot, and so lessen the generall charge.

The third is our constant resolution, that seeing our credits are so farre ingaged to the honourable Lords and the whole State, for the drawing this great Lottery, which we intend shall

[1] During Gates's governorship the prospects of the colony were much depressed by the mortality of the climate; and the cruelties perpetrated under the name of martial law deterred settlers from coming over. To raise money, resort was had to lotteries, but with poor results.

[2] Perhaps this word means distributers of lottery tickets.

be without delay, the 26. of June next, desiring all such as have undertaken with bookes to solicit their friends, that they will not with-hold their monies till the last moneth be expired, lest we be unwillingly forced to proportion a lesse value and number of our Blankes and Prises which hereafter followeth.

*Welcomes.*

| | Crownes. |
|---|---|
| To him that first shall be drawne out with a blanke, | 100 |
| To the second, | 50 |
| To the third, | 25 |
| To him that every day during the drawing of this Lottery, shall bee first drawne out with a blanke, | 10 |

*Prizes.*

| | Crownes. |
|---|---|
| 1 Great Prize of | 4500 |
| 2 Great Prizes, each of | 2000 |
| 4 Great Prizes, each of | 1000 |
| 6 Great Prizes, each of | 500 |
| 10 Prizes, each of | 300 |
| 20 Prizes, each of | 200 |
| 100 Prizes, each of | 100 |
| 200 Prizes, each of | 50 |
| 400 Prizes, each of | 20 |
| 1000 Prizes, each of | 10 |
| 1000 Prizes, each of | 8 |
| 1000 Prizes, each of | 6 |
| 4000 Prizes, each of | 4 |
| 1000 Prizes, each of | 3 |
| 1000 Prizes, each of | 2 |

*Rewards.*

| | Crownes. |
|---|---|
| To him that shall be last drawne out with a blanke, | 25 |
| To him that putteth in the greatest Lot, under one name, | 400 |
| To him that putteth in the second greatest number, | 300 |

To him that putteth in the third greatest number, 200
To him that putteth in the fourth greatest number, 100

If divers be of equall number, their rewards are to be divided proportionally.

*Addition of new Rewards.*

| | Crownes. |
|---|---|
| The blanke that shall bee drawne out next before the great Prize shall have | 25 |
| The blanke that shall be drawne out next after the said great Prize | 25 |
| The blancks that shall be drawne out immediately before the two next great Prizes, shall have each of them | 20 |
| The severall blankes next after them, each shall have | 20 |
| The severall blankes next before the foure great Prizes, each shall have | 15 |
| The severall blankes next after them, each shall have | 15 |
| The severall blankes next before the six great Prizes, each shall have | 10 |
| The severall blankes next after them, each shall have | 10 |

The prizes, welcomes, and rewards, shall be payed in ready Mony, Plate, or other goods reasonably rated; if any dislike of the plate or goods, he shall have mony, abating only the tenth part, except in small prizes of ten Crownes or under.

The mony for the Adventurers is to be paied to Sir Thomas Smith, Knight, and Treasurer for Virginia, or such Officers as he shall apoint in City or Country, under the common seale of the company for the receit thereof.

All prizes, welcomes and rewards drawne where ever they dwell, shall of the Treasurer have present pay, and whosoever under one name or poesie[1] payeth three pound in ready money, shall receive six shillings and eight pence, or a silver spoone of that value at his choice.

About this time it chanced a Spanish ship, beat too and againe before point Comfort, and at last sent a shore their

[1] "Posy" or motto used in place of an assumed name.

boat, as desirous of a Pilot. Captaine James Davis the governor, immediately gave them one: but he was no sooner in the boat, but a way they went with him, leaving three of their companions behind them; this sudden accident occasioned some distrust, and a strict examination of those three thus left, yet with as good usage as our estate could afford them. They only confessed, having lost their Admirall, accident had forced them into those parts; and two of them were Captaines, and in chiefe authority in the fleet: thus they lived till one of them was found to be an Englishman, and had been the Spaniards Pilot for England in 88.[1] and having here induced some male-contents, to beleeve his projects, to run away with a small barke, which was apprehended, some executed, and he expecting but the Hangmans curtesie, directly confessed that two or three Spanish ships was at Sea, purposely to discover the estate of the Colony: but their Commission was not to be opened till they arrived in the Bay, so that of any thing more he was utterly ignorant. One of the Spaniards at last dyed; the other was sent for England, but this reprieved, till Sir Thomas Dale hanged him at Sea in his voyage homeward: the English Pilot they carried for Spaine, whom after a long time imprisonment, with much sute[2] was returned for England.

Whilst those things were effecting, Sir Thomas Dale, having setled to his thinking all things in good order, made choice of one Master George Yearly, to be Deputy-Governour in his absence, and so returned for England; accompanied with Pocahontas the Kings Daughter, and Master Rolfe her husband: and arrived at Plimmoth the 12. of June. 1616.

*The government left to Captaine Yearly.*

Now a little to commentary upon all these proceedings, let me leave but this as a caveat by the way; if the alteration of government hath subverted great Empires, how dangerous

[1] 1588, the year of the Spanish Armada.

[2] Suit, *i.e.*, solicitation. For a better account of this episode, see the letter of Diego de Molina, on pp. 215–224, above, and the many documents from the Spanish archives printed by Brown in his *Genesis of the United States.*

is it then in the infancy of a common-weale? The multiplicity of Governors is a great damage to any State; but uncertaine daily changes are burdensome, because their entertainments are chargeable, and many will make hay whilst the sunne doth shine, how ever it shall faire with the generality.

This deare bought Land with so much bloud and cost, hath onely made some few rich, and all the rest losers. But it was intended at the first, the first undertakers should be first preferred and rewarded, and the first adventurers satisfied, and they of all the rest are the most neglected; and those that never adventured a groat, never see the Country, nor ever did any service for it, imploied in their places adorned with their deserts, and inriched with their ruines: and when they are fed fat, then in commeth others so leane as they were, who through their omnipotency doth as much. Thus what one Officer doth, another undoth, only ayming at their owne ends; thinking all the world derides his dignity, [who] cannot fill his Coffers being in authority with any thing. Every man hath his minde free, but he can never be a true member to that estate, that to enrich himselfe beggers all the Countrie. Which bad course, there are many yet in this noble plantation, whose true honour and worth as much scornes it, as the others loves it; for the Nobilitie and Gentrie, there is scarce any of them expects any thing but the prosperitie of the action: and there are some Merchants and others, I am confidently perswaded, doe take more care and paines, nay, and at their continuall great charge, than they could be hired to for the love of money; so honestly regarding the generall good of this great worke, they would hold it worse than sacrilege, to wrong it but a shilling, or extort upon the common souldier a penny. But to the purpose, and to follow the Historie.

Master George Yearly now invested Deputie Governour by Sir Thomas Dale, applied himselfe for the most part in planting Tobacco, as the most present commoditie they could devise for a present gaine, so that every man betooke himselfe to the best place he could for the purpose: now though Sir Thomas Dale had caused such an abundance of corne to be planted, that every man had sufficient, yet the supplies[1] were sent us, came so unfurnished, as quickly eased us of our superfluitie. To relieve their necessities, he sent to the Chickahamanias for the tribute Corne Sir Thomas Dale and Captaine Argall had conditioned for with them: But such a bad answer they returned him, that hee drew together one hundred of his best shot, with whom he went to Chickahamania; the people in some places used him indifferently, but in most places with much scorne and contempt, telling him he was but Sir Thomas Dales man, and they had payed his Master according to condition, but to give any to him they had no such order, neither would they obey him as they had done his Master; after he had told them his authoritie, and that he had the same power to enforce them that Dale had, they dared him to come on shore to fight, presuming more of his not daring, than their owne valours. Yearly seeing their insolencies, made no great difficultie to goe on shore at Ozinies, and they as little to incounter him: but marching from thence towards Mamanahunt, they put themselves in the same order they see us, lead by their Captaine Kissanacomen, Governour of Ozinies, and so marched close along by us, each as threatning other who should first begin. But that night we quartered against Mamanahunt, and they passed the River. The next day we followed them; there are few places in Virginia had then more plaine ground together, nor more plentie of Corne, which although it was but newly gathered, yet they had hid it in the woods where we could not finde it: a good time we spent thus in arguing the cause, the Salvages without feare standing in troupes amongst us, seeming as if their countenances had beene sufficient to dant us: what other practises they had I know not; but to prevent the worst, our Captaine caused us all to make ready, and upon the word, to let flie among them, where he appointed: others also he commanded to seize on them they could for prisoners; all which being done according to our direction, the Captaine gave the word, and

[1] Supplies (of men) which were sent, etc.

wee presently discharged, where twelve lay, some dead, the rest for life sprawling on the ground, twelve more we tooke prisoners, two whereof were brothers, two of their eight Elders, the one tooke by Sergeant Boothe, the other by Robert a Polonian. Neere one hundred bushels of Corne we had for their ransomes, which was promised the Souldiers for a reward, but it was not performed: now Opechankanough had agreed with our Captaine for the subjecting of those people, that neither hee nor Powhatan could ever bring to their obedience; and that he should make no peace with them without his advice: in our returne by Ozinies with our prisoners wee met Opechankanough, who with much adoe, fained with what paines hee had procured their peace, the which to requite, they called him the King of Ozinies, and brought him from all parts many presents of Beads, Copper, and such trash as they had. Here as at many other times wee were beholding to Captaine Henry Spilman our Interpreter, a Gentleman had lived long time in this Countrie, and sometimes a prisoner [1] among the Salvages; and done much good service, though but badly rewarded. From hence we marcht towards James towne, we had three Boats loaded with Corne and other luggage; the one of them being more willing to be at James towne with the newes than the other, was overset, and eleven men cast away with the Boat, Corne and all their provision. Notwithstanding this put all the rest of the Salvages in that feare, especially in regard of the great league we had with Opechankanough, that we followed our labours quietly, and in such securitie that divers salvages of other Nations, daily frequented us with what provisions they could get, and would guide our men on hunting, and oft hunt for us themselves. Captaine Yearly had a Salvage or two so well trained up to their peeces, they were as expert as any of the English, and one hee kept purposely to kill him fowle. There were divers others had Salvages in like manner for their men. Thus we lived together, as if wee had beene one people, all the time Captaine Yearley

[1] See p. 202, note 4.

staied with us, but such grudges and discontents daily increased among our selves, that upon the arrivall of Captaine Argall, sent by the Councell and Companie to bee our Governour, Captaine Yearley returned for England in the yeere 1617.[1]

From the writings of Captaine NATHANIEL POWELL, WILLIAM CANTRILL, Sergeant BOOTHE, EDWARD GURGANEY.

During this time, the Lady Rebecca, *alias* Pocahontas, daughter to Powhatan, by the diligent care of Master John Rolfe her husband and his friends, was taught to speake such English as might well bee understood, well instructed in Christianitie, and was become very formall and civill after our English manner; shee had also by him a childe which she loved most dearely, and the Treasurer and Company tooke order both for the maintenance of her and it, besides there were divers persons of great ranke and qualitie had beene very kinde to her; and before she arrived at London, Captaine Smith to deserve her former courtesies, made her qualities knowne to the Queenes most excellent Majestie and her Court, and writ a little booke[2] to this effect to the Queene: An abstract whereof followeth.

*To the most high and vertuous Princesse, Queene Anne*[3] *of Great Brittanie.*

MOST ADMIRED QUEENE:

The love I beare my God, my King and Countrie, hath so oft emboldened mee in the worst of extreme dangers, that now honestie doth constraine mee presume thus farre beyond my selfe, to present your Majestie this short discourse: if ingratitude be a deadly poyson to all honest vertues, I must

[1] Yeardley's government lasted one year, and the colony "lived in peace and the best plentye that ever it had till that time." *Breife Declaration.*

[2] Letter.

[3] Anne was the second daughter of Frederick II., king of Denmark, and married James I. in 1589. She died March 2, 1619.

bee guiltie of that crime if I should omit any meanes to bee thankfull. So it is,

That some ten yeeres agoe [1] being in Virginia, and taken prisoner by the power of Powhatan their chiefe King, I received from this great Salvage exceeding great courtesie, especially from his sonne Nantaquaus, the most manliest, comeliest, boldest spirit, I ever saw in a Salvage, and his sister Pocahontas, the Kings most deare and wel-beloved daughter, being but a childe of twelve or thirteene yeeres of age,[2] whose compassionate pitifull heart, of my desperate estate, gave me much cause to respect her: I being the first Christian this proud King and his grim attendants ever saw: and thus enthralled in their barbarous power, I cannot say I felt the least occasion of want that was in the power of those my mortall foes to prevent, notwithstanding al their threats. After some six weeks [3] fatting amongst those Salvage Courtiers, at the minute of my execution, she hazarded the beating out of her owne braines to save mine; and not onely that, but so prevailed with her father, that I was safely conducted to James towne: where I found about eight and thirtie miserable poore and sicke creatures, to keepe possession of all those large territories of Virginia; such was the weaknesse of this poore Commonwealth, as had the Salvages not fed us, we directly had starved.

And this reliefe, most gracious Queene, was commonly brought us by this Lady Pocahontas. Notwithstanding all these passages, when inconstant Fortune turned our peace to warre, this tender Virgin would still not spare to dare to visit us, and by her our jarres have beene oft appeased, and our wants still supplyed; were it the policie of her father thus to imploy her, or the ordinance of God thus to make her his instrument, or her extraordinarie affection to our Nation, I

[1] *I.e.*, December, 1607.

[2] She was consequently at the time of this letter (1616) twenty or twenty-one years old, which is confirmed by the inscription on the engraving by Simon de Passe, and on the original portrait in England, *Ætatis suæ* 21, *A*°. 1616.

[3] Or rather three weeks. Smith was absent from Jamestown from December 10, 1607, to January 2, 1608.

know not: but of this I am sure; when her father with the utmost of his policie and power, sought to surprize mee,[1] having but eighteene with mee, the darke night could not affright her from comming through the irkesome woods, and with watered eies gave me intelligence, with her best advice to escape his furie; which had hee knowne, hee had surely slaine her. James towne with her wild traine she as freely frequented, as her fathers habitation; and during the time of two or three yeeres, she next under God, was still the instrument to preserve this Colonie from death, famine and utter confusion; which if in those times, had once beene dissolved, Virginia might have line[2] as it was at our first arrivall to this day. Since then, this businesse having beene turned and varied by many accidents from that I left it at: it is most certaine, after a long and troublesome warre after my departure, betwixt her father and our Colonie; all which time shee was not heard of. About two yeeres after[3] shee her selfe was taken prisoner, being so detained neere two yeeres longer, the Colonie by that meanes was relieved, peace concluded; and at last rejecting her barbarous condition, was maried to an English Gentleman, with whom at this present she is in England; the first Christian ever of that Nation, the first Virginian ever spake English, or had a childe in mariage by an Englishman: a matter surely, if my meaning bee truly considered and well understood, worthy a Princes understanding.

Thus, most gracious Lady, I have related to your Majestie, what at your best leasure our approved Histories will account you at large, and done in the time of your Majesties life; and however this might bee presented you from a more worthy pen, it cannot from a more honest heart, as yet I never begged any thing of the state, or any: and it is my want of abilitie and her exceeding desert; your birth, meanes and authoritie; hir birth, vertue, want and simplicitie, doth make mee thus bold, humbly to beseech your Majestie to take this knowledge of her, though it be from one so unworthy to be the reporter,

[1] At Werowocomoco, about January 15, 1609.

[2] Lain.

[3] April, 1613. See above, p. 307.

as my selfe, her husbands estate not being able to make her fit to attend your Majestie. The most and least I can doe, is to tell you this, because none so oft hath tried it as my selfe, and the rather being of so great a spirit, how ever her stature:[1] if she should not be well received, seeing this Kingdome may rightly have a Kingdome by her meanes; her present love to us and Christianitie might turne to such scorne and furie, as to divert all this good to the worst of evill: where finding so great a Queene should doe her some honour more than she can imagine, for being so kinde to your servants and subjects, would so ravish her with content, as endeare her dearest bloud to effect that, your Majestie and all the Kings honest subjects most earnestly desire. And so I humbly kisse your gracious hands.

Being about this time preparing to set saile for New-England, I could not stay to doe her that service I desired, and she well deserved; but hearing shee was at Branford with divers of my friends, I went to see her. After a modest salutation, without any word, she turned about, obscured her face, as not seeming well contented; and in that humour her husband, with divers others, we all left her two or three houres, repenting my selfe to have writ she could speake English. But not long after, she began to talke, and remembered mee well what courtesies shee had done: saying, You did promise Powhatan what was yours should bee his, and he the like to you; you called him father being in his land a stranger, and by the same reason so must I doe you: which though I would have excused, I durst not allow of that title, because she was a Kings daughter; with a well set countenance she said,

Were you not afraid to come into my fathers Countrie, and caused feare in him and all his people (but mee), and feare you here I should call you father; I tell you then I will, and you shall call mee childe, and so I will bee for ever and ever your Countrieman. They did tell us alwaies you were dead, and I knew no other till I came to

[1] **Pocahontas was, therefore, not tall.**

Plimoth; yet Powhatan did command Uttamatomakkin to seeke you, and know the truth, because your Countriemen will lie much.

This Salvage, one of Powhatans Councell, being amongst them held an understanding fellow; the King purposely sent him, as they say, to number the people here, and informe him well what wee were and our state. Arriving at Plimoth, according to his directions, he got a long sticke, whereon by notches hee did thinke to have kept the number of all the men hee could see, but he was quickly wearie of that taske. Comming to London, where by chance I met him, having renewed our acquaintance, where many were desirous to heare and see his behaviour, hee told me Powhatan did bid him to finde me out, to shew him our God, the King, Queene, and Prince, I so much had told them of. Concerning God, I told him the best I could, the King I heard he had seene, and the rest hee should see when he would; he denied ever to have seene the King, till by circumstances he was satisfied he had: Then he replyed very sadly, You gave Powhatan a white Dog, which Powhatan fed as himselfe; but your King gave me nothing, and I am better than your white Dog.

The same time I staid in London, divers Courtiers and others, my acquaintances, hath gone with mee to see her, that generally concluded, they did thinke God had a great hand in her conversion, and they have seene many English Ladies worse favoured, proportioned, and behavioured; and as since I have heard, it pleased both the King and Queenes Majestie honourably to esteeme her, accompanied with that honourable Lady the Lady De la Ware, and that honourable Lord her husband, and divers other persons of good qualities, both publikely at the maskes and otherwise, to her great satisfaction and content, which doubtlesse she would have deserved, had she lived to arrive in Virginia.

*The government devolved to Captaine Samuel Argall, 1617.*

The Treasurer, Councell and Companie, having well furnished Captaine Samuel Argall, the Lady Pocahontas *alias*

Rebecca, with her husband and others, in the good ship called the *George*; it pleased God at Gravesend [1] to take this young Lady to his mercie, where shee made not more sorrow for her unexpected death, than joy to the beholders to heare and see her make so religious and godly an end. Her little childe Thomas Rolfe therefore was left at Plimoth with Sir Lewis Stukly, that desired the keeping of it. Captaine Hamar his [2] vice-Admirall was gone before, but hee found him at Plimoth. In March they set saile 1617. and in May he arrived at James towne, where hee was kindly entertained by Captaine Yearley and his Companie in a martiall order, whose right hand file was led by an Indian. In James towne he found but five or six houses, the Church downe, the Palizado's broken, the Bridge in pieces, the Well of fresh water spoiled; the Store-house they used for the Church; the market-place, and streets, and all other spare places planted with Tobacco: the Salvages as frequent in their houses as themselves, whereby they were become expert in our armes, and had a great many in their custodie and possession; the Colonie dispersed all about, planting Tobacco. Captaine Argall not liking those proceedings, altered them agreeable to his owne minde, taking the best order he could for repairing those defects which did exceedingly trouble us; we were constrained every yeere to build and repaire our old Cottages, which were alwaies a decaying in all places of the Countrie: yea, the very Courts of Guard built by Sir Thomas Dale, was ready to fall, and the Palizado's not sufficient to keepe out Hogs. Their number of people were about 400. but not past 200. fit for husbandry and tillage: we found there in all one hundred twentie eight cattell, and fourescore and eight Goats, besides innumerable numbers of Swine, and good plentie of Corne in some places, yet the next yeere [3] the Captaine sent out a Frigat and a Pinnace, that brought us neere six hundred bushels more, which did greatly relieve the whole Colonie. For from the tenants wee seldome had above foure hundred bushels of rent Corne to the store, and there was

[1] It is lately reported (July, 1907) that her grave and skeleton have been found there. [2] Argall's. [3] 1618.

not remaining of the Companies companie, past foure and fiftie men women and Children.

This yeere [1] having planted our fields, came a great drought; and such a cruell storme of haile, which did such spoile both to the Corne and Tobacco, that wee reaped but small profit: the Magazine that came in the *George*, being five moneths in her passage, proved very badly conditioned; but ere she arrived, we had gathered and made up our Tobacco, the best at three shillings the pound, the rest at eighteene pence.

To supply us, the Councell and Company with all possible care and diligence, furnished a good ship of some two hundred and fiftie tunne, with two hundred people and the Lord la Ware. They set saile in Aprill, and tooke their course by the westerne Iles,[2] where the Governour of the Ile of Saint Michael received the Lord la Ware, and honourably feasted him, with all the content hee could give him. Going from thence, they were long troubled with contrary winds, in which time many of them fell very sicke; thirtie died, one of which number was that most honourable Lord Governour the Lord la Ware, whose most noble and generous disposition is well knowne to his great cost, had beene most forward in this businesse for his Countries good. Yet this tender state of Virginia was not growne to that maturitie, to maintaine such state and pleasure as was fit for such a personage, with so brave and great attendance: for some small number of adventrous Gentlemen to make discoveries, and lie in Garrison ready upon any occasion to keepe in feare the inconstant Salvages, nothing were more requisite; but to have more to wait and play than worke, or more commanders and officers than industrious labourers was not so necessarie. For in Virginia, a plaine Souldier that can use a Pick-axe and spade, is better than five Knights, although they were Knights that could breake a Lance: for men of great place, not inured to those incounters, when they finde things not sutable, grow many times so discontented, they forget themselves, and oft become so carelesse, that a dis-

[1] Marginal reading, "1618. Sir Thomas Smith Treasurer." [2] Azores.

contented melancholy brings them to much sorrow, and to others much miserie.

At last they stood in for the coast of New-England; where they met a small Frenchman,[1] rich of Bevers and other Furres. Though wee had here but small knowledge of the coast nor countrie; yet they tooke such an abundance of Fish and Fowle, and so well refreshed themselves there with wood and water, as by the helpe of God thereby, having beene at Sea sixteene weekes, got to Virginia, who without this reliefe had beene in great danger to perish. The French-men made them such a feast, with such an abundance of varietie of Fish, Fowle and Fruits, as they all admired, and little expected that wild wildernesse could affoord such wonderfull abundance of plentie. In this ship came about two hundred men, but very little provision: and the ship called the *Treasurer* came in againe not long after with fortie passengers. The Lord la Wares ship lying in Virginia three moneths,[2] wee victualled her with threescore bushels of Corne, and eight Hogsheads of flesh, besides other victuall she spent whilest they tarried there: this ship brought us advice that great multitudes were a preparing in England to bee sent, and relied much upon that victuall they should finde here: whereupon our Captaine[3] called a Councell, and writ to the Councell here in England the estate of the Colonie, and what a great miserie would insue, if they sent not provision as well as people; and what they did suffer for want of skilfull husbandmen, and meanes to set their Ploughs on worke: having as good ground as any man can desire, and about fortie Bulls and Oxen; but they wanted men to bring them to labour, and Irons for the Ploughs, and harnesse for the Cattell. Some thirtie or fortie acres wee had sowne with one Plough, but it stood so long on the ground before it was reaped, it was most shaken; and the rest spoiled with the Cattell and Rats in the Barne, but no better Corne could bee for the quantitie.

[1] A small French ship.
[2] From August to November, 1618.
[3] Samuel Argall.

Richard Killingbeck being with the Captaine at Kekoughtan, desired leave to returne to his wife at Charles hundred,[1] hee went to James towne by water, there he got foure more to goe with him by land, but it proved that he intended to goe trade with the Indies [2] of Chickahamania: where making shew of the great quantitie of trucke they had, which the Salvages perceiving, partly for their trucke, partly for revenge of some friends they pretended should have beene slaine by Captaine Yearley; one of them with an English peece shot Killingbeck dead, the other Salvages assaulted the rest and slew them, stripped them, and tooke what they had. But fearing this murther would come to light, and might cause them to suffer for it, would now proceed to the perfection of villanie; for presently they robbed their Machacomocko house [3] of the towne, stole all the Indian treasure thereout, and fled into the woods, as other Indians related. On Sunday following, one Fairfax [4] that dwelt a mile from the towne, going to Church, left his wife and three small children safe at home, as he thought, and a young youth: she supposing praier to be done, left the children, and went to meet her husband; presently after came three or foure of those fugitive Salvages, entred the house, and slew a boy and three children: and also another youth that stole out of the Church in praier time, meeting them, was likewise murdered. Of this disaster the Captaine sent to Opechankanough for satisfaction, but he excused the matter, as altogether ignorant of it; at the same time the Salvages that were robbed were complaining to Opechankanough, and much feared the English would bee revenged on them; so that Opechankanough sent to Captaine

[1] Bermuda Hundred. [2] Indians.

[3] "Their Church and Storehouse," says the margin.

[4] In 1620 William Fairfax, yeoman and ancient planter, who "has remained 8 years in the country, and Margery, his wife, an old planter also that came into the country, married to said Fairfax," sold to Rev. Richard Buck twelve acres of land a mile from Jamestown, in the eastern part of the island, on which were "a dwelling house and another little house." (Virginia Land Grants.) In 1622 he was killed by the Indians, while living at the house of Ensign William Spence in Archer's Hope.

Argall, to assure him the peace should never be broken by him, desiring that he would not revenge the injurie of those fugitives upon the innocent people of that towne; which towne he should have, and sent him a basket of earth, as possession given of it, and promised, so soone as possibly they could catch these robbers, to send him their heads for satisfaction, but he never performed it.

SAMUEL ARGALL, JOHN ROLFE.

*A relation from Master John Rolfe, June 15, 1618.*

Concerning the state of our new Common-wealth, it is somewhat bettered, for we have sufficient to content our selves, though not in such abundance as is vainly reported in England. Powhatan died this last Aprill, yet the Indians continue in peace. Itopatin his second brother succeeds him, and both hee and Opechankanough have confirmed our former league. On the eleventh of May, about ten of the clocke in the night, happened a most fearefull tempest, but it continued not past halfe an houre, which powred downe hailestones eight or nine inches about,[1] that none durst goe out of their doores, and though it tore the barke and leaves of the trees, yet wee finde not they hurt either man or beast; it fell onely about James towne, for but a mile to the East, and twentie to the West there was no haile at all. Thus in peace every man followed his building and planting without any accidents worthy of note. Some private differences happened betwixt Captaine Bruster and Captaine Argall, and Captaine Argall and the Companie here in England; but of them I am not fully informed, neither are they here for any use, and therefore unfit to be remembered.[2] In December [3] one Captaine Stallings,

[1] Such storms were apparently more frequent in colonial days than in later times. There is record of a storm in 1667, which poured down hailstones so large that they beat holes in the roofs of the houses.

[2] Particulars of the suit of Brewster against Argall and of the relations between Argall and the company in London, may be found in the first volume of the *Records of the Virginia Company* (Washington, 1906), published by the Library of Congress from the manuscript in its possession. For the period 1619–1624, these records are the chief and authoritative source for the history of the Virginia Company.

[3] 1617.

an old planter in those parts, being imployed by them of the West countrie for a fishing voyage in New-England, fell foule of a Frenchman whom hee tooke, leaving his owne ship to returne for England, himselfe with a small companie remained in the French barke, some small time after upon the coast, and thence returned to winter in Virginia.

*The government surrendered to Sir George Yearley.*

For to begin with the yeere of our Lord, 1619,[1] there arrived a little Pinnace privatly from England about Easter [2] for Captaine Argall; who taking order for his affaires, within foure or five daies returned in her, and left for his Deputy, Captaine Nathaniel Powell. On the eighteenth of Aprill, which was but ten or twelve daies after, arrived Sir George Yearley, by whom we understood Sir Edwin Sandys was chosen Treasurer, and Master John Farrar his Deputy; and what great supplies was a preparing to be sent us, which did ravish us so much with joy and content, we thought our selves now fully satisfied for our long toile and labours, and as happy men as any in the world. Notwithstanding, such an accident hapned Captaine Stallings, the next day his ship was cast away, and he not long after slaine in a private quarrell. Sir George Yearly to beginne his government, added to be of his councell, Captaine Francis West, Captaine Nathaniel Powell, Master John Pory, Master John Rolfe, and Master William Wickam, and Master Samuel Macocke, and propounded to have a generall assembly with all expedition. Upon the twelfth of this Moneth, came in a Pinnace of Captaine Bar-

[1] The margin reads, "1619. Sir Edwin Sands [Sandys, then pronounced Sands] Treasurer. Master John Farer [Ferrar] Deputie." This marks a great turning-point in the history of the Virginia Company, Sir Thomas Smith and his party being defeated in the spring election, and the opposite party becoming dominant, under the leadership of the Earl of Southampton, Sir Edwin Sandys, and the Ferrars, John and Nicholas. The history of all these struggles may be traced in E. D. Neill's *Virginia Company of London* (Albany, 1869), and in the *Records of the Virginia Company.*

[2] Easter Sunday (old style) was March 28, in 1619.

graves;[1] and on the seventeenth Captaine Lownes,[2] and one Master Evans, who intended to plant themselves at Waraskoyack: but now Ophechankanough will not come at us, that causes us suspect his former promises.

In May came in the *Margaret* of Bristoll, with foure and thirty men, all well and in health; and also many devout gifts: and we were much troubled in examining some scandalous letters sent into England, to disgrace this Country with barrennesse, to discourage the adventurers, and so bring it and us to ruine and confusion. Notwithstanding, we finde by them of best experience, an industrious man not other waies imploied, may well tend foure akers of Corne, and 1000. plants of Tobacco; and where they say an aker will yeeld but three or foure barrels,[3] we have ordinarily foure or five, but of new ground six, seven, and eight, and a barrell of Pease and Beanes, which we esteeme as good as two of Corne, which is after thirty or forty bushels an aker, so that one man may provide Corne for five; and apparell for two by the profit of his Tobacco. They say also English Wheat will yeeld but sixteene bushels an aker, and we have reaped thirty: besides to manure the Land, no place hath more white and blew Marble[4] than here, had we but Carpenters to build and make Carts and Ploughs, and skilfull men that know how to use them, and traine up our cattell to draw them; which though we indevour to effect, yet our want of experience brings but little to perfection but planting Tobaco. And yet of that, many are so covetous to have much, they make little good; besides there are so many sofisticating Tobaco-mungers in England, were it never so bad, they would sell it for Verinas,[5] and the trash that remaineth should be Virginia: such devilish bad mindes we know some of our owne Country-men doe beare, not onely to the businesse, but also to our mother England her selfe; could they or durst they as freely defame her.

The 25. of June came in the *Triall* with Corne and Cattell

[1] Captain George Bargrave. [2] Captain Christopher Lawne.
[3] "A barrell they account foure bushels," says the margin.
[4] Marl. [5] A high-grade Cuban tobacco.

all in safety, which tooke from us cleerely all feare of famine; then our governour and councell caused Burgesses to be chosen in all places, and met at a generall Assembly, where all matters were debated thought [1] expedient for the good of the Colony, and Captaine Ward was sent to Monahigan [2] in new England, to fish in May, and returned the latter end of May, but to small purpose, for they wanted Salt. The *George* also was sent to New-found-land with the Cape Merchant: there she bought fish, that defraied her charges, and made a good voyage in seven weekes. About the last of August came in a dutch man of warre that sold us twenty Negars: [3] and Japazous King of Patawomeck, came to James towne, to desire two ships to come trade in his River, for a more plentifull yeere of Corne had not beene in a long time, yet very contagious, and by the trechery of one Poule, in a manner turned heathen, wee were very jealous [4] the Salvages would surprize us. The Governours have bounded foure Corporations; [5] which is [6] the Companies, the University, the Governours and Gleabe land. Ensigne Wil. Spencer, and Thomas Barret a Sergeant, with some others of the ancient Planters being set free, weare the first farmers that went forth; and have chosen places to their content: so that now knowing their owne land, they strive who should exceed in building and planting. The fourth of November, the *Bona nova* came in with all her people lusty and well; not long after one Master Dirmer [7] sent out by some

[1] That were thought. This is the general assembly whose records have been printed on previous pages of this volume, pp. 245–278.

[2] Monhegan Island, off the coast of Maine.

[3] This was the first introduction of negro slavery into Virginia. See Ballagh, *History of Slavery in Virginia*, pp. 6–9, and p. 282, *ante*.

[4] Fearful.

[5] Elizabeth City, James City, Charles City, and Henrico. See Tyler, *The Cradle of the Republic*, pp. 117, 118.

[6] In which are, etc. Sir Edwin Sandys had this spring proposed a university or college for Virginia, and a grant of land at Henrico had been made for its support.

[7] Thomas Dermer during this voyage sailed up the Hudson River, and after visiting Virginia sailed to England, where he brought news of the Dutch trading posts on the Hudson, and the value of the fur trade. Therefore

of Plimoth for New-England, arrived in a Barke of five tunnes, and returned the next Spring. Notwithstanding the ill rumours of the unwholsomnesse of James towne, the new commers that were planted at old Paspaheghe,[1] little more then a mile from it, had their healths better then any in the Country. In December, Captaine Ward returned from Patawomeck, the people there dealt falsly with him, so that hee tooke 800. bushels of Corne from them perforce. Captaine Woddiffe [2] of Bristol came in not long after, with all his people lusty and in health: and we had two particular Governours sent us, under the titles of Deputies to the Company, the one to have charge of the Colledge Lands, the other of the Companies.[3] Now you are to understand, that because there have beene many complaints against the Governors, Captaines, and Officers in Virginia: for buying and selling men and boies, or to bee set over from one to another for a yeerely rent, was held in England a thing most intolerable; or that the tenants or lawfull servants should be put from their places, or abridged their Covenants, was so odious, that the very report thereof brought a great scandall to the generall action. The Councell in England did send many good and worthy instructions for the amending of those abuses, and appointed a hundred men should at the Companies charge be allotted and provided to serve and attend the Governour during the time of his government, which number he was to make good at his departure,

Captain Samuel Argall, with many English planters, prepared to make a settlement on the Hudson, but in 1623 a number of French-speaking Walloons came over and constituted the first regular Dutch colony in America.

[1] "Old Paspahegh," where the Paspahegh Indians had their chief town previous to the arrival of the English, was the site of Argall's "Gift" or "Town."

[2] Captain John Woodlief arrived in Virginia in the *Margaret* of Bristol on December 4, 1619, bringing the first colony for Berkeley Hundred, established by a private company of which Sir William Throckmorton, Richard Berkeley, William Tracy, George Thorpe, and John Smyth of Nibley were the leading members.

[3] George Thorpe was appointed manager of the college lands (set aside this year for the support of a college), and Captain Thomas Newce manager of the company's lands.

and leave to his Successor in like manner; fifty to the Deputy-Governour of the College land, and fifty to the Deputy of the Companies land, fifty to the Treasurer, to the Secretary five and twenty, and more to the Marshall and Cape merchant; which they are also to leave to their successors; and likewise to every particular Officer such a competency, as he might live well in his Office, without oppressing any under their charge: which good law I pray God it be well observed, and then we may truly say in Virginia, we are the most happy people in the world.[1]

By me John Rolfe.

There went this yeere by the Companies records, 11. ships, and 1216. persons to be thus disposed on: Tenants for the Governors land fourescore, besides fifty sent the former spring; for the Companies land a hundred and thirty, for the College a hundred, for the Glebe land fifty, young women to make wives ninety,[2] servants for publike service fifty, and fifty more whose labours were to bring up thirty of the infidels children: the rest were sent to private Plantations.

Two persons unknowne have given faire Plate and Ornaments for two Communion Tables, the one at the College, the other at the Church of Mistris Mary Robinson,[3] who towards the foundation gave two hundred pound. And another unknowne person sent to the Treasurer five hundred and fifty pounds, for the bringing up of the salvage children in Christianity. Master Nicholas Farrar deceased, hath by his Will given three hundred pounds to the College, to be paid when

[1] The object of assigning men and land to the different standing officers was to save the people from being taxed for their support. The experiment, however, proved a failure, and the land thus reserved was ultimately granted away to private persons.

[2] These ninety young maidens were sold with their consent to the settlers as wives, at the cost of their transportation, viz.: one hundred and twenty pounds of tobacco (equivalent to $500 in present currency). Cargoes of this interesting merchandise continued to arrive for many years.

[3] This church was in Southampton Hundred; *i.e.*, the country from Weyanoke to Chickahominy River. There is still preserved a cup, the gift of Mrs. Mary Robinson to this church, with the hall-mark 1617.

there shall be ten young Salvages placed in it, in the meane time foure and twenty pound[1] yeerely to bee distributed unto three discreet and godly young men in the Colony, to bring up three wilde young infidels in some good course of life; also there were granted eleven Pattents, upon condition to transport people and cattle to increase the Plantations.[2]

*A desperat Sea-fight[3] betwixt two Spanish men of warre, and a small English ship, at the Ile of Dominica, going to Virginia, by Captaine Anthony Chester.*

Having taken our journey towards Virginia in the beginning of February, a ship called the *Margaret and John*, of one hundred and sixty tuns, eight Iron Peeces and a Falcon, with eightie Passengers besides Sailers; After many tempests and foule weather, about the foureteenth of March[4] we were in thirteene degrees and an halfe of Northerly latitude, where we descried a ship at hull; it being but a faire gale of wind, we edged towards her to see what she was, but she presently set saile, and ran us quickly out of sight. This made us keepe our course for Mettalina, and the next day passing Dominica, we came to an anchor at Guardalupo, to take in fresh water. Six French-men there cast away sixteene moneths agoe came aboord us; they told us a Spanish man of Warre but seven daies before was seeking his consort, and this was she we descried at hull. At Mevis we intended to refresh our selves,

[1] The interest on £300 at the rate of eight per cent., a rate then usual, and made the legal rate a few years later, by 21 Jac. I. c. 17.

[2] "But few performe them," says the margin.

[3] This sea-fight was accounted in its day among the most notable exploits of the English people. Two accounts were published, one at Amsterdam and the other at London. In 1707 there was printed in Dutch at Leyden an account which is said to have been "narrated by a distinguished passenger." See *William and Mary College Quarterly*, IX. 203–214. An account also was written by Thomas Hothersall "late zityson and grocer of London being an I witness and interpreter of the exploÿte." Brown MS. to editor. The quotation made by Brown in his *First Republic*, p. 415, was doubtless from this writer.

[4] The margin has the note, "1620. The Earle of Southampton Treasurer [*i.e.*, of the Virginia Company] and Master John Ferrar Deputy."

having beene eleven weeks [1] pestered in this unwholsome ship; but there we found two tall ships with the Hollanders colours; but necessitie forcing us on shore, we anchored faire by them, and in friendly manner sent to hale them: but seeing they were Spaniards, retiring to our ship, they sent such a volley of shot after us, that shot the Boat, split the Oares, and some thorow the clothes, yet not a man hurt; and then followed with their great Ordnance, that many times over-racked our ship, which being so cumbred with the Passengers provisions, our Ordinance was not well fitted, nor any thing as it should have beene. But perceiving what they were, we fitted our selves the best we could to prevent a mischiefe. Seeing them warp themselves to windward, we thought it not good to be boorded on both sides at an anchor; we intended to set saile, but that the Vice-Admirall battered so hard our starboord side, that we fell to our businesse, and answered their unkindnesse with such faire shot from a Demiculvering,[2] that shot her betweene wind and water, whereby she was glad to leave us and her Admirall together. Comming faire by our quarter, he tooke in his Holland flag, and put forth his Spanish colours, and so haled us.

We quietly and quickly answered him, both what wee were, and whither bound; relating the effect of our Commission, and the cause of our comming thither for water, and not to annoy any of the King of Spaines Subjects, nor any. She commanded us amaine [3] for the King of Spaine. We replied with inlarging the particulars what friends both the Kings our Masters were; and as we would doe no wrong, we would take none. They commanded us aboord to shew our Commission; which we refused, but if they would send their Boat to us willingly they should see it. But for answer they made two great shot at us, with a volley of small shot, which caused us to leave the decks; then with many ill words they laid us aboord,[4] which caused us to raise our maine saile, and give the word to our small shot which lay close and ready, that paid

[1] From February to April, 1620.

[2] A demi-culverin was a cannon of about 4000 pounds.

[3] To lower the top-sail.

[4] Ran alongside of us.

them in such sort, they quickly retired. The fight continued halfe an houre, as if we had beene invironed with fire and smoke, untill they discovered the waste of our ship naked, where they bravely boorded us loofe for loofe, hasting with pikes and swords to enter; but it pleased God so to direct our Captaine, and encourage our men with valour, that our pikes being formerly placed under our halfe deck, and certaine shot lying close for that purpose under the Port holes, encountred them so rudely, that their fury was not onely rebated, but their hastinesse intercepted, and their whole company beaten backe. Many of our men were hurt, but I am sure they had two for one.

In the end they were violently repulsed, untill they were reinforced to charge againe by their commands, who standing upon their honors, thought it a great indignity to be so affronted, which caused a second charge, and that answered with a second beating backe: whereat the Captaine grew inraged, and constrained them to come on againe afresh, which they did so effectually, that questionlesse it had wrought an alteration, if the God that tosseth Monarchies, and teareth Mountaines, had not taught us to tosse our Pikes with prosperous events, and powred out a volley of small shot amongst them, whereby that valiant Commander was slaine, and many of his Souldiers dropped downe likewise on the top of the hatches. This we saw with our eies, and rejoyced with it at our hearts, so that we might perceive good successe comming on, our Captaine presently tooke advantage of their discomfiture, though with much comiseration of that resolute Captaine, and not onely plied them againe with our Ordnance, but had more shot under the Pikes, which was bestowed to good purpose, and amazed our enemies with the suddennesse.

Amongst the rest, one Lucas, our Carpenters Mate, must not be forgotten, who perceiving a way how to annoy them; As they were thus puzled and in a confusion, drew out a Minion [1] under the halfe decke, and there bent it upon them in such a manner, that when it was fired, the cases of stones and

[1] A small cannon weighing about 1500 pounds and shooting a four-pound ball.

peeces of Iron fell upon them so thick, as cleared the decke, and slew many; and in short time we saw few assailants, but such as crept from place to place covertly from the fury of our shot, which now was thicker than theirs: for although as far as we may commend our enemies, they had done something worthy of commendations; yet either wanting men, or being overtaken with the unlooked for valour of our men, they now began to shrinke, and give us leave to be wanton with our advantage. Yet we could onely use but foure peece of Ordnances, but they served the turne as well as all the rest: for she was shot so oft betweene wind and water, we saw they were willing to leave us, but by reason she was fast in the latch of our cable, which in haste of weighing our anchor hung aloofe, she could not cleare her selfe as she wrought to doe, till one cut the Cable with an axe, and was slaine by freeing us. Having beene aboord us two houres and an halfe, seeing her selfe cleere, all the shot wee had, plaied on both sides, which lasted till we were out of shot; then we discovered the Vice-Admirall comming to her assistance, who began a farre off to ply us with their Ordnances, and put us in minde we had another worke in hand. Whereupon we separated the dead and hurt bodies, and manned the ship with the rest, and were so well incouraged wee waifed them amaine.[1] The Admirall stood aloofe off, and the other would not come within Falcon [2] shot, where she lay battering us till shee received another paiment from a Demiculvering, which made her beare with the shore for smooth water to mend her leakes. The next morning they both came up againe with us, as if they had determined to devour us at once, but it seemed it was but a bravado, though they forsooke not our quarter for a time within Musket shot; yet all the night onely they kept us company, but made not a shot. During which time we had leasure to provide us better than before: but God bethanked they made onely but a shew of another assault, ere suddenly the Vice-admirall fell a starne, and the other lay shaking in the wind, and so they both left

[1] Signalled them to come ahead.

[2] A falcon was a cannon weighing about 1000 pounds.

us. The fight continued six houres, and was the more unwelcome, because we were so ill provided, and had no intent to fight, nor give occasion to disturbe them. As for the losse of men, if Religion had not taught us what by the providence of God is brought to passe, yet daily experience might informe us, of the dangers of wars, and perils at sea, by stormes tempests, shipwracks, encounters with Pirats, meeting with enemies, crosse winds, long voiages, unknowne shores, barbarous Nations, and an hundred inconveniences, of which humane pollicies are not capable, nor mens conjectures apprehensive. We lost Doctor Bohun,[1] a worthy valiant Gentleman, (a long time brought up amongst the most learned Surgeons and Physitions in Netherlands, and this his second journey to Virginia:) and seven slaine out right; two died shortly of their wounds; sixteene was shot, whose limbs God be thanked was recovered without maime, and now setled in Virginia. How many they lost we know not, but we saw a great many lie on the decks, and their skuppers runne with bloud. They were about three hundred tunnes apeece, each [2] sixteene or twentie Brasse-peeces. Captaine Chester, who in this fight had behaved himselfe like a most vigilant, resolute, and a couragious souldier, as also our honest and valiant Master, did still so comfort and incourage us by all the meanes they could. At last, to all our great contents, we arrived in Virginia, and from thence returned safely to England.[3]

That most generous and most honourable Lord, the Earle of Southampton, being pleased to take upon him the title of Treasurer, and Master John Farrar his Deputy, with [4] such instructions as were necessary, and admonitions to all Officers

[1] Dr. Bohun received a mortal wound, and Captain Chester embraced him and exclaimed, "Oh, Dr. Bohun, what a disaster is this." The noble doctor replied, "Fight it out, my brave man, the cause is good, and the Lord receive my soul." Brown, *Genesis of the United States*, II. 830.

[2] *I.e.*, each had.

[3] Next follows in the *Generall Historie* (pp. 130–138 of the original), an alphabetical list of the adventurers for Virginia, or subscribers to the Virginia Company, here omitted.

[4] Sent.

to take heede of extortion, ingrosing commodities, forestalling of markets, especially to have a vigilant care,[1] the familiarity of the Salvages living amongst them made them not way to betray or surprize them, for the building of Guest-houses to relieve the weake in, and that they did wonder in all this time they had made no discoveries, nor knew no more then[2] the very place whereon they did inhabit, nor yet could ever see any returne for all this continuall charge and trouble; therefore they sent to be added to the Councell seven Gentlemen, namely Mr Thorp, Captaine Nuce, Mr Tracy, Captaine Middleton, Captaine Blount, Mr John Pountas, and Mr Harwood, with men, munition, and all things thought fitting; but they write from Virginia, many of the Ships were so pestred with diseased people, and thronged together in their passage, there was much sicknesse and a great mortality, wherefore they desired rather a few able sufficient men well provided, then great multitudes. And because there were few accidents[3] of note, but private advertisements by letters, we will conclude this yeere, and proceed to the next.

Collected out of the COUNCELS letters for Virginia.

The instructions and advertisements for this yeere[4] were both from England and Virginia, much like the last: only whereas before they had ever a suspicion of Opechankanough, and all the rest of the Salvages, they had an eye over him more then any; but now they all write so confidently of their assured peace with the Salvages, there is now no more feare nor danger either of their power or trechery; so that every man planteth himselfe where he pleaseth, and followeth his businesse securely. But the time of Sir George Yearley being neere expired, the Councel here made choise of a worthy young Gentleman Sir Francis Wyat to succeed him, whom they forthwith furnished and provided, as they had done his Predecessors, with all the necessary instructions all these times had

[1] Supply "that." [2] Than. [3] Happenings.

[4] The margin has the note, "**1621. The Earle of Southampton Treasurer. Master John Ferrar Deputy.**"

acquainted them, for the conversion of the Salvages; the suppressing of planting Tobacco, and planting of Corne; not depending continually to be supplied by the Salvages, but in case of necessity to trade with them, whom long ere this, it hath beene promised and expected should have beene fed and relieved by the English, not the English by them; and carefully to redresse all the complaints of the needlesse [1] mortality of their people: and by all diligence seeke to send something home to satisfie the Adventurers, that all this time had only lived upon hopes, grew so weary and discouraged, that it must now be substance that must maintaine their proceedings, and not letters, excuses and promises; seeing they could get so much and such great estates for themselves, as to spend after the rate of 100. pounds, 2, 3, 4, 5, 6, 7, 8, 9, 10. nay some 2000. or 3000.[2] pounds yearely, that were not worth so many pence when they went to Virginia, can scarce containe themselves either in diet, apparell, gaming, and all manner of such superfluity, within a lesse compasse than our curious, costly, and consuming Gallants here in England, which cannot possibly be there supported, but either by oppressing the Comminalty there, or deceiving the generality here (or both).

Extracted out of the COUNCELS Letters for Virginia.

From Virginia, by the relations of the Chieftains there, and many I have conferred with, that came from thence hither, I have much admired to heare of the incredible pleasure, profit and plenty this Plantation doth abound in, and yet could never heare of any returne but Tobacco: but it hath oft amazed me to understand how strangely the Salvages hath beene taught the use of our armes, and imploied in hunting and fowling with our fowling peeces; and our men rooting in the ground about Tobacco like Swine. Besides, that the

[1] It was, as observed before, a part of the council's policy to "promote" the country at the expense of the settlers.

[2] Three thousand pounds sterling at that time was equivalent to $75,000 in present values.

Salvages that doe little but continually exercise their bow and arrowes, should dwell and lie so familiarly amongst our men that practised little but the Spade; being so farre asunder, and in such small parties dispersed, and neither Fort, exercise of armes used, Ordnances mounted, Courts of guard,[1] nor any preparation nor provision to prevent a forraine enemy, much more the Salvages howsoever: for the Salvages uncertaine conformity I doe not wonder; but for their constancy and conversion, I am and ever have beene of the opinion of Master Jonas Stockam [2] a Minister in Virginia, who even at this time, when all things were so prosperous, and the Salvages at the point of conversion, against all their Governours and Councels opinions, writ to the Councell and Company in England to this effect.

*May 28, Master Stockams relation.*

We that have left our native country to sojourne in a strange land, some idle spectators, who either cowardly dare not, or covetously will not adventure either their purses or persons in so commendable a worke; others supporting Atlas of this almost unsupportable burdens as your selves, without whose assistance this Virginia Firmament, in which some, and I hope in short time will shine many more glorious Starres, though there be many Italiannated and Spaniolized Englishmen envies our prosperities, and by all their ignominious scandals they can devise seekes to dishearten what they can, those that are willing to further this glorious enterprize, to such I wish according to the decree of Darius, that whosoever is an enemy to our peace, and seeketh either by getting monipolicall paten[t]s, or by forging unjust tales to hinder our welfare, thath is house were pulled downe, and a paire of gallowes made of the wood, and he hanged on them in the place.

[1] Pickets.

[2] Jonas Stockden, son of William Stockden, of Berkswell in the county of Warwick, England, author of a letter several times printed, which asserted the futility of any attempt to civilize or convert the Indians until their head men were put to death. He appears to have been the earliest exponent of the idea that "the only good Indian is a dead Indian."

As for those lasie servants, who had rather stand all day idle, than worke, though but an houre in this Vineyard; and spend their substance riotously, than cast the superfluity of their wealth into your Treasury: I leave them, as they are, to the eternall Judge of the world. But you, right worthy, that hath adventured so freely; I will not examine, if it were for the glory of God, or your desire of gaine, which, it may be, you expect should flow unto you with a full tide; for the conversion of the Salvages, I wonder you use not the meanes,[1] I confesse you say well to have them converted by faire meanes, but they scorne to acknowledge it;[2] as for the gifts bestowed on them they devoure them, and so they would the givers if they could: and though they[3] have endevoured by all the meanes they could by kindnesse to convert them, they finde nothing from them but derision and ridiculous answers. We have sent boies amongst them to learne their Language, but they returne worse than they went; but I am no Statesman, nor love I to meddle with any thing but my Bookes, but I can finde no probability by this course to draw them to goodnesse: and I am perswaded if Mars and Minerva[4] goe hand in hand, they will effect more good in an houre, then those verball Mercurians[5] in their lives; and till their Priests and Ancients have their throats cut, there is no hope to bring them to conversion.

### *The government of Sir Francis Wyat.*[6]

About October arrived Sir Francis Wyat, with Master George Sands,[7] appointed Treasurer, Master Davison[8] Secre-

[1] *I.e.*, for their conversion. [2] *I.e.*, the fair means.

[3] Those in Virginia who were interested in the work.

[4] Force and learning. [5] Messengers.

[6] Sir Francis Wyatt was governor of Virginia from 1621 to 1626, and from 1639 to 1642. He was son of George Wyatt, Esquire, and grandson of Sir Thomas Wyatt, who was beheaded in the reign of Queen Mary for instigating a rebellion to prevent her marriage with Philip II. of Spain.

[7] George Sandys, the poet, brother of Sir Edwin Sandys, and youngest son of the archbishop of York. While in Virginia he experimented in raising silkworms, had charge of the glass factory, and wrote his translation of *Ovid*.

[8] Christopher Davison, eldest son of Sir William Davison, secretary of state under Queen Elizabeth. He died before 1624.

tary, Doctor Pot[1] the Physician, and Master Cloyburne the Surgian;[2] but much provision was very badly conditioned, nay the Hogs would not eat that Corne they brought, which was a great cause of their sicknesse and mortality; and whatsoever is said against the Virginia Corne, they finde it doth better nourish than any provision is sent thither. The Sailers still they complaine are much to blame for imbesling the provisions sent to private men, killing of Swine, and disorderly trucking; for which some order would be taken.

In them nine Ships that went with Sir Francis Wyat not one Passenger died. At his arrivall he sent Master Thorpe to Opechancanough, whom hee found much satisfied with his comming, to confirme their leagues as he had done his Predecessors, and so contented his people should coinhabit amongst them, and hee found more motions of Religion in him than could be imagined. Every man betaking himselfe to his quarter, it was ordered, that for every head they should plant but 1000. Plants of Tobacco, and upon each plant nine leaves, which will be about 100. weight; the Corne being appointed but at two shillings and six pence the bushell, required such labour, it caused most men neglect it, and depend upon trade: where were it rated at ten shillings the bushell, every man would indevour to have plenty to sell to the new commers, or any that wanted; and seldome any is transported from England, but it standeth in as much, besides the hazard; and other necessaries the Ships might transport of that burden. The 22. of November arrived Master Gookin out of Ireland, with fifty men of his owne, and thirty Passengers, exceedingly well furnished with all sorts of provision and cattle, and planted himselfe at Nupors-newes:[3] the Cotton trees in a yeere grew so thicke as ones arme, and so high as a man: here any thing

[1] Dr. John Pott, afterwards deputy-governor in 1629.

[2] This should be William Clayborne, the surveyor.

[3] This was the first settlement at Newport News. The name either is derived from that of Captain Newport, or means New Port Newce, if, as is sometimes said, Daniel Gookin came from Newcestown in Ireland. His son Daniel migrated later to Massachusetts, where he became a prominent public man, and died a major-general in 1687.

that is planted doth prosper so well as in no place better. For the mortality of the people accuse not the place, for of the old Planters and the families scarce one of twenty miscarries, onely the want of necessaries are the occasions of those diseases.[1] And so wee will conclude this yeere with the shipping and numbers sent.

Out of the COUNCELS Letters from Virginia.

This yeere was sent one and twenty saile of Ships that imployed more than 400. sailers and 1300. men, women and children of divers faculties, with fourescore cattle; the *Tiger* fell in the Turkes hands, yet safely escaped: and by the returne of their letters from thence, the company is assured there can bee no fitter places of Mines, Wood and Water for Iron than there; and the French men [2] affirme no Country is more proper for Vines, Olives, Silke, Rice and Salt, &c. of which the next yeere they promise a good quantity.

*Gifts.*

The Gentlemen and Mariners that came in the *Royall James* from the East-Indies, gave towards the building of a free Schoole 70 pound, eight shillings, and six pence; [3] and an unknowne person to further it, sent thirtie pounds; and another in like manner five and twentie pounds; another refusing to be made knowne, gave fortie shillings yeerely for a Sermon before the Virginia companie: also another that would not be knowne, sent for the College at Henrico, many excellent good religious bookes, worth ten pound, and a most curious

[1] Climatic influences were, nevertheless, the chief trouble, and the writer wisely limits the health of the place to the old planters, who by sickness had become "seasoned" to the malaria of the river.

[2] These men had been sent by the Virginia Company to instruct the settlers how to raise grapes and make wine. They were natives of Languedoc, and were seated at Buckroe, near Point Comfort.

[3] The Reverend Patrick Copeland or Copland had incited these East India voyagers to make this subscription, for the history of which see *Records of the Virginia Company,* I. 532.

Map of al that coast of America. Master Thomas Bargave [1] their Preacher there deceased, gave a Librarie valued at one hundred Markes: and the Inhabitants hath made a contribution of one thousand and five hundred pounds, to build a house for the entertaining of strangers. This yeere also there was much suing for Patents for Plantations, who promised to transport such great multitudes of people: there was much disputing concerning those divisions, as though the whole land had beene too little for them: six and twentie obtained their desires, but as yet not past six hath sent thither a man; notwithstanding many of them would have more, and are not well contented; whom I would intreat, and all other wranglers, to peruse this saying of honest Claudius.

See'st not the world of Natures worke, the fairest well, I wot,
How it, it selfe together ties, as in a true-loves knot.
Nor seest how th'Elements ayre combin'd, maintaine one constant plea,
How midst of heaven contents the Sunne, and shore containes the sea;
And how the aire both compasseth, and carrieth still earths frame,
Yet neither pressing burdens it, nor parting leaves the same.

*The observations of Master John Pory Secretarie of Virginia, in his travels.*

Having but ten men meanly provided, to plant the Secretaries land on the Easterne shore neere Acomack [2] (Captaine Wilcocks plantation), the better to secure and assist each other, Sir George Yearley intending to visit Smiths Iles,[3]

[1] The Reverend Thomas Bargrave was a brother of Captain George Bargrave, came out to Virginia in 1619, and died in 1621.

[2] The reference here is to the peninsula east of Chesapeake Bay, which the Indians called Accomac, now occupied by two counties of Virginia, Northampton and Accomac. Here in the early part of 1621 Sir George Yeardley laid out some of the company's land, and in the fall of 1621 John Pory completed the work by settling ten men thereon as tenants.

[3] Near Cape Charles. Here, in 1614, Sir Thomas Dale established a party of men under Lieutenant Craddock for the purpose of making salt out of sea water, and called the settlement Dale's Gift. It is probable, however, that the settlement was not continued.

fell so sicke that he could not, so that he sent me with Estinien Moll a French-man, to finde a convenient place to make salt in.

Not long after Namenacus the King of Pawtuxunt, came to us to seeke for Thomas Salvage[1] our Interpreter. Thus insinuating himselfe, he led us into a thicket, where all sitting downe, he shewed us his naked brest; asking if we saw any deformitie upon it, we told him, No; No more, said hee, is the inside, but as sincere and pure; therefore come freely to my Countrie and welcome: which wee promised wee would within six weekes after. Having taken a muster of the companies tenants; I went to Smiths Iles, where was our Salthouse: not farre off wee found a more convenient place, and so returned to James towne.

Being furnished the second time, wee arrived at Aquohanock, and conferred with Kiptopeke their King. Passing Russels Ile and Onaucoke,[2] we arrived at Pawtuxunt: the discription of those places, you may reade in Captaine Smiths discoveries, therefore needlesse to bee writ againe. But here arriving at Attoughcomoco the habitation of Namenacus, and Wamanato his brother, long wee staied not ere they came aboord us with a brasse Kettle, as bright without as within, ful of boyled Oisters. Strict order was given none should offend us, so that the next day I went with the two Kings a hunting, to discover what I could in their confines. Wamanato brought mee first to his house, where hee shewed mee his wife and children, and many Corne-fields; and being two miles within the woods a hunting, as the younger conducted me forth, so the elder brought me home, and used me as kindly as he could, after their manner. The next day, he presented me twelve Bever skinnes and a Canow, which I requited with such things to his content, that he promised to keepe them whilst hee lived, and burie them with him being dead. Hee much wondered at our Bible, but much more to heare it was the Law of our God, and the first Chapter of Genesis expounded

[1] Dr. Brown is inclined to think that Ensign Thomas Savage was the first permanent settler on the Eastern Shore. His son was John Savage, and the family is still represented in Virginia.

[2] Onancock.

of Adam and Eve, and simple mariage; to which he replyed, hee was like Adam in one thing, for he never had but one wife at once: but he, as all the rest, seemed more willing of other discourses they better understood. The next day, the two Kings with their people, came aboord us, but brought nothing according to promise; so that Ensigne Salvage challenged Namenacus the breach of three promises, *viz.* not in giving him a Boy, nor Corne though they had plentie, nor Moutapass (a fugitive called Robert Marcum, that had lived 5. yeeres amongst those northerly nations): which hee cunningly answered by excuses. Womanato it seemes, was guiltlesse of this falshood, because hee staied alone when the rest were gone. I asked him if he desired to bee great and rich; he answered, They were things all men aspired unto: which I told him he should be, if he would follow my counsell, so he gave me two tokens, which being returned by a messenger, should suffice to make him confident the messenger could not abuse us.

Some things being stolne from us, he tooke such order that they were presently restored, then we interchanged presents: in all things hee much admired our discretions, and gave us a guide that hee called brother, to conduct us up the River: by the way we met with divers that stil tould us of Marcum: and though it was in October, we found the Countrie very hot, and their Corne gathered before ours at James towne. The next day, we went to Paccamaganant, and they directed us to Assacomoco, where their King Cassatowap had an old quarrell with Ensigne Salvage, but now seeming reconciled, went with us, with another Werowance, towards Mattapanient, where they perswaded us ashore upon the point of a thicket; but supposing it some trecherie, we returned to our boat: farre we had not gone from the shore, but a multitude of Salvages sallied out of the wood, with all the ill words and signes of hostilitie they could. When wee saw plainly their bad intent, wee set the two Werowances at libertie, that all this while had line [1] in the Cabbin, as not taking any notice of their villanie,

2 A

[1] Lain.

because we would convert them by courtesie. Leaving them as we found them, very civill and subtill, wee returned the same way wee came to the laughing Kings on the Easterne shore, who told us plainly, Namanicus would also have allured him into his Countrie, under colour of trade, to cut his throat. Hee told us also Opechancanough had imployed Onianimo to kill Salvage; because he brought the trade from him to the Easterne shore, and some disgrace hee had done his sonne and some thirteene of his people before one hundred of those Easterlings,[1] in rescuing Thomas Graves whom they would have slaine: where hee and three more did challenge the thirteene Pamaunkes to fight, but they durst not; so that all those Easterlings so derided them, that they came there no more.

This Thomas Salvage, it is sixteene yeeres since he went to Virginia, being a boy, hee was left with Powhatan for Namontacke, to learne the language: and as this Author [2] affirmeth, with much honestie and good successe hath served the publike without any publike recompence, yet had an arrow shot through his body in their service. This laughing King at Accomack, tels us the land is not two daies journy over in the broadest place, but in some places a man may goe in halfe a day, betwixt the Bay and the maine Ocean, where inhabit many people; so that by the narrownesse of the Land there is not many Deere, but most abundance of Fish and Fowle. Kiptope [3] his brother rules as his Lieutenant, who seeing his younger brother more affected by the people than himselfe, freely resigned him the moitie of his Countrie, applying himselfe onely to husbandry and hunting, yet nothing neglected in his degree; nor is hee carelesse of any thing concernes the state, but as a vigilant and faithfull Counceller, as hee is an affectionated Brother, bearing the greater burden in government, though the lesser honour: where cleane contrary they on the Westerne shore,[4] the younger beares the charge, and the elder the dignitie. Those are the best husbands [5] of any Salvages

[1] Indians of the Eastern Shore. [2] John Pory. [3] Kiptopeke.

[4] *I.e.*, the main part of Virginia, on the western shore of Chesapeake Bay. [5] Providers.

we know: for they provide Corne to serve them all the yeare, yet spare; and the other not for halfe the yeare, yet want. They are the most civill and tractable people we have met with; and by little sticks will keepe as just an account of their promises, as by a tally. In their mariages they observe a large distance, as well in affinitie as consanguinitie; nor doe they use that devilish custome in making black Boyes.[1] There may be on this shore about two thousand people: they on the West would invade them, but that they want Boats to crosse the Bay; and so would divers other Nations, were they not protected by us. A few of the Westerly Runnagados had conspired against the laughing King: but fearing their treason was discovered, fled to Smiths Iles, where they made a massacre of Deere and Hogges; and thence to Rickahake, betwixt Cissapeack [2] and Nansamund, where they now are seated under the command of Itoyatin.[3] And so I returned to James Towne, where I found the government rendred to Sir Francis Wyat. In February [4] also he travelled to the South River Chawonock, some sixtie miles over land; which he found to be a very fruitfull and pleasant Country, yeelding two harvests in a yeare, and found much of the Silke grasse formerly spoken of, was kindly used by the people, and so returned.

*Captaine Each sent to build a Fort to secure the Countrey.*

It was no small content to all the Adventurers to heare of the safe arivall of all those ships and companies, which was thought sufficient to have made a Plantation of themselves: and againe to second them, was sent Captaine Each in the *Abigale*, a ship of three or foure hundred tunnes, who hath undertaken to make a Block-house amongst the Oyster banks, that shall secure the River. The furnishing him with Instruments, cost three hundred pounds; but the whole charge and

[1] The reference here is to the religious exercises dedicating boys to the priesthood. Strachey, *Historie of Travaile into Virginia*, p. 95.

[2] Chesapeake. [3] Otherwise called Itopatin, or Opitchapan.

[4] The margin has the note, "1622. The Earle of Southampton Treasurer, and Nicholas Farrar Deputy."

the ships returne, will be neere two thousand pounds. In her went Captaine Barwicke with five and twentie men for the building ships and Boats, and not other waies to be imploied: and also a selected number to build the East Indie Schoole,[1] but as yet from Virginia little returnes but private mens Tobacco, and faire promises of plentie of Iron, Silke, Wine, and many other good and rich commodities, besides the speedy conversion of the Salvages, that at first were much discouraged from living amongst them, when they were debarred the use of their peeces; therefore it was disputed as a matter of State, whether such as would live amongst them should use them or not, as a bait to allure them; or at least such as should bee called to the knowledge of Christ. But because it was a great trouble for all causes to be brought to James Towne for a triall, Courts were appointed in convenient places to releeve them: but as they can make no Lawes in Virginia till they be ratified here; so they thinke it but reason, none should bee inacted here without their consents, because they onely feele them, and must live under them. Still they complaine for want of Corne, but what must be had by Trade, and how unwilling any Officer when he leaveth his place, is to make good his number of men to his Successor, but many of them during their times to help themselves, undoes the Company: for the servants you allow them, or such as they hire, they plant on their private Lands, not upon that belongeth to their office, which crop alwaies exceeds yours, besides those which are your tenants to halfes, are forced to row them up and downe,[2] whereby both you and they lose more then halfe. Nor are those officers the ablest or best deserving, but make their

[1] This school was to be built at Charles City (City Point) and to have dependence on the college at Henrico. The first contribution came from some of the East India Company returning from India in the *Royal James*. See p. 350, note 3. Hence the name "East India School." A rector (Rev. Patrick Copland) for the college, a master and usher for the school, tenants for the college lands, and a manager for the same were selected and all but the rector sent to Virginia; but the Indian massacre of 1622 destroyed them all, and effectually crushed out the college and the school.

[2] Up and down the river, from one plantation to another.

experience upon the companies cost, and your land lies unmanured to any purpose, and will yeeld as little profit to your next new officers.

*The massacre upon the two and twentieth of March.*[1]

The Prologue to this Tragedy,[2] is supposed was occasioned by Nemattanow, otherwise called Jack of the Feather, because hee commonly was most strangely adorned with them; and for his courage and policy, was accounted amongst the Salvages their chiefe Captaine, and immortall from any hurt could bee done him by the English. This Captaine comming to one Morgans house, knowing he had many commodities that hee desired, perswaded Morgan to goe with him to Pamauke to trucke, but the Salvage murdered him by the way; and after two or three daies returned againe to Morgans house, where he found two youths his Servants, who asked for their Master: Jack replied directly he was dead; the Boyes suspecting as it was, by seeing him weare his Cap, would have had him to Master Thorp:[3] But Jack so moved their patience, they shot him; so he fell to the ground, put[4] him in a Boat to have him before the Governor, then seven or eight miles from them. But by the way Jack finding the pangs of death upon him, desired of the Boyes two things: the one was, that they would not make it knowne hee was slaine with a bullet; the other, to bury him amongst the English. At the losse of this Salvage, Opechankanough much grieved and repined, with great threats of revenge; but the English returned him such terrible answers, that he cunningly dissembled his intent, with the greatest signes he could of love and peace: yet within fourteene daies after he acted what followeth.

Sir Francis Wyat at his arrivall[5] was advertised,[6] he found the Countrey setled in such a firme peace, as most men there

[1] Good Friday.

[2] Marginal note in the original, "The death of Nematanow, writ by Master Wimp."

[3] George Thorpe, manager of the college lands.

[4] And they put him, etc.

[5] October, 1621.

[6] Informed.

thought sure and unviolable, not onely in regard of their promises, but of a necessitie. The poore weake Salvages being every way bettered by us, and safely sheltred and defended, whereby wee might freely follow our businesse: and such was the conceit of this conceited peace, as that there was seldome or never a sword, and seldomer a peece, except for a Deere or Fowle; by which assurances the most plantations were placed straglingly and scatteringly, as a choice veine of rich ground invited them, and further from neighbours the better. Their houses generally open to the Salvages, who were alwaies friendly fed at their tables, and lodged in their bed-chambers; which made the way plaine to effect their intents, and the conversion of the Salvages as they supposed.

Having occasion to send to Opechankanough about the middle of March, hee used the Messenger well, and told him he held the peace so firme, the sky should fall or [1] he dissolved it; yet such was the treachery of those people, when they had contrived our destruction, even but two daies before the massacre, they guided our men with much kindnesse thorow the woods, and one Browne that lived among them to learne the language, they sent home to his Master. Yea, they borrowed our Boats to transport themselves over the River, to consult on the devillish murder that insued, and of our utter extirpation, which God of his mercy (by the meanes of one of themselves converted to Christianitie) prevented; and as well on the Friday morning that fatall day, being the two and twentieth of March, as also in the evening before, as at other times they came unarmed into our houses, with Deere, Turkies, Fish, Fruits, and other provisions to sell us: yea in some places sat downe at breakfast with our people, whom immediatly with their owne tooles they slew most barbarously, not sparing either age or sex, man woman or childe; so sudden in their execution, that few or none discerned the weapon or blow that brought them to destruction. In which manner also they slew many of our people at severall works in the fields, well knowing in what places and quarters

[1] Before.

each of our men were, in regard of their familiaritie with us, for the effecting that great master-peece of worke their conversion: and by this meanes fell that fatall morning under the bloudy and barbarous hands of that perfidious and inhumane people, three hundred forty seven men, women and children; mostly by their owne weapons; and not being content with their lives, they fell againe upon the dead bodies, making as well as they could a fresh murder, defacing, dragging, and mangling their dead carkases into many peeces, and carrying some parts away in derision, with base and brutish triumph.

Neither yet did these beasts spare those amongst the rest well knowne unto them, from whom they had daily received many benefits; but spightfully also massacred them without any remorse or pitie: being in this more fell then Lions and Dragons, as Histories record, which have preserved their Benefactors; such is the force of good deeds, though done to cruell beasts, to take humanitie upon them, but these miscreants put on a more unnaturall brutishnesse then beasts, as by those instances may appeare.

That worthy religious Gentleman M. George Thorp, Deputie to the College lands, sometimes one of his Majesties Pensioners, and in command one of the principall in Virginia; did so truly effect [1] their conversion, that whosoever under him did them the least displeasure, were punished severely. He thought nothing too deare for them, he never denied them any thing; in so much that when they complained that our Mastives did feare [2] them, he to content them in all things, caused some of them to be killed in their presence, to the great displeasure of the owners, and would have had all the rest guelt to make them the milder, might he have had his will. The King [3] dwelling but in a Cottage, he built him a faire house after the English fashion: in which he tooke such pleasure, especially in the locke and key, which he so admired, as locking and unlocking his doore a hundred times a day, he thought no device in the world comparable to it.

[1] Affect. [2] Frighten. [3] Opechancanough.

Thus insinuating himselfe into this Kings favour for his religious purpose, he conferred oft with him about Religion, as many other in this former Discourse had done: and this Pagan confessed to him (as he did to them) our God was better then theirs, and seemed to be much pleased with that Discourse, and of his company, and to requite all those courtesies; yet this viperous brood did, as the sequell shewed, not onely murder him, but with such spight and scorne abused his dead corps as is unfitting to be heard with civill eares. One thing I cannot omit, that when this good Gentleman upon his fatall houre, was warned by his man, who perceiving some treachery intended by those hell-hounds, to looke to himselfe, and withall ran away for feare he should be apprehended, and so saved his owne life; yet his Master out of his good meaning was so void of suspition and full of confidence, they had slaine him or [1] he could or would beleeve they would hurt him. Captaine Nathaniel Powell [2] one of the first Planters, a valiant Souldier, and not any in the Countrey better knowne amongst them; yet such was the error of an overconceited power and prosperitie, and their simplicities, they not onely slew him and his family, but butcher-like hagled their bodies, and cut off his head, to expresse their uttermost height of cruelty. Another of the old company of Captaine Smith, called Nathaniel Causie, being cruelly wounded, and the Salvages about him, with an axe did cleave one of their heads, whereby the rest fled and he escaped: for they hurt not any that did either fight or stand upon their guard. In one place, where there was but two men that had warning of it, [they] defended the house against sixty or more that assaulted it. M. Baldwin at Warraskoyack,[3] his

[1] Before.

[2] He came with the first settlers in 1607 to Virginia, and for ten days acted as governor after the departure of Captain Samuel Argall for England at Easter in 1619. He married Joyce, daughter of William Tracy, one of the proprietors of Berkeley Hundred, who was massacred with her. His place of 600 acres called Powell Brook lay on the creek which bears his name not far from the mouth of the Appomattox River.

[3] The plantations in Isle of Wight County on the south side of the James from Lawne's Creek to Day's Point were called Warrascoyack.

wife being so wounded, she lay for dead; yet by his oft discharging of his peece, saved her, his house, himselfe, and divers others. At the same time they came to one Master Harisons house, neere halfe a mile from Baldwines, where was Master Thomas Hamer [1] with six men, and eighteene or nineteene women and children. Here the Salvages with many presents and faire perswasions, fained they came for Capt. Ralfe Hamer to go to their King, then hunting in the woods: presently they sent to him, but he not comming as they expected, set fire of a Tobacco-house, and then came to tell them in the dwelling house of it to quench it; all the men ran towards it but Master Hamer, not suspecting any thing, whom the Salvages pursued, shot them full of arrowes, then beat out their braines. Hamer having finished a letter hee was a writing, followed after to see what was the matter, but quickly they shot an arrow in his back, which caused him returne and barricado up the doores, whereupon the Salvages set fire on the house. Harisons Boy finding his Masters peece loaded, discharged it at randome, at which bare report the Salvages all fled, Baldwin still discharging his peece, and Mr. Hamer with two and twentie persons thereby got to his house, leaving their owne burning. In like manner, they had fired Lieutenant Basse [2] his house, with all the rest there about, slaine the people, and so left that Plantation.

Captaine Hamer all this while not knowing any thing, comming to his Brother that had sent for him to go hunt with the King, meeting the Salvages chasing some yet escaped, retired to his new house then a building, from whence he came; there onely with spades, axes, and brickbats, he defended himselfe and his Company till the Salvages departed. Not long after, the Master from the ship had sent six Musketiers, with which he recovered their Merchants store-house, where he armed ten more; and so with thirtie more unarmed workmen, found his Brother and the rest at Baldwins. Now seeing all they had was burnt and consumed, they repaired to James

[1] Brother of Captain Ralph Hamor.

[2] Nathaniel Basse, who had his settlement at Basse's Choice on the west side of Pagan River Bay.

Towne with their best expedition; yet not far from Martins hundred, where seventy three were slaine, was a little house and a small family, that heard not of any of this till two daies after.

All those, and many others whom they have as maliciously murdered, sought the good of those poore brutes, that thus despising Gods mercies, must needs now as miscreants be corrected by Justice: to which leaving them, I will knit together the thred of this discourse.

At the time of the massacre, there were three or foure ships in James River, and one in the next; and daily more to come in, as there did within foureteene daies after; one of which they indevoured to have surprised: yet were the hearts of the English ever stupid, and averted from beleeving any thing might weaken their hopes, to win them by kinde usage to Christianitie. But divers write from thence, that Almighty God hath his great worke in this Tragedy, and will thereout draw honor and glory to his name, and a more flourishing estate and safetie to themselves, and with more speed to convert the Salvage children to himselfe, since he so miraculously hath preserved the English; there being yet, God be praised, eleven parts of twelve remaining,[1] whose carelesse neglect of their owne safeties, seemes to have beene the greatest cause of their destructions: yet you see, God by a converted Salvage that disclosed the plot, saved the rest, and the Pinnace then in Pamaunkes River, whereof (say they) though our sinnes made us unworthy of so glorious a conversion, yet his infinite wisdome can neverthelesse bring it to passe, and in good time, by such meanes as we thinke most unlikely: for in the delivery of them that survive, no mans particular carefulnesse saved one person, but the meere goodnesse of God himselfe, freely and miraculously preserving whom he pleased.

The Letters of Master George Sands, a worthy Gentleman, and many others besides them returned, brought us this

[1] "Eleven parts of twelve" would be 3817 persons, which seems to be a great exaggeration. In March, 1622, there were only 1240 persons resident in Virginia, and of them 347 were killed by the Indians, March 22, which reduced the number to 893. Brown, *First Republic*, p. 464.

unwelcome newes, that hath beene heard at large in publike Court, that the Indians and they lived as one Nation: yet by a generall combination in one day plotted to subvert the whole Colony, and at one instant, though our severall Plantations were one hundred and fortie miles up on River on both sides.

But for the better understanding of all things, you must remember these wilde naked natives live not in great numbers together; but dispersed, commonly in thirtie, fortie, fiftie, or sixtie in a company. Some places have two hundred, few places more, but many lesse; yet they had all warning given them one from another in all their habitations, though farre asunder, to meet at the day and houre appointed for our destruction at al our several Plantations; some directed to one place, some to another, all to be done at the time appointed, which they did accordingly. Some entring their houses under colour of trading, so tooke their advantage; others drawing us abroad under faire pretences; and the rest suddenly falling upon those that were at their labours.

Six of the counsell[1] suffered under this treason, and the slaughter had beene universall, if God had not put it into the heart of an Indian, who lying in the house of one Pace, was urged by another Indian his Brother, that lay with him the night before, to kill Pace, as he should doe Perry which was his friend, being so commanded from their King: telling him also how the next day the execution should be finished. Perrys Indian presently arose and reveales it to Pace, that used him as his sonne; and thus them that escaped was saved by this one converted Infidell. And though three hundred fortie seven were slaine, yet thousands of ours were by the meanes of this alone thus preserved; for which Gods name be praised for ever and ever.

Pace upon this, securing his house, before day rowed to James Towne, and told the Governor of it, whereby they were prevented, and at such other Plantations as possibly intelligence could be given: and where they saw us upon our

[1] These were George Thorpe, Nathaniel Powell, John Berkeley, Samuel Macock, John Rolfe, Michael Lapworth.

guard, at the sight of a peece they ranne away; but the rest were most slaine, their houses burnt, such Armes and Munition as they found they tooke away, and some cattell also they destroied. Since, wee finde Opechankanough the last yeare [1] had practised with a King on the Easterne shore, to furnish him with a kind of poison, which onely growes in his Country to poison us. But of this bloudy acte never griefe and shame possessed any people more then themselves, to be thus butchered by so naked and cowardly a people, who dare not stand the presenting of a staffe in manner of a peece, nor an uncharged peece in the hands of a woman. (But I must tell those Authors, though some might be thus cowardly, there were many of them had better spirits.) [2]

Thus have you heard the particulars of this massacre, which in those respects some say will be good for the Plantation, because now we have just cause to destroy them by all meanes possible: but I thinke it had beene much better it had never happened, for they have given us an hundred times as just occasions long agoe to subject them, (and I wonder I can heare of none but Master Stockam and Master Whitaker of my opinion.) Moreover, where before we were troubled in cleering the ground of great Timber, which was to them of small use: now we may take their owne plaine fields and Habitations, which are the pleasantest places in the Countrey. Besides, the Deere, Turkies, and other Beasts and Fowles will exceedingly increase if we beat the Salvages out of the Countrey: for at all times of the yeare they never spare Male nor Female, old nor young, egges nor birds, fat nor leane, in season or out of season; with them all is one. The like they did in our Swine and Goats, for they have used to kill eight in tenne more then we, or else the wood would most plentifully abound with victuall; besides it is more easie to civilize them by conquest then faire meanes; for the one may be made at once, but their civilizing will require a long time and much industry. The manner how to suppresse them is so often related and approved, I omit it here: And you have twenty

[1] 1621.

[2] A comment by Smith.

examples of the Spaniards how they got the West-Indies, and forced the treacherous and rebellious Infidels to doe all manner of drudgery worke and slavery for them, themselves living like Souldiers upon the fruits of their labours. This will make us more circumspect, and be an example to posteritie: (But I say, this might as well have beene put in practise sixteene yeares agoe as now).

Thus upon this Anvill shall wee now beat our selves an Armour of proofe hereafter to defend us against such incursions, and ever hereafter make us more circumspect: but to helpe to repaire this losse, besides his Majesties bounty in Armes he gave the Company out of the Tower, and divers other Honorable persons have renewed their adventures, we must not omit the Honorable Citie of London, to whose endlesse praise wee may speake it, are now setting forward one hundred persons: and divers others at their owne costs are a repairing; and all good men doe thinke never the worse of the businesse for all these disasters.

What growing state was there ever in the world which had not the like? Rome grew by oppression, and rose upon the backe of her enemies: and the Spaniards have had many of those counterbuffes, more than we. Columbus, upon his returne from the West-Indies into Spaine, having left his people with the Indies, in peace and promise of good usage amongst them, at his returne backe found not one of them living, but all treacherously slaine by the Salvages. After this againe, when the Spanish Colonies were increased to great numbers, the Indians from whom the Spaniards for trucking stuffe used to have all their corne, generally conspired together to plant no more at all, intending thereby to famish them; themselves living in the meane time upon Cassava, a root to make bread, onely then knowne to themselves. This plot of theirs by the Spaniards oversight, that foolishly depended upon strangers for their bread,[1] tooke such effect, and brought them to such misery by the rage of famine, that they spared no un-

[1] "A lamentable example too oft approved [*i.e.*, proved]," says the margin.

cleane nor loathsome beast, no not the poisonous and hideous Serpents, but eat them up also, devouring one death to save them from another; and by this meanes their whole Colony well-neere surfeted, sickned and died miserably. And when they had againe recovered this losse, by their incontinency an infinite number of them died on the Indian disease, we call the French Pox, which at first being a strange and an unknowne malady, was deadly upon whomsoever it lighted. Then had they a little flea called Nigua, which got betweene the skinne and the flesh before they were aware, and there bred and multiplied, making swellings and putrifactions, to the decay and losse of many of their bodily members.

Againe, divers times they were neere undone by their ambition, faction, and malice of the Commanders. Columbus, to whom they were also much beholden, was sent with his Brother in chaines into Spaine; and some other great Commanders killed and murdered one another. Pizzaro was killed by Almagros sonne, and him Vasco [1] beheaded; which Vasco was taken by Blasco, and Blasco was likewise taken by Pizzaros Brother: And thus by their covetous and spightfull quarrels, they were ever shaking the maine pillars of their Common-weale. These and many more mischiefes and calamities hapned them, more then ever did to us, and at one time being even at the last gaspe, had two ships not arrived with supplies as they did, they were so disheartned, they were a leaving the Countrey: yet we see for all those miseries they have attained to their ends at last, as is manifest to all the world, both with honour, power, and wealth; and whereas before few could be hired to goe to inhabit there, now with great sute they must obtaine it; [2] but where there was no honesty, nor equity, nor sanctitie, nor veritie, nor pietie, nor good civilitie in such a Countrey, certainly there can bee no stabilitie.

Therefore let us not be discouraged, but rather animated by those conclusions, seeing we are so well assured of the

[1] By Vasco the writer means Vaca de Castro, Pizarro's successor as governor of Peru; by Blasco, the viceroy Blasco Nuñez Vela.

[2] Permission to go.

goodnesse and commodities may bee had in Virginia; nor is it to be much doubted there is any want of Mines of most sorts, no not of the richest, as is well knowne to some yet living that can make it manifest when time shall serve: and yet to thinke that gold and silver Mines are in a country otherwise most rich and fruitfull, or the greatest wealth in a Plantation, is but a popular error; as is that opinion likewise, that the gold and silver is now the greatest wealth of the West Indies at this present. True it is indeed, that in the first conquest the Spaniards got great and mighty store of treasure from the Natives, which they in long space had heaped together; and in those times the Indians shewed them entire and rich Mines, which now by the relations of them that have beene there, are exceedingly wasted, so that now the charge of getting those Metals is growne excessive, besides the consuming the lives of many by their pestilent smoke and vapours in digging and refining them, so that all things considered, the cleere gaines of those metals, the Kings part defraied, to the Adventurers is but small, and nothing neere so much as vulgarly is imagined. And were it not for other rich Commodities there that inrich them, those of the Contraction House [1] were never able to subsist by the Mines onely; for the greatest part of their Commodities are partly naturall, and partly transported from other parts of the world, and planted in the West-Indies, as in their mighty wealth of Sugar canes, being first transported from the Canaries; and in Ginger and other things brought out of the East-Indies, in their Cochanele, Indicos, Cotton, and their infinite store of Hides, Quick-silver, Allum, Woad, Brasill woods, Dies, Paints, Tobacco, Gums, Balmes, Oiles, Medicinals and Perfumes, Sassaparilla, and many other physicall drugs: These are the meanes whereby they raise that mighty charge of drawing out their gold and silver to the great and cleare revenue of their King. Now seeing the most of

[1] "Contraction" for "Contractation." The Casa de Contratacion at Seville was the India House of Spain, where the Board of Colonial Trade held its sessions and administered in economic respects the Spanish colonial empire.

those commodities, or as usefull, may be had in Virginia by the same meanes, as I have formerly said; let us with all speed take the priority of time, where also may be had the priority of place, in chusing the best seats of the Country; which now by vanquishing the salvages, is like to offer a more faire and ample choice of fruitfull habitations, then hitherto our gentlenesse and faire comportments could attaine unto.

*The numbers that were slaine in those severall Plantations.*

| | | |
|---|---|---|
| 1 | At Captaine Berkleys Plantation, himselfe and 21. others, seated at the Falling-Crick, 66. miles from James City. | 22 |
| 2 | Master Thomas Sheffelds Plantation, some three miles from the Falling-Crick, himselfe and 12. others. | 13 |
| 3 | At Henrico Iland, about two miles from Sheffelds Plantation. | 6 |
| 4 | Slaine of the College people, twenty miles from Henrico. | 17 |
| 5 | At Charles City, and of Captaine Smiths men. | 5 |
| 6 | At the next adjoyning Plantation. | 8 |
| 7 | At William Farrars house. | 10 |
| 8 | At Brickley hundred,[1] fifty miles from Charles City, Master Thorp and | 10 |
| 9 | At Westover, a mile from Brickley. | 2 |
| 10 | At Master John Wests Plantation. | 2 |
| 11 | At Captaine Nathaniel Wests Plantation. | 2 |
| 12 | At Lieutenant Gibs his Plantation. | 12 |
| 13 | At Richard Owens house, himselfe and | 6 |
| 14 | At Master Owen Macars house, himselfe and | 3 |
| 15 | At Martins hundred, seven miles from James City. | 73 |
| 16 | At another place. | 7 |
| 17 | At Edward Bonits [2] Plantation. | 50 |
| 18 | At Master Waters his house, himselfe [3] and | 4 |
| 19 | At Apamatucks River, at Master Perce his Plantation, five miles from the College. | 4 |

[1] Berkeley Hundred. [2] Bennett's.
[3] This was a mistake. Edward Waters escaped.

20 At Master Macocks Divident, Captaine Samuel Macock and 4
21 At Flowerda hundred, Sir George Yearleys Plantation. 6
22 On the other side opposite to it. 7
23 At Master Swinhows house, himselfe and 7
24 At Master William Bickars house, himselfe and 4
25 At Weanock, of Sir George Yearleys people. 21
26 At Powel Brooke, Captaine Nathaniel Powel, and 12
27 At South-hampton hundred. 5
28 At Martin Brandons hundred. 7
29 At Captaine Henry Spilmans house. 2
30 At Ensigne Spences house. 5
31 At Master Thomas Perse his house by Mulbery Ile, himselfe and 4

The whole number 347.

Men in this taking bettered with affliction,
Better attend, and mind, and marke Religion,
For then true voyces issue from their hearts.
Then speake they what they thinke in inmost parts,
The truth remaines, they cast off fained Arts.

This lamentable and so unexpected a disaster caused them all beleeve the opinion of Master Stockam, and drave them all to their wits end. It was twenty or thirty daies ere they could resolve what to doe, but at last it was concluded, all the petty Plantations should be abandoned, and drawne onely to make good five or six places, where all their labours now for the most part must redound to the Lords of those Lands where they were resident. Now for want of Boats, it was impossible upon such a sudden to bring also their cattle, and many other things, which with much time, charge and labour they had then in possession with them; all which for the most part at their departure was burnt, ruined and destroyed by the Salvages. Only Master Gookins at Nuports-newes would not obey the Commanders command in that, though hee had scarce five and thirty of all sorts [1] with him, yet he thought

[1] Boys and men.

himselfe sufficient against what could happen, and so did to his great credit and the content of his Adventurers. Master Samuel Jorden gathered together but a few of the straglers about him at Beggers-bush, where he fortified and lived in despight of the enemy. Nay, Mistrisse Proctor, a proper, civill, modest Gentlewoman did the like, till perforce the English Officers forced her and all them with her to goe with them, or they would fire her house themselves; as the Salvages did when they were gone, in whose despight they had kept it and what they had, a moneth or three weekes after the Massacre; which was to their hearts a griefe beyond comparison, to lose all they had in that manner, onely to secure others pleasures.

Now here in England it was thought,[1] all those remainders might presently have beene reduced into fifties or hundreds in places most convenient with what they had, having such strong houses as they reported they had, which with small labour might have beene made invincible Castles against all the Salvages in the Land: and then presently raised a company, as a running Armie to torment the Barbarous and secure the rest, and so have had all that Country betwixt the Rivers of Powhatan and Pamaunke to range and sustaine them: especially all the territories of Kecoughtan, Chiskact and Paspahege, from Ozenies to that branch of Pamaunke, comming from Youghtanund, which strait of land is not past 4. or 5. miles, to have made a peninsula much bigger then the Summer Iles, invironed with the broadest parts of those two maine Rivers, which for plenty of such things as Virginia affords is not to be exceeded, and were it well manured, more then sufficient for ten thousand men. This, were it well understood, cannot but be thought better then to bring five or six hundred to lodge and live on that, which before would not well receive and maintaine a hundred, planting little or nothing, but spend that they have upon hopes out of England, one evill begetting another, till the disease is past cure. There-

[1] The margin has a note against this paragraph, "The opinion of Captaine Smith."

fore it is impossible but such courses must produce most fearefull miseries and extreme extremities; if it prove otherwise, I should be exceeding glad. I confesse I am somewhat too bold to censure other mens actions being not present, but they have done as much of me; yea many here in England that were never there, and also many there that knowes little more then their Plantations, but as they are informed: and this doth touch the glory of God, the honour of my Country, and the publike good so much, for which there hath beene so many faire pretences, that I hope none will be angry for speaking my opinion; seeing the old Proverbe doth allow losers leave to speake, and Du Bartas [1] saith,

Even as the wind the angry Ocean moves,
Wave hunteth Wave, and Billow Billow shoves,
So doe all Nations justell each the other,
And so one people doe pursue another,
And scarce a second hath the first unhoused,
Before a third him thence againe have roused.

Amongst the multitude of these severall Relations, it appeares Captaine Nuse [2] seeing many of the difficulties to ensue, caused as much Corne to be planted as he could at Elizabeths city, and though some destroyed that they had set, fearing it would serve the Salvages for Ambuscadoes, trusting to releefe by trade, or from England (which hath ever beene one cause of our miseries, for from England wee have not had much: and for trading, every one hath not Ships, Shalops, Interpreters, men and provisions to performe it; and those that have, use them onely for their owne private gaine, not the publike good), so that our beginning this yeere doth cause many to distrust the event of the next. Here wee will leave Captaine Nuse for a while, lamenting the death of Captaine Norton, a valiant industrious Gentleman, adorned with many good qualities, besides Physicke and Chirurgery, which for

[1] Guillaume du Bartas, whose epic, *La Création*, translated into English by Joshua Sylvester, was one of the most popular poems of the time.

[2] Captain Thomas Newce, a member of the Council.

the publike good he freely imparted to all *gratis*, but most bountifully to the poore; and let us speake a little of Captaine Croshaw amongst the midst of those broiles in the River of Patawomeke.

Being in a small Barke called the *Elizabeth*, under the command of Captaine Spilman, at Cekacawone,[1] a Salvage stole aboord them, and told them of the Massacre; and that Opechancanough had plotted with his King and Countrey to betray them also, which they refused: but them of Wighcocomoco at the mouth of the river had undertaken it. Upon this Spilman went thither, but the Salvages seeing his men so vigilant and well armed, they suspected themselves discovered, and to colour their guilt, the better to delude him, so contented his desire in trade, his Pinnace was neere fraught; but seeing no more to be had, Croshaw went to Patawomek, where he intended to stay and trade for himselfe, by reason of the long acquaintance he had with this King that so earnestly entreated him now to be his friend, his countenancer, his Captaine and director against the Pazaticans, the Nacotchtanks,[2] and Moyaons his mortall enemies. Of this oportunity Croshaw was glad, as well to satisfie his owne desire in some other purpose he had, as to keepe the King as an opposite to Opechancanough, and adhere him unto us, or at least make him an instrument against our enemies; so onely Elis Hill stayed with him, and the Pinnace returned to Elizabeths City; here shall they rest also a little, till we see how this newes was entertained in England.

It was no small griefe to the Councell and Company, to understand of such a supposed impossible losse, as that so many should fall by the hands of men so contemptible; and yet having such warnings, especially by the death of Nemattanow, whom the Salvages did thinke was shot-free,[3] as he had perswaded them, having so long escaped so many dangers without any hurt. But now to leape out of this labyrinth of melancholy, all this did not so discourage the noble adventurers, nor divers others still to undertake new severall Plantations;

[1] Chicacoan. [2] Nacostans. [3] Immune from shot.

but that divers ships were dispatched away, for their supplies and assistance thought sufficient. Yet Captaine Smith did intreat and move them to put in practise his old offer; seeing now it was time to use both it and him, how slenderly heretofore both had beene regarded, and because it is not impertinent to the businesse, it is not much amisse to remember what it was.[1]

*The project and offer of Captaine John Smith, to the Right Honourable and Right Worshipfull Company of Virginia.*

If you please I may be transported with a hundred Souldiers and thirty Sailers by the next Michaelmas,[2] with victuall, munition, and such necessary provision; by Gods assistance, we would endevour to inforce the Salvages to leave their Country, or bring them in that feare and subjection that every man should follow their businesse securely. Whereas now halfe their times and labours are spent in watching and warding, onely to defend, but altogether unable to suppresse the Salvages: because every man now being for himselfe will be unwilling to be drawne from their particular labours, to be made as pack-horses for all the rest, without any certainty of some better reward and preferment then I can understand any there can or will yet give them.

These [3] I would imploy onely in ranging the Countries, and tormenting the Salvages, and that they should be as a running Army till this were affected; and then settle themselves in some such convenient place, that should ever remaine a garison of that strength, ready upon any occasion against the Salvages, or any other for the defence of the Countrey, and to see all the English well armed, and instruct them their use.[4] But I would have a Barke of one hundred tunnes, and meanes to build sixe or seven Shalops, to transport them where there should bee occasion.

Towards the charge, because it is for the generall good, and what by the massacre and other accidents, Virginia is

[1] The *Records of the Virginia Company* seem to contain no trace of these proposals of Smith, nor of the response to them which follows.

[2] September 29, 1622. [3] *I.e.*, soldiers. [4] *I.e.*, in the use of firearms.

disparaged, and many men and their purses much discouraged, however a great many doe hasten to goe, thinking to bee next heires to all the former losses, I feare they will not finde all things as they doe imagine; therefore leaving those gilded conceits, and dive into the true estate of the Colony; I thinke if his Majestie were truly informed of their necessitie, and the benefit of this project, he would be pleased to give the custome [1] of Virginia; and the Planters also according to their abilities would adde thereto such a contribution, as would be fit to maintaine this garison till they be able to subsist, or cause some such other collections to be made, as may put it with all expedition in practice: otherwise it is much to be doubted, there will neither come custome, nor any thing from thence to England within these few yeares.

Now if this should be thought an imploiment more fit for ancient [2] Souldiers there bred, then such new commers as may goe with me; you may please to leave that to my discretion, to accept or refuse such voluntaries, that will hazard their fortunes in the trialls of these events, and discharge such of my company that had rather labour the ground then subdue their enemies: what releefe I should have from your Colony I would satisfie, and spare them (when I could) the like courtesie. Notwithstanding these doubts, I hope to feede them as as well as defend them, and yet discover you more land unknowne then they all yet know, if you will grant me such priviledges as of necessity must be used.

For against any enemy we must be ready to execute the best can be devised by your state there, but not that they shall either take away my men, or any thing else to imploy as they please by vertue of their authority: and in that I have done somewhat for New-England as well as Virginia, so I would desire liberty and authority to make the best use I can of my best experiences, within the limits of those two Patents, and to bring them both in one Map, and the Countries betwixt them, giving alwaies that respect to the Governors and government, as an Englishman doth in Scotland, or a Scotch-

[1] Custom-house dues.

[2] Experienced.

man in England, or as the regiments in the Low-countries[1] doe to the Governors of the Townes and Cities where they are billited, or in Garrison, where though they live with them, and are as their servants to defend them, yet not to be disposed on at their pleasure, but as the Prince and State doth command them. And for my owne paines in particular I aske not any thing but what I can produce from the proper labour of the Salvages.

### *Their Answer.*

I cannot say, it was generally for the Company, for being published in their Court,[2] the most that heard it liked exceeding well of the motion, and some would have been very large Adventurers in it, especially Sir John Brookes and Master David Wyffin, but there were such divisions amongst them, I could obtaine no answer but this, the charge would be too great; their stocke was decayed, and they did thinke the Planters should doe that of themselves if I could finde meanes to effect it; they did thinke I might have leave of the Company, provided they might have halfe the pillage, but I thinke there are not many will much strive for that imploiment, for except it be a little Corne at some time of the yeere is to be had, I would not give twenty pound for all the pillage is to be got amongst the Salvages in twenty yeeres: but because they supposed I spake only for my owne ends, it were good those understand providents [3] for the Companies good they so much talke of, were sent thither to make triall of their profound wisdomes and long experiences.

About this time also was propounded a proposition concerning a Sallery of five and twenty thousand pounds to be raised out of Tobacco, as a yeerely pension to bee paid to certaine Officers for the erecting a new office, concerning the sole importation of Tobacco, besides his Majesties custome, fraught, and all other charges. To nominate [4] the undertakers, fa-

[1] *I.e.*, the British auxiliary troops which for many years were maintained in the service of the Dutch Republic.

[2] Stockholders' meeting.

[3] Understanding providents, *i.e.*, wise providers.

[4] Name.

vourers and opposers, with their arguments (*pro*) and (*con*) would bee too tedious and needlesse being so publikely knowne; the which to establish, spent a good part of that yeere, and the beginning of the next. This made many thinke wonders of Virginia, to pay such pensions extraordinary to a few here that were never there, and also in what state and pompe some Chieftaines and divers of their associates live in Virginia; and yet no money to maintaine a Garrison, pay poore men their wages, nor yet five and twenty pence to all the Adventurers here, and very little to the most part of the Planters there, bred such differences in opinion it[1] was dissolved.

Now let us returne to Captaine Croshaw at Patawomek, where he had not beene long ere Opechancanough sent two baskets of beads to this King, to kill him and his man, assuring him of the Massacre he had made, and that before the end of two Moones there should not be an Englishman in all their Countries: this fearefull message the King told this Captaine, who replied, he had seene both the cowardise and trechery of Opechancanough sufficiently tried by Captaine Smith,[2] therefore his threats he feared not, nor for his favour cared, but would nakedly fight with him or any of his with their owne swords; if he were slaine, he would leave a letter for his Country men to know, the fault was his owne, not the Kings. Two daies the King deliberated upon an answer, at last told him the English were his friends, and the Salvage Emperour Opitchapam, now called Toyatan, was his brother; therefore there should be no bloud shed betwixt them: for hee returned the Presents, willing the Pamaunkes to come no more in his Country, lest the English, though against his will, should doe them any mischiefe.

Not long after, a Boat going abroad to seeke out some releefe amongst the Plantations, by Nuports-newes met such ill weather, though the men were saved they lost their boat, which the storme and waves cast upon the shore of Nandsamund: where Edward Waters one of the three that first stayed

[1] The charter.

[2] At Pamunkey in 1609.

in Summer Iles, and found the great peece of Amber-greece, dwelling in Virginia at this Massacre, hee and his wife these Nandsamunds kept Prisoners till it chanced they found this Boat; at which purchase they so rejoyced, according to their custome of triumph, with songs, dances and invocations. They were so busied, that Waters and his wife found opportunity to get secretly into their Canow, and so crossed the River to Kecoughtan, which is nine or ten miles: whereat the English no lesse wondred and rejoyced, then the Salvages were madded with discontent. Thus you may see how many desperate dangers some men escape, when others die that have all things at their pleasure.

All men thinking Captaine Croshaw dead, Captaine Hamer arriving with a Ship and a Pinnace at Patawomeke, was kindly entertained both by him[1] and the King; that Don Hamar told the King he came for Corne; the King replied hee had none, but the Nacotchtanks and their confederats had, which were enemies both to him and them; if they would fetch it, he would give them 40. or 50 choise Bow-men to conduct and assist them. Those Salvages, with some of the English, they sent; who so well played their parts, they slew 18. of the Nacotchtanks,[2] some write but 4. and some they had a long skirmish with them; where the Patawomeks were so eager of revenge, they drive them not onely out of their towne, but all out of sight through the woods; thus taking what they liked, and spoiling the rest, they retired to Patawomek, where they left Captaine Croshaw, with foure men more, the rest set saile for James towne. Captaine Croshaw now with five men and himselfe found night and day so many Alarums, he retired into such a convenient place, that with the helpe of the Salvages, hee had quickly fortified himselfe against all those wilde enemies. Captaine Nuse his Pinnace meeting Hamar by the way, understanding all this, came to see Captaine Croshaw: after their best enterchanges of courtesies, Croshaw writ to Nuse the estate of the place where he was, but understanding by them the poore estate of the Colony, offered if they would send

[1] Croshaw. [2] Necostans.

him but a bold Shallop, with men, armes and provision for trade, the next Harvest he would provide them Corne sufficient, but as yet it being but the latter end of June, there was little or none in all the Country.

This being made knowne to the Governour and the rest, they sent Captaine Madyson with a ship and pinnace, and some six and thirtie men: those Croshaw a good time taught the use of their armes, but receiving a letter from Boyse his Wife,[1] a prisoner with nineteene more at Pamaunke, to use meanes to the Governour for their libertie; So hee dealt with this King, hee got first two of his great men to goe with him to James towne, and eight daies after to send foure of his counsell to Pamaunke, there to stay till he sent one of his two to them, to perswade Opachankanough to send two of his with two of the Patawomekes, to treat about those prisoners, and the rest should remaine their hostage at Pamaunke. But the Commanders, at James towne, it seemes, liked not of it, and so sent the Patawomekes backe againe to their owne Countrie, and Captaine Croshaw to his owne habitation.

All this time we have forgot Captaine Nuse,[2] where we left him but newly acquainted with the Massacre, calling all his next adjoyning dispersed neighbours together, he regarded not the pestring his owne house, nor any thing to releeve them, and with all speed entrenched himselfe, mounted three peece of Ordnance, so that within 14. daies, he was strong enough to defend himselfe from all the Salvages, yet when victuall grew scant, some that would forrage without order, which he punished, neere occasioned a mutiny. Notwithstanding, he behaved himselfe so fatherly and kindly to them all, they built two houses for them he daily expected from England, a faire Well of fresh water mantled with bricke, because the River and Cricks are there brackish or salt; in all which things he plaied the Sawyer, Carpenter, Dauber, Laborer, or any thing; wherein though his courage and heart were steeled, he found his body was not made of Iron, for hee had many

[1] Sarah, the wife of Cheney Boys.

[2] He commanded at Elizabeth City.

sicknesses, and at last a Dropsie, no lesse griefe to himselfe, then sorrow to his Wife and all under his government. These crosses and losses were no small increasers of his malady, nor the thus abandoning our Plantations, the losse of our Harvest, and also Tobacco which was as our money; the Vineyard our Vineyetours [1] had brought to a good forwardnesse, bruised and destroyed with Deere, and all things ere they came to perfection, with weeds, disorderly persons or wild beasts; so that as we are I cannot perceive but the next yeere [2] will be worse, being still tormented with pride and flattery, idlenesse and covetousnesse, as though they had vowed heere to keepe their Court with all the pestilent vices in the world for their attendants, inchanted with a conceited statelinesse, even in the very bottome of miserable senselesnesse.

Shortly after, Sir George Yearly and Captaine William Powel [3] took each of them a company of well disposed Gentlemen and others to seeke their enemies. Yearley ranging the shore of Weanock, could see nothing but their old houses which he burnt, and so went home: Powel searching another part, found them all fled but three he met by chance, whose heads hee cut off, burnt their houses, and so returned; for the Salvages are so light and swift, though wee see them (being so loaded with armour) they have much advantage of us though they be cowards.

I confesse this is true,[4] and it may cause some suppose they are grown invincible: but will any goe to catch a Hare with a Taber and a Pipe? for who knowes not though there be monsters both of men and beasts, fish and fowle, yet the greatest, the strongest, the wildest, cruellest, fiercest and

[1] The French vinedressers at Buckroe. [2] 1623.

[3] Captain William Powell came to Virginia with Gates in 1611, and in 1616 was made captain of the fort at Jamestown. Pace first told him of the plot of the Indians in 1622 to murder the whites. When they appeared before the fort in the morning, he dispersed them with the ordnance. He held lands afterward in Surry County, which appears to have been named after his native county in England.

[4] Against this paragraph the original has the marginal note, "The opinion of Captaine Smith." With the next paragraph we return to narratives by dwellers in Virginia, edited by Smith.

cunningest, by reason, art and vigilancy, courage and industry hath beene slaine, subjected or made tame: and those are still but Salvages as they were, onely growne more bold by our owne simplicities, and still will be worse and worse till they be tormented with a continuall pursuit, and not with lying inclosed within Palizados, or affrighting them out of your sights, thinking they have done well [who] can but defend themselves: and to doe this to any purpose, will require both charge, patience and experience. But to their proceedings.

About the latter end of June, Sir George Yearley accompanied with the Councell, and a number of the greatest Gallants in the Land, stayed three or four daies with Captaine Nuse, he making his moane to a chiefe man amongst them for want of provision for his Company, the great Commander replied hee should turne them to his greene Corne, which would make them plumpe and fat: these fields being so neere the Fort, were better regarded and preserved then the rest, but the great mans command, as we call them, were quickly obeied, for though it was scarce halfe growne either to the greatnesse or goodnesse, they devoured it greene though it did them small good. Sir George with his company went to Accomack to his new Plantation, where he staied neere six weekes:[1] some Corne he brought home; but as he adventured for himselfe, he accordingly enjoyed the benefit. Some pety Magazines[2] came this Summer, but either the restraint by Proclamation, or want of Boats, or both, caused few but the Chieftaines to be little better by them. So long as Captaine Nuse had any thing we had part; but now all being spent, and the people forced to live upon Oisters and Crabs, they became so faint no worke could be done; and where the Law was, no worke, no meat, now the case is altered, to no meat, no worke: some small quantity of Milke and Rice the Captaine had of his owne, and that he would distribute *gratis* as he saw occasion; I say *gratis*, for I know no place else, but it was sold for ready paiment. Those eares of Corne that had escaped till August, though not ripe

[1] His descendants intermarried with most of the families of the Eastern Shore.

[2] Private stores.

by reason of the late planting, the very Dogs did repaire to the Corne fields to seeke them as the men till they were hanged: and this I protest before God is true that I have related, not to flatter Nuse, nor condemne any, but all the time I have lived in Virginia, I have not seene nor heard that any Commander hath taken such continuall paines for the publike, or done so little good for himselfe; and his vertuous wife was no lesse charitable and compassionate according to her power. For my owne part, although I found neither Mulberies planted, houses built, men nor victuall provided, as the honourable Adventurers did promise mee in England; yet at my owne charge, having made these preparations, and the silk-Wormes ready to be covered, all was lost, but my poore life and children, by the Massacre, the which as God in his mercy did preserve, I continually pray we may spend to his glory. The 9. of September, we had an alarum, and two men at their labours slaine; the Captaine,[1] though extreme sicke, sallied forth, but the Salvages lay hid in the Corne fields all night, where they destroyed all they could, and killed two men more. Much mischiefe they did to Master Edward Hills cattle, yet he alone defended his house though his men were sicke and could doe nothing, and this was our first assault since the Massacre.

About this time Captaine Madyson passed by us, having taken Prisoners, the King of Patawomek, his sonne, and two more, and thus it happened. Madyson not liking so well to live amongst the Salvages as Croshaw did, built him a strong house within the Fort, so that they were not so sociable as before, nor did they much like Poole the Interpre[te]r. Many Alarums they had, but saw no enemies: Madyson before his building went to Moyaones, where hee got provision for a moneth, and was promised much more; so he returned to Patawomek and built this house, and was well used by the Salvages. Now by the foure great men the King sent to Pamaunke for the redemption of the Prisoners, Madyson sent them a letter, but they could neither deliver it nor see them: so long they stayed that the King grew doubtfull of their bad

[1] Newce.

usage, that hee swore by the Skyes, if they returned not well, he would have warres with Opechankanough so long as he had any thing. At this time two of Madysons men ranne from him, to finde them he sent Master John Upton and three more with an Indian guide to Nazatica,[1] where they heard they were. At this place was a King beat out of his Country by the Necosts,[2] enemies to the Patawomeks; this expulsed King though he professed much love to the Patawomeks, yet hee loved not the King because he would not helpe him to revenge his injuries, but to our Interpreter Poole hee protested great love, promising if any treason were, he would reveale it; our guide conducted this *Bandyto* [3] with them up to Patawomek and there kept him; our Fugitives we found the Patawomeks had taken and brought home, and the foure great men returned from Pamaunke. Not long after, this expulsed King desired private conference with Poole, urging him to sweare by his God never to reveale what hee would tell him, Poole promised he would not; then quoth this King, those great men that went to Pamaunke, went not as you suppose they pretended, but to contract with Opechankanough how to kill you all here, and these are their plots.

First, they will procure halfe of you to goe a fishing to their furthest towne, and there set upon them, and cut off the rest; if that faile, they will faine a place where are many strangers would trade their Furres, where they will perswade halfe of you to goe trade, and there murder you and kill them at home; and if this faile also, then they will make Alarums two nights together, to tire you out with watching, and then set upon you, yet of all this, said he, there is none acquainted but the King and the great Conjurer.

This being made known to the Captain, we all stood more punctually upon our guard, at which the Salvages wondering, desired to know the cause; we told them we expected some assault from the Pamaunkes, whereat they seemed contented;

[1] Country of the Necostans, where Washington now stands.
[2] Necostans, sometimes called Anacostans.
[3] Bandit, Indian robber.

and the next day the King went on hunting with two of our men, and the other a fishing and abroad as before, till our Shallop returned from James towne with the two Salvages sent home with Captaine Croshaw: by those the Governour sent to Madyson, that this King should send him twelve of his great men; word of this was sent to the King at another towne where he was, who not comming presently with the Messenger, Madyson conceited [1] hee regarded not the message, and intended as he supposed the same treason. The next morning the King [2] comming home, being sent for, he came to the Captaine and brought him a dish of their daintiest fruit; then the Captaine fained his returne to James towne, the King told him he might if he would, but desired not to leave him destitute of aid, having so many enemies about him; the Captaine told him he would leave a guard, but intreated his answer concerning the twelve great men for the Governour; the King replied, his enemies lay so about him he could not spare them; then the Captaine desired his sonne and one other; my sonne, said the King, is gone abroad about businesse, but the other you desire you shall have, and that other sits by him, but that man refused to goe, whereupon Madyson went forth and locked the doore, leaving the King, his sonne, and foure Salvages, and five English men in the strong house, and setting upon the towne with the rest of his men, slew thirty or forty men, women and children. The King demanding the cause, Poole told him the treason, crying out [3] to intreat the Captaine cease from such cruelty: but having slaine and made flye all in the towne, hee [4] returned, taxing the poore King of treason, who denied to the death not to know of any such matter, but said, This is some plot of them that told it, onely to kill mee for being your friend. Then Madyson willed him, to command none of his men should shoot at him as he went aboord, which he presently did, and it was performed: so Madyson departed, leading the King, his sonne, and two more to his ship, promising when all his men were shipped, he should

[1] Concluded.

[2] *I.e.*, the king of the Potomacs.

[3] And he (the Indian) cried out.

[4] *I.e.*, Captain Madison.

returne at libertie; notwithstanding he brought them to James towne, where they lay some daies, and after were sent home by Captaine Hamer, that tooke Corne for their ransome, and after set saile for New found Land.

But, alas the cause of this was onely this
They understood, nor knew what was amisse.

Ever since the beginning of these Plantations, it hath beene supposed the King of Spaine would invade them, or our English Papists indevour to dissolve them. But neither all the Counsels of Spaine, nor Papists in the world could have devised a better course to bring them all to ruine, then thus to abuse their friends, nor could there ever have beene a better plot, to have overthrowne Opechankanough then Captaine Croshaws, had it beene fully managed with expedition. But it seemes God is angry to see Virginia made a stage where nothing but murder and indiscretion contends for victory.

Amongst the rest of the Plantations all this Summer little was done, but securing themselves and planting Tobacco, which passes there as current Silver, and by the oft turning and winding [1] it, some grow rich, but many poore: notwithstanding ten or twelve ships or more hath arrived there since the massacre, although it was Christmas ere any returned, and that returne greatly revived all mens longing expectation here in England: for they brought newes, that notwithstanding their extreme sicknesse many were recovered, and finding the Salvages did not much trouble them, except it were sometimes some disorderly straglers they cut off. To lull them the better in securitie, they sought no revenge till their Corne was ripe, then they drew together three hundred of the best Souldiers they could, that would leave their private businesse, and adventure themselves amongst the Salvages to surprise their Corne, under the conduct of Sir George Yearley, being imbarked in convenient shipping, and all things necessary for the enterprise; they went first to Nandsamund, where the people set fire on their owne houses, and spoiled what they could, and then fled

[1] *I.e.*, handling.

with what they could carry; so that the English did make no slaughter amongst them for revenge. Their Corne fields being newly gathered, they surprized all they found, burnt the houses remained unburnt, and so departed. Quartering about Kecoughtan, after the Watch was set, Samuell Collyer one of the most ancientest Planters, and very well acquainted with their language and habitation, humors and conditions, and Governor of a Towne, when the Watch was set, going the round, unfortunately by a Centinell that discharged his peece, was slaine.

Thence they sailed to Pamaunke, the chiefe seat of Opechankanough, the contriver of the massacre: the Salvages seemed exceeding fearefull, promising to bring them Sara,[1] and the rest of the English yet living, with all the Armes, and what they had to restore, much desiring peace, and to give them any satisfaction they could. Many such devices they fained to procrastinate the time ten or twelve daies, till they had got away their Corne from all the other places up the River, but that where the English kept their quarter: at last, when they[2] saw all those promises were but delusions, they seised on all the Corne there was, set fire on their houses: and in following the Salvages that fled before them, some few of those naked Devils had that spirit, they lay in ambuscado, and as our men marched discharged some shot out of English peeces, and hurt some of them flying at their pleasures where they listed, burning their empty houses before them as they went, to make themselves sport: so they escaped, and Sir George returned with Corne, where for our paines we had three bushels apeece, but we were enjoyned before we had it, to pay ten shillings the bushell for fraught and other charges. Thus by this meanes the Salvages are like as they report, to endure no small misery this Winter, and that some of our men are returned to their former Plantations.

What other passages or impediments hapned in their proceedings, that they were not fully revenged of the Salvages

[1] Sara Boys, who had been made a captive.

[2] *I.e.*, the English.

before they returned, I know not;[1] nor could ever heare more, but that they supposed they slew two, and how it was impossible for any men to doe more then they did: yet worthy Ferdinando Courtus[2] had scarce three hundred Spaniards to conquer the great Citie of Mexico, where thousands of Salvages dwelled in strong houses. But because they were a civilised people, had wealth, and those meere Barbarians[3] as wilde as beasts have nothing; I intreat your patience to tell you my opinion: which if it be Gods pleasure I shall not live to put in practice, yet it may be hereafter usefull for some; but howsoever I hope not hurtfull to any, and this it is.

Had these three hundred men beene at my disposing, I would have sent first one hundred to Captaine Rawley Chroshaw to Patawomek, with some small Ordnance for the Fort, the which but with daily exercising them, would have struck that love and admiration into the Patawomeks, and terror and amazement into his enemies, which are not farre off, and most seated upon the other side the River, they would willingly have beene friends, or have given any composition they could, before they would be tormented with such a visible feare.

Now though they be generally perfidious, yet necessity constraines those to a kinde of constancy because of their enemies, and neither my selfe that first found them, Captaine Argall, Chroshaw, nor Hamar, never found themselves in fifteene yeares trials: nor is it likely now they would have so hostaged their men, suffer the building of a Fort, and their women and children amongst them, had they intended any villany; but suppose they had, who would have desired a better advantage then such an advertisement, to have prepared the Fort for such an assault, and surely it must be a poore Fort they could hurt, much more take, if there were but five men in it durst discharge a peece: Therefore a man not well knowing their conditions, may be as wel too jealous as too carelesse. Such another Lope Skonce[4] would I have had at Onawmanient, and one hundred men more to have made

[1] Again we have the marginal note, "The opinion of Captaine Smith."
[2] Cortés. [3] *I.e.*, the Indians of Virginia. [4] A fort.

such another at Atquacke upon the River of Toppahanock,[1] which is not past thirteene miles distant from Onawmanient:[2] each of which twelve men would keepe, as well as twelve thousand, and spare all the rest to bee imploied as there should be occasion. And all this with these numbers might easily have beene done, if not by courtesie, yet by compulsion, especially at that time of September when all their fruits were ripe, their beasts fat, and infinite numbers of wilde Fowle began to repaire to every creeke, that men if they would doe any thing, could not want victuall. This done, there remained yet one hundred who should have done the like at Ozinieke,[3] upon the River of Chickahamania, not past six miles from the chiefe habitations of Opechankanough. These small Forts had beene cause sufficient to cause all the Inhabitants of each of those Rivers to looke to themselves. Then having so many Ships, Barks, and Boats in Virginia as there was at that present, with what facility might you have landed two hundred and twentie men, if you had but onely five or six Boats in one night; forty to range the branch of Mattapanyent, fortie more that of Youghtanund, and fortie more to keepe their randivous at Pamaunke it selfe. All which places lie so neere, they might heare from each other within foure or five houres; and not any of those small parties, if there were any valour, discretion, or industry in them, but as sufficient as foure thousand, to force them all to contribution, or take or spoile all they had. For having thus so many convenient randevous to releeve each other, though all the whole Countries had beene our enemies, where could they rest, but in the depth of Winter we might burne all the houses upon all those Rivers in two or three

[1] Rappahannock.

[2] An Indian district on the south side of the Potomac where the county of King George now is.

[3] The Chickahominy River, after emerging from the swamps around Richmond, flows parallel to the James until it reaches a station on the Chesapeake and Ohio Railroad, known as Lanexa, the site of the Indian village of Ozinies or Ozinieke, from which it flows at nearly right angles to its former course eight miles to the James River. From Lanexa to the York the distance is not more than six miles.

daies? Then without fires they could not live, which they could not so hide but wee should finde, and quickly so tire them with watching and warding, they would be so weary of their lives, as either fly all their Countries, or give all they had to be released of such an hourely misery. Now if but a small number of the Salvages would assist us, as there is no question but divers of them would; And to suppose they could not be drawne to such faction, were to beleeve they are more vertuous then many Christians, and the best governed people in the world, All the Pamaunkes might have beene dispatchd as well in a moneth as a yeare, and then to have dealt with any other enemies at our pleasure, and yet made all this toile and danger but a recreation.

If you think this strange or impossible, 12 men with my selfe I found sufficient, to goe where I would adaies,[1] and surprise a house with the people, if not a whole towne, in a night, or incounter all the power they could make, as a whole Army, as formerly at large hath beene related: And it seemes by these small parties last amongst them, by Captaine Crashow, Hamar, and Madyson, they are not growne to that excellency in policy and courage but they might bee encountred, and their wives and children apprehended. I know I shall bee taxed for writing so much of my selfe: but I care not much, because the judiciall know there are few such Souldiers as are my examples, have writ their owne actions, nor know I who will or can tell my intents better then my selfe.

Some againe finde as much fault with the Company for medling with so many Plantations together, because they that have many Irons in the fire some must burne; but I thinke no if they have men enow know how to worke them, but howsoever, it were better some burne then have none at all. The King of Spaine regards but how many powerfull Kingdomes he keepes under his obedience, and for the Salvage Countries he hath subjected, they are more then enow for a good Cosmographer to nominate,[2] and is three Mole-hills so much to us, and so many Empires so little for him? For my

[1] Any day. [2] Enumerate.

owne part, I cannot chuse but grieve, that the actions of an Englishman should be inferior to any, and that the command of England should not be as great as any Monarchy that ever was since the world began, I meane not as a Tyrant to torment all Christendome, but to suppresse her disturbers, and conquer her enemies.

For the great Romans got into their hand  
The whole worlds compasse, both by Sea and Land,  
Or any seas, or heaven, or earth extended,  
And yet that Nation could not be contented.

Much about this time, arrived a small Barke of Barnestable, which had beene at the Summer Iles, and in her Captaine Nathaniel Butler,[1] who having beene Governour there three yeares, and his Commission expired, he tooke the opportunity of this ship to see Virginia. At James Towne he was kindly entertained by Sir Francis Wyat the Governour. After he had rested there fourteene daies, he fell up with his ship to the River of Chickahamania, where meeting Captaine William Powell, joyning together such forces as they had to the number of eighty, they set upon the Chickahamanians, that fearefully fled, suffering the English to spoile all they had, not daring to resist them. Thus he returned to James towne, where hee staied a moneth, at Kecoughtan as much more, and so returned for England.[2]

But riding at Kecoughtan, Master John Argent, sonne to Doctor Argent, a young Gentleman that went with Captaine Butler from England to this place, Michael Fuller, William Gany, Cornelius May, and one other going ashore with some goods late in a faire evening, such a sudden gust did arise, that drive [3] them thwart the River, in that place at least three or foure miles in bredth, where the shore was so shallow at a low water, and the Boat beating upon the Sands, they left her,

[1] His tract, *The Unmasking of Virginia,* was a cause of much trouble to the Virginia Company. See its *Records,* and the next piece in this volume

[2] February, 1623.

[3] Drove.

wading neere halfe a mile, and oft up to the chin. So well it hapned, Master Argent had put his Bandileir of powder in his hat, which next God was all their preservations: for it being February, and the ground so cold, their bodies became so benumbed, they were not able to strike fire with a steele and a stone hee had in his pocket; the stone they lost twice, and thus those poore soules groping in the darke, it was Master Argents chance to finde it, and with a few withered leaves, reeds, and brush, make a small fire, being upon the Chisapeaks shore, their mortall enemies, great was their feare to be discovered. The joyfull morning appearing, they found their Boat and goods drive ashore, not farre from them, but so split shee was unserviceable: but so much was the frost, their clothes did freeze upon their backs, for they durst not make any great fire to dry them, lest thereby the bloudy Salvages might discry them, so that one of them died the next day; and the next night, digging a grave in the Sands with their hands, buried him. In this bodily feare they lived and fasted two daies and nights, then two of them went into the Land to seeke fresh water; the others to the Boat to get some meale and oyle. Argent and his Comrado found a Canow, in which they resolved to adventure to their ship, but shee was a drift in the River before they returned. Thus frustrate of all hopes, Captaine Butler the third night ranging the shore in his Boat to seeke them, discharged his Muskets; but they supposing it some Salvages had got some English peeces, they grew more perplexed then ever: so he returned and lost his labour. The fourth day they unloaded their Boat, and stopping her leakes with their handkerchiefes, and other rags, two rowing, and two bailing out the water; but farre they went not ere the water grew upon them so fast, and they so tired, they thought themselves happy to be on shore againe, though they perceived the Indians were not farre off by their fires. Thus at the very period of despaire, Fuller undertooke to sit a stride upon a little peece of an old Canow; so well it pleased God the wind and tide served, by padling with his hands and feet in the water, beyond all expectation God so guided him three or foure houres upon this boord, he arrived at their ship, where they no lesse amazed then he tired, they tooke him in. Presently as he had concluded with his Companions, he caused them discharge a peece of Ordnance if he escaped: which gave no lesse comfort to Master Argent and the rest, then terror to those Plantations that heard it, (being late) at such an unexpected alarum; but after with warme clothes and a little strong water they had a little recovered him, such was his courage and care of his distressed friends, he returned that night againe with Master Felgate to conduct him to them: and so giving thanks to God for so hopelesse a deliverance, it pleased his Divine power, both they and their provision came safely aboord, but Fuller they doubt will never recover his benumbed legs and thighes.

Now before Butlers arrivall in England, many hard speeches were rumored against him for so leaving his charge, before he received order from the Company. Divers againe of his Souldiers as highly commended him, for his good government, art, judgement and industry. But to make the misery of Virginia appeare that it might be reformed in time, how all those Cities, Townes, Corporations, Forts, Vineyards, Nurseries of Mulberies, Glasse-houses, Iron forges, Guest-houses, Silke-wormes, Colleges, the Companies great estate, and that plenty some doe speake of here, are rather things in words and paper then in effect, with divers reasons of the causes of those defects; if it were false, his blame nor shame could not be too much: but if there bee such defects in the government, and distresse in the Colony, it is thought by many it hath beene too long concealed, and requireth rather reformation then disputation: but however, it were not amisse to provide for the worst, for the best will help it selfe. Notwithstanding, it was apprehended so hardly, and examined with that passion, that the brute thereof was spread abroad with that expedition, it did more hurt then the massacre; and the fault of all now by the vulgar rumour, must be attributed to the unwholesomnesse of the ayre, and barrennesse of the Countrey: as though all England were naught, because the Fens and Marshes are unhealthy; or barren, because some will lie under windowes and starve in Cheapside, rot in Goales, die in the street, high-waies, or any where, and use a thousand devices to maintaine themselves in those miseries, rather then take any paines to live as they may by honest labour, and a great part of such like are the Planters of Virginia, and partly the occasion of those defailements.

In the latter end of this last yeare, or the beginning of this,[1] Captaine Henrie Spilman a Gentleman, that hath lived in those Countries thirteene or fourteene yeares, one of the best Interpreters in the Land, being furnished with a Barke and six and twentie men, hee was sent to trucke in the River of Patawomek, where he had lived a long time amongst the Salvages. Whether hee presumed too much upon his acquaintance amongst them, or they sought to be revenged of any for the slaughter made amongst them by the English so lately, or hee sought to betray them, or they him, are all several relations, but it seemes but imaginary: for they returned, report they left him ashore about Patawomek, but the name of the place they knew not, with one and twentie men, being but five in the Barke. The Salvages, ere they suspected any thing, boorded them with their Canowes, and entred so fast, the English were amazed, till a Sailer gave fire to a peece of Ordnance onely at randome; at the report whereof, the Salvages leapt over-boord, so distracted with feare, they left their Canowes and swum a shore; and presently after they heard a great brute [2] amongst the Salvages a shore, and saw a mans head throwne downe the banke. Whereupon they weighed Anchor and returned home, but how he was surprised or slaine, is uncertaine.

Thus things proceed and vary not a jot,
Whether we know them, or we know them not.

[1] Marginal reading, "1623. The Earle of Southampton Treasurer."
[2] Noise.

*A particular of such necessaries as either private families, or single persons, shall have cause to provide to goe to Virginia, whereby greater numbers may in part conceive the better how to provide for themselves.*

*Apparell.*[1]

| | |
|---|---|
| A Monmoth Cap. | 1*s.* 10*d.* |
| 3 falling bands. | 1*s.* 3*d.* |
| 3 shirts. | 7*s.* 6*d.* |
| 1 Waste-coat. | 2*s.* 2*d.* |
| 1 suit of Canvase. | 7*s.* 6*d.* |
| 1 suit of Frize.[2] | 10*s.* |
| 1 suit of Cloth. | 15*s.* |
| 3 paire of Irish stockings. | 4*s.* |
| 4 paire of shooes. | 8*s.* 8*d.* |
| 1 paire of garters. | 10*d.* |
| 1 dozen of points.[3] | 3*d.* |
| 1 paire of Canvas sheets. | 8*s.* |
| 7 ells of Canvas to make a bed and boulster, to be filled in Virginia, serving for two men. | 8*s.* |
| 5 ells of course Canvas to make a bed at Sea for two men. | 5*s.* |
| 1 course rug at sea for two men. | 6*s.* |
| | 4*l.* |

*Victuall for a whole yeare for a man, and so after the rate for more.*

| | |
|---|---|
| 8 bushels of meale. | 2*l.* |
| 2 bushels of pease. | 6*s.* |
| 2 bushels of Otemeale. | 9*s.* |
| 1 gallon of *Aquavitae.* | 2*s.* 6*d.* |
| 1 gallon of oyle. | 3*s.* 6*d.* |
| 2 gallons of Vineger. | 2*s.* |
| | 3*l.* 3*s.* |

*Armes for a man; but if halfe your men be armed it is well, so all have swords and peeces.*

| | |
|---|---|
| 1 Armor compleat, light. | 17*s.* |
| 1 long peece five foot and a halfe, neere Musket bore. | 1*l.* 2*s.* |
| 1 Sword. | 5*s.* |
| 1 Belt. | 1*s.* |
| 1 Bandilier.[4] | 1*s.* 6*d.* |
| 20 pound of powder. | 18*s.* |
| 60 pound of shot or | |

[1] The margin explains, "Apparrell for one man, and so after the rate for more."

[2] Frieze, a coarse woollen cloth.

[3] Laces for fastening the clothing.

[4] Bandoleer, a broad leather belt formerly worn by soldiers over the left shoulder.

Lead, Pistoll and Goose shot. 5*s.*

3*l.* 9*s.* 6*d.*

*Tooles for a family of six persons, and so after the rate for more.*

5 broad howes at 2*s.* a peece. 10*s.*
5 narrow howes at 16*d.* a peece. 6*s.* 8*d.*
2 broad axes at 3*s.* 8*d.* a peece. 7*s.* 4*d.*
5 felling axes at 18*d.* a peece. 7*s.* 6*d.*
2 steele handsawes at 16*d.* a piece. 2*s.* 8*d.*
2 two handsawes[1] at 5*s.* a peece. 10*s.*
1 whipsaw, set and filed; with box, file and wrest. 10*s.*
2 hammers 12*d.* a peece. 2*s.*
3 shovels at 18*d.* a peece. 4*s.* 6*d.*
2 spades at 18*d.* a peece. 3*s.*
2 Augers at 6*d.* peece. 1*s.*
6 Chissels at 6*d.* a peece. 3*s.*
2 Percers stocked 4*d.* a peece. 8*d.*
3 Gimblets at 2*d.* a peece. 6*d.*
2 Hatchets at 21*d.* a peece. 3*s.* 6*d.*
2 frowes[2] to cleave pale 18*d.* each. 3*s.*
2 hand Bills 20*d.* a peece. 3*s.* 4*d.*
1 Grindstone. 4*s.*
Nailes of all sorts to the value of 2*l.*
2 Pickaxes. 3*s.*

6*l.* 2*s.* 8*d.*

*Household implements for a family of six persons, and so for more or lesse after the rate.*

1 Iron pot. 7*s.*
1 Kettell. 6*s.*
1 large Frying-pan. 2*s.* 6*d.*
1 Gridiron. 1*s.* 6*d.*
2 Skellets. 5*s.*
1 Spit. 2*s.*
Platters, dishes, spoones of wood. 4*s.*

1*l.* 8*s.*

For Sugar, Spice, and Fruit, at Sea for six men. 12*s.* 6*d.*

So the full charge after this rate for each person, will

[1] *I.e.*, two two-hand saws.
[2] A wedge-shaped tool for splitting rails or staves.

amount to about the summe of 12*l*. 10*s*. 10*d*.
The passage of each man is 6*l*.
The fraught of these provisions for a man, will be about halfe a tun, which is 1*l*. 10*s*.
So the whole charge will amount to about 20*l*.

Now if the number be great; Nets, Hooks, and Lines, but Cheese, Bacon, Kine and Goats must be added. And this is the usuall proportion the Virginia Company doe bestow upon their Tenents they send.

*A briefe relation written by Captaine Smith to his Majesties Commissioners for the reformation of Virginia, concerning some aspersions against it.*

Honourable Gentlemen, for so many faire and Navigable Rivers so neere adjoyning, and piercing thorow so faire a naturall Land, free from any inundations, or large Fenny unwholsome Marshes, I have not seene, read, nor heard of: And for the building of Cities, Townes, and Wharfage, if they will use the meanes, where there is no more ebbe nor floud, Nature in few places affoords any so convenient. For salt Marshes or Quagmires, in this tract of James Towne River I know very few; some small Marshes and Swamps there are, but more profitable than hurtfull: and I thinke there is more low Marsh ground betwixt Eriffe and Chelsey,[1] then Kecoughton and the Falls, which is about one hundred and eighty miles by the course of the River.

Being enjoyned by our Commission not to unplant nor wrong the Salvages, because the channell was so neere the shore, where now is James Towne, then a thick grove of trees; wee cut them downe, where the Salvages pretending as much kindnesse as could bee, they hurt and slew one and twenty of us in two houres. At this time our diet was for most part water and bran, and three ounces of little better stuffe in bread for five men a meale; and thus we lived neere three

[1] Erith and Chelsea are on the Thames, the one below London, the other above.

moneths: our lodgings under boughes of trees, the Salvages being our enemies, whom we neither knew nor understood; occasions I thinke sufficient to make men sicke and die.

Necessity thus did inforce me with eight or nine, to try conclusions amongst the Salvages, that we got provision which recovered the rest being most sicke. Six weeks [1] I was led captive by those Barbarians, though some of my men were slaine, and the rest fled; yet it pleased God to make their great Kings daughter the means to returne me safe to James towne, and releeve our wants: and then [2] our Common-wealth was in all eight and thirty, the remainder of one hundred and five.

Being supplied with one hundred and twenty, with twelve men in a boat of three tuns, I spent fourteene weeks in those large waters; the contents of the way of my boat protracted by the skale of proportion, was about three thousand miles, besides the River we dwell upon: where no Christian knowne ever was, and our diet for the most part what we could finde, yet but one died.

The Salvages being acquainted, that by command from England we durst not hurt them, were much imboldned; that famine and their insolencies did force me to breake our Commission and instructions; cause Powhatan fly his Countrey, and take the King of Pamaunke Prisoner; and also to keepe the King of Paspahegh in shackels, and put his men to double taskes in chaines, till nine and thirty of their Kings paied us contribution, and the offending Salvages sent to James towne to punish at our owne discretions: in the two last yeares I staied there, I had not a man slaine.

All those conclusions being not able to prevent the bad events of pride and idlenesse, having received another supply of seventie, we were about two hundred in all, but not twentie work-men: In following the strict directions from England to doe that was impossible at that time; So it hapned, that neither wee nor they had any thing to eat but what the Countrey afforded naturally; yet of eightie who lived upon Oysters

[1] Three weeks, rather,—from December 10, 1607, to January 2, 1608.
[2] January 2, 1608. Brown, *Genesis of the United States*, I. 175.

in June and July,[1] with a pint of corne a week for a man lying under trees, and 120 for the most part living upon Sturgion, which was dried til we pounded it to powder for meale, yet in ten weeks but seven died.

It is true, we had of Tooles, Armes, and Munition sufficient, some Aquavitae, Vineger, Meale, Pease, and Otemeale, but in two yeares and a halfe not sufficient for six moneths; though by the bils of loading the proportions sent us, would well have contented us: notwithstanding we sent home ample proofes of Pitch, Tar, Sope Ashes, Wainskot, Clapboord, Silke grasse, Iron Ore, some Sturgion and Glasse, Saxefras, Cedar, Cypris, and blacke Walnut; crowned Powhatan; sought the Monacans Countrey, according to the instructions sent us, but they caused us neglect more necessary workes: they had better have given for Pitch and Sope ashes one hundred pound a tun in Denmarke: Wee also maintained five or six severall Plantations.[2]

James towne being burnt, wee rebuilt it and three Forts more: besides the Church and Store-house, we had about fortie or fiftie severall houses to keepe us warme and dry, invironed with a palizado of fourteene or fifteene foot, and each as much as three or foure men could carrie. We digged a faire Well of fresh water in the Fort, where wee had three Bulwarks, foure and twentie peece of Ordnance (of Culvering, Demiculvering, Sacar and Falcon), and most well mounted upon convenient plat-formes: planted one hundred acres of Corne.[3] We had but six ships to transport and supply us, and but two hundred seventy seven men, boies, and women: by whose labours Virginia being brought to this kinde of perfection, the most difficulties past, and the foundation thus laid by this small meanes; yet because we had done no more, they called in our Commission, tooke a new in their owne names, and appointed us neere as many offices and Officers as I had

[1] 1609.

[2] In May, 1609, Smith divided the settlers into small parties, but it was to escape starvation rather than to establish settlements.

[3] In the earlier narratives the area of cultivation was put at forty acres.

Souldiers, that neither knew us nor wee them, without our consents or knowledge. Since,[1] there have gone more then one hundred ships of other proportions, and eight or ten thousand people. Now if you please to compare what hath beene spent, sent, discovered, and done this fifteene yeares, by that we did in the three first yeares: and every Governor that hath beene there since, give you but such an account as this, you may easily finde what hath beene the cause of those disasters in Virginia.

Then came in Captaine Argall, and Mr Sedan, in a ship of Mr Cornelius, to fish for Sturgion; who had such good provision, we contracted with them for it, whereby we were better furnished then ever.

Not long after came in seven ships, with about three hundred people; but rather to supplant us then supply us: their Admirall with their authoritie being cast away in the Bermudas, very angry they were we had made no better provision for them. Seven or eight weekes we withstood the inundations of these disorderly humors, till I was neere blowne to death with Gun-powder, which occasioned me to returne for England.

In the yeare 1609 about Michaelmas, I left the Countrey, as is formerly related, with three ships, seven Boats, Commodities to trade, harvest newly gathered, eight weeks provision of Corne and Meale, about five hundred persons, three hundred Muskets, shot powder and match with armes for more men then we had. The Salvages their language and habitation well knowne to two hundred expert Souldiers; Nets for fishing, tooles of all sorts, apparell to supply their wants: six Mares and a Horse, five or six hundred Swine, many more Powltry, what was brought or bred, but victuall, there remained.

Having spent some five yeares, and more then five hundred pounds in procuring the Letters Patents and setting forward, and neere as much more about New England, &c. Thus these nineteene yeares I have here and there not spared any thing

[1] *I.e.*, by 1624.

according to my abilitie, nor the best advice I could, to perswade how those strange miracles of misery might have beene prevented, which lamentable experience plainly taught me of necessity must insue, but few would beleeve me till now too deerely they have paid for it. Wherefore hitherto I have rather left all then undertake impossibilities, or any more such costly taskes at such chargeable rates: for in neither of those two Countries have I one foot of Land, nor the very house I builded, nor the ground I digged with my owne hands, nor ever any content or satisfaction at all. And though I see ordinarily those two Countries shared before me by them that neither have them nor knowes them, but by my descriptions: Yet that doth not so much trouble me, as to heare and see those contentions and divisions which will hazard if not ruine the prosperitie of Virginia, if present remedy bee not found, as they have hindred many hundreds, who would have beene there ere now, and makes them yet that are willing to stand in a demurre.

For the Books and Maps I have made, I will thanke him that will shew me so much for so little recompence; and beare with their errors till I have done better. For the materials in them I cannot deny, but am ready to affirme them both there and here, upon such grounds as I have propounded: which is to have but fifteene hundred men to subdue againe the Salvages, fortifie the Countrey, discover that yet unknowne, and both defend and feed their Colony, which I most humbly refer to his Majesties most judiciall judgement, and the most honourable Lords of his Privy Councill, you his trusty and well-beloved Commissioners, and the Honourable company of Planters and well-willers to Virginia, New-England and Sommer-Ilands.

*Out of these Observations it pleased his Majesties Commissioners for the reformation of Virginia, to desire my answer to these seven Questions.*

Quest. 1. *What conceive you is the cause the Plantation hath prospered no better since you left it in so good a forwardnesse?*

*Answ.* Idlenesse and carelesnesse brought all I did in three yeeres, in six moneths to nothing; and of five hundred I left, scarce threescore remained; and had Sir Thomas Gates not got from the Bermudas, I thinke they had beene all dead before they could be supplied.

Quest. 2. *What conceive you should be the cause, though the Country be good, there comes nothing but Tobacco?*

*Answ.* The oft altering of Governours it seemes causes every man make use of his time, and because Corne was stinted at two shillings six pence the bushell, and Tobacco at three shillings the pound; and they value a mans labour a yeere worth fifty or threescore pound, but in Corne not worth ten pound, presuming Tobacco will furnish them with all things: now make a mans labour in Corne worth threescore pound, and in Tobacco but ten pound a man, then shall they have Corne sufficient to entertaine all commers, and keepe their people in health to doe any thing; but till then, there will be little or nothing to any purpose.

Quest. 3. *What conceive you to have beene the cause of the Massacre, and had the Salvages had the use of any peeces in your time, or when, or by whom they were taught?*

*Answ.* The cause of the Massacre was the want of marshall discipline; and because they would have all the English had by destroying those they found so carelesly secure, that they were not provided to defend themselves against any enemy; being so dispersed as they were. In my time, though Captaine Nuport furnished them with swords by truck, and many fugitives did the like, and some Peeces they got accidentally: yet I got the most of them againe; and it was death to him that should shew a Salvage the use of a Peece. Since, I understand, they became so good shot, they were imployed for Fowlers and Huntsmen by the English.

Quest. 4. *What charge thinke you would have setled the government both for defence and planting when you left it?*

*Answ.* Twenty thousand pound would have hyred good labourers and mechanicall men, and have furnished them with cattle and all necessaries; and 100. of them would hav done more then a thousand of those that went: though the Lord Laware, Sir Ferdinando Waynman, Sir Thomas Gates and Sir Thomas Dale were perswaded to the contrary; but when they had tried, they confessed their error.

Quest. 5. *What conceive you would be the remedy and the charge?*

*Answ.* The remedy is to send Souldiers and all sorts of labourers and necessaries for them, that they may be there by next Michaelmas,[1] the which to doe well will stand you in five thousand pound: but if his Majesty would please to lend two of his Ships to transport them, lesse would serve; besides the benefit of his grace to the action would encourage all men.

Quest. 6. *What thinke you are the defects of the government both here and there?*

*Answ.* The multiplicity of opinions here, and Officers there, makes such delaies by questions and formalitie, that as much time is spent in complement as in action; besides, some are so desirous to imploy their ships, having six pounds for every Passenger, and three pounds for every tun of goods, at which rate a thousand ships may now better be procured then one at the first, when the common stocke defrayed all fraughts, wages, provisions and Magazines, whereby the Ships are so pestred, as occasions much sicknesse, diseases and mortality: for though all the Passengers die they are sure of their fraught; and then all must be satisfied with Orations, disputations, excuses and hopes. As for the letters of advice from hence, and their answers thence, they are so well written, men would beleeve there were no great doubt of the performance, and that all things were wel, to which error here they have beene ever much subject; and there not to beleeve, or not to releeve the true and poore estate of that Colony, whose fruits were commonly spent before they were ripe, and this losse is nothing to them here, whose great estates are not sensible of the losse of their adventures, and so they thinke, or will not take notice; but it is so with all men. But howsoever they thinke or dispose of all things at their pleasure, I

[1] 1624.

am sure not my selfe onely, but a thousand others have not onely spent the most of their estates, but the most part have lost their lives and all, onely but to make way for the triall of more new conclusions: and he that now will adventure but twelve pounds ten shillings, shall have better respect and as much favour then he that sixteene yeere agoe adventured as much, except he have money as the other hath; but though he have adventured five hundred pound, and spent there never so much time, if hee have no more and not able to begin a family of himselfe, all is lost by order of Court.

But in the beginning it was not so, all went then out of one purse, till those new devices have consumed both mony and purse; for at first there were but six Patentees, now more then a thousand; then but thirteene Counsailors, now not lesse then an hundred: I speake not of all, for there are some both honourable and honest, but of those Officers which did they manage their owne estates no better then the affaires of Virginia, they would quickly fall to decay so well as it. But this is most evident, few Officers in England it hath caused to turne Banquerupts, nor for all their complaints would leave their places; neither yet any of their Officers there, nor few of the rest but they would be at home. But fewer Adventurers here will adventure any more till they see the businesse better established, although there be some so wilfully improvident they care for nothing but to get thither, and then if their friends be dead, or want themselves, they die or live but poorely for want of necessaries, and to thinke the old Planters can releeve them were too much simplicity; for who here in England is so charitable to feed two or three strangers, have they never so much; much lesse in Virginia where they want for themselves. Now the generall complaint saith, that pride, covetousnesse, extortion and oppression in a few that ingrosses all, then sell all againe to the comminalty at what rate they please (yea even men, women and children for who will give most), occasions no small mischiefe amongst the Planters.

As for the Company, or those that doe transport them, provided of necessaries, God forbid but they should receive their charges againe with advantage,[1] or that masters there should not have the same privilege over their servants as here: but to sell him or her for forty, fifty, or threescore pounds, whom the Company hath sent over for eight or ten pounds at the most, without regard how they shall be maintained with apparell, meat, drinke and lodging, is odious, and their fruits sutable: therefore such merchants it were better they were made such merchandize themselves, then suffered any longer to use that trade, and those are defects sufficient to bring a well setled Common-wealth to misery, much more Virginia.

Quest. 7. *How thinke you it may be rectified?*

*Answ.* If his Majestie would please to intitle it to his Crowne,[2] and yearely that both the Governours here and there may give their accounts to you, or some that are not ingaged in the businesse, that the common stocke bee not spent in maintaining one hundred men for the Governour, one hundred for two Deputies, fifty for the Treasurer, five and twenty for the Secretary, and more for the Marshall and other Officers who were never there nor adventured any thing; but onely preferred by favour to be Lords over them that broke the ice and beat the path, and must teach them what to doe. If any thing happen well, it is their glory; if ill, the fault of the old directors, that in all dangers must endure the worst, yet not five hundred of them have so much as one of the others. Also that there bee some present course taken to maintaine a Garrison to suppresse the Salvages, till they be able to subsist, and that his Majesty would please to remit his custome; or it is to be feared they will lose custome and all, for this cannot be done by promises, hopes, counsels and countenances, but with sufficient workmen and meanes to maintaine them: not such delinquents as here cannot be ruled by all the lawes in England. Yet when the foundation is laid, as I have said, and a common-wealth established, then such there may better be constrained to labour then here; but to rectifie a commonwealth with debaushed people is impossible, and no wise man would throw himselfe into such a society, that intends honestly

[1] Profit.

[2] Resume Virginia to himself.

and knowes what he undertakes. For there is no Country to pillage as the Romans found: all you expect from thence must be by labour.

For the government I thinke there is as much adoe about it as the Kingdomes of Scotland and Ireland, men here conceiting Virginia as they are, erecting as many stately Offices as Officers with their attendants, as there are labourers in the Countrey: where a Constable were as good as twenty of their Captaines; and three hundred good Souldiers and labourers better then all the rest, that goe onely to get the fruits of other mens labours by the title of an office. Thus they spend Michaelmas rent in Mid-summer Moone, and would gather their Harvest before they have planted their Corne.

As for the maintenance of the Officers, the first that went never demanded any, but adventured good summes: and it seemes strange to me, the fruits of all their labours, besides the expence of an hundred and fifty thousand pounds, and such multitudes of people, those collaterall Officers could not maintaine themselves so well as the old did; and having now such liberty to doe to the Salvages what they will, the others had not.[1] I more then wonder they have not five hundred Salvages to worke for them towards their generall maintenance; and as many more to returne some content and satisfaction to the Adventurers, that for all their care, charge and diligence, can heare nor see nothing but miserable complaints: therefore under your correction to rectifie all, is with all expedition to passe the authority to them who will releeve them, lest all bee consumed ere the differences be determined. And except his Majestie undertake it, or by Act of Parlament some small tax may be granted throughout his Dominions, as a Penny upon every Poll, called a head-penny; two pence upon every Chimney, or some such collection might be raised, and that would be sufficient to give a good stocke, and many servants to sufficient men of any facultie, and transport them freely for paying onely homage to the Crowne of England, and such

[1] Which the others had not.

duties to the publike good as, their estates increased, reason should require. Were this put in practice, how many people of what quality you please, for all those disasters would yet gladly goe to spend their lives there, and by this meanes more good might be done in one yeere, then all those pety particular undertakings will effect in twenty.

For the Patent the King may, if he please, rather take it from them that have it, then from us who had it first; pretending to his Majesty what great matters they would doe, and how little we did: and for any thing I can conceive had we remained still as at first, it is not likely we could have done much worse; but those oft altering of governments are not without much charge, hazard and losse. If I be too plaine, I humbly crave your pardon; but you requested me, therefore I doe but my duty. For the Nobility, who knowes not how freely both in their Purses and assistances many of them have beene to advance it, committing the managing of the businesse to inferiour persons: amongst whom questionlesse also many have done their utmost best, sincerely and truly according to their conceit, opinion and understanding; yet grosse errors have beene committed, but no man lives without his fault. For my owne part, I have so much adoe to amend my owne, I have no leisure to looke into any mans particular,[1] but those in generall I conceive to be true. And so I humbly rest

Yours to command,

J. S.

Thus those discords, not being to be compounded among themselves; nor yet by the extraordinary diligences, care and paines of the noble and right worthy Commissioners, Sir William Jones, Sir Nicholas Fortescue, Sir Francis Goston, Sir Richard Sutton, Sir Henry Bourgchier and Sir William Pit: a Corante[2] was granted against Master Deputy Farrar,

[1] Particular fault.

[2] A *quo warranto*. For the events attending the dissolution of the Virginia Company, see Miss Kingsbury's introduction to the *Records*, and Neill's *Virginia Company of London*.

and 20. or 30. others of that party, to plead their causes before the right Honourable the Lords of His Majesties Privy Councell. Now notwithstanding all the Relations, Examinations, and intercepting of all Letters whatsoever came from thence, yet it seemes they were so farre unsatisfied and desired to know the truth, as well for the preservation of the Colony, as to give content and doe all men right, they sent two Commissioners strictly to examine the true estate of the Colony. Upon whose returne after mature deliberation, it pleased his royall Majesty to suppresse the course of the Court at Deputy Farrars: and that for the present ordering the affaires of Virginia, untill he should make a more full settlement thereof, the Lord Viscount Mandevile, Lord President of his Majesties Privie Councell, and also other Privy Councellors, with many understanding Knights and Gentlemen, should every Thursday in the afternoone meet at Sir Thomas Smiths in Philpot lane: where all men whom it should concerne may repaire, to receive such directions and warrant for their better security; as more at large you may see in the Proclamation to that effect, under the great Seale of England, dated the 15. of July, 1624.[1] But as for the relations last returned, what numbers they are, how many Cities, Corporations, townes, and houses, cattle and horse they have; what fortifications or discoveries they have made, or revenge upon the Salvages; who are their friends or foes; or what commodities they have more then Tobacco; and their present estate or what is presently to be put in execution: in that the Commissioners are not yet fully satisfied in the one, nor resolved in the other, at this present time when this went to the Presse, I must intreat you pardon me till I be better assured.

Thus far I have travelled in this Wildernesse of Virginia, not being ignorant for all my paines this discourse will be wrested, tossed and turned as many waies as there is leaves; that I have writ too much of some, too little of others, and many

[1] In Hazard's *Historical Collections*, I. 183, or Rymer's *Fœdera*, XVII. 609.

such like objections. To such I must answer, in the Companies name I was requested to doe it, if any have concealed their approved experiences from my knowledge, they must excuse me: as for every fatherles or stolne relation, or whole volumes of sofisticated rehearsals, I leave them to the charge of them that desire them. I thanke God I never undertooke any thing yet any[1] could tax me of carelesnesse or dishonesty, and what is hee to whom I am indebted or troublesome? Ah! were these my accusers but to change cases and places with me but 2. yeeres, or till they had done but so much as I, it may be they would judge more charitably of my imperfections. But here I must leave all to the triall of time, both my selfe, Virginia's preparations, proceedings and good events; praying to that great God the protector of all goodnesse to send them as good successe as the goodnesse of the action and Country deserveth, and my heart desireth.

[1] Wherein any.

# THE VIRGINIA PLANTERS' ANSWER TO CAPTAIN BUTLER, 1623

## INTRODUCTION

Captain Nathaniel Butler served as governor of the Bermuda Islands from the spring of 1619 to October, 1622, during which time he got into trouble by extorting money from some Spaniards who had been shipwrecked there. He spent the winter of 1622–1623 in Virginia, and on his return to England in the spring presented to the king a document called "The Unmasked face of our Colony in Virginia as it was in the Winter of the yeare 1622." After this no more was heard of the complaint which the Spanish minister had lodged against him for his conduct in the Bermudas. The company, deeming it necessary to reply to Butler at once, drew up the paper below and sent out and secured the affidavits of each of the persons in London best acquainted with Virginia affairs. As far as Butler's attack proved anything, it showed how much credit the managers of the company deserved for having rescued the colony from the depths of despair to which it had been brought by the evils of the old government of martial law.

The text of this document is taken from the "court books" of the Virginia Company preserved in the Library of Congress. It occurs in *The Records of the Virginia Company of London* (Washington, 1906), II. 381–385. It was first printed by Neill in his *Virginia Company of London*, pp. 395–404. Butler's paper is embodied in it.

L. G. T.

# THE VIRGINIA PLANTERS' ANSWER TO CAPTAIN BUTLER, 1623

*The Answers of divers Planters that have long lived in Virginia, as alsoe of sundry Marriners and other persons that have bene often at Virginia unto a paper intituled: The Unmasked face of our Colony in Virginia, as it was in the Winter of the yeare 1622.*

1. I FOUNDE the Plantacions generally seated uppon meere Salt marishes full of infectious Boggs and muddy Creekes and Lakes, and therby subjected to all those inconveniences and diseases which are soe commonly found in the moste Unsounde and most Unhealthy parts of England wherof everie Country and Clymate hath some.

Answere 1. Wee say that there is no place inhabited but is conveniently habitable. And for the first [1] plantacion w$^{ch}$ is Kiccoutan against w$^{ch}$ (if any be) most exception may be made, itt is every way soe well disposed that in that place well governed men may enjoy their healthes and live as plentifully as in any parte of England or other his Ma$^{ties}$ Dominions, yett that there are Marishes in some places wee acknowledge; Butt soe as they are more Comodious for divers good respects and uses then if they were wantinge.[2] As for Boggs wee knowe of none in all the Country and for the rest of the Plantacions as Newports News, Blunt poynt, Wariscoyake, Martins Hundred, Paspahey, and all the Plantacions right over against James Citty, and all the Plantacions above these w$^{ch}$ are many,

[1] *I.e.*, the plantation nearest the mouth of the river.

[2] Eastern Virginia is intersected with great numbers of creeks and rivers, lined with marshes, the favorite resorts of sora, ducks, and other toothsome birds.

they are verie fruitfull and pleasant Seates, free from Salt Marishes being all on the fresh River, and they are all verie healthfull and high land except James Citty w[ch] is yett as high as Debtforde or Radclyffe.[1]

2. I founde the shores and sides of those partes of the Mayne River where our Plantacions are setled every wher soe shallow as noe Boates can approach the shores, soe that besides the difficulty daunger and spoile of goods in the Landinge of them the people are forced to a Continuall wadinge and wettinge of themselves and that in the prime [2] of winter when the Shipps commonly arrive, and therby gett such vyolent surfetts of colde uppon colde as seldom leave them until they leave to live.

Answere 2. That generally for the Plantacions att all times from halfe ffloud to halfe ebb any boate that drawes betwixt three and 4 foote water may safely com in and Land their goods dry on Shore w[th]out wadinge and for further Cleeringe of these false objeccons, the Seamen there doe at all times deliver the goods they bringe to the Owners dry on Shore, wherby itt plainely appeares not any of the Country people there inhabitinge are by this meanes in daunger of their lives, And at a great many Plantacions belowe James Citty and allmost all above they may att all times Land dry.[3]

3. The new people that are yearly sent over which arrive here for the most part very Unseasonably in Winter, finde neither Guest house, Inne nor any the like place to shroud themselves in at their arrivall, noe not soe much as a stroake given towards any such charitable worke soe that many of them by want hereof are not onely seen dyinge under hedges and in the woods but beinge dead ly some of them many dayes Unregarded and Unburied.

Answere 3. To the first they Answere that the winter is the most healthfull time and season for arrivall of new Commers.

[1] This answer could hardly be made in truth. The climate of the James River was undoubtedly very deadly to the newcomers. Conditions have changed since that day, because of the opening of the forests. Deptford and Ratcliff were on the Thames near London.

[2] Middle.

[3] This description accords with the modern topography.

True itt is that as yett ther is noe Guesthouse or place of interteynm$^{t}$ for Strangers. Butt wee averr that itt was a late intent and had by this time been putt in practise to make a generall gatheringe for the buildinge of such a Convenient house, w$^{ch}$ by this time had been in good fowardnes had itt not pleased God to suffer this Disaster to fall out by the Indians. But although there be no publique Guesthouse yett are new Commers entertayned and lodged and provided for by the Governo$^{r}$ in pryvate houses; And for any dyinge in the feilds through this defecte and lying unburied, wee are altogether ignorant, yett that many dy suddenly by the hand of God, wee often see itt to fall out even in this flourishinge and plentifull Citty in the middest of our streets. As for dyinge under hedges there is no hedge in all Virginia.

4. The Colony was this winter in much distress of victuall soe that English meale was soulde at the rate of thirtie shillings [1] a bushell their owne native Corne called Maize at ten and fifteen shillings the bushell, The w$^{ch}$ howsoever itt lay heavy uppon the shoulders of the Generallytie it may be suspected not to be unaffected by some of the chiefe, for they only haveinge the means in these extremities to trade for Corne with the Natives doe herby ingrosse all into their hands and soe sell yt abrode at their owne prices, and my selfe have heard from the mouth of a prime one amonst them that hee would never wish that their owne Corne should be cheaper among them then eight shillings the bushell.

Answere 4. True itt is that English meale hath of late since the Massacre been sould for Tenn pounds of Tobacco the bushell w$^{ch}$ no understandinge man can there value above fifteen shillings sterlinge, and here we finde (w$^{th}$out a Massacre) by the judgment of God for our murmuringe att plentie Wheat hath this yeare been sould and still is in many places at three times the rate itt hath borne w$^{th}$in two or three years last past; And againe Indian corne hath heretofore comonly been sould after the rate of five shillings the bushell. And farther meale bore so high a price this year as itt cost ready mony in

[1] About $30 in present values.

England together w^th^ the fraight and other charges neer uppon twelve shillinges, soe that if itt were sould at Tenn pounds of Tobacco ther will not be gayned twenty in the hundred.

5. Ther Howses are generally the worst that ever I sawe the meanest Cottages in England beinge every way equall (if not superior) with the most of the beste, And besides soe improvidently and scatteringly are they seated one from an other as partly by theire distance but especially by the interposicion of Creeks and Swamps as they call them they offer all advantages to their savadge enimys and are utterly deprived of all suddaine recollection of themselves uppon any tearmes whatsoever.

Answere 5. First that the houses there were most built for use, and not for ornament, and are soe farr from beinge soe meane as they are reported that throughout his Ma^ts^ Dominions here all labouringe mens houses (w^ch^ wee cheifly professe our selvs to be) are in no wise generally for goodnes to be compared unto them. And for the howses of men of better Ranke and quallety they are soe much better and convenyent that noe man of quallety w^th^out blushinge can make excepcion against them; Againe for the Creeks and Swamps every man ther that cannott goe by Land hath either a Boate or a Conoa for the Conveyinge and speedy passage to his neighbors house. As for Cottages ther are none in Virginia, that they knowe.

6. I found not the least peec of Fortification, Three Peeces of Ordinance onely mounted at James Citty and one at Flowerdue Hundred,[1] but never a one of them serviceable Soe that itt is most certaine that a smale Barke of one hundred Tunns may take its time to pass up the River in spite of them and comminge to an Anchor before the Towne may beate all their houses downe aboute their eares and so forceinge them to retreat into the Woods, may land under the favour of their Ordinance and rifle the Towne at pleasure.

[1] Flowerdew Hundred was about twenty miles from Jamestown up the river on the south side. It was at this time the property of Sir George Yeardley, who in 1621 erected on a point of land the first windmill in the United States. This point is yet known as "Windmill Point."

Answere 6. Itt is true ther is as yett no other artificiall Fortificacions then Pallisadoes wherof allmoste everie Plantacion hath one, and divers of them hath Trenches, And this last yeare Cap$^{t}$ Eache was sent for that purpose. As for great Ordinance there are fower peeces mounted att James Citty and all serviceable, ther are six Mounted at Flowerdue hundred all of them likewise serviceable, And three mounted att Kiccoutan and all of them serviceable, there are likewise att Newporte Newes three, all of them serviceable, ther are likewise att Henrico seaven peeces and at Charles hundred two, and in other places, besides Fowlers and Murders [1] at divers places.

7. Expectinge accordinge to their printed Bookes [2] a great fowardnes of divers and sundry Comodities, At myne arrivall I found not any one of them so much as in any towardnes [3] of being. For the Iron workes were utterly wasted and the men dead, The Furnaces for Glass and Pots at a stay and in a smale hope, As for the rest they were had in a generall derision even amongst themselves, and the Pamphlets that had published here beinge sent thither by Hundreds wer laughed to scorne, and every base fellow boldly gave them the Lye in divers perticulers, Soe that Tobacco onely was the buisines and for ought that I could here every man madded upon that, and lyttle thought or looked for any thinge else.

Answere 7. That the Country yields divers usefull and rich Commodities w$^{ch}$ by reason of the Infancie of the Plantacion, and this unexpected Massacre cannot yett be brought to perfeccon, and is no lesse hindred by the emulous and envious reports of ill willers whose pryvate ends by time wilbe discovered and by God recompensed. And wee doe further answer that this Country is a moste fruitfull Country and doth certainely produce divers rich Comodities. Itt is true that the Ironworks are wasted and the men dead, but that was by the Massacre w$^{ch}$ if itt had not happened ther had been a good proofe of that Comodity, for the works wer in a very great forwardnes. As for Vines likewise ther were divers Vine-yeards planted in sundry places, butt all of them putt back by the Massacre,

[1] Murderers (cannon). [2] Circulars or pamphlets. [3] Forwardness.

butt for the peoples derydinge of these Comodities or the books sent by the Comp[a]: wee have never heard of any such scoffinge or derisions, butt as the Governor and Counsell ther are very desirous and have sett forth Proclamacions to cause all men to sett both Vines and Mulbery Trees, so the people generally are very desyrous and forward to rayse those former Commodities of Wine and Silke and likewise divers other good Comodities.[1]

8. I found the Antient Plantations of Henrico and Charles Citty wholly quitted and lefte to the spoile of the Indians, who not onely burned the houses saide to be once the best of all others, but fell uppon the Poultry, Hoggs, Cowes, Goates and Horses wherof they killed great numbers to the greate griefe as well as ruine of the Olde Inhabitants, whoe stick not to affirme that these were not onely the best and healthiest parts of all others, but might allsoe by their naturall strength of scituacion have been the most easefully preserved of all the rest.

9. Wheras accordinge to his Ma[ties] gratious Letters Patents his People in Virginia are as neer as possibly may be to be governed after the excellent Lawes and Customes of Englande, I found in the Government there not onely ignorant and enforced strayings in diver particulers, but willfull and intended ones;[2] Insomuch as some who urged due conformity have in contempt been tearmed men of Lawe, and were excluded from those rights which by orderly proceedings they were elected and sworne unto here.

10. There havinge been as it is thought not fewer than Tenn thousand soules transported thither ther are not through the aforenamed abuses and neglects above Two thousand of them at the present to be found alive, many of them alsoe in a

[1] Nevertheless, Butler was very near right when he gave the emphasis to tobacco; and doubtless for many years the culture of tobacco was too absorbing.

[2] Butler means that he found that the orders of the company, which promised a government after the excellent laws and customs of England, were wilfully disregarded.

sickly and desperate estate:[1] Soe that itt may undoubtedly [be] expected that unlesse the Confusions and pryvate ends of some of the Company here, and the bad executions in secondinge them by their Agents there be redressed with speed by some divine and supreame hand, that in steed of a Plantacion it will shortly gett the name of a Slaughterhouse, and soe justly become both odious to our selves and contemptible to all the worlde.

Answere. All these wee leave to be answered by the Governor and Company some of them beinge unfitt to be determyned of by us. And for the last wee being ignorant how many have been transported or are now lyvinge there.

Wee whose names are hereunder and hereafter written have uppon mature deliberacion and after full examinacion and consideracion of the premises, drawne upp these answers beinge such as we finde in our consyencies to be true, and shall att all times justifie them uppon our oathes. In wittnes wherof wee have hereunder sett our hands.[2]

[1] The Virginia Company afterwards undertook to answer these three last charges. The condition of the plantations at Henrico and Charles City was ascribed to an Indian massacre, which was unavoidable. There was nothing in the charge of arbitrary rule, which had no better ground than the exclusion of Butler's unjust claim to a seat in the council. As to the number of emigrants, it did not exceed 6000, of whom 2500 had been sent over during the twelve years of Sir Thomas Smith; 2500, and not 2000, still survived.

[2] Upon this follow sixteen attestations by persons who had lived in Virginia or mariners who had visited the country, all of whom declare the answers above given to be truthful.

# THE TRAGICAL RELATION OF THE VIRGINIA ASSEMBLY, 1624

# INTRODUCTION

THE effort of the faction of Sir Thomas Smith in the Virginia Company to secure a dissolution was heartily reprobated by the Virginia Assembly, and in January, 1624, they drew up a paper denouncing the administration of Sir Thomas Smith and extolling that of Sandys and Southampton. The exact truth cannot be expected of such a paper, but after its perusal there can be but one opinion of the merits of the two parties. The original is in the Library of Congress, Division of Manuscripts. The text which follows has been carefully collated with this original. The document was first printed in Neill's *Virginia Company of London*, pp. 407–411.

L. G. T.

# THE TRAGICAL RELATION OF THE VIRGINIA ASSEMBLY, 1624

*The answere of the Generall Assembly in Virginia to a Declaratione of the state of the Colonie in the 12 yeers of Sr Thomas Smiths Government, exhibited by Alderman Johnson*[1] *and others.*

Holdinge it a sinne against God, and our owne sufferinge, to suffer the World to be abused w[th] untrue reportes, and to give unto vice the reward of vertue, we in the name of the whole Colonie of Virginia, in our generall assembly, many of us having beene eye witnesses and patients[2] of those tymes have framed out of our duty to this country, and love unto truth, this Dismaskinge of those prayses w[ch] are contayned in the foresaide declarationes.

In those 12 yeers of S[r] Tho: Smith his goverment, we averr that the Colony for the most parte remayned in great want and misery under most severe and Crewell lawes sent over in printe,[3] and contrary to the expresse Letter of the Kinge in his most gracious Charter, and as mercylessly executed, often times without tryall or Judgment. The allowance in those tymes for a man was only eight ounces of meale and half a pinte of pease

[1] Alderman Robert Johnson of London was one of the leading members of the Smith faction in the company, and had been deputy-treasurer under Smith. He took a leading part in procuring the dissolution of the company.

[2] Sufferers.

[3] These printed laws, entitled *Laws Divine, Morall and Martiall* (London, 1612; reprinted in Force's *Tracts*, Washington, 1844, Vol. III.) were promulgated by Sir Thomas Gates at Jamestown for the first time, May 24, 1610. They were afterwards enlarged by Sir Thomas Dale, who introduced the martial code contained in the thirty-two articles of war of the army of the Netherlands, with the cognizance of Sir Thomas Smith, the treasurer of the company.

for a daye, the one and the other mouldy, rotten, full of Cobwebs and Maggotts loathsome to man and not fytt for beasts, w^ch^ forced many to flee for reliefe to the Savage Enemy, who being taken againe were putt to sundry deaths as by hanginge, shooting and breakinge uppon the wheele and others were forced by famine to filch for their bellies, of whom one for steelinge of 2 or 3 pints of oatemeale had a bodkinge thrust through his tounge and was tyed w^th^ a chaine to a tree untill he starved, yf a man through his sicknes had not been able to worke, he had noe allowance at all, and soe consequently perished. Many through these extremities, being weery of life, digged holes in the earth and there hidd themselves till they famished.

Wee cannott for this our scarsitie blame our Comanders heere, in respect that o^r^ sustenance was to come from England, for had they at that time given us better allowance we had perished in generall, soe lamentable was our scarsitie that we were constrayned to eate Doggs, Catts, ratts, Snakes, Toadstooles, horse hides and w^t^ nott, one man out of the mysery that he endured, killinge his wiefe powdered [1] her upp to eate her, for w^ch^ he was burned. Many besides fedd on the Corps of dead men, and one who had gotten unsatiable, out of custome to that foode could not be restrayned, untill such tyme as he was executed for it, and in deede soe miserable was our estate, that the happyest day that ever some of them hoped to see, was when the Indyans had killed a mare, they [2] wishinge whilst she was a boylinge that S^r^ Tho: Smith were uppon her backe in the kettle.

And wheras it is afirmed that there were very fewe of his Ma^ties^ subjects left in those dayes, and those of the meanest ranke, we answere that for one that now dyes, there then perished five, many beinge of Auncyent Howses and borne to estates of 1000^li^ by the yeere, some more some lesse, who likewyse perished by famine. Those who survived, who had both adventured theire estates and personnes, were Constrayned to serve the Colony, as yf they had been slaves, 7 or 8 yeers for

[1] Salted.

[2] The desperate settlers.

their freedomes, who underwent as harde and servile labor as the basest Fellow that was brought out of Newgate.

And for discovery we saye that nought was discovered in those 12 yeers, and in these 4 or 5 last yeers much more then formerly.[1]

For o[r] howses and churches in those tymes they were soe meane and poore by resone of those calamities that they could not stand above one or two yeers, the people never goinge to woorke but out of the bitterness of theire spiritts threatninge execrable curses uppon Sr: Thomas Smith, nether could a blessinge from god be hoped for in those buildings w[ch] were founded uppon the bloud of soe many Christians.[2]

The Townes were only James Cyttie, Henryco, Charles hundred, West and Sherley hundred, and Kicoughtan, all w[ch] in those tymes were ruined alsoe, unlesse some 10 or 12 howses in the Corporatione of James Cyttie. At this present tyme are 4 for every one that were then, and forty times exceedinge in goodnesse.[3] Fortifications there were non at all against the foraigne enemy, and those that were against the domestick very few and contemptible. Bridges there was only one w[ch] also decayde in that tyme.[4] Yf through the forsaid calamities many had not perished we doupt not but there might have been many more than 1000 people in the lande when Sr Thomas Smith left the Goverment.

But we conceive that when Sr George Yardly arrived Govno[r] hee founde not above 400,[5] most of those in want of

[1] "Discoveries" (*i.e.*, explorations) were made in both periods. Long before Sir Thomas Smith's term expired, all of eastern Virginia was well known to the settlers; Delaware Bay had been visited, and the Bermuda Islands settled. The discoveries made in the four or five last years were probably those of John Pory.

[2] The houses were made of green wood, which soon decayed.

[3] The houses at this time were made of seasoned timbers.

[4] In 1611 Sir Thomas Dale made a bridge, *i.e.*, a wharf, above where the church tower now stands at Jamestown, on which to land goods from the ships. This was the "bridge" referred to.

[5] This was the number on the public plantations, but the private settlements had 600 more, making 1000 in all. *Abstract of Proceedings of the Virginia Company of London*, I. 65.

corne, nearly destitute of cattle, swyne, poultrey and other necessary provisions to nourishe them. Ministers to instruct the people there were some whose sufficyentcie and abilitie we will not tax, yet divers of them had no Orders.

We knowe not at any time that we exceeded in Armes, Powder and munitions, yet that in qualitie almost altogether uselesse. We acknowledg in those times there was a tryall made of divers staple Comodities, the Colony as then not havinge meanes to proceede therin, we hope in tyme there may be some better progressions be made, and had it not beene for the Massacre, many by this had beene brought to perfectione. As for boats in the tyme of that Govermte, there was only one left that was servicable in the Colonie, for w^ch^ one besides 4 or 5 shipps and pynnaces, there are now not soe fewe as 40, the barques and barges that then were built in number fewe, so unwillinglie and weakly by the people effected, that in the same time they also perished.

We never perceaved that the natives of the Countrey did voluntarily yeeld them selves subjects to our gracyous Sovraigne, nether that they took any pride in that title, nor paide at any tyme any contrybutione of corne for sustentation of the Colony, nor could we at any tyme keepe them in such good respect of correspondency as we became mutually helpful each to the other but contrarily what at any was done proceeded from feare and not love, and their corne procured by trade or the sworde.

To w^t^ grouth of perfectione the Colony hath attayned at the end of those 12 yeers wee conceave may easily be judged by w^t^ we have formerly saide. And rather then to be reduced to live under the like Govment we desire his Ma^tie^ that Commissioners may be sent over, w^th^ authoritie to hange us.

Alderman Johnson, one of the Authors of this Declaratione, hath reasone to comend him [1] to whose offences and infamies he is so inseparably chained.

By the generall report of the Country w^ch^ we never hard contradicted, we affirme this to be true wherof all or the most

[1] *I.e.*, Sir Thomas Smith.

parte were eye witnesses or resident in the Country when every particuler within written were effected.

Francis Wyatt
George Sandis
John Pott
John Powntis
Roger Smith
Raphe Hamor
Wm. Tucker
Wm. Peerce
Rawley Croshaw
Samuel Mathews
Jabez Whittaker
John Willcox
Nicholas Marten
Edward Blany
Isack Madisone

Clement Dilke
Luke Boyse
John Utie
John Chew
Richard Stephens
John Southerne
Samuel Sharpe
Henry Watkins
Nathanell Causey
Richard Bigge
Richard Kingswell
John Pollington
Robert Addams
Gabriell Holland
Thomas Marlott

# THE DISCOURSE OF THE OLD COMPANY, 1625

# INTRODUCTION

THE government of Virginia under the first charter (1606) was that of a supreme council in England appointed by the king and a subordinate council in Virginia; and neither the Virginia Company nor the settlers had any political authority. Under the second charter (1609), the government was centred in England in a treasurer and council, who selected a governor for Virginia having authority independent of the local council. The third charter (1612) vested the authority in England in the company and, as a consequence, parties arose. On the question of governing the colony, the company soon divided into two factions, — one in favor of continuing martial law, at the head of which was Sir Robert Rich, afterwards Earl of Warwick, and the "Country" or "Patriot Party" in favor of ending the system of servitude. The latter party was led by Sir Thomas Smith, who had been treasurer ever since 1609, Sir Edwin Sandys, Henry Wriothesley, Earl of Southampton, Sir John Danvers, and John and Nicholas Ferrar. In 1618 Sir Thomas Smith was deposed from his office, and Sandys made treasurer, which so offended Smith that he joined forces with the court party. After a year Sandys, finding himself an object of disfavor with the king, stepped aside, and the Earl of Southampton, who agreed with Sandys in all his views, was appointed and kept in office till the company's dissolution. The five years' rule of the patriot party was a period of extraordinary activity in Virginia affairs, and the plans of Sandys and Southampton were remarkably statesmanlike and far-reaching. But the calamities of epidemics and an Indian massacre, which could not be prevented, made them a prey to all kinds of attack.

At the suggestions of Lionel Cranfield, the crafty Earl of Middlesex, they were induced to apply to King James for the monopoly of the sale of tobacco in England, and they became entangled in a quarrel, which was fanned to a white heat by the intrigues of Count Gondomar, the Spanish minister. The court party took the matter to the king, and after a long agitation the charter was revoked. After this the king appointed a commission, consisting in part of members of the court party, to take charge of Virginia affairs, but on his death, the next year, King Charles, his son, revoked the former royal commission and intrusted affairs relating to Virginia to a committee of the Privy Council, who ignored the Smith party and called the Sandys party into consultation. These last presented a paper in April, 1625, called "The Discourse of the Old Company," in which they gave a full history of affairs, and petitioned to be reincorporated. Charles was not indisposed to grant the request, but postponed the matter from time to time till sentiment in the colony, which once favored the company, became adverse to it, as the Virginians found that they enjoyed a larger degree of liberty under the neglect of the king than under the care of the company.

The document is reprinted, by permission, from the *Virginia Magazine of History*, I. 155–167, 287–302. The last part of it, not narrative, but containing suggestions as to future government, etc., has been omitted. The original is in the Public Record Office in London.

L. G. T.

# THE DISCOURSE OF THE OLD COMPANY, 1625

*May it please your Lop*$^{s}$[1]

WHEN last we attended this Honourable Board y$^{or}$ Lop$^{p}$ required two things at our hands to be presented this day in writing to your Lop$^{s}$.

The first, our opinion touching the best forme of Government to be made for Virginia; the second, as to such contract touching Tobacco w$^{th}$ his Ma$^{tie}$ as might both uphold his former Revenue, and not be grievous to the Plantations.

Concerning the former of w$^{ch}$ proposicions, wee humbly crave leave thus much to deliver w$^{th}$out offence, that it came altogether unexpected to us: who brought w$^{th}$ us, a strong and confirmed resolucion, not to intermedle any more in the business of Virginia, so soyled and wronged by the partie opposite, and now reduced to extreame terms allmost past recovery and wherein all our former labours, cares, and expenses had receaved by the practise and procurement of these men, the undeserved reward of rebuke and disgrace.

Notw$^{th}$standing, whome wee have alwayes found just and hono$^{ble}$ and if happily some good may rebound thereby to that now distressed and languishing Plantation, w$^{ch}$ hath bin heretofore so deare unto us, and w$^{ch}$ gave so great hope of honour to this Kingdome, and might have bin in these tymes of warrly[2] preparations, of so great use and service to his Mat$^{ie}$ if it had bin so cherished and strengthened by these men, as when they gayned the government, they pretended and promised, we wised[3] and designed: We here present in all humbleness our deliberate opinion touching the forme of Government

[1] Lordships.

[2] Warlike. England was then at war with Spain.

[3] Wished.

now fittest to be established for the restoring and reviving of that Plantation, if it be possible yet to be recovered. Wherein wee thinke it requisite, that yo$^{r}$ Lop$^{s}$ in the first place be truly informed, of the state of that Colony, what before it was, and what now it is, according unto the best advertisements from thence received.

The Plantation now in Virginia, began about the yeare 1606 and continued about twelve yeares under the Governem$^{t}$ of the selfe same handes, whereinto it was first intrusted by the Kings Ma$^{tie}$ the most Royall founder of this noble worke. The perticular carriages of this first Governem$^{t}$ are too long, and would bee too displeasing to yo$^{r}$ Lopp$^{s}$ eares. But in Generall such it was, as the now Earle of Middlesex then Lo: high Treasurer [1] (being an ancient adventurer and councellor for Virginia) informed yo$^{r}$ Lop$^{s}$ sitting in Counsell the 5th of March, 1622, when he told Alderman Johnson, That in former yeares when he the said alderman was Deputie, and the business was in other hands, it was carried leaudly,[2] so that if they should be called to an accompt for it, their Estates would not answere it.

What his Lo$^{pp}$ delivered as his owne censure, was truly the opinion of the whole company of Adventurers here in England: And w$^{th}$ them doth the Colonie concure having the last yeare by their Vice admirall sent a writing [3] signed by the hands of the Generall Assembly, and directed to his Ma$^{tie}$, wherein having declared: The manner of Those Twelve yeares Governem$^{t}$, they conclude w$^{th}$ these words, full of passion and griefe; and rather then to be reduced to live under the like Government, wee desire his Ma$^{tie}$ that Commissioners may be sent over with authoritie to hang us. Of this quallitie was the first Governem$^{t}$ And answerable to fforme, were the effects, as the Generall Assemblie having by oath examined the particulars, sett downe in their Declaration directed to his late Mat$^{ie}$.

[1] Lionel Cranfield, Earl of Middlesex, lord high treasurer from 1621 to his impeachment in 1624.

[2] Lewdly.

[3] This was the paper entitled *The Tragical Declaration.*

1. For People then alive about the nomber of 400.[1]

2. Very many of them in want of corne, utterly destitute of cattle, swine, Poultry and other provisions to nourish them.

3. As for Fortificacon agaynst a forraigne enemy there was none at all, onely foure pieces mounted, but altogether unserviceable.

4. There was only eight Plantacions, all w[ch] were but poorely housed, and ill fortified agaynst the Savages.

5. Onely one old friggott belonging to the Sumer Ilandes, one shallop, one shippboate, and two small boats belonging to private men.

6. Three ministers in orders and Two w[th]out.

7. No comoditie on foote save Tobacco.

8. The Indians in doubtful Termes.

This as they report was the true estate of the Plantacons at the Twelve yeares end. To w[ch] being added the other condicon of the colonie, w[ch] in other writinges they expresse:

1. That they lived or rather suffered under Martial lawe.

2. Under a most extorting Governour there whome by 24 bundles of depositions they have accused of strange depredacons.

3. Under most oppressive orders hence, to the breach of all faith and honesty.

4. W[th]out confort of wives or servants.

5. W[th]out assurance of their estates.

6. There beinge no Dividents of Land laid out.[2]

7. W[th]out assurance of their Libties, being violently deteyned as serv[ts] beyond their convenented tymes.

We may truly affirme, that the intencons of the people in Virginia, were no wayes to settle there a colonie, but to gett

[1] At Easter, 1619, about the time Sir George Yeardley arrived, there were one thousand people in Virginia — four hundred on the public plantations and six hundred on the private.

[2] The joint-stock partnership expired November 30, 1616, and Captain Samuel Argall was sent to Virginia with instructions to give every settler his own private dividend. But Argall disregarded his orders and kept the people in servitude until he was superseded by Yeardley. Sir Thomas Smith was, therefore, not fairly responsible for the whole dismal picture drawn above.

a little wealth by Tobacco, then in price, and to return for Englande.

As for the Adventurers here the greatest part were long before beaten out as from an hopeless Action. In w^ch^ regard there was ffifteene thousand pounds of mens subscripcons w^ch^ by no means they could bee procured to pay in; sundry of them alleaging in theer answers in chancery upon their oathes, the misimployment of the monyes, and ill keeping of the accounts. Those few that followed the business, upon some hope to reforme it, were (by the Governours here, for their owne perticuler ends as is conceaved, for, to theire owne private benefitt it was only sutable) directed to bestowe their moneyes in adventuringe by way of Magazine,[1] upon two comodities onely, Tobacco and Sassafras matters of present proffitt, but no wayes foundacons of a future state. Soe that of a merchantlike Trade there was some probbillitie at least for a while; but of a Plantation there was none at all, neither in the course nor in the intencons either of the Adventurers here or the colonie there.

In this estate and condicon was the action lefte by the First to the second Governm^t^ w^ch^ began in the yeare 1619 by the choice of S^r^ Edwin Sandis for Treasurer. To whome the yeare followinge succeed^d^ the Earle of Southampton.

1. Under whose Governm^t^ by Gods blessing the Plantation soe prospered as by the end of the yeare 1621 the nomber of people was encreased, there, to be about Two thousand.

2. The number of Neat cattle, besides Goates and Swine, eight hundred.

3. The number of Housinge was proporcionably encreased, and the manner of building much bettered.

4. The number of Boats was Ten tymes multiplyed, and w^ch^ was much more, there were fower Shippes belonging to the Colonie.

5. Ther were sent more than eight able ministers.

[1] Particular merchants would make up a fund and send over a ship with goods to exchange for tobacco and sassafras. This was called a magazine.

6. With great care and cost there were procured men skilfull in sawing Milles from Hambrough.[1]

7. Vigneroones from Lanquedock:[2] In divers places of the Colonie, Vineyards beganne, some of them conteyinge Ten thousand plants.

8. Store of silkeworme-seed sent.

9. And the Iron-workes brought after five thousand pounds expences to that assured perfection, as w[th] in Three months they promised to send home great quantities.

10. Many new Plantations were made.

11. All men had sufficiency of corne.

12. And many Great plenty of cattle, swyne and Poultrie, and other good provisions.

13. The mortalitie w[ch] had raigned the two first yeares, (w[ch] at that tyme was generall over all America) was at last ceased.

14. Soe that by this sodayne and unexpected advancement of Plantation in these things, together with the redresse of all former Grievances: supplies of young women for wives, and of youthes for serv[ts] being sent them.

15. The bloudy Lawes being silenced and their Governemt ordered like to that of this Kingdom.

16. Provisions being made for the mayntennce of Officers that they should not need to prey upon the people: And the like done for the ministers:

17. The libertie of a Generall assembly being granted them, whereby they find out and execute those things as might best tend to their good.

18. The Estates of Land by just Dividends being surely conveyed:

19. A ffree Trade from hense for all sorts of people being permitted, whereby they were eeven to superfluity furnished w[th] all necessaries:

The Colony grewe into an opinion that they were the happiest people in the world, w[ch] meeting here at home w[th] the experience of most Noble Demeanor on the Companies part,

[1] Hamburg. [2] Vinedressers from Languedoc.

agaynst w^ch^ Envy itselfe could not finde any shadowe of calamny or offence: the reputacon of this action grew to such an height, as not only the old Adventurers renewed their zeale of their first Loves, but great numbers of new came dayly in w^th^ assurance to expend large somes in the business.

And for the Plant^rs^ to goe in person, not only here at home Thousands of choise people offred themselves: but out of Ireland went divers shipps, and more were followinge: Three hundred ffamilies French and Dutch in the yeare 1621 made request to the state, that they might plant in Virginia;[1] whither not long before, condempned persons had refused to go with pardon of their Lives.

The great amendment in this and in all other parts of this Action, made the Earle of Middlesex say at yo^r^ honob^le^ Board, That in these latter tymes the Plantation by the good carriage had thriven and prospered beyond beliefe and allmost miraculouslie.

This wee cannot but esteeme an hono^ble^ testimony proceeding from our most heavy enemy, who had himselfe layde in o^r^ way soe many great Rubbs and Difficulties, as hee might well say, It was by miracle wee over passed them.

The first yeare, directly agaynst his Ma^ts^ L'res Pattents, and consequently against Laws, by the judgment of the then Attorney-Generall, exceedingly over burdeninge our Commoditie:

The second yeare to the Kings great dammage and abuse of the whole Kingdome procuringe an utter banishment of our Tobacco:

And the third yeare enforcinge us to bring all in, onely to the enrichm^t^ of his private friends. But besides these; we were continually struglinge w^th^ a most malicious faction w^th^in

[1] They were Walloons, Huguenots, driven from Europe by persecution. Not liking the terms offered by the Virginia Company, they entered into negotiation with the Dutch West India Company, and in 1623 went to New York. Some few, nevertheless, came to Virginia. Among these was Nicholas Marlier (generally rendered Martian), who was the first patentee of the land where Yorktown is now located. He was an ancestor of George Washington.

our owne Body here; yet through all these difficulties did we wrestle by Gods blessing, with the expence of lesse then ffower and twenty thousands pounds of the Public stock. For howso-ever your Lop$^{s}$ have been enformed, the very thruth w$^{ch}$ we shall alwayes make good is, that there was not receaved from the Lottaries in the tyme of this latter Governem$^{t}$ any more than Twenty one thousand seaven hundred sixty six poundes nyne shillings Two pence. By the expence of w$^{ch}$ some together w$^{th}$ about Three thousand pounds receaved from the Collections, wee brought the Colony to those Termes wee have related. And if in the Declaration sent to his Ma$^{tie}$ the last yeare, the colony have made a right and perfect calculacon, wee affirme unto yo$^{r}$ Lop$^{s}$ that in the first Three yeares of this latter Governement the company sent as many shipps in nomber, but of greater burthen; as many people in nomber, but much better provided, as were sent in the first Twelve years. Yet had the latter Governem$^{t}$ under Twenty fower Thousand poundes, and S$^{r}$ Thomas Smith receaved above Three score and ffifteene thousand pounds, of publique stock. Soe that wee may truly affirme through Gods blessing w$^{th}$ a Third part of the money, and in a fourth part of the tyme, wee brought the Plantation to foure tymes the nomber of men that Sr Thomas Smith left it in, and in all other parts incomparably better.

The Plantation being growne to this height by the end of the year 1621, it pleased God in his secrett judgment to give leave to the enemies thereof, by many powerfull and most wicked meanes to bring it downe agayne to the ground. The first Blowe was a most blowdy massacre, when by the Treacherous cruelty of the savages about 400 of o$^{r}$ People were slayne, upon the 22th of March 1621.[1] The terror whereof w$^{th}$ the losse of much cattle and other substance, and a sodayne alteracon of the state of all things, so dismaide the whole Colony, as they allmost gave themselves for gone. But then appeared both the love of the Company to the Plantation and their great abilettie

[1] At this time it was usual in England to regard the new year as beginning on March 25. We should date the massacre March 22, 1622.

to goe through therewith: when in supply of this Loss, and for the encouragement of the Colony, they did send that yeare to Virginia 16 ships and 800 people and that altogether at the charges of private Adventurors. For the publique stock being utterly exhaust the yeare before was not able to contribute 500*l.* towards all this charge.

But this cruell Tragedy of the massacre was second[d] by Two other sharpe Calamities in the very neck one of another:

First, scarcitie in the Colony by being putt off from their Grounds prepared, together w[th] the losse of their season and much seed; besides that through the troublesomnes of those tymes, they could not freely imploy themselves in plantinge thereof, no not in those their scanted grounds, many Plantacions being drawne into few places for their better defence. W[ch] pestringe of themselves did likewise breed contagious sicknesse; w[ch] being encreased by the Infection brought in by some shipps, there dyed that yeare of mortallitie neere upon 600 more: and the Colony passed much hardnesse in their victuall, by reason of the miscarriage of one of their shippes, w[ch] the Company sett forth w[th] above 500*l.* worth of meale and other provisions: But the shipp being blowne up w[th] Powder at the Summer Islandes, the Provisions were lost, and never came to Virginia.

Notwithstandinge these things were most grievous to the Company here; yett were they no wayes of Discouragement, but rather seemed to add heat to their former zeale: so as by the beginning of the year 1623 there appeared in readinesse and preparation to go to Virginia, double that nomber of people and Adventurers that any former yeare had carried. When on a sodayne the Plantation itselfe was by Captaine Butler in a certayne writinge Intituled The unmaskinge of Virginia, soe fowly disgraced, and the present miseries thereof so farr amplified above Truth, and the future hopes there of so belowe all good meanings derided and villified by divers ill willers of the Action especially some discontented members of the Company, as the greatest part of the intended supplies for New Plantations, gave over, as some of themselves will testify to yor Lops, yet notwthstandinge, the united Body of the Company did even that year, 1623, send out eleven Shipps, stored wth supplies of victuall and provisions: although by many cruell encounters of the opposites, they were so hindered and dejected, directly wth Intention to make them abandon the busines. But the welfare of the Plantacon and the mayntennce of their own honour and credit, did prevaile so wth the company that though wth certainty of their owne extreame loss, they passed in the aboundance of supply, not only the necessitis of the Colony, but even the unreasonable demaunds of their opposite: Having in fower days space that was given them after the notice of the Colonies want, procured the underwriting of fower thousand pounds Adventure: wch the Honoble Board of the privy Counsell was pleased wth much Noble favour highly to approve.

As for the people that went that yeare in those eleven ships the nomber was not above 260, and those procured not wthout difficulty, so much had the disgrace of the Plantation spread amongst the comon sort of people.

Neither could it be prevented by the companie although they used all possible dilligence; solliciting the Comissioners then appointed by his Matie by a publique examinacon of Captayne Butlers reporte, to clear the truth. But they would by no meanes bee drawne thereunto. As for the companie it selfe, their proceedings and demeanors were so approbriously calumniatd as deprived them both of abillitie and credite to doe any good herein: but wth much sorrowe to behold how sencibly and dangerously the good opinion of this Action decayed; so that Preachers of note in the Cittie that had begun in this latter Governemt to pray continually for Virginia, lefte quite the remembrance of it; finding the Action to growe either odious or contemptible in mens minds: wch yet but a little before was of that esteeme as divers on their death beds gave great Lagacies to the furtherance thereof; and even from the East Indies by way of contribucon, hath bin sent by the ffactors and poore marriners above 1000 marks, so farr was the reputacon of this action spread, by the prosperinge thereof under the latter Governem$^{t}$ and by their zealous and sollicitous endeavours. W$^{ch}$ although by the continuall encrease of further suffringes, their pattent being called in question, receaved a sore check: yet not w$^{th}$standing their owne Innocencie giving them courage and hope that they should overcome all w$^{th}$ honour and thanks of the state: there were ffive shipps provided for this last yeare, 1624, whereof one of them since the Companies disolucon hath given over her voyage: the other ffoure have proceeded, although w$^{th}$ much difficulty, in regard that a great part of the Passengers that afore intended to goe, fell off. Whereby two of the shippes w$^{ch}$ had their comissions from the late companie in May last could not gett away till the end of this last yeare, the one in ffebruary, the other in March last.[1]

Thus have wee given yo$^{r}$ Lop$^{s}$ a true Informacon, both of the growth and languishinge of the Virginia Plantacion, in these ffive latter yeares Governemt: wherein no incombrances, no calamities whatsoever could keepe it soe downe, but that it did yearely advance itselfe w$^{th}$ a most remarkable growth whilst the carefull Nurse and tender mother the Company was permitted to governe it.

Though contagion and sword destroyed many people: yet whilst the nomber of new did doubly supply those that fayled it cannot be said, but the action was in a thriving, in a prosperous course; though not in a cleare or easy. Then began it to stand when the Companie was troubled; to stagger, when they were disgrac'd and discountenanced; to sinck, when they were terrifyed w$^{th}$ affreightment of dissolucon; since w$^{ch}$ tyme there hath bin nothing at all done towards the recovery of helping it forward, but much towards the hindrenge and bringing it lower.

The poor supply of people and shippes that are gone, are but the remaynder of the late Companies cares and loves. The settlers out of the best of them doe affirme, that if they had not been so farr engaged before the unexpected dissolucon of the late Companie, they would have drawne back their ad-

[1] *I.e.*, in 1625.

ventures and People. When they shall arive in Virginia they will not bring eith comfort or supply to the Colonie: but only add to their Calamitie, to their grief.

The first Shipp went in August, victualled only for Three months; the next in October; neither of them were arived the 25th of ffebruary last. Whereby they must needs come into Virginia in most miserable distresse.

The other two went out soe meanly provid[d] that however their voyage shal be, they cannot but prove an insupported charge to the Colony, much disfurnished by the victualling of divers shipps lately returned thence, and so ill provided by a deceptful cropp, w[ch] seemed large, but proved scant, as wee dare not acquaynt yo[r] Lop[s] what experience perswades us, That there is like to followe in the Colonie some great distresse for victualls except by speedy supply hence they be relieved.

There is likewise in the Colony a most dangerous want of Powder, so great, as if the savages should but knowe advantage they have thereby they might easily in one day destroy all o[r] people.

There is most extreame want of hose, shoes, and all apparell, even to a dangerous empeachement of their healthes: and that so generall, as the provisions carried in these late shipps, will not as farr as wee cann learne, supply the Tenth part of their necessities. The want of such wonted supplies, will undoubtedly much dismay and deject the Colony. But when they shall understand of the Companies dissolucon, for the continuance of whose Governem[t] and the Liberties they enjoyed under them, they were most importunate suitors to his Ma[tie] and that they are returned under those handes w[ch] they so much abhorred:[1] Wee doubt no possible meanes will be found to keepe the greatest and best part of the Colonie from imediatly cominge away. For wee are credibly informed, that some of the chiefs, have allready by sellinge of their Estates, made preparacon upon the first notice of the change, to leave the Country. But when further they shall heare the newes

[1] *I.e.*, under the control of Sir Thomas Smith, the chief manager of the company during the first twelve years.

of the late contract,[1] whereby all their hopes shal be quite extinguished and all possibilitie of subsistance taken from them, wee cannot thinke that any will stay behinde that shall not be kept by force.

But howsoever it shall happen: sure we are that by these alteracons and courses, the mindes of the Planters wil be filled w^th^ such Jealousies and suspicions as it wil be a long while ere they wil be reduced to a firm resolucon of setting up the Rest of their Lives and hopes, in the Colony: which w^th^ all humble duty we are bold to say hath bin and will ever bee a disposition most pernicious to the establishing of the Plantation: And the overcoming thereof by the Company, we hold to have bin one of the greatest services that they did. This wee conceave to be the state of the Colonie now in Virginia w^ch^ though they should be persuad^d^ or forced to stay yet w^th^-out supply of others sent hence, they must needs come to nothinge in a very short space, although they had noe other enemy.

As for adventuringe hence, what by the disgracinge of the Action itselfe, and the undeserved suffrings of the late Companie, the businesse is brought to such a stand, as seemes incredible: there being no preparacon that wee can heare of not only of any shipp, but of any man to goe to Virginia whereas comonly for divers yeares before, there were foure or five shipps in readinesse, and as many hundreds of men, at this tyme of the yeare.

So that even in that reguard also the Colony will find themselves both in great discomfort and in great danger. For although formerly they had no Forte on the Land to hinder a forraigne enemy: yet especially in the latter tymes, there was such a boundance of shipping comminge and goinge continually to Virginia that there hath bin sometymes told seaventeen sayle

[1] The reference here is to a contract authorized by the king, with a Mr. Ditchfield, by which the crop of tobacco, for the first two years, was to be limited to 200,000 pounds, for which he was to pay the planters at the rate of 2*s*. 4*d*. per pound for the higher grades, and 1*s*. 4*d*. for the lower. Four hundred thousand pounds were not deemed enough at these rates. Bruce, *Economic History of Virginia*, I. 278.

together in James River. Whereby besides that it was a continuall terror to the Natives it would have bin a difficult thinge to endamage the Colonie, w$^{th}$out the power both of many shipps, and many souldiers, W$^{ch}$ was amongst divers others, a very mayne securitie and encouragement to persuade men boldly to goe to Virginia. But that and all other helpes being now foyled or much empayred although the nomber of men be at least Three tymes as many as when wee undertooke the Governem$^{t}$; yet will wee Ingenuously yield, that equall thanks and equall honour wil be due to them, who shall now recover and restore it to that prosperous and flourishing estate to w$^{ch}$ by Gods blessinge o$^{r}$ cares and labours had brought it, untill it was marred by them, who as appeares never loved it, but for their owne indirect ends, w$^{ch}$ they have industriously pursued. Thus much touching the present estate of the Plantation, and the late generall decay thereof.

Wherein wee hope yo$^{r}$ Lop$^{s}$ will excuse both our playnes[1] and prolixitie, tending to no other end, but only to present unto yo$^{r}$ Lop$^{s}$ viewe the cleare state and true neture of the Disease; that so yo$^{r}$ Lop$^{s}$ in yo$^{r}$ great wisdome may the better discerne and provide the proper remedies. Towards w$^{ch}$ since yo$^{r}$ Lop$^{s}$ have bin also pleased to require some preparative as it were of o$^{r}$ opinions: wee will now humbly apply our selves to that consideration w$^{th}$out w$^{ch}$ all the rest were but griefe and labour.

And here first wee are in duety forced to deliver unto yo$^{r}$ Lo$^{ps}$, that the restoring, supporting and re advancem$^{t}$ of that Plantation, wee hold to bee a worke, though of great necessitie for the honour, yea and service of his Ma$^{tie}$, these tymes considered: yet w$^{th}$ all of soe extreame difficultie, that it is not to be rashly and unadvisedly undertaken, but w$^{th}$ great circumspection, care, and preparacon, with assurance also of great assistance.

For not to insist much, upon the nature and greatnes of the worke, so remote from the favourers, so vicine[2] to mighty maligners of it: and inded fitter for the power and purse of a

[1] Plainness.

[2] Neighboring.

Great Prince and State, then of private Adventure$^{rs}$, and those allready exhaust and tyred; the wounds w$^{ch}$ since that great wound of the Massacre, it hath more lately receaved, from their handes whome it least beseemed, are still so wide and bleedinge, that unlesse his Ma$^{tie}$, and yo$^{r}$ Lo$^{ps}$ as deputed from him, shall vouchsafe to apply a soveraine hand for the healing of them, wee are resolute of opinion, that it is impossible, the Plantation carried as formerly by private persons, should either prosper or long subsist: Those woundes wee conceave are these. First the generall disreputacon of the Business (Reputation being a principall pillar of all great actions) and that partly by some errors, neglects and disasters, but principally by the late faction, though of a few and small Adventurers yet strongly and strangely inanimated and supported agaynst the great Body of Companie: whereof in fien also by undermining misinformacons they have wrought the Disolucon; and consequently lefte all, both Adventurers and Planters, in an utter uncertaynty of their Rights, Titles and Possessions: though promise was made that they should be reassured to them, w$^{ch}$ these men have neglected to see performed.

Secondly the great discouragem$^{t}$ of sundry not of the meanest both Adventurers and Planters, some of them persons, and others also of good qualitie: by whose cares and labours, together w$^{th}$ their friends and purses, the Plantation having formerly receaved no small encrease and benefit, to the Planters great comfort and content (w$^{ch}$ they have not forborne from tyme to tyme to declare): yet have they by the unjust calumnies and clamors of these men, bin continually prosecuted w$^{th}$ all variety of extremitie, to the rewarding of them with evill for their good deservings, and to the disheartening of all other, to succeed in like care and industry.

Thirdly the present extreame povertie and consumpcon of the Plantacion being for want of the accustomed yearly supplies, reduced to that paucetie of men and want of all sorts well neere of necessary provision, that it cannot be restored but w$^{th}$ an huge expence, no less allmost then to sett up a new Plantation.

Nowe touching the disreputacon of the Action, and the generall dishearteninge of the Adventurers and Planters, such especially as have spared neither paynes nor expence, for the recovering, supporting and advancinge the Plantation: We humbly crave yo$^{r}$ Lop$^{s}$ favourable patience, though wee somewhat enlarge our selves in this place, to present in part the Injustice and greaveousnes of those wounds to the hono$^{ble}$ minds and skillfull hands of yo$^{r}$ Lop$^{s}$: Seeing that in our understandinge the curing of them by yo$^{r}$ Lop$^{s}$, may be a meanes to revive agayne the generally deaded hearts of both Adventurers and Planters and to adde a new lustre and grace to the Action.

Amongst the many glorious workes of the late Kinge, there was none more eminent, then his Gracious enclination, together w$^{th}$ the propagation of Christian Religion, to advance and sett forward a new Plantacion in the new world, W$^{ch}$ purpose of his continued till the last, manifested by his Ma$^{t}$ many publique and private speeches by divers L'res of his, and by his sundry Proclamacons, so that their faults are farr the greater, who, as imediatly shal be declared, did malitiously and cunningly pervert those Gracious intencons of his Mat$^{ie}$ by scandalizing the Government as it then stood, as neither convenient here nor likely there to advance the prosperitie of the Colonie; and by insinuating assurances, that they themselves would mayntayne that worke by better meanes. Which his Ma$^{tie}$ conceavinge (as it was reason) they would not so boldly have promised of themselves, being so great a worke unlesse they had had both knowledge and meanes to goe thorough w$^{th}$ it; did also believe: and so they became the undertakers. And now, as it hath bin ever farr from o$^{r}$ practize and agaynst o$^{r}$ present desires to fall upon the persons of any men, where necessitie and justice of the cause doth not necessarilie require it: yet at this tyme it is impossible to cleare this pointe to yo$^{r}$ Lop$^{s}$ without naming some of their persons and particularizing their Actions. About six yeares agoe, when by reason of the apparant misprosperinge of the Plantation, and the fowlnes of the Accounts here, (the then Treasurer being Governour of ffower or ffive other Companies,[1] w^ch^ excused his neglect of attending this business,) the Governem^t^ of the Companie was translated from S^r^ Thomas Smith and Alderman Johnson, into S^r^ Edwin Sandis, and after into the Earle of Southampton's hands and their deputies: it is notoriously knowne how they w^th^ Captayne Argoll and other friends, partly peradventure through discontent for being removed from their places, but principally through feare, (their accounts, depredacons, Piracies and misgovernem^t^ being now questioned before the Counsell and in the Companies Courts) perpetuall disturbed and disgraced by severall wayes, both to his Ma^tie^ and to the world, all the present proceedings of the Companie, to the great disheartninge of the Companie here, and no small disadvantage of the Colonie. And of this, and of the bad effects of it, all our bookes and memories are full. But yet by God's assistance, and the unwearied courage of the Companie; wee ridd out this storme. The next blowe, as wee had reason to believe, proceeding by their underhand raysinge of new spiritts, drawne to disturbe us for their owne gayne was the bringing in of new and severall projects concerning Tobacco: w^ch^ was for the instant the only comoditie whereby the Planters mayntayned themselves, and so under colour of advancing profitt to his Ma^tie^ sometimes (as hath been before touched) wee were forbidden to bring in any Tobacco, sometimes to bring in but a small quantitie, and sometimes comaunded to bring in all. W^ch^ varying directions did so distract and confound the Adventurers and Planters, that it had in a manner ruyned the Plantation.

But yet by Gods assistance, and the constancy of the Companie, wee ridd out this storme also. The instruments in this worke that especiallie appeared, were the then S^r^ Lionell Cranfield,[2] Mr. Jacob and some others: to the extreame damage of the Company, enrichement of themselves, and deceyt of his Ma^tie^ as was at large expressed and offered to be proved in the

[1] Sir Thomas Smith was presiding officer of the East India, Muscovy, Northwest Passage, and Somers Islands companies, as well as of the Virginia Company.

[2] Afterward Earl of Middlesex and lord high treasurer.

last Parliament. Thirdly by the procuremen$^{t}$ of that part, divers scandalous peticons agayns$^{t}$ the company in generall, and many in perticuler did putt us to much vexacon and trouble. But their accusacons were so fals, that wee also overcame this Third assault.

After this another stratagem was obtruded upon us, under pretence of friendship and love of the Plantation. The Earle of Middlesex then Lo: high Treasurer of England who in respect of his place, was to take into his consideracon all thinges that had relacon to his Ma$^{ts}$ revennue, did first propound to S$^{r}$ Edwin Sandis, and afterwards to the Ea: of Southampton, the Lo: Cavendish and S$^{r}$ Edwin Sandis together that the King, he knewe, had by S$^{r}$ Thomas Smithes meanes and Alderman Johnsons, and some great friends and instruments of theires bin strangely possessed agaynst the forme of our Governmen$^{t}$, and the consequences of it: and particularly that they had made such advantage by traducing the names of the Earle of Southampton and S$^{r}$ Edwin Sandis, that the business of the Plantacon fared the worse for their sakes. That he had already in Generall spoken w$^{th}$ his Ma$^{tie}$ and assured him, that the whispers and relacons of those men, had an eye to their owne safetie, and not the Colonie's good; and that thereupon the King referred the whole consideracon of the Plantation, and what was best to be done, to his care.

Upon this he propounded unto those before named, that the best way to engage the Kinge in his care of the Plantations, and to make it impossible for any hereafter to disturbe the Companie, as they had formerly done, was to thinke of some such meanes, whereby the profit of his Ma$^{tie}$, and the good of the Plantation, might hand in hand goe together. And to speake truth; though those he spoke w$^{th}$ all, were at first very unwilling to swallowe this guilded pill, as having heard of the stile he used in negotiating other businesses of this nature: yet he was so full of protestacons in it, ever pretending the Companies good, and w$^{th}$ all procured further intimacon to the Earle of Southampton, that no service of his could be more acceptable to his Ma$^{tie}$ then this now propounded: that upon these protestacons and assurance they engaged themselves to treat of a contract between his Ma[tie] and the companies. In the making whereof, the said Earle of Midd. remembered not his promised care of the Plantations; but in truth from one degree to another, wrested us to such condicons and such a rate, as was very dammeagh to the Plantacions. But upon serious debate in maney and full Courts, upon the whole matter wee were resolved, considering the protection of the Colonies, and favour promised; and to be free from those frequent projects that in former tymes had soe much wronged and disturbed us, to accept an hard bargayne: conceavinge that though it were not so good as wee desired, and was fitt to have bin offered; yet by it we shall be in a better case and way of benefitting the Plantations, then formerly wee were.

And so in Michealmas terme, 1622, this contract w[ch] began to be treated of in Easter terme, was concluded by the subscription of the Earle of Middlesex his hand, and by sending the company word, that that day the whole Counsell board had given their assent thereunto, w[ch] was the first tyme the Company understood that they had heard of the matter. The contract thus concluded, a great Tempest arose by what secrett cause and underhand procurement, wee may guess, but not affirm. But in a Court of the Company upon the 4th of December following, one Mr. Wrote[1] Cosen Germane to the Earle of Middlesex, (discontent[d] also that he was passed over in the election of Officers) did w[th] a passionate and blasting speech, inveigh agaynst the Contract, and the managing thereof w[th] sallary: agaynst the proceeding in the Treaty of it, as that it had bin unduly and unjustly carried, that men had bin overawed, and that it had bin procured to private ends. Whereof not being able to make any shadowe of proofe and persisting still in his violent and contemptuous Demeande, upon a full hearinge he was thrust out of the Companie, and upon that ground joyned himself to S[r] Thomas Smith, Alderman Johnson

[1] Samuel Wrote was son of Robert Wrote of Gunton, in Suffolk, England. He was a leading opponent of the Sandys-Southampton faction, and because of his violent language was suspended by them from the company.

and that opposite party and drewe also with him Two more of his Companions, and so now made shewe of a formall party agaynst the Company. But for all this, wee still mayntayned the reputacon of o^r^ proceedings. The next of o^r^ troubles in order, (proceeding from what secrett cause, that w^ch^ follows will give yo^r^ Lop^s^ more reason of conjecture, then wee will now affirme) was, that this opposite party then attayned to about 25 in nomber, had some secrett encouragem^t^ or other given them, directly to oppugne the Contract; w^ch^ as is before declared was so formally made: and gave some reasons in writing agaynst it to the then Lord Tre^r^; who receaving them, gave the company first suspicon of double intelligence and indirectness in his dealinges.

But howsoever, the Earle of Southampton, the Lo: Cavendish, S^r^ Edwin Sandis, and some other, being called by the Earle of Middlesex to his Chamber at Whitehall, then thought, that they had given such answers to them, as that his Lop^p^ rested satisfied. But his Lop^p^ after, speaking w^th^ the Earle: of Southampton and the rest before named, told them that they that had opposed, were a clamorous Company, and that to make the business goe current, it were best that their objections and o^r^ answers should be heard at the Counsell table. And upon hearing thereof, their accusacons, and o^r^ answers, the Earle of Middlesex, who assumed the chief knowledge and care of that business, did in the close of that hearinge use the words formerly rehearsed, of the leaud [1] carriage in former tymes, and of the latter in a manner miraculous recoverie.

A greater testimony of o^r^ integritie and their guilt, could not be given. But as the sequall will manifest, and as wee have since found in other of his Lop^s^ proceedings, he meant to loose nothing by those words. Howsoever it was, and whatsoever wee suspect, not intending now to dive into those misaries, from that day forward, to the Conclusion of this business he professedly made himselfe the patron to that side, and enemy to the company, for w^ch^ wee appeal to yo^r^ Lop^s^ better knowledge. Afterwards about that Contract were divers meetings

[1] Lewd.

before the Lords, where it was principally inveighed agaynst by S'r Nathaniell Rich; speaking agaynst the injustice and unconscionablenes of it; protesting that he had ever sold his Tobacco for ffive shillings a pound one w$^{th}$ another, and that every pound cost him Two shillings six pence in the Sumer Islands: and now to give a Third away to the King and peradventure the price not to be much higher was agaynst justice and conscience. And here by the way, wee humbly crave leave to say thus much, that his conscience now serves him in this new Contract, to force the Planter and the Adventurer to sell their Tobacco, the best sort 2$^{s}$4$^{d}$ and the second sort at sixteene pence a pound. But upon that former Demonstrative Argument of his, though it were so fully answered as nothing could be more, yet the Earle of Middlesex took his ground to condemn the contract he had signed, as hurtfull to the Plantacions; and to commaund the companies to thinke of propounding a better, and to bring it in writing w$^{th}$in Two daies: w$^{ch}$ was accordingly done: and therein shewed that the hardnesse of this contract, was not by the Companies proposition, but by his Lop$^{s}$ pressure. And therefore urged what had bin offered to his Lop$^{s}$ at the first; that his Ma$^{tie}$ would be contented w$^{th}$ a fourth and not require a third of o$^{r}$ Tobacco. To w$^{ch}$ in great scorne his Lop$^{p}$ replyed that take Two pence out of six pence their would remayne a Groat. But the last Parliament saw that his best invention, was by adding 3£ to 40$^{s}$ to make up ffive pounds. But in conclusion that Contract was dissolved, and a commaund laid upon the Companies by his Lop$^{s}$ procurement to bring all o$^{r}$ Tobaccoes in, under colour that Three pence custom was abated; whereas in truth by his admitting also of all Spanish Tobacco, upon S'r John Wolstenholmes [1] motion wee could not vent a third part of it here: and so by computacon, in respect of the quantitie unvented, wee paid neere doouble as much as before: w$^{ch}$ was his only favour to the Plantations.

The contract thus dissolved as publiquely damageable by the incouragement of the Earle of Middlesex, and industry of

[1] A leading member of the company.

the ffive and twenty before menconed, (that so place might be made for this latter contract, so privately beneficiall, for so by the effect it hath appeared): the Governm$^{t}$ was now likewise to be questioned and altered, or else they compassed not their ends. Which to bring about, these two wayes were used. First a peticion was delivered to his Ma$^{ty}$ by Alderman Johnson, in the name of the rest, inveighing against the latter Governm$^{t}$ and magnifying the former. And in the end, desiring a commission to examine the proceedings of those last ffower.

This peticon was by the Company at large answered to his Ma$^{tie}$ and wee joyned in the point of having o$^{r}$ actions examined by the Comission: but w$^{ch}$ all thought it just, and desired, that their Twelve years Govermen$^{t}$ before might be also examined: w$^{ch}$ accordingly was ordered. The second means used by them, was to rayse up Captayne Butler, who hasting from the Summer Islands to Virginia, where he stayed but a few weeks, upon his returne delivered to his Ma$^{tie}$ a paper called The unmasking of Virginia. The substance of w$^{ch}$ was first the dispraise of the country and making of it an unfit place for any English Colony; and next scandalizing the Governm$^{t}$ of it, both here, and there. What concerned the colonie, was proved to be false by fforty witnesses: who chaunced to be in Towne then, and had bin often and long in the Colonie: And was endeavoured to be mayntayned by him by two meanes only: one by practizing to gett the hands of Two men unto it, to whome he owed money and deferred payment: who when they heard it read in Co$^{rt}$, protested that they never saw what they sett their hands to, and that Capt: Butler told them it was a Paper, w$^{ch}$ he would shew the King for the good of the Plantation: and desired the companies pardon; for whatever was there said was false. Secondly, he would made it to have bin better believed, by a forged L$^{re}$ w$^{ch}$ hee brought to Sr. John Bourchire from his daughter Mrs. Whittakers:[1] who

[1] Probably the wife of Jabez Whittaker, a member of the council of Virginia and brother of Rev. Alexander Whittaker, formerly of Coxendale on James River.

knew it was not her hand. This was alleddged at the counsell Table: and Capt: Butler answered that she was sick and dictated it to him, and he wrote it. But since, both shee and her husband being come over, they bothe forsweare it, and say it was none of her doing nor direction. But howsoever, by these meanes the opposite party thus farre obteyned their ends, that by the Defamation, and this trouble ensuinge, a very great nomber that intended to have gone over, were descouraged.

But yet for all this, the Companie knewe their cause to be just and justifiable, that they did not abandon it: but prepared themselves to give divers charges before the commission$^{rs}$, agayns$^{t}$ divers of the partie opposite; and professed themselves ready to make their owne defence whensoever they should be charged. But whilst the comission sate farther to descourage us, first all o$^{r}$ Bookes, and after the minutes of them were sent far away from us; that none of the L'res that then came from Virginia were to be seene by us, being all seazed on by the Comission$^{rs}$. But touching the rest of the caridge of that comission, because it was at large delivered in Parliment, and offered to be proved, if further proceedinge in that businesse had not bin forborne upon a L're written to the house from His Ma$^{tie}$ wee will now to yo$^{r}$ Lo$^{ps}$ say only this: That whatsoever was brought by us concerninge accounts, depredacon, misgovernement, and divers other crimes, agaynst perticuler persons, was by this comission, (especially directed by the Earle of Midd.) shuffled of for all the tyme, till the comission was even at the end nothing done upon them. And on the contrary, whatsoever could be gathered out of the fragments of L'res from discontented persons in Virginia concerning either the place, or governem$^{t}$ was diligently collected by them, and receaved by the Earle of Middlesex as a great testimony agaynst us; and would not take those other L'res for proof w$^{ch}$ wee ever guided o$^{r}$ selves by; and came from the Governour and counsell there. And lastly some three dayes before their Comission ended, they putt us on a sodayne to answere to 39 Articles, or else they would take them pro confesso. This they thought for us impossible to doe. But wee deceaved their expectacon; and they could not find in the least perticuler, any just ground to make any report agaynst us.[1]

By all this the Earle of Middlesex and that partie, perceaving the companie would not be beaten off a good cause; there was a practise to try whether wee had rather part from the business, or from our mony. Where upon wee were called before the Counsell agayne, and there that side as compassionate affecters of the Plantation, urged the want of corne and other necessaries there, and that they were like to perish for want of provisions. The Earle of Midd. replied, it was a matter of so great importance, and concerned the lives of so many of the King's subjects, that if the Companie would not presently take order for sending supplies, the state would call in their Pattent. Whereupon the Companie conceaving that if they did send supplyes, their Pattent would not be taken from them, underwritt to a Roule (though they knewe the necessitie was nothing so great) foure thousand and odd pounds, w$^{ch}$ was paid and sent: and those Gentlemen that before seemed so zealous, subscribed Twelve pounds, and paid it not. Upon w$^{ch}$ comparison wee leave it to yo$^{r}$ Lop$^{s}$ to judge w$^{ch}$ party was the true father of this child. This then not succeeding according to their desires, certayne obscure persons were found out by the Earle of Midd., to be sent into Virginia, as Comission$^{rs}$ for these two ends, as wee have since found. First to sifte out what they could agaynst the forme of o$^{r}$ Governm$^{t}$ here and there: and next to persuade the people to become Peticon to his Ma$^{tie}$ for a newe [2] W$^{ch}$ succeeded not according to their expectacon. For by the Colonies Peticons, answeres to those papers that had bin delivered agaynst them, and divers other remonstrances to his Ma$^{tie}$ from a Generall Assembly there they shewed the misery wherein they lived, or rather languished

[1] The answer was prepared by Sir Edwin Sandys, Nicholas Ferrar, and Lord Cavendish, who scarcely slept in the interval. Carter's *Ferrar*, p. 71.

[2] Form of government.

in S'r Thomas Smithe's tyme; and their happy estate in this latter Government: concludinge that if his Ma$^{tie}$ intended to alter the Government, and put it into the former hands, their humble suite to him was; That Comission$^{rs}$ might be sent over to another purpose before declared. The writinges themselves will manifest this more at large. These comissioners thus sent to Virginia, the Earle of Midd. and the rest were not idle in further distractinge the Companie, to give their assent for surrendring their Pattent, and altringe the forme of Governm$^{t}$; and a newe one was proposed. W$^{ch}$ according to order they takinge into consideracon, w$^{th}$ duetie refused: rendring also in writing the reasons of their refusall. Whereupon a Quo Warranto was directed by the Earle of Midd. suggestion for the calling in of their Pattent.

In the meanetime, to affright men, both from cominge to and much more from speaking in Courts, mens wordes were then carped at and complayned of: and their persons by the Earle of Midd. prosequution, were upon quick hearinge sent to prison.

Yet for all this the Comp$^{n}$ stood to their owne Justificacon, and defence of their Pattent. Now Mr. Atturney,[1] according to the duty of his place and instructions given him, urged the misgovernem$^{t}$ of the Companie, and consequently the ruyne of the Plantation. To w$^{ch}$ point we were willinge to joyne issue. But afterwards in o$^{r}$ reply to his pleadinge w$^{th}$out further enquiry of the former allegation, advantage was taken upon o$^{r}$ mispleading, and in fine w$^{th}$out any farther ground that wee knowe of, the Patent was Trinity terme following, condemned: But for anything that we have yet seene no judgment entered. Yo$^{r}$ Lop$^{s}$ by the perticulers before related do see by what courses wee were reduced to this extremitie. One thinge yet wee thinke most necessary to adde; It hath bin said by many, and perticulerly by some principall persons of the opposite partie, that the dissolutions of these Plantacons was part of the Count of Gondomars Instructions. And cer-

[1] Thomas Coventry, knighted in 1617, appointed attorney-general January 11, 1621, lord keeper in 1625, and died in 1640.

taynely wee found his activenes in negotiatinge here, such, that in bringing about his owne ends, he could create here, instruments of o$^{r}$selves agaynst our selves. Wee say not that he and other Spanish Ministers practised thus amongst us. These two only perticulers, wee crave leave to offer unto yo$^{r}$ Lop$^{s}$ Judgem$^{ts}$. When S'r Samuell Argoll some six or seaven yeares since, was vehemently complayned agaynst by Padre Maestro and the Spanish secretarie then here for Piracie agaynst the Kinge of Spaines subjects in the West Indies he no sooner came home from Virginia, and appeared an opposite to the present Company, who questioned him for divers misdemeanors and amongst others for this; but the heate of the Spanish accusacon did presently cease. Our second observacon is this, yo$^{r}$ Lop$^{s}$ cannot but remember, w$^{th}$ what extreame earnestnes the Count of Gondomar and afterwards Don Carlo di Coloma,[1] inveighed agaynst Capt. Butler whilst he was in Summer Islands about the Spanish wrack. And so violent were they about it that the Lo: Stewart, now w$^{th}$ God, and the Lo: Chamberlaine, were entreated to come on purpose to the Sumer Islands company, about that business. And a comission was directed by the Lords of the Counsell, to examine the truth of the cause in the Sumer Islands. W$^{ch}$ Captain Butler having been forewarned by some friends of his left his Governmen$^{t}$ before he had leave, and before the arrivall of the Comission: Having first there endeavoured to alienate the minds of the people from the forme of Governmen$^{t}$ here. But he was no sooner come home, and delivered to his Ma$^{tie}$ The unmasking of Virginia before spoken of, but there was an end of Don Carlo Di Colomas prosecution. Wee have related the particulars; and make no application.

As for the late Comission,[2] w$^{ch}$ hath suceeded in the place of the Companies; if wee might have seen the business seriously

[1] Spanish ambassador after Gondomar.

[2] On June 24, 1624, shortly after the decision of Chief-Justice Ley revoking the charter, the king appointed a commission of sixteen persons, among whom were Sir Thomas Smith and other opponents of Sandys and Southampton, to take charge temporarily of Virginia affairs; and on July 15, 1624, he enlarged this commission by forty more persons.

taken into the Grave cares and prosequuted w[th] the Noble paynes of those most hono[ble] personages, whose names are inserted in the sayd Comission: wee should have hoped to have seene some good effect befitting their great and eminent worth. But whilst their more weighty affairs have hindered them the business hath bin principally carried only by those persons that were the chiefe opposers of the late Comp: ffor although there be named divers worthy Gentlemen, and Citizens likewise, in the Comission: yet as wee understand, the most of them have forborne altogether to appeare at any meeting. Wherefore when either in o[r] wordes or thoughts, wee complayne of any proceedings of the late Comission wee alwayes except both all the persons of Honour and indifferency: and only intend those others, whose stomacks were so great, as they durst undertake the overthrowinge of the late Companie; and yet their harts so narrow, as they have not dared to adventure all of them during these Nyne moneths, so far as wee can learne, one five pounds to the advancem[t] or subsistance of the Plantation.

By the publique L'res of the Governour, delivered them in July last, they understood of the extreame want of Powder in the Colonie: and were often told from us of the great danger that might ensue thereby: Yet did they neglect the sending of any in the shipp or in the second: but about Christmas, and since in March they have sent a small quantitie, obteyned by his late Ma[ts] guifts (as wee heare) out of the Tower.

This did not the late Company: who upon notice of the massacre, did by the first ship send 42 Barrels of Powder; for halfe whereof the Officers having disturbed the money, are yet unsatisfied.

Whereas all the ffower shippes now sent, were prepared in the Comp[ns] tyme; these last Comissioners callinge in the Comissions graunted them by the late Company, made them take new as from themselves that so they might glory upon anothers foundacon. But whilst they thus hunted after windy ambition, hindringe the two first shipps from takinge a faire winde; they have bin the causes of all the lamentable calamities and distresses, w$^{ch}$ in so long voyages must needs befall them.

The principal scope of his late Ma$^{ts}$ comission to them, as wee understand was that they should finde a better forme of Governem$^{t}$ for the Plantacions advancement; and therein is especially promised the conservacon of every mans right. Intentions worthy the wisedome and Justice of so great a Prince. But as farr as wee can understand these comissioners have done nothing towards either of these ends: But quite contrary to the second.

By an unknown contract, w$^{ch}$ themselves will not so much as declare much less are able to defend; they have sought to have amongst themselves, twice as much upon every mans goods, as they will leave to the Owner thereof. And although they say only three of them are Contractors yet wee cannot believe it, having observed the ends of some of them for many years, to have constantly bin bent to the compassinge of some such advantage, as they have now by this bargayne gayned. It is constantly reported that they have liberally given that w$^{ch}$ was not their owne, to those who have no right thereto; as namely the Colonies kine to S'r Samuell Argoll and Mr. Woodall surgeon to S'r Thomas Smith. But this and all their other proceedings are kept in great secrett: w$^{ch}$ breeds suspicon that they have not bin good: else why doe they fly the Light? This is cleane contrary to the use of the late Company: who did all things in publique w$^{ch}$ was a cause of as great satisffacon, as this of distaste.

And as in this, so in all other thinges do they proceed cleane contrary to all right in o$^{r}$ understandinge. They publish their Intention of employinge S'r Samuell Argoll and Captaine Butler for Governours agayne in the Plantations agaynst whome the Colony hath professed open enmity. How they should make the Colony encrease by these means, w$^{ch}$ will bring home most of them that are there allready wee cannot imagine.

Neither are S'r Thomas Smith nor Alderman Johnson fitt or likely men to reunite the late Companie, or to drawe them onto any thing for the Plantations advancement, since as the whole world knowes the late Company have not only allwayes conceaved extreamly ill of them but in the yeare 1623 putt up publique accusations agaynst them, of very dangerous Consequence. As for the Colony yo$^{r}$ Lop$^{s}$ have formerly heard their like opinions.

Nor cann the late Companie conceave Mr. Wrote a fitt Instrum$^{t}$ to sett forward the business; whome they thought unworthy to bee of their Societie.

Nor that those who out of pretence for New Englands good, have truly wronged Virginia should now runne right way for the behalfe thereof. Nor in sum that those who have little or no interest in the Plantation should be so sencible of it as were fitt. In w$^{ch}$ number wee accompte S'r Nathaniell Rich; who to our knowledge hath not adventured any thinge for the good thereof but contrary wise hath been so perpetuall a hinderer and disturber of the Action, that the body of the Company, addressed a Peticon of Complainte, to the last Parliament, cravinge justice against him, for his injurious and most unworthy practices.

Nor that they that meane not to adventure anythinge, will be able to persuade others to doe that w$^{ch}$ themselves forbeare.

Nor that ever they will do the adventurers of the late Companie, right, in matters of their Estates, that have so violently endeavoured to do them wrong in their Honors Reputacons, having intended as themselves wright, a Reformacon and correction of the Original court bookes of the late Companie then possessed by them, if they could have gott into their hands certayne copies of them w$^{ch}$ Mr. Necholas Ferrar late Deputy at his owne charges caused to be transcribd.[1] But before there severe order came to him he had delivered his copys to the Earle of Southampton: who sent the comissioners word, that

[1] These copies are the identical volumes now possessed by the Library of Congress (having come to it from the library of President Jefferson) and recently put into print.

he would as soone part w$^{th}$ the evidences of his Land, as w$^{th}$ the said Copies, being the evidence of his honour in that Service: So by this meanes have the Original Court bookes yet escaped purging: And w$^{th}$ all duety wee humbly beseech yo$^{r}$ Lop$^{s}$ that they may hereafter be protected from it: And that howsoever yo$^{r}$ Lop$^{s}$ shall please for the future to dispose of the Companie, that the records of their past Actions may not be corrupted and falsified.

As for their resolucions of orderinge the business, wee cannot say anythinge, because wee heare nothing, and we doubt they meane nothinge ffor all that wee heare tends only to nothing. They dislike the sending of nombers of men. They professe the reducinge of all trading to a Joynt stock or Magazine: w$^{ch}$ courses in o$^{r}$ judgements tend directly to the subversion of the Plantation at least to the appropriatinge of it to themselves which to have bin the mayne end of some of them, the late Counsell and Companie for Virginia, have upon strong presumpcon bin long agoe induced to believe: and therefore have now thought themselves bound to declare it, that yo$^{r}$ Lop$^{s}$ in yo$^{r}$ Noble wisedomes may make such due prevencon as shall be fitt: Humbly beseechinge, that this perticular examinacon of their Actions and persons, may not be interpreted to proceed from private spleene, but only from a sincere desire of the Plantations advancement.

Wee doubt and feare, that we have wearied yo$^{r}$ Lop$^{s}$ w$^{t}$ the large relation of the proceedings of these men, wee meane the partie opposite to the late Companie and Colonie. Whereby as they have laid all kind of Disreputacion upon the Action, and made that in the estimacon of the world vilde and contemptible, w$^{ch}$ before was held worthy, beneficiall, and honourable: so by their manifold and incessant practises, to wrong and oppress, to defame and disgrace, by unjust and unworthy aspirsions, and contumelies, (and that by word and writing over all the kingdome) the innocency of men zealous for the good of Virginia, for no other fault save only for their love of right and justice; they have bredd a great disheartninge and discouragemt of many the most forward and most constant adventurers whose industry also and labours bin of great use to the Plantation, All w$^{ch}$ being wearied out w$^{th}$ their mallice and injuries and loath to spend more of their lives in so unthankfull a service, are humble suitors unto yo$^{r}$ Lo$^{ps}$, that they may be spared from all farther employment in this Action. And that if these men will now at length apply themselves seriously to the businnes of the Colonies both w$^{th}$ their paynes and purses, w$^{ch}$ they have hitherto spared and undertake, (w$^{ch}$ they owe to his Ma$^{tie}$ and the State) the repairinge those ruynes of the Plantation, whereof they have bin the chiefe cause and instruments: the Government thereof may, as it is, be continued in them, giving fitt securitie for so great a debt and duty. For wee protest unto yo$^{r}$ Lo$^{ps}$ upon our truth and fidelitie that if his Ma$^{ty}$ may be served, the Colony secured and cherished, justice duly administred, mens rights and states preserved, innocent men not oppressed, and malefactors not protected and rewarded: wee shall be so farr from envying the glory of their Governement, that extinguishinge for ever the memory of all their former inguries, wee will be ready to doe them all fitt service that they shall require.

# INDEX

Abbay, Thomas, 160; publishes Smith's manuscripts, 75; dedications written by, 77–78, 119–121.
Abbot, Jeffrey, 76, 140, 162; sent to punish the conspirators, 189; character, 303.
*Abigale*, ship, 355.
Accomac Indians, 89; fishing methods, 103; character, 354–355.
Accomack, company's land at, 351, 351 n.
Acohanocks, 89.
Acorns, uses, 90, 91.
Acquaviva, Father Claude, letter to, 228.
Acquintanacksuaks, 87.
Acrigge, George, 162.
Adams, Robert, 169, 426.
Aguiar, Don Rodrigo de, 291.
Alberton, Robert, 140.
Algernourne Fort, 11, 200; described, 223.
Alicock, Jeremy, 126.
*American Anthropologist*, 113 n.
Amocis, Indian spy, Smith tests the honesty of, 68–69.
Anacostans, 202. *See* Nacostans.
Anchanachuck, 49.
Anne, queen of Great Britain, 325 n.; Smith's letter to, 325.
Anone, 49.
Apokant, location, 42.
Appomattox Indians, 47, 84, 85, 113; Percy visits, 14, 14 n.; Smith entertained by, 34, 40, 54; Dale's conquest of, 305–306.
Appomattox River, 14 n., 83; discovery of, 161.
Aquia Creek, *see* Quia Creek.
Aquohanock, 352.
Arber, Edward, ed., *Works* of Captain John Smith, 4, 75, 291.
*Archaeologia Americana*, 4.
Archer, Gabriel, 125, 191; wounded by the Indians, 10, 32; returns to England, 71 n.; censures Smith, 52; Smith's injustice toward, 75; attempted abandonment of the colony, 130; opposition to the government, 194; conspiracy of, 196; *A Relatyon of the Discovery of our River*, 34 n.
Archer's Hope, discovered, 14.
Archer's Hope Creek, 15 n.
Argall, Samuel, 239; arrival at Jamestown, 189; French settlements destroyed by, 189 n., 227, 313; is despatched to the Bermudas, 202; deputy-governor of Virginia, 207; trading expeditions, 212, 213; petition for the discharge of bonds issued to, 275–276; settlement established by, 275 n.; encourages slave-trade, 282–283; expedition to the Potomac River, 300, 307; return to England, 317, 335; contribution to the *Generall Historie*, 328–334; government, 330, 433 n.; petitions the Council for supplies, 332; seeks redress for the murder of certain colonists, 333; trouble with the Virginia Company, 334, 334 n.; opinion of the Indians, 386; furnishes supplies for the colonists, 398; accusations against, 455; enmity of the colonists for, 457.
Argall's Gift, 338 n.; delegates from, 250.
Argall's Town, petition of the inhabitants of, 275–276; location, 275 n.
Argent, John, adventure, 389.
Arrohateck, 113; Smith at, 33, 33 n., 34.
Arrohateck Indians, 84.
Arsek Indians, 143.
Asbie, John, death, 20.
Ascacap, Indian village, Smith visits, 41.
Atlamuspincke, Indian village, 41.
Atquacke, 387.
Atquanachuke Indians, 89, 150.

Azores, Argall sails for, 211, 231; Lord Delaware at, 331.

Baggly, Anthony, 162, 163.
Bagnall, Anthony, 147.
Baldwin, rescues his wife, 360.
Ballagh, *History of Slavery in Virginia*, 337 n.
Baltimore, Lord, boundary of Maryland determined by, 86 n.
Bancroft, George, 248.
Bargrave, Captain George, 335–336; privileges granted to, 267.
Bargrave, Thomas, gift to the college, 351; death, 351 n.
Barnes, Joseph, 76, 119.
Barnes, Robert, 140.
Barret, Thomas, 337.
Bartas, Guillaume du, *La Création*, 371, 371 n.
Basse, Nathaniel, Indian attack upon, 361, 361 n.
Bathori, Sigismund, rewards Smith, 27.
Bayley, William, 140.
Beast, Benjamin, 21.
Becam, *see* Vieques.
Beckwith, William, 140.
Bedle, Gabriell, 159.
Beheathland, Robert, 126, 134, 162, 170, 172, 173.
Belfield, Richard, 140.
Bell, Henry, 160.
Bentley, William, 140, 162, 188.
Berkeley Hundred, first colony for, 338 n.
Berkeley, John, murdered by the Indians, 363 n.
Berkeley, Richard, 338 n.
Bermuda City, 306 n.
Bermuda Hundred, 34 n., 312, 333.
Bermuda Islands, 411; Sir Thomas Gates shipwrecked on, 201; provisions sought from, 202; English colonization of, 219; fortress at, 219 n.; described, 220; history of, 296 n.; Sir George Somers at, 300.
Biard, Father Pierre, letter of, 228–234; settlement of, 227; capture, 229; is taken to Virginia, 230; experiences before reaching France, 233.
Bigge, Richard, 426.
Birds, abundance of, 9, 37; kinds, 15
Black River, 84 n.
Blany, Edward, 426.
Bloodroot, uses, 93.
Blount, Captain, member of the council, 345.
Blount Point, 412.
Bohun, Laurence, physician to Delaware, 210, 210 n.; death, 344, 344 n.
*Bole Armoniac*, 82, 87, 143.
*Bonanova*, ship, 337.
Booth, John, 140, 324; contribution to the *Generall Historie*, 316–325.
Bourchier, Sir Henry, 405.
Bourchier, Sir John, 451.
Bourne, James, 140, 141, 147, 162.
Box, William, contribution to the *Generall Historie*, 297–301.
Boys, Cheney, 378 n.
Boys, John, 256; elected a burgess, 250.
Boys, Luke, 426.
Boys, Sarah, a captive among the Indians, 378, 378 n., 385, 385 n.
Bradford, William, friendship of, for Pory, 281.
Bradley, Thomas, 160.
Brandon, delegates from, 250.
Bread, Indian manner of making, 18.
Brereton, *Briefe and True Relation*, 21 n.
Brewster, William, 125; death, 20; trouble with Argall, 334, 334 n.
Brinton, Edward, 126, 162, 169, 170.
Brislow, Richard, 140.
Brookes, Edward, 126; death, 8.
Brookes, Sir John, 125; approves Smith's proposals, 375.
Brown, Alexander, *First Republic*, 304 n., 340 n., 362 n.; *Genesis of the United States*, 208, 217, 227, 297 n., 302, 321 n., 344 n., 396.
Browne, Edward, 358; death, 21.
Bruce, *Economic History of Virginia*, 442 n.
Brumfield, James, 126.
Buck, Richard, 333; opens the Virginia assembly, 248, 251, 251 n.
Buckler, Andrew, 153.
Burket, William, 140.
Burrows, Anne, 160.
Burrows, John, 160.
Burton, George, 159, 162.

Butler, Nathaniel, arrival, 389; searches for Argent, 390; rumors concerning, 391; governor of the Bermuda Islands, 411; the Virginia planters' answer to, 412-418; attacks the Virginia government, 438, 439; forgery of, 452; accusations against, 455; enmity of the colonists for, 457; "The Unmasked Face of Our Colony in Virginia as it Was in the Winter of the Yeare 1622," 389 n., 411, 451, 452.

Callicut, William, discovers silver, 156.
Canada, 105 n.
Canaries, John Smith arrives at, 32; colonists at, 122.
Cantrill, William, 140, 141; contribution to the *Generall Historie*, 316-325.
Capp, William, 256; elected a burgess, 250.
Cappahowasicke, 50; location, 50 n.
Capper, Thomas, 126.
Carayon, Father Auguste, S. J., *Première Mission des Jésuites au Canada*, 227.
Carleton, Sir Dudley, Pory's letter to, 282.
Carter, *Ferrar*, 453 n.
Cary, Henry, first Lord Hunsdon, 207.
Cary, Katherine, 207.
Cassatowap, quarrel with Thomas Savage, 353.
Cassen, George, 126; murder, 116.
Cassen, Thomas, 126.
Cassen, William, 126.
Castro, Vasco de, murder, 366.
Catataugh, 115.
Causey, Nathaniel, 426; murdered by the Indians, 360.
Causey, William, 140.
Cavendish, Lord, accusations against, 447, 449; efforts to retain the charter, 453 n.
Cecocawone, 145.
Champlain, Samuel de, *Voyages*, 150 n.
Charles I., king of Great Britain, 81 n.
Charles, Cape, 81.
Charles City, 306 n., 356 n., 418 n.; incorporated, 337, 337 n.; abandoned, 417.
Charles Hundred, 424.
Charter of Orders, Laws, and Privileges, 255, 256-257; adoption, 259; results of the revocation of, 400; history of the revocation, 450-455.
Chawonock, 163; described, 355.
Chawonoke Indians, 89.
Chesapeake Bay, Percy enters, 9; Smith anchors in, 32; natives of, attack colonists, 48; described, 81, 82, 222, 223; Smith explores, 141-151.
Chesapeake Indians, 84.
Chesapeake, town of, discovered, 89.
Chester, Captain Anthony, 344 n.; contribution to the *Generall Historie*, 340-344; voyage to Virginia, 340-344; fight with two Spanish men-of-war, 341-344.
Chew, John, 426.
Chicacoan Indians, 86, 372.
Chickahominies, 84; choose Opechancanough for king, 35 n.; Smith's expedition to, 39-40, 129, 157; colonists assisted by, 39 n.; trading methods of, 57; conspire against the colonists, 67-70; governors of, 84; character, 183-184; law concerning, 262; conclude a peace with Dale, 310-311; attacks upon, 323-324, 389; attack the colonists, 333.
Chickahominy River, 84, 157 n., 387; Smith explores, 41-43, 130, 387 n.
Chippokes Creeks, 83 n.
Cinquoateck, Smith anchors at, 60, 61.
City Point, 306 n., 356; delegates from, 249.
Clarke, John, 160.
Clayborne, William, 349.
Clergy, laws concerning, 271-272, 273.
Clovill, Eustis, 126.
Coan River, 86 n.
Coe, Thomas, 134, 140, 162, 177; failure to kill Smith, 196, 196 n.; report of, 198.
Cole, Edward, plot, 303 n., 304; execution, 304 n.
College, land grant for, 337, 337 n.; means of supporting, 338; contributions to, 350-351.

Collier, Samuel, 126, 153; remains with Powhatan, 163; death, 385.
Collings, Henry, 159.
Coloma, Don Carlo di, accuses Butler of piracy, 455.
*Colonial Records of Virginia, Senate Document Extra*, 248.
Columbus, Christopher, 77, 78; colony of, 365; imprisonment, 366.
Comfort, Cape, named, 11.
Commissioners for the Reformation of Virginia, questions put to Smith by, 399–405.
Copeland, Patrick, 356; starts subscription for a free school, 350 n.
Copper, desire of Indians for, 307.
Corn, 95–97; efforts to obtain, 37, 161, 165, 176, 323–324; rats devour, 185; price of, 414–415.
Cornelius, 398.
Cortes, Hernando, discoveries of, 301; conquest of Mexico, 386.
Cotten, Robert, 141.
Cotton, abundance of, 7; prodigious growth of, 349.
Council of New England, 191 n.
Council of Virginia, alters its government, 191; attitude toward Powhatan's coronation, 152–153; extract from a declaration by, 301–302; extract from a letter by, 345–347; policy of, 346, 346 n.
Couper, Thomas, 126.
Coventry, Sir Thomas, opposition to the company, 454, 454 n.
Craddock, Lieutenant, 141 n.
Cranfield, Lionel, *see* Middlesex, Earl of.
Crofts, Richard, 126.
Croshaw, Raleigh, 159, 162, 170, 173, 175, 204, 204 n., 383, 426; voyage to the Potomac, 372; experiences among the Indians, 376–378; plot to overthrow Opechancanough, 384; opinion of the Indians, 386, 388.
Cuba, 219, 219 n.
Cutler, Robert, 140.
Cuttatawomen, 47, 86.

Dale, Lady, privileges granted to, 267.
Dale, Sir Thomas, 401; arrival at Jamestown, 302, 320; political positions, 202 n.; establishes a settlement, 141, 305; deputy-governor of Virginia, 207; censures the colonists, 208; government of the colony, 220 n., 302–303, 303 n., 304; treatment of French prisoners, 230; Rolfe's letter to, 239–244; seeks a ransom for Pocahontas, 308; concludes a peace with the Indians, 309–311; private property instituted by, 312; a proposal to marry the daughter of Powhatan, 314–315; letter of, 316; return to England, 321.
Danvers, Sir John, political leadership, 429.
Dauxe, John, 160.
Davidson, Christopher, secretary for Virginia, 348, 348 n.
Davis, Captain James, 200; arrival, 294; Spanish spies arrested by, 321.
Davis, Thomas, elected a burgess, 250.
Dawson, William, 140.
Deane, Charles, editor of the *True Relation*, 29.
De Bry, map of, 53.
Delaware, Lady, friendship for Pocahontas, 237; privileges granted to, 267; presents Pocahontas at court, 329.
Delaware, Lord, 401; sails for England, 3, 211, 301; governor of Virginia, 191, 191 n.; arrival at Jamestown, 202, 297; biographical sketch of, 207; censures the colonists, 208; severe experiences at Jamestown, 210; government, 299; builds new forts, 300; death, 331; *Relation*, 208, 209–214.
Dermer, Thomas, arrival, 337; voyage up the Hudson, 337 n.
Dilke, Clement, 426.
*Discovery*, ship, 122 n.
Ditchfield, government contract with, 442 n.
Dixon, John, 229.
Dixon, Richard, 126.
Dods, John, 126, 162.
Dole, Richard, 141.
Dominica, Percy anchors at, 5 n.; Smith sails for, 32; colonists at, 122; sea-fight at, 340–344.
Dowman, William, 160.

Downs, Percy anchors in, 5; Smith encounters dangers in, 32.
Dowse, Thomas, 160, 256; makes known Volda's conspiracy, 189; elected a burgess, 249.
Drake, Sir Francis, circumnavigation of the globe, 59 n.
Dutchmen, allies of the savages, 170, 177, 188, 189; assist Powhatan, 175, 180–182.
Du Thet, settlement of, 227; death, 229.
Dyer, William, 134; conspiracy of, 186; failure to kill Smith, 196 n.; report of, 198.

Each, Captain, 416; sent to build a fort, 355.
East India School, 356, 356 n.
Edmonds, Sir Thomas, 207, 208.
Edward, Ould, 126.
Elizabeth City, 372; delegates from, 250; named, 259; incorporated, 337, 337 n.; Newce fortifies, 378.
Elizabeth, queen of Great Britain, 207.
Elizabeth River, 84 n.
*Elizabeth*, ship, 372.
Ellis, David, 162.
Emry, Thomas, 126; on the Chickahominy, 43.
Essex, Earl of, Lord Delaware implicated in rebellion of, 207.
Evans, 336.

Fairfax, Margery, death, 333.
Fairfax, William, Indians murder the family of, 333, 333 n.
Falls, the, of the James River, 48, 124; proposed expedition beyond, 64–65; West's settlement at, 192, 193; attack of the savages at, 301.
Fayal, 232.
Feld, Thomas, 141.
Felgate, Captain, 391.
Ferrar, John, 340 n., 406; deputy-governor, 335, 335 n., 344, 345 n.; privileges granted to, 405; political leadership, 429.
Ferrar, Nicholas, Jr., 247, 458; political leadership, 335 n., 429; bequests, 339–340; efforts to retain the charter, 453 n.
Fetherstone, Richard, 140, 141, 147.
Fish, abundance of, 81; kinds, 95.
Florida, 80.
Flowerdew Hundred, delegates from, 250; fortifications, 415, 416; location, 415 n.
Flowre, George, death, 20.
Force, Peter, *Historical Tracts*, 302 n., 422 n.
Ford, Robert, 125, 162, 170, 175.
Forest, George, 140.
Forest, Mistress, 160.
Forest, Thomas, 160.
Fort Charles, 223 n., 300.
Fortescue, Sir Nicholas, 405.
Fort Henry, 224, 300.
Fortress Monroe, 11 n.
Fox, Thomas, 160.
Francis, 169, 181.
Fuller, Michael, adventure, 389–391.

Galthorpe, Stephen, 21.
Gany, William, adventure, 389–391.
Garnett, Thomas, accusation against, 268.
Garret, William, 126.
Gates, Sir Thomas, 401; political positions, 191, 191 n.; arrival at Jamestown, 201, 296, 304; deputy-governor of Virginia, 207; censures the colonists, 208; meeting with Lord Delaware, 212; government of the colony, 220 n., 318 n.; is despatched to England for help, 202; returns to England, 300.
*George*, ship, 330, 331, 337.
Gibbes, Lieutenant, elected a burgess, 250.
Gipson, Thomas, 160, 162.
Glass, 416; factory for making, 348 n.
Gold, 152; craze for, among the settlers, 136, 138; Molina's report concerning, 219.
Golding, George, 126.
Gondomar, Count, intrigues of, 430; instructions, 454; accuses Argall of piracy, 455.
*Goodspeed*, ship, 122 n.
Goodyson, Ramon, 140.
Gookin, Daniel, 369; establishes a settlement at Newport News, 349.
Gore, Thomas, 20 n., 21, 126.
Gosnold, Anthony, 125, 126, 132, 134; death, 174.

Gosnold, Bartholomew, 125; voyage to New England, 21 n.; contention of, over location of settlement, 33; arouses interest in the Virginia expedition, 121–122; is chosen as councillor, 123; death, 21, 36, 71 n., 128.
Goston, Sir Francis, 405.
Gourgaing, elected a burgess, 250.
Gradon, Richard, 140.
Graves, Thomas, 159, 256; elected a burgess, 250; rescue, 354.
Griswold, ed., Delaware's *Relation*, 208.
Gryvill, William, 140.
Guadeloupe, hot bath at, 6–7, 122; Chester anchors at, 340.
Gudderington, John, 159.
Guercheville, Madame de, assists Biard, 227.
Guiacum, tree, 7.
Gurganey, Edward, 140; contribution to the *Generall Historie*, 316–325.

Hakluyt, Richard, 179, 179 n.; map of, 53 n.
Hall, William, 209.
Hamor, Ralph, 312 n., 316 n., 317, 426; visit to Powhatan, 313–316; sails for Virginia, 330; Indian attack upon, 361, 361 n.; entertained by the king of the Potomacs, 377; voyage to Newfoundland, 384; opinion of the Indians, 386, 388; *A True Discourse of the Present Estate of Virginia and the Successes of the Affaires there till the* 18 *of June*, 1614, 238, 302, 302 n., 309 n.; contribution to the *Generall Historie*, 302–316.
Hamor, Thomas, 361, 361 n.
Hampton River, 11 n.
Hancock, Nicholas, 160, 162.
Hardwin, 160.
Harford, John, 141.
Harington, Edward, 21.
Harper, John, 140.
Harwood, member of the council, 345.
Haryson, Harmon, 159.
Hassinnunga Indians, 105.
Hazard, Ebenezer, *Historical Collections*, 406 n.
Hellyard, 160.
Henrico, 424; early settlement at, 224, 224 n.; delegates from, 249; described, 305; incorporated, 337; land grant at, for a university, 337 n.; abandonment, 417; condition of, 418 n.
Henry, son of James I., 81 n.
Henry, Cape, 81; named, 11; Smith touches, 32.
Herd, John, 126.
Heriots, 89.
Hill, Elis, 372.
Hill, George, 140.
Hills, Edward, 381.
Hog Island, 174, 297; blockhouse at, 185.
Holland. Gabriell, 426.
Hope, Thomas, 119, 134, 140.
Hothersall, Thomas, account of the sea-fight at Dominica, 340 n.
Houlgrave, Nicholas, 126.
Hoult, John, 159.
Hunt, Robert, 125, 132, 135, 160; sickness, 122.

Iguanas, found, 8, 122.
Indians, dress, 6, 12, 13–14, 48, 88, 99–100, 110; religion, 6, 20, 23, 51, 108–113, 355, 355 n.; remedies, 108; treatment of prisoners, 115–116; treatment of their sick, 51; war-paint, 100; weapons, 6, 17, 102–103, 142; customs, 6, 56, 101, 114–115, 377; ceremonies, 12, 48, 51, 54, 110–112, 153–154; werowances, 15 n., 49 n., 84, 105, 112–113, 115; conversion, 345–346, 347, 347 n., 348, 356, 362; occupations, 18, 101; manner of life, 101, 363; cabins, 100–101, 114; canoes, 103; character, 6, 63, 99, 386, 388; government, 52, 113–114, 115; agricultural methods, 95–97; methods of tattooing their bodies, 6, 19; dances, 12; difference between the married and unmarried, 19; longevity, 19; oaths, 20; language, 89; hunting methods, 103–105; physical characteristics, 99; food, 102; methods of warfare, 105–107; music, 107; manner of trading, 108; mode of burial, 109; priests, 110; marriage, 355; refusal to trade with colonists, 157, 159, 160–161; learn

the use of firearms, 346; attacks of, 10, 32, 35, 43–44, 138; massacre of the colonists by, 357–373, 400, 437, 444; peace with, 345, 358; laws concerning, 262, 264, 269–270, 273.
Irrohatock Indians, 85.
Isabella, of Spain, 77, 78.
Isle of St. Michael, governor of, entertains Lord Delaware, 331.
Itopatin, 355; succeeds Powhatan, 334.

Jackson, John, 250, 256.
Jacob, Thomas, 21, 446.
James City, *see* Jamestown.
James I., king of Great Britain, 325 n.
James River, 413 n.; explorations up, 17–18, 33–35, 123–124; described, 17–18, 34; Spanish ships in, 217.
Jamestown Peninsula, 185 n.
Jamestown, settlement at, 15, 15 n., 33, 123; described, 19, 306; burning of the fort at, 52, 135, 397; country surrounding, 64 n.; location, 84, 412, 413; proceedings of the colony at, 119–204; arrival of the first supply at, 52, 132–137; the second supply reaches, 152; arrival of the first woman at, 155; life at, 156–158, 397; the third supply reaches, 191, 292; aid sent to, 203, 331–332; condition of affairs at, 21–22, 36–38, 41, 71, 127–128, 179–180, 184–187, 197–198, 198 n., 200, 201, 208, 212–214, 220–221, 283–286, 285 n., 286 n., 292, 294–296, 299–300, 301, 302 n., 326, 330–331, 332, 334, 338, 347, 384, 395, 400, 414, 422–425; houses, 415, 424; government, 247, 296, 312, 337, 338–339, 400–405; meeting of Virginia assembly at, 248, 249, 337; fortifications, 415, 416; dissentions at, 191–192, 196, 197; young women sold to the settlers at, 339; Indians attack, 35; delegates from, 249; number of inhabitants in, 224; incorporated, 337, 337 n.
Japazaws, betrays Pocahontas, 307; seeks trade with the colonists, 337.
Jarnette, D. C. de, 248.
Jefferson, 250, 256.
*John and Francis*, vessel, 71 n.
Johnson, Robert, 425, 432, 446, 447, 448; efforts to dissolve the Virginia Company, 422, 422 n.; petition, 451; accusations against, 457.
Johnson, William, 126, 140.
Jones, Sir William, 405.
Jordan, Samuel, 249, 256, 370.

Keale, Richard, 141, 147.
Kecoughtan, Indian village, 11, 37, 377, 389, 424; described, 38; natives of, befriend colonists, 48; Smith reaches, 146, 163; *see also* Elizabeth City.
Kecoughtan Indians, 13 n., 84.
Keffer, Peter, 140.
Kekataugh, 165; entertains Smith, 46; trade with Smith, 60.
Kendall, George, 125; conviction of, 21; shot as a conspirator, 41, 71 n.; his chosen councillor, 123; deposed, 36, 128; conspires against Smith, 129.
Kerby, Captain, traffics in slaves, 282 n.
Killingbeck, Richard, 140; death, 333.
Kingsbury, Susan M., Introduction to the *Records of the Virginia Company*, 405 n.
Kingston, Ellis, 22, 22 n.
Kingswell, Richard, 426.
Kiptopeke, conference with Pory, 352; character, 354.
Kiskiack or Chiskiack Indians, 50, 85; religion, 51; Smith visits, 61; conspiracy of, 67–70.
Kissanacomen, fight with Yeardley, 323.
Kitchin, plot, 303 n., 304; execution, 304 n.
Knollys, Sir Francis, 207.
Kuscarawaoke Indians, 89.
Kuskaranaocke River, 143.

Lambert, Thomas, 162.
Lane, Sir Ralph, 89, 143.
Lanexa, 41, 387.
Lapworth, Michael, murdered by the Indians, 363 n.
Lavander, Thomas, 160.

Lawne, Captain Christopher, 256, 336; elected a burgess, 250.
Lawne's Hundred, delegates from, 250; law concerning, 266.
*Laws Divine, Morall and Martiall* (London, 1612), 422 n.
Laxon, William, 126, 185.
Laydon, John, 126, 160.
Leds, Timothy, 140.
Lembri, Francisco, arrest as a spy, 217; execution, 222 n.; experiences as a spy, 321.
Lewes, John, 141.
Ley, Henry, chief-justice, 159, 187; revokes the charter, 455 n.
Limbo Isles, 143.
London Company, *see* Virginia Company.
Lottery, determination of the council concerning, 317; reasons for instituting, 318; rules, 319–320; receipts from, 437.
Love, William, 126, 162.
Lowicke, Michaell, 160.
Lucas, 342.
Lynnhaven River, Percy enters, 10.

Macanoe, confession of, 69.
McDonald, Angus, 248.
Machot, Indian village, 309.
Macocke, Samuel, member of the council, 335; murdered by the Indians, 363 n.
Madison, Isaac, 426; adventures of, 378; attacks the Potomacs, 381–438.
Maestro, Padre, accuses Argall of piracy, 455.
Maine, expeditions to, 202, 203.
Maize, 12.
Mallard, Thomas, 160; makes known Volda's conspiracy, 189.
Mamanahunt, Indian village, Smith arrives at, 40, 323.
Manakin Indians, 34 n.
Mandeville, Lord Viscount, 406.
Mangoage Indians, search for Raleigh's colony among, 89, 188.
Mannahock Indians, 47, 86, 89, 105.
Manosquosick, Indian village, location, 40, 40 n.
Mansa, Indian village, Smith at, 40.
Mantivas, carries provisions to Smith, 58–59.
Marcum, Robert, Thomas Savage seeks, 353.
*Margaret and John*, ship, 336, 338 n., 340.
Marlott, Thomas, 426.
Marraughtacum, 47.
Marriage, law concerning, 273.
Marten, Nicholas, 426, 436 n.
Martha's Vineyard, 227.
Martin, George, 126.
Martin, John, 125, 126, 128; death, 21; sickness, 36, 37; opposes sending a pinnace to England, 41; is elected councillor, 52, 123, 252; willingness of, to attempt expedition beyond the Falls, 65; quarrels with Smith, 66 n.; returns to England, 71 n.; is appointed president, 192; resignation, 193; opposition to the government, 194; decisions concerning the patent of, 253–255, 260–262, 262 n.; accusations against, 269.
Martinique, Percy at, 5 n.
Martin's Hundred, 412; delegates from, 250; law concerning, 266.
Mason, Dorothea, 237.
Massachusetts Historical Society, *Collections*, 281.
Massawomeke Indians, 88, 89, 105, 106, 143, 144, 150.
Massé, Father Enemond, 228; settlement of, 227; embarkation, 229.
Massinnacack Indians, 105.
Mathews, Samuel, 426.
Mattalunt, Indian village, 41.
Mattapony, Indian village, 387; Smith discovers, 41; Smith seeks corn in, 176.
Mattapony Indians, 67–70, 85, 87, 113.
Mattapony River, 46, 85.
Maxes, Thomas, 159.
May, Cornelius, adventure, 389–391.
May, William, 140.
Menapacute or Menapacant, Indian village, Smith is conducted to, 46; Newport sails for, 60.
Mettalina, 340.
Mevis, *see* Nevis.
Michael, 140.
Middlesex, Earl of, 430, 432, 432 n., 436; efforts to secure the tobacco

contracts, 446–450; accuses Sandys, 449; efforts to revoke the charter, 452–454.
Middleton, Captain, member of the council, 345.
Midwinter, Francis, 126.
Miler, Richard, 140.
Milman, 160.
Molina, Don Diego de, experiences in Virginia, 217, 222, 223; urges Spanish king to destroy the English colony, 218, 221; letter of, 218–224, 321 n.; arrest, 321.
Molynex, Richard, 140.
Momford, Thomas, 141, 147.
Mona, Percy arrives at, 8.
Monacan Indians, 83, 89, 105, 106.
Monahassanuggs, 105.
Mone, Captain, 194.
Monhegan Island, Captain Ward visits, 337, 337 n.
Monica, 9, 9 n., 48; Newport sets out to discover, 155; Smith secures, 165.
Monts, Sieur de, settlement of, 227.
Mooney, James, *The Powhatan Confederacy, Past and Present*, 113 n.
Morattico, Lane discovers, 143.
Moraughtacunds, 86.
Moreno, Antonio, 220.
Morgan, death, 357.
Morinogh, Indian village, Smith enters, 41.
Morish, Edward, 20, 20 n.
Morrell, 160.
Morton, Matthew, wounded by Indians, 32.
Morton, Ralph, 140, 141.
Mouhemenchughes, 105.
Mounslic, Thomas, 21.
Mount Desert Island, destruction of the settlement at, 189 n., 227, 228–229.
Mountains, of Virginia, 82.
Mouton, Thomas, death, 22.
Moyaon Indians, 41, 372, 381.
Moyowances, 86.
Moysenock, Indian village, Smith reaches, 41.
Mulberry trees, 90, 391, 417; law as to planting, 264–265.
Mussels, abundance of, 10, 34.
Mutton, Richard, 126.
Nacostans, 86, 372, 382; attack upon, 377.
Namenacus, Pory visits, 352; Thomas Savage accuses, 353; treachery of, 354.
Namontack, aids Smith, 53, 56; is given to Newport, 134; is returned to Powhatan, 67, 154; death, 313 n.
Nansemond Indians, 84; refuse to trade with colonists, 160; Edward Waters captured by, 376–377; Yeardley attacks, 384–385.
Nansemond River, 84; Smith discovers, 61; described, 62–63, 63 n.; explorations up, 303.
Nantaquaus, friendship for Smith, 53, 56, 326.
Nause Indians, 143.
Nautaquake, 143.
Nautaughtacunds, 47, 86.
Nazatica, 382.
Nechanichock, Indian village, 41.
Negroes, introduction into the colony, 282 n., 337.
Neill, Edward D., *Virginia Company of London*, 297 n., 335 n., 405 n., 411, 421.
Nelson, Captain, reaches Virginia, 64, 130, 137; refuses to go beyond the Falls, 65; sails for England, 71.
Nelstrop, Rowland, 140.
Nemattanow, 372; death, 357.
Nevis, 7 n., 211, 340.
New France, northern boundary of Virginia, 80; Jesuits in, 228.
Newce, Captain Thomas, manager of the company's lands, 338 n.; member of the council, 345; industry of, 371, 371 n., 378; Croshaw asks aid of, 377; illness, 379; liberality of, 380; character, 381.
Newfoundland, Hamor sails for, 384.
Newport, Christopher, transports the colonists to Virginia, 122; explores James River, 33–34, 123–124; sails for England, 19, 35, 125, 125 n., 137, 159; returns to Virginia, 52, 61, 132; visits Powhatan, 53–60, 133–135; arranges for Powhatan's coronation, 152–155; voyage to Monacan, 155–156; promises to send

supplies, 20; rescues Smith, 28, 48; gives a boy to Powhatan, 56; is chosen councillor, 123; private commission, 152; friendship for Powhatan, 167; sells swords to the Indians, 400; *Relatyon*, 4.
Newport News, 412; settlement at, 349; named, 349 n.
Nickoles, John, 140.
Nonsuch, fort, 195.
Northampton County, 351 n.
Norton, Thomas, 159; death, 371.

Ocanahonan, inhabitants of, 45, 46.
Ocanindge, discourse concerning peace, 183.
Oconor, Dius, 160.
Onancock, 352.
Onawmanient, Indian village, 386.
Onawmanient Indians, 86.
Onianimo, purposes to kill Savage, 354.
Opechancanough, 115, 165, 378; second successor of Powhatan, 35 n.; holds Smith a prisoner, 44–48; to assist in the war against the Monacums, 59; entertains Smith, 60; asks the release of his friends, 69; entertains Newport, 135; conference with Smith, 170; Smith overpowers, 172–173; visit to Smith, 175; Spelman gives information to, 274–275; becomes the king of Ozinies, 324; promises to avenge the murder of certain colonists, 333; confirms the peace with the colonists, 334, 349; suspicions aroused by, 345; conspiracy against Savage, 354; treachery, 357, 372, 376, 382; leads in the great massacre, 358; plot to overthrow, 384.
Opitchapam, 115, 165, 376; trades with Smith, 60.
Opussoquionuske, Queen, 34 n.
Oraniocke, Indian village, Smith visits, 40.
Orapakes, Indian village, 85, 85 n., 114.
Outponcas, 105.
Ovid, Sandys's, 348 n.
Oysters, abundance of, 10.
Ozinies, 89, 323, 324, 387.

Paccamaganant, Pory at, 353.
Pace, informs the governor of the Indian uprising, 363, 379 n.
Paltsits, Victor H., 76 n.
Pamacacack Indians, 86.
Pamunkey River, 46, 46 n., 362, 370; described, 50, 85.
Pamunkeys, 85, 113, 388; friendship of, for the colonists, 35–36; country of, 35 n.; character, 63; conspiracy of, 67–70, 376; certain colonists imprisoned by, 378; Yeardley attacks, 385.
Pananuaioc, 53 n.
Panawicke, 53.
Pansarowmana, is given to Newport, 61.
Parahunt, son of Powhatan, 33 n.
Parker, William, recovered, 315, 316.
Part, John, 160.
Partridge, 194.
Paspaheghe Indians, 84; entertain Percy, 13; visit Percy, 15–16, 17; colonists trade with, 39; colonists befriended by, 48, 53; conspiracy of, 67–70; removal of, to Sandy Point, 275 n.; Percy's attack upon, 300.
Paspihegh, Bay of, 39.
Passe, Simon de, 237, 326.
Patuxent Indians, 87; aid sought by, 105–106; Pory visits, 352.
Patuxent River, described, 87; Smith explores, 150.
Pawlett, 256; elected a burgess, 250.
Payankatank River, 48; Smith explores, 150.
Pazatican Indians, 372.
Pearls, found, 10, 34.
Pecock, Nathaniel, 126, 162.
Peirce, Captain William, 140, 237, 426
Peirce, Jane, 237.
Pembroke, 232.
Pennington, Robert, death, 21.
Percy, George, 125; biographical sketch of, 3; sails from London, 5; in the West Indies, 6–9; enters Chesapeake Bay, 9; explores the shores, 10–14; visits Indian chiefs, 12–14; builds fortification, 15; explores the James River, 17; returns to settlement, 18; wretched condition of, 21–22; visits the

Chickahominies, 157; voyage in search of provisions, 161–173; appointment as president, 196; deputy-governor of Virginia, 212; illness, 200, 294; attacks the Paspaheghs, 300; *Observations*, 3, 5–23.
Perez, Marco Antonio, death, 222.
Perkins, Francis, 140.
Persey, Abraham, view concerning the tobacco law, 259, 260.
Phelps, Thomas, 160.
Phettiplace, Michael, 140, 162.
Phettiplace, William, 76, 119, 121, 134, 140, 162, 195 n.; voyage to the Pamunkey country, 170, 170 n.; contribution to the *Proceedings of the English Colony*, 151–200.
Philpot, Henry, 159.
Phitz-James, Captain, 194.
*Phoenix*, vessel, 27, 64, 64 n., 71 n., 137, 141.
Piankatank River, 48; Smith explores, 150.
Pickhouse, Dru, 21, 125.
Pierse, Thomas, sergeant of the general assembly, 251.
Pinkerton, J., *General Collection of Voyages*, 291.
Pising, Edward, 126, 147, 162, 163.
Pit, Sir William, 405.
Pizarro, murder, 366.
Plymouth, England, Dale reaches, 321.
Plymouth, Mass., Pory aids the colonists at, 281.
Pocahontas, Smith rescued by, 28, 326, 327; sent as a peacemaker to Jamestown, 69, 139; is returned to Powhatan, 70; friendship for Smith, 199; Spelman rescued by, 295; marriage, 237, 251, 310, 327; Rolfe's reasons for marrying, 239–244; capture, 307–308, 327; baptism, 316; visit to England, 321, 325; education, 325; presentation at court, 329; death, 330.
Pochins, son of Powhatan, 11 n.
Pocoughtronack, description of, 49.
Point Comfort, fort at, 200, 200 n., 212, 223; Spanish ships at, 217, 218, 320.
Polentine, John, elected a burgess, 249.
Pollington, John, 426.
Poole, Robert, 381; accusations of, against Spelman, 274–275; treachery of, 337; makes known the plot of the Indians, 382.
Port Royal, colony at, 227, 230; destruction of the settlement at, 189, 231, 313.
Porto Rico, 8 n., 219, 219 n.
Pory, John, 151, 162; speaker of the assembly, 248, 251, 255; biographical sketch, 281; illness, 283; visits many Indian chiefs, 352–355; letter of, 282–287; observations of, 351–355; *Proceedings of the Virginia Assembly*, 245–278; translation of Leo Africanus, 281.
Pory, Peter, 140.
Potapacos, 86.
Potomac Indians, wars of, 49; number of, 86; ask aid of Smith, 105–106; attack the Nacostans, 377; attempt to liberate Sarah Boys, 378; Madison attacks, 381–384.
Potomac River, described, 86; source of, 105; Smith explores, 144–145; country surrounding, 213; trading expeditions to, 202, 300, 307, 372.
Pott, John, 426; arrival at Jamestown, 349; deputy-governor, 349 n.
Pott or Pots, Richard, 76, 119, 121, 140, 195 n.; compiles Smith's manuscript, 75; contribution to the *Proceedings of the English Colony*, 179–200.
Pountas or Powntis, John, member of the council, 345, 426.
Poutrincourt, Sieur de, reëstablishes the colony at Port Royal, 227.
Powell Brook, 360 n.
Powell, Captain William, 160, 170, 172, 173, 256, 389; elected a burgess, 249; petition of, 268; political offices, 268 n.; payment made to, 275–276; expedition against the savages, 379; in command at Jamestown, 379 n.
Powell, Henry, 162.
Powell, John, 140, 141.
Powell, Nathaniel, 76, 119, 121, 126, 134, 147, 162, 194; contribution to the *Proceedings of the English Colony*, 121–204; account of the explorations in Chesapeake Bay, 151; search for Raleigh's lost

colony, 188; contribution to the *Generall Historie*, 316–325; deputy-governor, 335, 360 n.; murdered by the Indians, 360, 363 n.

Powhatan, Smith meets, 46; friendship of, for colonists, 52–53, 396; Smith entertained by, 54–60; Smith trades with, 57–58; war plans, 59; treachery of, 67–70, 168–170; sends Pocahontas to Smith, 69; territories of, 113; personal appearance, 114; character, 115–116; conquers the Payankatanks, 116; colonists aided by, 131; entertains Newport, 134–135; conspiracy of, 138–139; coronation, 152–155, 399; policy of, to starve the colonists, 157; Smith's determination to surprise, 161; conference with Smith, 164–168; designs against Smith, 174, 181, 327, 327 n.; abandons Merocomoco, 177; Ratcliffe slain by, 200; refusal to trade with colonists, 295; attitude respecting the capture of Pocahontas, 308; concludes a peace with Dale, 309–310; captures Smith, 326; death, 334.

Powhatan, Indian town, 33, 34, 34 n., 84, 85, 113; Smith attempts to buy, 193; colonists take possession of, 195.

Powhatan Creek, location, 84.

Powhatan Indians, 89, 105, 124; war methods of, 106–107.

Powhatan River, 370; described, 83–85.

Prat, John, 162.

Pretty, George, 140.

Price, revolt of, 303.

Proctor, Mistress, 370.

Prodger, Richard, 140.

Profit, Jonas, 126, 141, 147, 162.

*Prosperus*, ship, 274.

Purchas, Samuel, *Pilgrimes*, 3, 208; marginal note by, 5 n.; prints Percy's *Observations*, 3; an abridgment of Smith's *Description of Virginia*, 75.

Quentin, Father Jacques, 229; settlement of, 227.

Quia Creek, 86 n.

Quiyough, *see* Quia Creek.

Quiyoughcohanock River, 83.

Quiyoughcohanocks, 13 n., 84; Smith visits, 39; assist the colonists, 188.

Quiyoughquosicke, Indian deity, 51.

Raleigh, Sir Walter, 89; lost colony of, 152, 163, 188.

Ramirez, Captain Diego, relation of, 219.

Ransacke, Abraham, 140.

Rappahannock Indians, Percy entertained by, 13; friendship of, for the colonists, 20; Smith visits, 47; number of, 86.

Rappahannock River, 89, 105, 387; discovery, 47; described, 86; Smith explores, 150.

Rasawrack, Smith is taken a prisoner to, 44.

Ratcliffe, John, 125; sickness, 36; president of the colony, 22, 37, 128; in authority at Jamestown, 71 n.; is chosen councillor, 123; attempted abandonment of the colony, 130; extravagance, 141; deposed, 147; imprisonment, 151; enmity toward Smith, 194, 196; fort built by, 200; is sent to Point Comfort, 294; death, 37, 200, 295.

Rawhunt, 69.

Read, James, 126, 141, 162.

Rice, John Holt, ed., *Works* of Captain John Smith, 291.

Rich, Sir Nathaniel, opposition to the tobacco contract, 450; accusations against, 458.

Rich, Sir Robert, *see* Warwick, Earl of.

Richards Cliffs, 143.

Rickahake, 355.

Righkahauck, Indian village, 41.

Roanoke, lost colony of, 17 n.

Robinson, Conway, 248.

Robinson, John, 126; with Smith on the Chickahominy, 43; death, 44.

Robinson, Mary, donates a fund for a church, 339, 339 n.

Rodes, Christopher, 140.

Rodes, William, 20 n., 21, 126.

Roffingham, elected a burgess, 250.

Rolfe, John, biographical sketch of, 237; letter to Sir Thomas Dale, 239–244; reasons for marrying Poca-

hontas, 239–244; petition, 269; contribution to the *Generall Historie*, 302–316, 328–339; marriage to Pocahontas, 310, 327; educates Pocahontas, 316; visit to England, 321.
Rolfe, Thomas, 238, 330.
Rolfe's Creek, 185 n.
Rose, 160.
Rosingham, Ensign, 256.
*Royall James*, ship, 350.
Russawmeake, 105.
Russell, John, 156, 159, 162, 163.
Russell, Robert, 140.
Russell, Walter, 76, 119, 121, 146, 170, 175; contribution to the *Proceedings of the English Colony*, 141–147; discovers the designs of the savages, 171.
Russell, William, 159.
Russell's Isles, 142, 352.
Rymer, *Fœdera*, 406.

Sabbath, law concerning, 273.
Sagadahock, *see* Maine.
Saint Croix Island, French settlement at, 230; destruction of the settlement at, 227, 313.
St. Michael, island, 331.
St. Sauveur, 230 n.
Salt-works, 352.
Sambage, William, 159.
Samuell, 170.
Sands, Thomas, 126.
Sandy Point, 13 n.; Paspahegh Indians remove to, 275 n.
Sandys, Sir Edwin, 429; treasurer, 335; policy toward the colonists, 247; political leadership, 335 n.; efforts to establish a university, 337 n.; government, 293, 421, 434, 446; accusations against, 447; efforts to retain the charter, 453 n.
Sandys, George, treasurer, 348, 426; experiments, 348 n.; report concerning the Indians, 363.
Santa Maria, *see* Chesapeake Bay.
Santo Domingo, 219, 219 n.
*Sarah Constant*, ship, 122 n.
Sassafras, 434, 434 n.
Savage, Richard, 140, 170.
Savage, Thomas, interpreter, 140; is given to Powhatan by Newport, 56, 134; is returned to Jamestown, 68; accompanies Hamor to Powhatan, 313; Namenacus seeks, 352; first permanent settler on the Eastern Shore, 352 n.; quarrels with Indian chiefs, 353; conspiracy against, 354.
School, free, subscription for, 350, 350 n.
Scot, Nicolas, 126, 160.
Scrivener, Matthew, 140; becomes president of the colony, 37 n., 147; is elected councillor, 52; accompanies Smith to Powhatan, 53; experiences in a bog, 58; traffics with Indian chiefs, 60; accompanies Newport, 61, 133–135; trouble with the Indians, 66; in authority at Jamestown, 71 n.; accompanies Smith to Nansamund, 160; is left in charge at Jamestown, 161; death, 174.
*Sea Venture*, ship, 191 n.
Secowocomoco Indians, 86.
Sedan, 398.
Shackaconias, 105.
Sharpe, Samuel, 249, 256, 426.
Shelley, Walter, 250, 256; death, 260, 260 n.
Sherley, Sir Thomas, 207.
Shortridge, Geoffery, 160, 162.
Sicklemore, John, *see* Ratcliffe, John.
Sicklemore, Michael, 140, 141, 147, 162, 163; failure to find Raleigh's colony, 188.
Silk, attempt to make, 90, 348 n.; law concerning the manufacture of, 265.
Silkworms, destruction, 381.
Silver, discovered, 156.
Simonds, Doctor William, 140, 294, 294 n., 297; revises Smith's manuscript, 75; contribution to the *Proceedings of the English Colony*, 179–204, 297 n.; contribution to the *Generall Historie*, 294–297; death, 22.
Small, Robert, 126, 141.
Smith, Alice, mother of Captain John Smith, 27.
Smith, George, father of Captain John Smith, 27.
Smith, Captain John, *True Relation*, 4, 28, 30–71; *Map of Virginia*, 28,

191; *Generall Historie of Virginia, New England and the Summer Isles*, 5 n., 28, 31, 208, 217, 294–407; critical estimate of his works, 29; *Mappe of the Bay and River*, 75, 76; letter of, to Sir Edward Semer, 76–77; *Description of Virginia*, 80–118; *Proceedings of the English Colonies in Virginia*, 119–204; *A Description of New England*, 191; *New England's Trials*, 191; *True Travels*, 28, 291; letter of, to Queen Anne, 325–328.

Smith, Captain John, biographical sketch of, 27–28; reaches Chesapeake Bay, 32; establishes a settlement, 33; explores James River, 33–34, 123–124; return to the fort, 35, 52, 61, 177; illness, 36; trades with the Indians, 37–38; goes on trading expedition, 39–40; explores the Chickahominy River, 41–43; capture, 44, 396; experiences as a prisoner, 45–51, 130–131; at Werowocomoco, 47, 163; conference with Powhatan, 48–49; visits Powhatan, 53–60, 133–135; promises of, to Powhatan, 55; trades with Powhatan, 57, 59; in a bog, 58; is entertained by Opechancanough, 60; trouble with the Indians, 63, 66–70; quarrels with Martin, 66 n.; savages ask aid of, 105–106; censures his enemies, 117–118; sails for Virginia, 122; arrest, 124–125, 124 n.; accuses Wingfield, 127; conspiracy against, 129, 196; rebuilds the fort, 137; treatment of the Indians, 138–139, 177–178, 182–183; first voyage to the Chesapeake Bay, 141–147; on the Potomac, 145; second voyage to the Chesapeake Bay, 147–151; among the Toghwoghs, 149–150; president of the colony, 151; management of the colony, 151, 156, 179–180, 186–187, 190, 192; attitude toward Powhatan's coronation, 152–155; visits the Chickahominy Indians, 157; efforts to depose, 158; voyage to the Pamunkey country, 161–173; conference with Powhatan, 164–168; reaches the Pamunkey country, 170; discourse with Opechancanough, 170–173; attempt to poison, 176; fight with the king of Paspahegh, 181; makes peace with the Indians, 183; Volda's treachery made known to, 189; departure for the Falls, 193; is injured by gunpowder, 195, 398; sails for England, 196; character, 197; accusations against, 198–199; censures the colonists, 208; comments on the revocation of the charter, 293; visit to Pocahontas, 328; opinion concerning the defence of the colony, 370, 370 n.; proposal, 373–375; opinion concerning the Indians, 379–380; opinion concerning the attacks upon the Indians, 379, 379 n., 385–389, 385 n.; reviews his administration, 398–399; answers to the questions of the Commissioners, 399–405; opinion as to the government of Virginia, 400–407.

Smith, Roger, 426.

Smith, Sir Thomas, 306 n., 418 n.; treasurer of Virginia, 320, 331 n.; political defeat, 335 n.; efforts to secure the dissolution of the Virginia Company, 421; government, 422–425, 437, 454, 455 n.; political leadership, 429; deposed, 446, 446 n.; commissioner of Virginia, 455; accusations against, 457.

Smith's Fort, 185 n.

Smith's Island, 141, 141 n., 355; saltworks at, 352.

Smyth, John, of Nibley, 338 n.

Smyth's Hundred, delegates from, 250; law concerning, 266.

Snarsbrough, Francis, 126.

Somers, Sir George, political positions, 191, 191 n.; arrival at Jamestown, 201, 296; return to England, 202; death, 203; at the Bermudas, 300.

Soraphanigh Indians, 143.

South Sea, 152; belief concerning, 59 n.; report of, 147; English designs concerning, 219.

Southampton, Earl of, treasurer, 247, 344, 345 n.; political leadership, 429; administration of, 293,

421, 434–436, 446; accusations, 447, 449.
Southampton Hundred, 339 n., 250 n.
Southerne, John, 426.
Spanish Colonies, condition of, 365–366.
Sparkes, Michael, goes as messenger to Powhatan, 310.
Speareman, John, 140.
Spelman, Captain Henry, 723; death, 202 n., 392; punishment, 274–275; rescue, 295; assists Argall, 300; good services of, 324.
Spence, William, 140, 256, 312, 337; elected a burgess, 249.
Stacy, Robert, elected a burgess, 250.
Stalling, Daniel, 140; voyage to New England, 334; death, 335.
Stegarake Indians, 105.
Stephens, Richard, 426.
Stockden, Jonas, relation of, 347–348; opinion as to the Indians, 347 n., 364, 369.
Strachey, William, *Historie of Travaile into Virginia*, 355 n.
Studley, Thomas, 21 n., 76, 119, 121, 126; death, 21; narratives concerning Jamestown, 121–139, 139 n.; contribution to the *Proceedings of the English Colony*, 121–139.
Sturgeon, abundance of, 84–85.
Sturgeon Point, 13 n.
Summer Islands, 28, 291, 371 n., 438, 450, 451, 455.
Susquehanna Indians, described, 87–88; domain of, 89, 149; physical characteristics, 99; ask aid of Smith, 105–106.
Sutton, Sir Richard, 405.

Taler, William, 160.
Tankard, William, 126, 162.
Tauxenent Indians, 86.
Tauxsnitanias, 105.
Taverner, John, 134, 140.
Tavin, Henry, 126.
Tegoneaes, 105.
Terceras, *see* Azores.
*Terra Sigillata*, 50, 66, 82.
Thorpe, George, 357 n.; manager for the college lands, 338 n ; member of the council, 345; visits Opechancanough, 349; treatment of the Indians, 359; murdered by the Indians, 360, 363 n.
Throckmorton, Kellam, 20 n., 21, 126.
Throckmorton, Sir William, 338 n.
Thwaites, R. G., *Jesuit Relations*, 227.
*Tiger*, ship, 350.
Tobacco, price of, 259, 450; great fortunes from, 346; used as currency, 384; reasons for the small profit from, 400; sole attention of the colonists given to, 416, 417 n., 434; laws concerning, 266, 267–268, 349; contract, 431, 442, 446–451.
Tockwogh Indians, 89; ask aid of Smith, 105–106.
Tockwogh River, 148.
Todkill, Anas, 76, 119, 121, 126, 134, 141, 147, 170; narratives concerning Jamestown, 132 n., 137–179; search for Raleigh's lost colony, 188; contribution to the *Proceedings of the English Colony*, 132–179.
Tooker, William Wallace, 33 n., 39 n., 62 n.
Toppahanock River, *see* Rappahannock River.
Towtales, Lawrence, 140.
Toyatan, 376.
Tracy, Joyce, murdered by the Indians, 360 n.
Tracy, William, member of the council, 338 n., 345; murdered by the Indians, 360 n.
*Tragical Declaration*, 432 n.
*Treasurer*, ship, 282, 332; first negro slaves brought over by, 282 n.
*Triall*, ship, 337.
Tropic of Cancer, Percy passes, 9.
Tucker, Daniel, 159.
Tucker, Captain William, 250, 256, 426.
Twine, John, clerk of the general assembly, 251.
Tyler, Lyon G., editor of the Virginia Narratives, 4; *England in America*, 286 n.; *The Cradle of the Republic*, 337 n.

Unger, William, 126.
University, *see* College.
Uphu, David, 160.
Upton, John, 382.

**Utie**, John, 426.
Uttamatomakkin, visit to England, 329.
Uttamussick, wigwams at, 35 n.; Indian temple at, 109.

Vela, Blasco Nuñez, 366.
Velasco, Don Alonzo de, letter to, 217.
Ven, Nicholas, 140.
Vere, 140.
Vieques, Percy near, 8 n.
Virgin Islands, Percy at, 8 n.
Virginia Assembly, proceedings of, 249–278; preliminaries, 251; order concerning Captain Ward, 252; committees, 255–256; petitions, 257–259, 276–278; decisions as to Captain Martin's Patent, 260–262; laws based on instructions from England, 262–268; laws proposed by individual burgesses, 268–274; remuneration of the officers determined by, 276; adjournment, 277; denounces Sir Thomas Smith's administration, 421; *The Tragical Relation of*, 419–426.
Virginia, boundaries, 80; climate, 81, 413–414; physical contour, 82, 412–413; rivers, 83–89; trees, 90; fruits, 91; herbs, 92–93; animals, 93–94; birds, 94; fishes, 95; commercial advantages, 97–98; inhabitants, 98–108; religion, 108–113; natural advantages, 213, 220, 283, 286, 395; fertility of the soil, 336, 350; houses, 415, 424; fortifications, 415, 424; government, 113–118, 249–278, 400–405, 417, 417 n., 429, 433, 437, 456–460; condition of affairs, 379, 380–381, 414, 417–418, 422–425, 431, 433–436, 438–443, 444; difficulties in settling, 177–179; courts established in, 356; commodities, 367–368; commission appointed to govern, 455–460, 455 n.; Indian massacre, 357–373, 437, 444; after effects of the massacre, 373–374; manufactures, 416–417; large immigration to, 350, 417–418, 436; false reports concerning, 336, 391–392, 439–440, 444, 451.
Virginia Company, 207–209, 221 n., 250 n., 372, 429; opposes Argall, 334, 334 n.; sends Frenchmen to instruct colonists how to raise grapes, 350, 350 n.; Smith's proposal to, 373–375; reply of, to Smith's proposal, 375; dissensions, 375–376; outfit furnished the colonists by, 393–395; dissolution, 405, 421, 422; journals of, or *Records* of, 292, 334 n., 335 n., 350 n., 373 n., 389, 405 n., 411; *Abstract of Proceedings*, 424 n.; *Briefe Declaration*, 212 n., 220 n., 325 n.; *A True and Sincere Declaration of the Estate of the Colony of Virginia*, 294 n., 302 n.; *Nova Britannia*, 294 n.
*Virginia Magazine of History*, 255 n., 258, 430.
Volda, William, conspiracy of, 188–189; escape, 190.

Wahunsonacock, name given by the Indians to their ruling chief, 113.
Wainman, Sir Ferdinando, 202, 401.
Waldo, Captain Richard, 153, 157, 159, 160, 161; member of the council, 152, 171 n.; death, 174.
Waler, John, 126.
Walker, George, 21, 160.
Walnuts, uses, 91.
Wamanato, entertains Pory, 352; innocence, 353.
Ward, William, 140, 147, 162, 256; elected a burgess, 250; is denied a seat in the assembly, 251; order concerning, 252; voyage to New England, 337; experiences on the Potomac, 338.
Ward's Plantation, delegates from, 250.
Warraskoyack, Indian town, location of, 38, 360 n., 412.
Warraskoyack Indians, 83, 84.
Warwick, Earl of, 237, 247, 429.
Washer, Ensign, elected a burgess, 250.
Washington, George, 436 n.
Waters, Edward, escape, 377.
Watkins, Henry, 426.
Watkins, James, 140, 141, 144, 147, 162.
Watson, Thomas, supposed author of *A True Relation*, 27; books wrong-

fully printed under the name of, 31.
Waynman, Sir Ferdinando, 202, 401.
Webbe, Thomas, 126, 194; revolt of, 303.
Wecuttanow, attempt of, to poison Smith, 176.
Weeks, S. B., *The Lost Colony of Roanoke: Its Fate and Survival*, 17 n.
Welbie, William, 209.
Weraskoyack, warns Smith, 162.
Werawhone, Indian village, Smith at, 40.
Werowance, 15 n., 49 n., 84, 105; Indian belief concerning, 112–113; power of, 115.
Werowocomoco, 114; Smith arrives at, 47, 53, 61, 134, 163; location, 47 n., 85; Powhatan's triumph at, 116.
West, Francis, 159, 162, 170, 172, 175, 176, 208, 294, 295; efforts to obtain provisions, 186; settlement of, 192, 192 n., 193; attitude toward mutinous colonists, 195; experiences among the savages, 200; member of the council, 335.
West, Henry, fourth Lord Delaware, 207.
West, John, 208.
West, Nathaniel, 208.
West, Thomas, second Lord Delaware, 207.
West, Thomas, third Lord Delaware, *see* Delaware, Lord.
West, William, 208.
West Hundred, 424.
West Indies, colonists at, 122; Lord Delaware in, 207.
Weyanoke Indians, Smith among the, 34–35; territory of, 34 n.; return to Jamestown, 68; number of, 84.
Whitaker, Alexander, 305, 305 n., 451 n.; remarks of, 316; complaints, 317, 317 n.; opinion concerning the Indians, 316, 364.
Whitaker, Jabez, 426, 451 n.
Whitaker, Mrs., 451.
White Oak Swamp, Smith captured at, 44 n., 85 n.
White, William, 126, 194; reports of, concerning Indian customs, 23.
Whonkentyaes, 105.
Wickam, William, member of council, 335.
Wiffin, David, approves Smith's proposal, 375.
Wiffin, Richard, 76, 119, 134, 140, 170 n., 174, 177; contribution to the *Proceedings of the English Colony*, 151–179; sent to punish the conspirators, 189.
Wighcocomoco Indians, 86; physical characteristics, 99.
Wighcocomoco River, 142.
Wilcox, John, 426.
Wilkinson, William, 126.
*William and Mary College Quarterly*, 340.
Williams, 160.
Williamsburg, 14 n.
Wimp, 357 n.
Wingfield, Edward Maria, 125; deposed, 22, 37, 127–128; biographical sketch of, 22 n.; fined for Smith's arrest, 28; president of the colony, 33, 123; accusations made against, 36, 36 n., 127; leaves Jamestown, 71 n.; Smith's injustice toward, 75; conspires against Smith, 129; *Discourse of Virginia*, 4, 36 n.
Winne, Captain Peter, 157, 159, 160, 161, 169, 183; member of the council, 152, 171 n.; dealings with the Dutchmen, 181, 182; death, 187.
Wollystone, Hugh, 159.
Wolstenholme, Sir John, position as to the tobacco contract, 450, 450 n.
Wood, Captain, 194.
Woodall, 457.
Woodlief, Captain John, arrival at Jamestown, 338, 338 n.
Worley, Richard, 140, 162.
Wotton, Thomas, 126.
Wriothesley, Henry, *see* Southampton, Earl of.
Wrote, Samuel, suspended from the company, 448, 448 n.; character, 458.
Wyatt, Sir Francis, arrival at Jamestown, 348; succeeds Yeardley, 345.
Wyles, Bishop, 140.
Wynne, Hugh, 160.

Yarington, George, 159, 162.
Yeardley, Sir George, deputy-governor

of Virginia, 207, 321; government, 247, 322, 325 n., 335; summons the Virginia assembly, 249; political positions, 249 n.; fight with the Chickahominies, 323–324; return to England, 325; illness, 351–352; expedition against the Indians, 379, 384–386; at Accomac, 380; arrival, 424.

Yonge, William, 140.

Youghtanund Indians, 85; conspiracy of, 67–70.

Youghtanund, Indian village, 50, 113, 176, 387.